W9-ANM-718

Related Books of Interest

A Practical Guide to Distributed Scrum

By Elizabeth Woodward, Steffan Surdek, and Matthew Ganis

ISBN-13: 978-0-13-704113-8

This is the first comprehensive, practical guide for Scrum practitioners working in large-scale distributed environments. Written by three of IBM's leading Scrum practitioners—in close collaboration with the IBM QSE Scrum Community of more than 1,000 members worldwide—this book offers specific, actionable guidance for everyone who wants to succeed with Scrum in the enterprise.

Readers will follow a journey through the lifecycle of a distributed Scrum project, from envisioning products and setting up teams to preparing for Sprint planning and running retrospectives. Using real-world examples, the book demonstrates how to apply key Scrum practices, such as look-ahead planning in geographically distributed environments. Readers will also gain valuable new insights into the agile management of complex problem and technical domains.

Agile Career Development
Lessons and Approaches from IBM

By Mary Ann Bopp, Diana A. Bing, Sheila Forte-Trammell

ISBN-13: 978-0-13-715364-0

Supercharge Performance by Linking Employee-Driven Career Development with Business Goals

How do you make career development work for both the employee and the business? IBM® has done it by tightly linking employee-driven career development programs with corporate goals. In *Agile Career Development*, three of IBM's leading HR innovators show how IBM has accomplished this by illustrating various lessons and approaches that can be applied to other organizations as well. This book is for every HR professional, learning or training manager, executive, strategist, and any other business leader who wants to create a high-performing organization.

Related Books of Interest

Implementing the IBM® Rational Unified Process® and Solutions

By Joshua Barnes
ISBN-13: 978-0-321-36945-1

This book delivers all the knowledge and insight you need to succeed with the IBM Rational Unified Process and Solutions. Joshua Barnes presents a start-to-finish, best-practice roadmap to the complete implementation cycle of IBM RUP—from projecting ROI and making the business case through piloting, implementation, mentoring, and beyond. Drawing on his extensive experience leading large-scale IBM RUP implementations and working with some of the industry's most recognized thought leaders in the Software Engineering Process world, Barnes brings together comprehensive "lessons learned" from both successful and failed projects. You'll learn from real-world case studies, including actual project artifacts.

Work Item Management with IBM Rational ClearQuest and Jazz

A Customization Guide

By Shmuel Bashan and David Bellagio
ISBN-13: 978-0-13-700179-8

The Complete Guide to Managing Work Items and Workflow with IBM® Rational® ClearQuest® and IBM Rational Team Concert™

Work items are the lifeblood of software and hardware development. They tell development teams exactly who is doing what, which issues are resolved, which remain unresolved, and which products are impacted. In large, team-based projects, however, managing work items can be difficult. Now, two IBM Rational experts show how to simplify and improve every aspect of work item management with IBM Rational ClearQuest and the powerful and collaborative Jazz™-based products: IBM Rational Team Concert (RTC) and IBM Rational Quality Manager.

IBM Press™

Related Books of Interest

Software Test Engineering with IBM Rational Functional Tester
The Definitive Resource

By Chip Davis, Daniel Chirillo, Daniel Gouveia, Fariz Saracevic, Jeffrey B. Bocarsley, Larry Quesada, Lee B. Thomas, and Marc van Lint
ISBN-13: 978-0-13-700066-1

If you're among the thousands of developers using IBM Rational Functional Tester (RFT), this book brings together all the insight, examples, and real-world solutions you need to succeed. Eight leading IBM testing experts thoroughly introduce this state-of-the-art product, covering issues ranging from building test environments through executing the most complex and powerful tests. Drawing on decades of experience with IBM Rational testing products, they address both technical and nontechnical challenges and present everything from best practices to reusable code.

Enterprise Master Data Management
An SOA Approach to Managing Core Information

Dreibelbis, Hechler, Milman, Oberhofer, van Run, Wolfson

ISBN-13: 978-0-13-236625-0

The Business of IT
How to Improve Service and Lower Costs

Robert Ryan, Tim Raducha-Grace

ISBN-13: 978-0-13-700061-6

An Introduction to IMS
Your Complete Guide to IBM Information Management Systems, 2nd Edition

Barbara Klein, et al.

ISBN-13: 978-0-13-288687-1

Dynamic SOA and BPM
Best Practices for Business Process Management and SOA Agility

Marc Fiammante

ISBN-13: 978-0-13-701891-8

Outside-in Software Development
A Practical Approach to Building Successful Stakeholder-based Products

Carl Kessler, John Sweitzer

ISBN-13: 978-0-13-157551-6

Praise for *Disciplined Agile Delivery*

"Finally, a practical down-to-earth guide that is true to agile values and principles while at the same time acknowledging the realities of the business and the bigger picture. You will find no purist dogma here, nor any hype or hyperbole. Ambler and Lines show how to navigate the varied contexts and constraints of both team-level and enterprise-level needs to hit the agile 'sweet spot' for your team and attain the real benefits of sustainable agility. I wish I'd had this book ten years ago!"
—**Brad Appleton**, agile/lean development champion for a large fortune 150 telecommunications company

"We have found the guidance from *Disciplined Agile Delivery* to be a great help in customizing our PMO governance for agile projects at CP Rail. The book will definitely be on the must-read list for teams using agile delivery."
—**Larry Shumlich**, project manager coach, Canadian Pacific Railway

"This book is destined to become the de facto standard reference guide for any organization trying to apply agile/scrum in a complex environment. Scott and Mark provide practical guidance and experiences from successful agile teams on what it takes to bring an end-to-end agile delivery lifecycle to the enterprise."
—**Elizabeth Woodward**, IBM agile community leader, coauthor of
A Practical Guide to Distributed Scrum

"There are many ways to achieve the benefits of agility, so it's really encouraging to see a pragmatic and usable 'umbrella' description that encapsulates most of these without becoming a diluted kind of 'best of' compilation, or a one-size-fits-all. Great reading for anyone orientating themselves in an ever-growing and complex field."
—**Nick Clare**, agile coach/principal consultant, Ivar Jacobson International

"Scott and Mark have compiled an objective treatment of a tough topic. Loaded with insights from successful application under game conditions, this book strikes a good balance between progressive agilists looking to accelerate change and conservative organizational managers looking for scalable solutions."
—**Walker Royce**, chief software economist, IBM

"*Disciplined Agile Delivery*, a hybrid and experience-based approach to software delivery, reflects the growing trend toward pragmatism and away from the anti-syncretism that has plagued the software development industry for over 40 years. I commend Scott and Mark for writing this book and showing the leadership necessary to take our profession to the next level."
—**Mark Kennaley**, CTO, Software-Development-Experts.com;
author of *SDLC 3.0: Beyond a Tacit Understanding of Agile*

"I've seen 'certified agile' run rampant in an organization and create more severe problems than it solved. Finally, we have a definitive source on how to apply agile pragmatically with discipline to deliver success. Thanks, Scott and Mark."
—**Carson Holmes**, EVP, service delivery, Fourth Medium Consulting, Inc.

Disciplined Agile Delivery

Disciplined Agile Delivery

A Practitioner's Guide to Agile Software Delivery in the Enterprise

Scott Ambler and Mark Lines

IBM Press
Pearson plc
Upper Saddle River, NJ • Boston • Indianapolis • San Francisco
New York • Toronto • Montreal • London • Munich • Paris • Madrid
Cape Town • Sydney • Tokyo • Singapore • Mexico City

Ibmpressbooks.com

IBM Press Program Managers: Steven Stansel, Ellice Uffer
Cover design: IBM Corporation
Publisher: Paul Boger
Marketing Manager: Stephane Nakib
Publicist: Heather Fox
Acquisitions Editor: Bernard Goodwin
Managing Editor: Kristy Hart
Designer: Alan Clements
Project Editor: Betsy Harris
Copy Editor: Geneil Breeze
Indexer: Erika Millen
Compositor: Nonie Ratcliff
Proofreader: Debbie Williams
Manufacturing Buyer: Dan Uhrig

Published by Pearson plc
Publishing as IBM Press

IBM Press offers excellent discounts on this book when ordered in quantity for bulk purchases or special sales, which may include electronic versions and/or custom covers and content particular to your business, training goals, marketing focus, and branding interests. For more information, please contact:

U. S. Corporate and Government Sales
1-800-382-3419
corpsales@pearsontechgroup.com

For sales outside the U. S., please contact:

International Sales
international@pearsoned.com

Library of Congress Cataloging-in-Publication data is on file.

ISBN-13: 978-0-13-281013-5
ISBN-10: 0-13-281013-1

Text printed in the United States on recycled paper at R.R. Donnelley in Crawfordsville, Indiana.
First printing June 2012

For Olivia, who will always be my little pumpkin. —Scott

To my beautiful family, Louise, Brian, and Katherine,
for your love and support. I am truly blessed… —Mark

Contents

Part 2: People First

Part 3: Initiating a Disciplined Agile Delivery Project

Part 4: Building a Consumable Solution Incrementally

Part 5: Releasing the Solution

Part 6: Disciplined Agile Delivery in the Enterprise

Foreword

The process wars are over, and agile has won. While working at Forrester, we observed that agile methods had gone mainstream, with the majority of organizations saying that they were using agile on at least 38% of their projects. But the reality of agile usage, as Scott and Mark point out, is far from the original ideas described by the 17 thought leaders in 2001. Instead, agile is undermined by organizational inertia, politics, people's skills, management practices, vendors, and outsourced development. I observed that the reality of agile was something more akin to *water-scrum-fall*—water-scrum describing the inability of an organization to start any project without a lengthy phase up front that defined all the requirements, planning the project in detail, and even doing some of the design. Scrum-fall defines the release practices operated by most organizations in which software is released infrequently, with costly and complex release practices that include manual deployments and testing. Water-scrum-fall is not all bad, with some benefits to the development team working in an iterative, scrum-based way, but water-scrum-fall does not release the power of agile. Enterprise agile not only creates the most efficient software development process but more importantly delivers software of greater business value. It is my assertion that scaled, enterprise-level agile is therefore not just important for your software-delivery organization but crucial for business success. Fixing water-scrum-fall will increase business value and enable organizations to compete. And this book provides a framework to make that happen.

In this book, Scott and Mark, two very experienced software-delivery change agents, describe a detailed framework for how to scale agile to the enterprise. They show how change leaders can amplify agile, making it not just about teams but about the whole value stream of software delivery. In many books about agile adoption, the really tricky problems associated with governance and organizational control are often side-stepped, focusing on why it is stupid to do something rather than how to change that something. Scott and Mark have not done this. They have focused clearly on the gnarly problems of scale, describing practical ways of fixing governance models, staffing issues, and management approaches. Their use of lean positions their framework in a broader context, allowing change leaders to not only improve their delivery capability but also connect it directly to business value. But be warned: These problems are not easily solved, and adopting these ideas does not just require agile skills but also draws on other process models, change techniques, and good engineering practices.

Scott and Mark not only made me think, but they also reminded me of lots of things that I had forgotten—things that the agile fashion police have made uncool to talk about. This book is not about fashionable agile; it is about serious change, and it should be required reading for any change leader.

Dave West @davidjwest
Chief Product Officer, Tasktop, and former VP and Research Director, Forrester Research

Preface

The information technology (IT) industry has an embarrassing reputation from the perspective of our customers. For decades we have squandered scarce budgets and resources, reneged on our promises, and delivered functionality that is not actually needed by the client. An outsider looking at our profession must be truly baffled. We have so many process frameworks and various bodies of knowledge such that we ourselves have difficulty keeping up with just the acronyms, let alone the wealth of material behind them. Consider: PMBOK, SWEBOK, BABOK, ITIL®, COBIT, RUP, CMMI, TOGAF, DODAF, EUP, UML, and BPMN, to name a few. Even within the narrow confines of the agile community, we have Scrum, XP, CI, CD, FDD, AMDD, TDD, and BDD, and many others. There is considerable overlap between these strategies but also considerable differences. We really need to get our act together.

Why Agile?

On traditional/classical projects, and sadly even on "heavy RUP" projects, basic business and system requirements often end up written in multiple documents in different fashions to suit the standards of the various standards bodies. Although in some regulatory environments this proves to be good practice, in many situations it proves to be a huge waste of time and effort that often provides little ultimate value—you must tailor your approach to meet the needs of your situation.

Fortunately, agile methods have surfaced over the past decade so that we can save ourselves from this madness. The beauty of agile methods is that they focus us on delivering working software of high business value to our customers early and often. We are free to adjust the project objectives at any time as the business needs change. We are encouraged to minimize documentation, to minimize if not eliminate the bureaucracy in general. Who doesn't like that?

More importantly, agile strategies seem to be working in practice. Scott has run surveys[1] within the IT industry for several years now, and he has consistently found that the agile and iterative strategies to software development have consistently outperformed both traditional and ad-hoc strategies. There's still room for improvement, and this book makes many suggestions for such improvements, but it seems clear that agile is a step in the right direction. For example, the 2011 IT Project Success Survey revealed that respondents felt that 67% of agile projects were considered successful (they met all of their success criteria), 27% were considered challenged (they delivered but didn't meet all success criteria), and only 6% were considered failures. The same survey showed that 50% of traditional projects were considered successful, 36% challenged, and 14% failures. The 2008 IT Project Success survey found that agile project teams were much more adept at delivering quality solutions, good return on investment (ROI), and solutions that stakeholders wanted to work with and did so faster than traditional teams. Granted, these are averages and your success at agile may vary, but they are compelling results. We're sharing these numbers with you now to motivate you to take agile seriously but, more importantly, to illustrate a common theme throughout this book: We do our best to shy away from the overly zealous "religious" discussions found in many software process books and instead strive to have fact-based discussions backed up by both experiential and research-based evidence. There are still some holes in the evidence because research is ongoing, but we're far past the "my process can beat up your process" arguments we see elsewhere.

Alistair Cockburn, one of the original drafters of the Agile Manifesto, has argued that there are three primary aspects of agile methodologies:

- Self-discipline, with Extreme Programming (XP) being the exemplar methodology
- Self-organization, with Scrum being the exemplar methodology
- Self-awareness, with Crystal being the exemplar methodology

As you'll see in this book, Disciplined Agile Delivery (DAD) addresses Cockburn's three aspects.

Why Disciplined Agile Delivery?

Although agile strategies appear to work better than traditional strategies, it has become clear to us that the pendulum has swung too far the other way. We have gone from overly bureaucratic and document-centric processes to almost nothing but code. To be fair, agile teams do invest in planning, although they are unlikely to create detailed plans; they do invest in modeling, although are unlikely to create detailed models; they do create deliverable documentation (such as operations manuals and system overview documents), although are unlikely to create detailed specifications. However, agile teams have barely improved upon the results of iterative approaches. The 2011 IT

---

1. The original questions, source data (without identifying information due to privacy concerns), and summary slide decks for all surveys can be downloaded free of charge from www.ambysoft.com/surveys/.

Project Success survey found that 69% of iterative projects were considered successful, 25% challenged, and 6% failures, statistically identical results as agile projects. Similarly, the 2008 IT Project Success survey found that agile and iterative teams were doing statistically the same when it came to quality, ability to deliver desired functionality, and timeliness of delivery and that agile was only slightly better than iterative when it came to ROI. The reality of agile hasn't lived up to the rhetoric, at least when we compare agile strategies with iterative strategies. The good news is that it is possible to do better.

Our experience is that "core" agile methods such as Scrum work wonderfully for small project teams addressing straightforward problems in which there is little risk or consequence of failure. However, "out of the box," these methods do not give adequate consideration to the risks associated with delivering solutions on larger enterprise projects, and as a result we're seeing organizations investing a lot of effort creating hybrid methodologies combining techniques from many sources. The Disciplined Agile Delivery (DAD) process framework, as described in this book, is a hybrid approach which extends Scrum with proven strategies from Agile Modeling (AM), Extreme Programming (XP), and Unified Process (UP), amongst other methods. DAD extends the construction-focused lifecycle of Scrum to address the full, end-to-end delivery lifecycle[2] from project initiation all the way to delivering the solution to its end users. The DAD process framework includes advice about the technical practices purposely missing from Scrum as well as the modeling, documentation, and governance strategies missing from both Scrum and XP. More importantly, in many cases DAD provides advice regarding viable alternatives and their trade-offs, enabling you to tailor DAD to effectively address the situation in which you find yourself. By describing what works, what doesn't work, and more importantly why, DAD helps you to increase your chance of adopting strategies that will work for you.

Indeed there are an increasing number of high-profile project failures associated with agile strategies that are coming to light. If we don't start supplementing core agile practices with a more disciplined approach to agile projects at scale, we risk losing the hard-earned momentum that the agile pioneers have generated.

This book does not attempt to rehash existing agile ideas that are described in many other books, examples of which can be found in the references sections. Rather, this book is intended to be a practical guide to getting started today with agile practices that are structured within a disciplined approach consistent with the needs of enterprise-scale, mission-critical projects.

What Is the History?

The Disciplined Agile Delivery (DAD) process framework began as a concept in 2007 that Scott worked on in his role as chief methodologist for agile and lean at IBM® Rational®. He was working with customers around the world to understand and apply agile techniques at scale, and he

---

2. A full system/product lifecycle goes from the initial idea for the product, through delivery, to operations and support and often has many iterations of the delivery lifecycle. Our focus in DAD is on delivery, although we discuss how the other aspects of the system lifecycle affect the delivery lifecycle.

noticed time and again that organizations were struggling to adopt mainstream agile methods such as Extreme Programming (XP) and Scrum. At the same time Mark, also working with organizations to adopt and apply agile techniques in practice, observed the same problems. In many cases, the organization's existing command-and-control culture hampered its adoption of these more chaordic techniques. Furthermore, although many organizations were successful at agile pilot projects, they struggled to roll out agile strategies beyond these pilot teams. A common root cause was that the methods did not address the broader range of issues faced by IT departments, let alone the broader organization. Something wasn't quite right.

Separately we began work on addressing these problems, with Scott taking a broad approach by observing and working with dozens of organizations and Mark taking a deep approach through long-term mentoring of agile teams at several organizations. In 2009 Scott led the development of the DAD process framework within IBM Rational, an effort that continues to this day. This work included the development of DAD courseware, whitepapers, and many blog postings on IBM developerWorks®.[3]

What About Lean?

There are several reasons why lean strategies are crucial for DAD:

- Lean provides insights for streamlining the way that DAD teams work.
- Lean provides a solid foundation for scaling DAD to address complex situations, a topic we touch on throughout the book but intend to address in greater detail in a future book.
- Lean principles explain why agile practices work, a common theme throughout this book.
- Lean strategies, particularly those encapsulated by Kanban, provide an advanced adoption strategy for DAD.

So why aren't we writing about Disciplined Lean Development (DLD) instead? Our experience is that lean strategies, as attractive and effective as they are, are likely beyond all but a small percentage of teams at this time. Perhaps this "small" percentage is 10% to 15%—it's certainly under 20%—but only time will tell. We've found that most development teams are better served with a lightweight, end-to-end process framework that provides coherent and integrated high-level advice for how to get the job done without getting bogged down in procedural details. Having said that, many of the options that we describe for addressing the goals of the DAD process framework are very clearly lean in nature, and we expect that many teams will evolve their process from a mostly agile one to a mostly lean one over time.

DAD is the happy medium between the extremes of Scrum, a lightweight process framework that focuses on only a small part of the delivery process, and RUP, a comprehensive process framework that covers the full delivery spectrum. DAD addresses the fundamentals of agile

---

3. https://www.ibm.com/developerworks/mydeveloperworks/blogs/ambler/

delivery while remaining flexible enough for you to tailor it to your own environment. In many ways, Scrum taught agilists how to crawl, DAD hopes to teach agilists how to walk, and agility@scale and lean approaches such as Kanban will teach us how to run.

How Does This Book Help?

We believe that there are several ways that you'll benefit from reading this book:

- It describes an end-to-end agile delivery lifecycle.
- It describes common agile practices, how they fit into the lifecycle, and how they work together.
- It describes how agile teams work effectively within your overall organization in an "enterprise aware" manner, without assuming everyone else is going to be agile, too.
- It uses consistent, sensible terminology but also provides a map to terminology used by other methods.
- It explains the trade-offs being made and in many cases gives you options for alternative strategies.
- It provides a foundation from which to scale your agile strategy to meet the real-world situations faced by your delivery teams.
- It goes beyond anecdotes to give fact-based reasons for why these techniques work.
- It really does answer the question "how do all these agile techniques fit together?"

Where Are We Coming From?

Both of us have seen organizations adopt Scrum and extend it with practices from XP, Agile Modeling, and other sources into something very similar to DAD or to tailor down the Unified Process into something similar to DAD. With either strategy, the organizations invested a lot of effort that could have been easily avoided. With DAD, we hope to help teams and organizations avoid the expense of a lengthy trial-and-error while still enabling teams to tailor the approach to meet their unique situation.

Scott led the development of DAD within IBM Rational and still leads its evolution, leveraging his experiences helping organizations understand and adopt agile strategies. This book also reflects lessons learned from within IBM Software Group, a diverse organization of 27,000 developers worldwide, and IBM's Agile with Discipline (AwD) methodology followed by professionals in IBM Global Service's Accelerated Solution Delivery (ASD) practice. In the autumn of 2009 DAD was captured in IBM Rational's three-day "Introduction to Disciplined Agile Delivery" workshop. This workshop was rolled out in the first quarter of 2010 to IBM business partners, including UPMentors, and Mark became one of the first non-IBMers to be qualified to deliver the workshop. Since then, Mark has made significant contributions to DAD, bringing his insights and experiences to bear.

What's The Best Way to Read this Book?

Most people will want to read this cover to cover. However, there are three exceptions:

- Experienced agile practitioners can start with Chapter 1, "Disciplined Agile Delivery in a Nutshell," which overviews DAD. Next, read Chapter 4, "Roles, Rights, and Responsibilities," to understand the team roles. Then, read Chapters 6 through 19 to understand in detail how DAD works.

- Senior IT managers should read Chapter 1 to understand how DAD works at a high level and then skip to Chapter 20, "Governing Disciplined Agile Teams," which focuses on governing[4] agile teams.

- People who prefer to work through an example of DAD in practice should read the case study chapters first. These are: Chapter 12, "Initiating a Disciplined Agile Delivery Project—Case Study"; Chapter 17, "Case Study: Construction Phase"; and Chapter 19, "Case Study: Transition Phase."

We hope that you embrace the core agile practices popularized by leading agile methods but choose to supplement them with some necessary rigor and tooling appropriate for your organization and project realities.

Incidentally, a portion of the proceeds from the sale of this book are going to the Cystic Fibrosis Foundation and Toronto Sick Kid's Hospital, so thank you for supporting these worthy causes.

The Disciplined Agile Delivery Web Site

www.DisciplinedAgileDelivery.com is the community Web site for anything related to DAD. Mark and Scott are the moderators. You will also find other resources such as information on DAD-related education, service providers, and supporting collateral that can be downloaded. We invite anyone who would like to contribute to DAD to participate as a blogger. Join the discussion!

---

4. Warning: Throughout the book we'll be using "agile swear words" such as governance, management, modeling, and yes, even the D-word—documentation. We'd like to apologize now for our use of foul language such as this.

Abbreviations Used in This Book

AD	Agile Data
AM	Agile Modeling
AMDD	Agile Model Driven Development
ASM	Agile Scaling Model
ATDD	Acceptance test driven development
AUP	Agile Unified Process
AwD	Agile with Discipline
BABOK	Business Analysis Book of Knowledge
BDD	Behavior driven development
BI	Business intelligence
BPMN	Business Process Modeling Notation
CASE	Computer aided software engineering
CD	Continuous deployment
CI	Continuous integration
CM	Configuration management
CMMI	Capability Maturity Model Integrated
COBIT	Control Objectives for Information and Related Technology
DAD	Disciplined Agile Delivery
DDJ	Dr. Dobb's Journal
DevOps	Development operations
DI	Development intelligence
DODAF	Department of Defense Architecture Framework
DSDM	Dynamic System Development Method
EUP	Enterprise Unified Process
EVM	Earned value management
FDD	Feature Driven Development
GQM	Goal question metric
HR	Human resources
IT	Information technology
ITIL	Information Technology Infrastructure Library
JIT	Just in time

MDD	Model driven development
MMR	Minimally marketable release
NFR	Non-functional requirement
NPV	Net present value
OSS	Open source software
PMBOK	Project Management Book of Knowledge
PMO	Project management office
ROI	Return on investment
RRC	Rational Requirements Composer
RSA	Rational Software Architect
RTC	Rational Team Concert™
RUP	Rational Unified Process
SCM	Software configuration management
SDLC	System development lifecycle
SLA	Service level agreement
SWEBOK	Software Engineering Book of Knowledge
TCO	Total cost of ownership
TDD	Test-driven development
TFD	Test first development
TOGAF	The Open Group Architecture Framework
T&M	Time and materials
TVO	Total value of ownership
UAT	User acceptance testing
UML	Unified Modeling Language
UI	User interface
UP	Unified Process
UX	User experience
WIP	Work in progress
XP	Extreme Programming

Acknowledgments

We'd like to thank the following people for their feedback regarding this book: Kevin Aguanno, Brad Appleton, Ned Bader, Joshua Barnes, Peter Bauwens, Robert Boyle, Alan L. Brown, David L. Brown, Murray Cantor, Nick Clare, Steven Crago, Diana Dehm, Jim Densmore, Paul Gorans, Leslie R. Gornig, Tony Grout, Carson Holmes, Julian Holmes, Mark Kennaley, Richard Knaster, Per Kroll, Cherifa Liamani, Christophe Lucas, Bruce MacIsaac, Trevor O. McCarthy, M.K. McHugh, Jean-Louise Marechaux, Evangelos Mavrogiannakis, Brian Merzbach, Berne C. Miller, Mike Perrow, Andy Pittaway, Emily J. Ratliff, Oliver Roehrsheim, Walker Royce, Chris Sibbald, Lauren Schaefer, Paul Sims, Paula Stack, Alban Tsui, Karthikeswari Vijayapandian, Lewis J. White, Elizabeth Woodward, and Ming Zhi Xie.

We'd also like to thank the following people for their ideas shared with us in online forums, which were incorporated into this book: Eric Jan Malotaux, Bob Marshall, Valentin Tudor Mocanu, Allan Shalloway, Steven Shaw, Horia Slusanschi, and Marvin Toll.

About the Authors

Scott W. Ambler is Chief Methodologist for IT with IBM Rational, working with IBM customers around the world to help them to improve their software processes. In addition to Disciplined Agile Delivery (DAD), he is the founder of the Agile Modeling (AM), Agile Data (AD), Agile Unified Process (AUP), and Enterprise Unified Process (EUP) methodologies and creator of the Agile Scaling Model (ASM). Scott is the (co-)author of 20 books, including *Refactoring Databases*, *Agile Modeling*, *Agile Database Techniques*, *The Object Primer,* 3rd Edition, and *The Enterprise Unified Process*. Scott is a senior contributing editor with *Dr. Dobb's Journal*. His personal home page is www.ambysoft.com.

Mark Lines co-founded UPMentors in 2007. He is a disciplined agile coach and mentors organizations on all aspects of software development. He is passionate about reducing the huge waste in most IT organizations and demonstrates hands-on approaches to speeding execution and improving quality with agile and lean techniques. Mark provides IT assessments and executes course corrections to turn around troubled projects. He writes for many publications and is a frequent speaker at industry conferences. Mark is also an instructor of IBM Rational and UPMentors courses on all aspects of software development. His Web site is www.UPMentors.com. Mark can be reached at Mark@UPMentors.com.

CHAPTER 1

Disciplined Agile Delivery in a Nutshell

For every complex problem there is a solution that is simple, neat, and wrong. —*H L Mencken*

The agile software development paradigm burst onto the scene in the spring of 2001 with the publication of the Agile Manifesto (www.agilemanifesto.org). The 17 authors of the manifesto captured strategies, in the form of four value statements and twelve supporting principles, which they had seen work in practice. These strategies promote close collaboration between developers and their stakeholders; evolutionary and regular creation of software that adds value to the organization; remaining steadfastly focused on quality; adopting practices that provide high value and avoiding those which provide little value (e.g., work smarter, not harder); and striving to improve your approach to development throughout the lifecycle. For anyone with experience on successful software development teams, these strategies likely sound familiar.

Make no mistake, agile is not a fad. When mainstream agile methods such as Scrum and Extreme Programming (XP) were introduced, the ideas contained in them were not new, nor were they even revolutionary at the time. In fact, many of them have been described in-depth in other methods such as Rapid Application Development (RAD), Evo, and various instantiations of the Unified Process, not to mention classic books such as Frederick Brooks' *The Mythical Man Month*. It should not be surprising that working together closely in collocated teams and collaborating in a unified manner toward a goal of producing working software produces results superior to those working in specialized silos concerned with individual rather than team performance. It should also come as no surprise that reducing documentation and administrative bureaucracy saves money and speeds up delivery.

While agile was once considered viable only for small, collocated teams, improvements in product quality, team efficiency, and on-time delivery have motivated larger teams to take a closer look at adopting agile principles in their environments. In fact, IBM has teams of several hundred people, often distributed around the globe, that are working on complex products who are applying agile techniques—and have been doing so successfully for years. A recent study conducted by the *Agile Journal* determined that 88% of companies, many with more than 10,000 employees, are using or evaluating agile practices on their projects. Agile is becoming the dominant software development paradigm. This trend is also echoed in other industry studies, including one conducted by *Dr. Dobb's Journal (DDJ)*, which found a 76% adoption rate of agile techniques, and within those organizations doing agile, 44% of the project teams on average are applying agile techniques in some way.

Unfortunately, we need to take adoption rate survey results with a grain of salt: A subsequent *Ambysoft* survey found that only 53% of people claiming to be on "agile teams" actually were. It is clear that agile methods have been overly hyped by various media over the years, leading to abuse and misuse; in fact, the received message regarding agile appears to have justified using little or no process at all. For too many project teams this resulted in anarchy and chaos, leading to project failures and a backlash from the information technology (IT) and systems engineering communities that prefer more traditional approaches.

Properly executed, agile is not an excuse to be undisciplined. The execution of mainstream agile methods such as XP for example have always demanded a disciplined approach, certainly more than traditional approaches such as waterfall methods. Don't mistake the high ceremony of many traditional methods to be a sign of discipline, rather it's a sign of rampant and often out-of-control bureaucracy. However, mainstream agile methods don't provide enough guidance for typical enterprises. Mature implementations of agile recognize a basic need in enterprises for a level of rigor that core agile methods dismiss as not required such as governance, architectural planning, and modeling. Most mainstream agile methods admit that their strategies require significant additions and adjustments to scale beyond teams of about eight people who are working together in close proximity. Furthermore, most Fortune 1000 enterprises and government agencies have larger solution delivery teams that are often distributed, so the required tailoring efforts can prove both expensive and risky. The time is now for a new generation of agile process framework.

Figure 1.1 shows a mind map of the structure of this chapter. We describe each of the topics in the map in clockwise order, beginning at the top right.

THE BIG IDEAS IN THIS CHAPTER

- People are the primary determinant of success for IT delivery projects.
- Moving to a disciplined agile delivery process is the first step in scaling agile strategies.
- Disciplined Agile Delivery (DAD) is an enterprise-aware hybrid software process framework.
- Agile strategies should be applied throughout the entire delivery lifecycle.
- Agile teams are easier to govern than traditional teams.

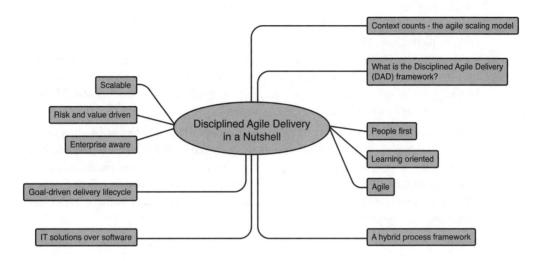

Figure 1.1 Outline of this chapter

Context Counts—The Agile Scaling Model

To understand the need for the Disciplined Agile Delivery (DAD) process framework you must start by recognizing the realities of the situation you face. The Agile Scaling Model (ASM) is a contextual framework that defines a roadmap to effectively adopt and tailor agile strategies to meet the unique challenges faced by an agile software development team. The first step to scaling agile strategies is to adopt a disciplined agile delivery lifecycle that scales mainstream agile construction strategies to address the full delivery process from project initiation to deployment into production. The second step is to recognize which scaling factors, if any, are applicable to your project team and then tailor your adopted strategies to address the range of complexities the team faces.

The ASM, depicted in Figure 1.2, defines three process categories:

1. **Core agile development.** Core agile methods—such as Scrum, XP, and Agile Modeling (AM)—focus on construction-oriented activities. They are characterized by value-driven lifecycles where high-quality potentially shippable software is produced on a regular basis by a highly collaborative, self-organizing team. The focus is on small (<15 member) teams that are collocated and are developing straightforward software.

2. **Agile delivery.** These methods—including the DAD process framework (described in this book) and Harmony/ESW—address the full delivery lifecycle from project initiation to production. They add appropriate, lean governance to balance self-organization and add a risk-driven viewpoint to the value-driven approach to increase the chance of project success. They focus on small-to-medium sized (up to 30 people) near-located teams (within driving distance) developing straightforward solutions. Ideally DAD teams are small and collocated.

3. **Agility@scale.** This is disciplined agile development where one or more scaling factors apply. The scaling factors that an agile team may face include team size, geographical distribution, organizational distribution (people working for different groups or companies), regulatory compliance, cultural or organizational complexity, technical complexity, and enterprise disciplines (such as enterprise architecture, strategic reuse, and portfolio management).

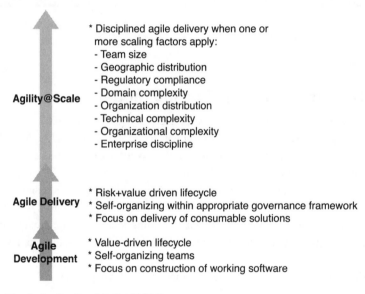

Figure 1.2   The Agile Scaling Model (ASM)

This book describes the DAD process framework. In most cases we assume that your team is small (<15 people) and is either collocated or near-located (within driving distance). Having said that, we also discuss strategies for scaling agile practices throughout the book. The DAD process framework defines the foundation to scale agile strategies to more complex situations.

What Is the Disciplined Agile Delivery (DAD) Process Framework?

Let's begin with a definition:

> The Disciplined Agile Delivery (DAD) process framework is a people-first, learning-oriented hybrid agile approach to IT solution delivery. It has a risk-value lifecycle, is goal-driven, is scalable, and is enterprise aware.

From this definition, you can see that the DAD process framework has several important characteristics:

- People first
- Learning oriented
- Agile
- Hybrid
- IT solution focused
- Goal-driven
- Delivery focused
- Enterprise aware
- Risk and value driven
- Scalable

To gain a better understanding of DAD, let's explore each of these characteristics in greater detail.

People First

Alistair Cockburn refers to people as "non-linear, first-order components" in the software development process. His observation, based on years of ethnographic work, is that people and the way that they collaborate are the primary determinants of success in IT solution delivery efforts. This philosophy, reflected in the first value statement of the Agile Manifesto, permeates DAD. DAD team members should be self-disciplined, self-organizing, and self-aware. The DAD process framework provides guidance that DAD teams leverage to improve their effectiveness, but it does not prescribe mandatory procedures.

The traditional approach of having formal handoffs of work products (primarily documents) between different disciplines such as requirements, analysis, design, test, and development is a very poor way to transfer knowledge that creates bottlenecks and proves in practice to be a huge source of waste of both time and money. The waste results from the loss of effort to create interim documentation, the cost to review the documentation, and the costs associated with updating the documentation. Yes, some documentation will be required, but rarely as much as is promoted by traditional techniques. Handoffs between people provide opportunities for misunderstandings and injection of defects and are described in lean software development as one of seven sources of waste. When we create a document we do not document our complete understanding of what we are describing, and inevitably some knowledge is "left behind" as tacit knowledge that is not passed on. It is easy to see that after many handoffs the eventual deliverable may bear little resemblance to the original intent. In an agile environment, the boundaries between disciplines should be torn down and handoffs minimized in the interest of working as a team rather than specialized individuals.

In DAD we foster the strategy of cross-functional teams made up of cross-functional people. There should be no hierarchy within the team, and team members are encouraged to be cross-functional in their skillset and indeed perform work related to disciplines other than their specialty. The increased understanding that the team members gain beyond their primary discipline results in more effective use of resources and reduced reliance on formal documentation and handoffs.

As such, agile methods deemphasize specific roles. In Scrum for instance, there are only three Scrum team roles: ScrumMaster, product owner, and team member. Nonteam roles can be extended to stakeholder and manager. The primary roles described by DAD are stakeholder, team lead, team member, product owner, and architecture owner. These roles are described in detail in Chapter 4, "Roles, Rights, and Responsibilities."

Notice that tester and business analyst are not primary roles in the DAD process framework. Rather, a generic team member should be capable of doing multiple things. A team member who specializes in testing might be expected to volunteer to help with requirements, or even take a turn at being the ScrumMaster (team lead). This doesn't imply that everyone needs to be an expert at everything, but it does imply that the team as a whole should cover the skills required of them and should be willing to pick up any missing skills as needed. However, as you learn in Chapter 4, DAD also defines several secondary roles often required in scaling situations.

Team members are often "generalizing specialists" in that they may be a specialist in one or more disciplines but should have general knowledge of other disciplines as well. More importantly, generalizing specialists are willing to collaborate closely with others, to share their skills and experiences with others, and to pick up new skills from the people they work with. A team made up of generalizing specialists requires few handoffs between people, enjoys improved collaboration because the individuals have a greater appreciation of the background skills and priorities of the various IT disciplines, and can focus on what needs to be done as opposed to focusing on whatever their specialties are.

However, there is still room for specialists. For example, your team may find that it needs to set up and configure a database server. Although you could figure it out yourselves, it's probably easier, faster, and less expensive if you could have someone with deep experience help your team for a few days to work with you to do so. This person could be a specialist in database administration. In scaling situations you may find that your build becomes so complex that you need someone(s) specifically focused on doing just that. Or you may bring one or more business analyst specialists onto the team to help you explore the problem space in which you're working.

DAD teams and team members should be

- Self-disciplined in that they commit only to the work they can accomplish and then perform that work as effectively as possible
- Self-organizing, in that they estimate and plan their own work and then proceed to collaborate iteratively to do so
- Self-aware, in that they strive to identify what works well for them, what doesn't, and then learn and adjust accordingly

Although people are the primary determinant of success for IT solution delivery projects, in most situations it isn't effective to simply put together a good team of people and let them loose on the problem at hand. If you do this then the teams run several risks, including investing significant time in developing their own processes and practices, ramping up on processes or practices that more experienced agile teams have discovered are generally less effective or efficient, and not adapting their own processes and practices effectively. We can be smarter than that and recognize that although people are the primary determinant of success they aren't the only determinant. The DAD process framework provides coherent, proven advice that agile teams can leverage and thereby avoid or at least minimize the risks described previously.

Learning Oriented

In the years since the Agile Manifesto was written we've discovered that the most effective organizations are the ones that promote a learning environment for their staff. There are three key aspects that a learning environment must address. The first aspect is domain learning—how are you exploring and identifying what your stakeholders need, and perhaps more importantly how are you helping the team to do so? The second aspect is process learning, which focuses on learning to improve your process at the individual, team, and enterprise levels. The third aspect is technical learning, which focuses on understanding how to effectively work with the tools and technologies being used to craft the solution for your stakeholders.

The DAD process framework suggests several strategies to support domain learning, including initial requirements envisioning, incremental delivery of a potentially consumable solution, and active stakeholder participation through the lifecycle. To support process-focused learning DAD promotes the adoption of retrospectives where the team explicitly identifies potential process improvements, a common agile strategy, as well as continued tracking of those improvements. Within the IBM software group, a business unit with more than 35,000 development professionals responsible for delivering products, we've found that agile teams that held retrospectives improved their productivity more than teams that didn't, and teams that tracked their implementation of the identified improvement strategies were even more successful. Technical learning often comes naturally to IT professionals, many of whom are often eager to work with and explore new tools, techniques, and technologies. This can be a double-edged sword—although they're learning new technical concepts they may not invest sufficient time to master a strategy before moving on to the next one or they may abandon a perfectly fine technology simply because they want to do something new.

There are many general strategies to improve your learning capability. Improved collaboration between people correspondingly increases the opportunities for people to learn from one another. Luckily high collaboration is a hallmark of agility. Investing in training, coaching, and mentoring are obvious learning strategies as well. What may not be so obvious is the move away from promoting specialization among your staff and instead fostering a move toward people with more robust skills, something called being a generalizing specialist (discussed in greater detail in Chapter 4). Progressive organizations aggressively promote learning opportunities for their people outside their specific areas of specialty as well as opportunities to actually apply these new skills.

If you're experienced with, or at least have read about, agile software development, the previous strategies should sound familiar. Where the DAD process framework takes learning further is through enterprise awareness. Core agile methods such as Scrum and XP are typically project focused, whereas DAD explicitly strives to both leverage and enhance the organizational ecosystem in which a team operates. So DAD teams should both leverage existing lessons learned from other agile teams and also take the time to share their own experiences. The implication is that your IT department needs to invest in a technology for socializing the learning experience across teams. In 2005 IBM Software Group implemented internal discussion forums, wikis, and a center of competency (some organizations call them centers of excellence) to support their agile learning efforts. A few years later they adopted a Web 2.0 strategy based on IBM Connections to support enterprise learning. When the people and teams within an organization choose a learning-oriented approach, providing them with the right tools and support can increase their success.

Agile

The DAD process framework adheres to, and as you learn in Chapter 2, "Introduction to Agile and Lean," enhances, the values and principles of the Agile Manifesto. Teams following either iterative or agile processes have been shown to produce higher quality solutions, provide greater return on investment (ROI), provide greater stakeholder satisfaction, and deliver these solutions quicker as compared to either a traditional/waterfall approach or an ad-hoc (no defined process) approach. High quality is achieved through techniques such as continuous integration (CI), developer regression testing, test-first development, and refactoring—these techniques, and more, are described later in the book. Improved ROI comes from a greater focus on high-value activities, working in priority order, automation of as much of the IT drudgery as possible, self-organization, close collaboration, and in general working smarter not harder. Greater stakeholder satisfaction is increased through enabling active stakeholder participation, by incrementally delivering a potentially consumable solution each iteration, and by enabling stakeholders to evolve their requirements throughout the project.

A Hybrid Process Framework

DAD is the formulation of many strategies and practices from both mainstream agile methods as well as other sources. The DAD process framework extends the Scrum construction lifecycle to address the full delivery lifecycle while adopting strategies from several agile and lean methods. Many of the practices suggested by DAD are the ones commonly discussed in the agile community—such as continuous integration (CI), daily coordination meetings, and refactoring—and some are the "advanced" practices commonly applied but for some reason not commonly discussed. These advanced practices include initial requirements envisioning, initial architecture envisioning, and end-of-lifecycle testing to name a few.

The DAD process framework is a hybrid, meaning that it adopts and tailors strategies from a variety of sources. A common pattern that we've seen time and again within organizations is that they adopt the Scrum process framework and then do significant work to tailor ideas from other sources to flesh it out. This sounds like a great strategy. However, given that we repeatedly see new organizations tailoring Scrum in the same sort of way, why not start with a robust process framework that provides this common tailoring in the first place? The DAD process framework adopts strategies from the following methods:

- **Scrum.** Scrum provides an agile project management framework for complex projects. DAD adopts and tailors many ideas from Scrum, such as working from a stack of work items in priority order, having a product owner responsible for representing stakeholders, and producing a potentially consumable solution every iteration.
- **Extreme Programming (XP).** XP is an important source of development practices for DAD, including but not limited to continuous integration (CI), refactoring, test-driven development (TDD), collective ownership, and many more.
- **Agile Modeling (AM).** As the name implies, AM is the source for DAD's modeling and documentation practices. This includes requirements envisioning, architecture envisioning, iteration modeling, continuous documentation, and just-in-time (JIT) model storming.
- **Unified Process (UP).** DAD adopts many of its governance strategies from agile instantiations of the UP, including OpenUP and Agile Unified Process (AUP). In particular these strategies include having lightweight milestones and explicit phases. We also draw from the Unified Process focus on the importance of proving that the architecture works in the early iterations and reducing much of the business risk early in the lifecycle.

- **Agile Data (AD).** As the name implies AD is a source of agile database practices, such as database refactoring, database testing, and agile data modeling. It is also an important source of agile enterprise strategies, such as how agile teams can work effectively with enterprise architects and enterprise data administrators.

- **Kanban.** DAD adopts two critical concepts—limiting work in progress and visualizing work—from Kanban, which is a lean framework. These concepts are in addition to the seven principles of lean software development, as discussed in Chapter 2.

The concept of DAD being a hybrid of several existing agile methodologies is covered in greater detail in Chapter 3, "Foundations of Disciplined Agile Delivery."

OUR APOLOGIES

Throughout this book we'll be applying agile swear words such as *phase*, *serial*, and yes, even the "G word"—*governance*. Many mainstream agilists don't like these words and have gone to great lengths to find euphemisms for them. For example, in Scrum they talk about how a project begins with Sprint 0 (DAD's Inception phase), then the construction sprints follow, and finally you do one or more hardening/release sprints (DAD's Transition phase). Even though these sprint categories follow one another this clearly isn't serial, and the Scrum project team clearly isn't proceeding in phases. Or so goes the rhetoric. Sigh. We prefer plain, explicit language.

IT Solutions over Software

One aspect of adopting a DAD approach is to mature your focus from producing software to instead providing solutions that provide real business value to your stakeholders within the appropriate economic, cultural, and technical constraints. A fundamental observation is that as IT professionals we do far more than just develop software. Yes, software is clearly important, but in addressing the needs of our stakeholders we often provide new or upgraded hardware, change the business/operational processes that stakeholders follow, and even help change the organizational structure in which our stakeholders work.

This shift in focus requires your organization to address some of the biases that crept into the Agile Manifesto. The people who wrote the manifesto (which we fully endorse) were for the most part software developers, consultants, and in many cases both. It was natural that they focused on their software development strengths, but as the ten-year agile anniversary workshop (which Scott participated in) identified, the agile community needs to look beyond software development.

It's also important to note that the focus of this book is on IT application development. The focus is not on product development, even though a tailored form of DAD is being applied for that within IBM, nor is it on systems engineering. For agile approaches to embedded software development or systems engineering we suggest you consider the IBM Harmony process framework.

Goal-Driven Delivery Lifecycle

DAD addresses the project lifecycle from the point of initiating the project to construction to releasing the solution into production. We explicitly observe that each iteration is *not* the same. Projects do evolve and the work emphasis changes as we move through the lifecycle. To make this clear, we carve the project into phases with lightweight milestones to ensure that we are focused on the right things at the right time. Such areas of focus include initial visioning, architectural modeling, risk management, and deployment planning. This differs from mainstream agile methods, which typically focus on the construction aspects of the lifecycle. Details about how to perform initiation and release activities, or even how they fit into the overall lifecycle, are typically vague and left up to you.

Time and again, whenever either one of us worked with a team that had adopted Scrum we found that they had tailored the Scrum lifecycle into something similar to Figure 1.3, which shows the lifecycle of a DAD project.[1] This lifecycle has several critical features:

- **It's a delivery lifecycle.** The DAD lifecycle extends the Scrum construction lifecycle to explicitly show the full delivery lifecycle from the beginning of a project to the release of the solution into production (or the marketplace).

- **There are explicit phases.** The DAD lifecycle is organized into three distinct, named phases, reflecting the agile coordinate-collaborate-conclude (3C) rhythm.

- **The delivery lifecycle is shown in context.** The DAD lifecycle recognizes that activities occur to identify and select projects long before their official start. It also recognizes that the solution produced by a DAD project team must be operated and supported once it is delivered into production (in some organizations called operations) or in some cases the marketplace, and that important feedback comes from people using previously released versions of the solution.

- **There are explicit milestones.** The milestones are an important governance and risk reduction strategy inherent in DAD.

The lifecycle of Figure 1.3, which we focus on throughout this book, is what we refer to as the basic agile version. This is what we believe should be the starting point for teams that are new to DAD or even new to agile. However, DAD is meant to be tailored to meet the needs of your situation. As your team gains more experience with DAD you may choose to adopt more and more lean strategies, and may eventually evolve your lifecycle into something closer to what you see in

---

1. Granted, in this version we're using the term "iteration" instead of "sprint," and "work item list" instead of "product backlog."

Figure 1.4. A primary difference of this lean version of the DAD lifecycle is that the phase and iteration cadence disappears in favor of a "do it when you need to do it" approach, a strategy that works well only for highly disciplined teams.

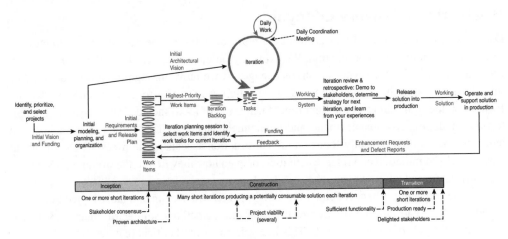

Figure 1.3   The Disciplined Agile Delivery (DAD) lifecycle

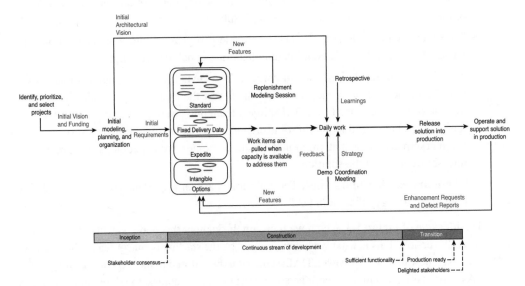

Figure 1.4   A lean version of the DAD lifecycle

One of the challenges with describing a process framework is that you need to provide sufficient guidance to help people understand the framework, but if you provide too much guidance you become overly prescriptive. As we've helped various organizations improve their software processes over the years, we've come to the belief that the various process protagonists are coming from one extreme or the other. Either there are very detailed processes descriptions (the IBM Rational Unified Process [RUP] is one such example), or there are very lightweight process descriptions, with Scrum being a perfect example. The challenge with RUP is that many teams do not have the skill to tailor it down appropriately, often resulting in extra work being performed. On the other hand many Scrum teams had the opposite problem with not knowing how to tailor it up appropriately, resulting in significant effort reinventing or relearning techniques to address the myriad issues that Scrum doesn't cover (this becomes apparent in Chapter 3). Either way, a lot of waste could have been avoided if only there was an option between these two extremes.

To address this challenge the DAD process framework is goals driven, as summarized in Figure 1.5. There are of course many ways that these goals can be addressed, so simply indicating the goals is of little value. In Chapters 6 through 19 when we describe each of the phases in turn, we suggest strategies for addressing the goals and many times discuss several common strategies for doing so and the trade-offs between them. Our experience is that this goals-driven, suggestive approach provides just enough guidance for solution delivery teams while being sufficiently flexible so that teams can tailor the process to address the context of the situation in which they find themselves. The challenge is that it requires significant discipline by agile teams to consider the issues around each goal and then choose the strategy most appropriate for them. This may not be the snazzy new strategy that everyone is talking about online, and it may require the team to perform some work that they would prefer to avoid given the choice.

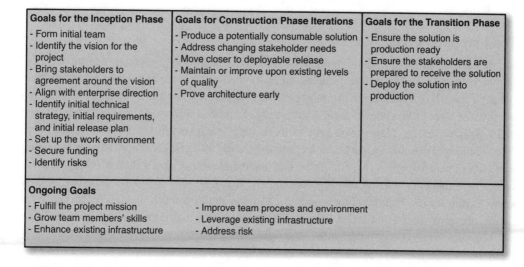

Goals for the Inception Phase	Goals for Construction Phase Iterations	Goals for the Transition Phase
- Form initial team - Identify the vision for the project - Bring stakeholders to agreement around the vision - Align with enterprise direction - Identify initial technical strategy, initial requirements, and initial release plan - Set up the work environment - Secure funding - Identify risks	- Produce a potentially consumable solution - Address changing stakeholder needs - Move closer to deployable release - Maintain or improve upon existing levels of quality - Prove architecture early	- Ensure the solution is production ready - Ensure the stakeholders are prepared to receive the solution - Deploy the solution into production

Ongoing Goals

- Fulfill the project mission
- Grow team members' skills
- Enhance existing infrastructure

- Improve team process and environment
- Leverage existing infrastructure
- Address risk

Figure 1.5 Goals addressed throughout a DAD project

Figure 1.5 doesn't provide a full listing of the goals your team will address. There are several personal goals of individuals, such as specific learning goals and the desire for interesting work, compensation, and public recognition of their work. There are also specific stakeholder goals, which will be unique to your project.

THE AGILE 3C RHYTHM

Over the years we've noticed a distinct rhythm, or cadence, at different levels of the agile process. We call this the agile 3C rhythm, for coordinate, collaborate, and conclude. This is similar conceptually to Deming's Plan, Do, Check, Act (PDCA) cycle where coordinate maps to plan, collaborate maps to do, and conclude maps to check and act. The agile 3C rhythm occurs at three levels in the DAD process framework:

1. **Release.** The three phases of the delivery lifecycle—Inception, Construction, Transition—map directly to coordinate, collaborate, and conclude, respectively.

2. **Iteration.** DAD construction iterations begin with an iteration planning workshop (coordinate), doing the implementation work (collaborate), and then wrapping up the iteration with a demo and retrospective (conclude).

3. **Day.** A typical day begins with a short coordination meeting, is followed by the team collaborating to do their work, and concludes with a working build (hopefully) at the end of the day.

Let's overview the DAD phases to better understand the contents of the DAD process framework.

The Inception Phase

Before jumping into building or buying a solution, it is worthwhile to spend some time identifying the objectives for the project. Traditional methods invest a large amount of effort and time planning their projects up front. Agile approaches suggest that too much detail up front is not worthwhile since little is known about what is truly required as well as achievable within the time and budget constraints. Mainstream agile methods suggest that very little effort be invested in up-front planning. Their mantra can be loosely interpreted as "let's just get started and we will determine where we are going as we go." To be fair, some agile teams have a short planning iteration or do some planning before initiating the project. "Sprint 0" is a common misnomer used by some Scrum teams. Extreme Programming (XP) has the "Planning Game." In fact, a 2009 Ambysoft survey found that teams take on average 3.9 weeks to initiate their projects. In DAD, we recognize the need to point the ship in the right direction before going full-speed ahead—typically between a few days and a few weeks—to initiate the project. Figure 1.6 overviews the potential activities that occur during Inception, described in greater detail in Chapters 6 through 12. This phase ends when the team has developed a vision for the release that the stakeholders agree to and has obtained support for the rest of the project (or at least the next stage of it).

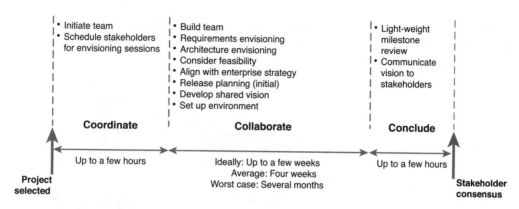

Figure 1.6   Inception phase overview

The Construction Phase

The Construction phase in DAD is the period of time during which the required functionality is built. The timeline is split up into a number of time-boxed iterations. These iterations, the potential activities of which are overviewed in Figure 1.7, should be the same duration for a particular project and typically do not overlap. Durations of an iteration for a certain project typically vary from one week to four weeks, with two and four weeks being the most common options. At the end of each iteration a demonstrable increment of a potentially consumable solution has been produced and regression tested. At this time we consider the strategy of how to move forward in the project. We could consider executing an additional iteration of construction, and whether to deploy the solution to the customer at this time. If we determine that there is sufficient functionality to justify the cost of transition, sometimes referred to as minimally marketable release (MMR), then our Construction phase ends and we move into the Transition phase. The Construction phase is covered in greater detail in Chapters 13 through 17.

The Transition Phase

The Transition phase focuses on delivering the system into production (or into the marketplace in the case of a consumer product). As you can see in Figure 1.8 there is more to transition than merely copying some files onto a server. The time and effort spent transitioning varies from project to project. Shrink-wrapped software entails the manufacturing and distribution of software and documentation. Internal systems are generally simpler to deploy than external systems. High visibility systems may require extensive beta testing by small groups before release to the larger population. The release of a brand new system may entail hardware purchase and setup while updating an existing system may entail data conversions and extensive coordination with the user community. Every project is different. From an agile point of view, the Transition phase ends when the stakeholders are ready and the system is fully deployed, although from a lean point of view, the phase ends when your stakeholders have worked with the solution in production and are delighted by it. The Transition phase is covered in greater detail in Chapters 18 and 19.

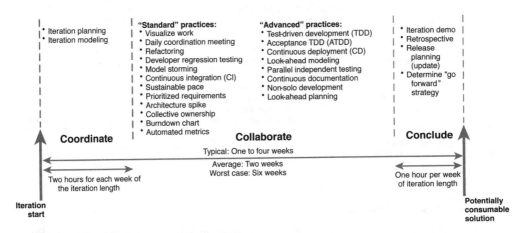

Figure 1.7   Construction iteration overview

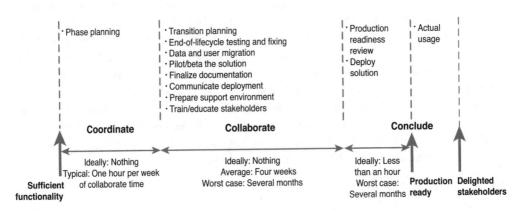

Figure 1.8   Transition phase overview

Some agilists will look at the potential activities listed in Figure 1.8 and ask why you couldn't do these activities during construction iterations. The quick answer is yes, you should strive to do as much testing as possible throughout the lifecycle and you should strive to write and maintain required documentation throughout the lifecycle, and so on. You may even do some stakeholder training in later construction iterations and are more likely to do so once your solution has been released into production. The more of these things that you do during the Construction phase, the shorter the Transition phase will be, but the reality is that many organizations require end-of-lifecycle testing (even if it's only one last run of your regression test suite), and there is often a need to tidy up supporting documentation. The November 2010 Ambysoft Agile State of the Art survey found that the average transition/release phase took 4.6 weeks.

Enterprise Aware

DAD teams work within your organization's enterprise ecosystem, as do other teams, and explicitly try to take advantage of the opportunities presented to them—to coin an environmental cliché "disciplined agilists act locally and think globally." This includes working closely with the following: enterprise technical architects and reuse engineers to leverage and enhance[2] the existing and "to be" technical infrastructure; enterprise business architects and portfolio managers to fit into the overall business ecosystem; senior managers who should be governing the various teams appropriately; operations staff to support your organization's overall development and operations (DevOps) efforts; data administrators to access and improve existing data sources; IT development support people to understand and follow enterprise IT guidance (such as coding, user interface, security, and data conventions to name a few); and business experts who share their market insights, sales forecasts, service forecasts, and other important concerns. In other words, DAD teams should adopt what Mark refers to as a "whole enterprise" mindset.

WHAT IS APPROPRIATE GOVERNANCE?

Effective governance strategies should enhance that which is being governed. An appropriate approach to governing agile delivery projects, and we suspect other types of efforts, is based on motivating and then enabling people to do what is right for your organization. What is right of course varies, but this typically includes motivating teams to take advantage of, and to evolve, existing corporate assets following common guidelines to increase consistency, and working toward a shared vision for your organization. Appropriate governance is based on trust and collaboration. Appropriate governance strategies should enhance the ability of DAD teams to deliver business value to their stakeholders in a cost effective and timely manner.

Unfortunately many existing IT governance strategies are based on a command-and-control, bureaucratic approach that often proves ineffective in practice. Chapter 20, "Governing Disciplined Agile Teams," explores appropriate governance, the impact of traditional governance strategies, and how to adopt an appropriate governance strategy in greater detail.

With the exception of startup companies, agile delivery teams do not work in a vacuum. Often existing systems are currently in production, and minimally your solution shouldn't impact them. Granted, hopefully your solution will leverage existing functionality and data available in

---

2. Disciplined agile teams strive to reduce the level of technical debt in your enterprise by adopting the philosophy of mature campers and hikers around the world: Leave it better than how you found it.

production so there will always be at least a minor performance impact without intervention of some kind. You will often have other teams working in parallel to your team, and you may want to take advantage of a portion of what they're doing and vice versa. Your organizations may be working toward a vision to which your team should contribute. A governance strategy might be in place, although it may not be obvious to you, which hopefully enhances what your team is doing.

Enterprise awareness is an important aspect of self-discipline because as a professional you should strive to do what's right for your organization and not just what's interesting for you. Teams developing in isolation may choose to build something from scratch, or use different development tools, or create different data sources, when perfectly good ones that have been successfully installed, tested, configured, and fine-tuned already exist within the organization. We can and should do better by doing the following:

- **Leveraging enterprise assets.** There may be many enterprise assets, or at least there should be, that you can use and evolve. These include common development guidelines, such as coding standards, data conventions, security guidelines, and user interface standards. DAD teams strive to work to a common infrastructure; for example, they use the enterprise-approved technologies and data sources whenever possible, and better yet they work to the "to be" vision for your infrastructure. But enterprise assets are far more than standards. If your organization uses a disciplined architecture-centric approach to building enterprise software, there will be a growing library of service-based components to reuse and improve upon for the benefit of all current and future solutions. To do this DAD teams collaborate with enterprise professionals—including enterprise architects, enterprise business modelers, data administrators, operations staff, and reuse engineers—throughout the lifecycle and particularly during Inception during envisioning efforts. Leveraging enterprise assets increases consistency and thereby ease of maintenance, decreases development costs and time, and decreases operational costs.

- **Enhancing your organizational ecosystem.** The solution being delivered by a DAD team should minimally fit into the existing organizational ecosystem—the business processes and systems supporting them—it should better yet enhance that ecosystem. To do this, the first step is to leverage existing enterprise assets wherever possible as described earlier. DAD teams work with operations and support staff closely throughout the lifecycle, particularly the closer you get to releasing into production, to ensure that they understand the current state and direction of the organizational ecosystem. DAD teams often are supported by an additional independent test team—see Chapter 15, "A Typical Day of Construction"—that performs production integration testing (among other things) to ensure that your solution works within the target production environment it will face at deployment time.

- **Sharing learnings.** DAD teams are learning oriented, and one way to learn is to hear about the experiences of others. The implication is that DAD teams must also be prepared to share their own learnings with other teams. Within IBM we support agile discussion forums, informal presentations, training sessions delivered by senior team members, and internal conferences to name a few strategies.

- **Open and honest monitoring.** Although agile approaches are based on trust, smart governance strategies are based on a "trust but verify and then guide" mindset. An important aspect of appropriate governance is the monitoring of project teams through various means. One strategy is for anyone interested in the current status of a DAD project team to attend their daily coordination meeting and listen in, a strategy promoted by the Scrum community. Although it's a great strategy we highly recommend, it unfortunately doesn't scale very well because the senior managers responsible for governance are often busy people with many efforts to govern, not just your team. In fact Scott found exactly this in the 2010 How Agile Are You? survey. Another approach, one that we've seen to be incredibly effective, is for DAD teams to use instrumented and integrated tooling, such as Rational Team Concert (RTC), which generates metrics in real time that can be displayed on project dashboards. You can see an example of such a dashboard for the Jazz™ team itself at www.jazz.net, a team following an open commercial strategy. Such dashboards are incredibly useful for team members to know what is going on, let alone senior managers. A third strategy is to follow a risk-driven lifecycle, discussed in the next section, with explicit milestones that provide consistent and coherent feedback as to the project status to interested parties.

Risk and Value Driven

The DAD process framework adopts what is called a risk/value lifecycle, effectively a lightweight version of the strategy promoted by the Unified Process (UP). DAD teams strive to address common project risks, such as coming to stakeholder consensus around the vision and proving the architecture early in the lifecycle. DAD also includes explicit checks for continued project viability, whether sufficient functionality has been produced, and whether the solution is production ready. It is also value driven, a strategy that reduces delivery risk, in that DAD teams produce potentially consumable solutions on a regular basis.

It has been said "attack the risks before they attack you." This is a philosophy consistent with the DAD approach. DAD adopts what is called a risk-value driven lifecycle, an extension of the value-driven lifecycle common to methods such as Scrum and XP. With a value-driven lifecycle you produce potentially shippable software every iteration or, more accurately from a DAD perspective, a potentially consumable solution every iteration. The features delivered represent those in the requirements backlog that are of highest value from the perspective of the stakeholders. With a risk-value driven lifecycle you also consider features related to risk as high priority items, not just high-value features. With this in mind we explicitly address risks common to IT delivery projects as soon as we possibly can. Value-driven lifecycles address three important risks—the risk of not delivering at all, the risk of delivering the wrong functionality, and political risks resulting from lack of visibility into what the team is producing. Addressing these risks is a great start, but it's not the full risk mitigation picture.

First and foremost, DAD includes and extends standard strategies of agile development methods to reduce common IT delivery risks:

- **Potentially consumable solutions.** DAD teams produce potentially consumable solutions every construction iteration, extending Scrum's strategy of potentially shippable software to address usability concerns (the consumability aspect) and the wider issue of producing solutions and not just software. This reduces delivery risk because the stakeholders are given the option to have the solution delivered into production when it makes sense to do so.

- **Iteration demos.** At the end of each construction iteration the team should demo what they have built to their key stakeholders. The primary goal is to obtain feedback from the stakeholders and thereby improve the solution they're producing, decreasing functionality risk. A secondary goal is to indicate the health of the project by showing their completed work, thereby decreasing political risk (assuming the team is working successfully).

- **Active stakeholder participation.** The basic idea is that not only should stakeholders, or their representatives (i.e., product owners), provide information and make decisions in a timely manner, they can also be actively involved in the development effort itself. For example, stakeholders can often be actively involved in modeling when inclusive tools such as paper and whiteboards are used. Active stakeholder involvement through the entire iteration, and not just at demos, helps to reduce both delivery and functionality risk due to the greater opportunities to provide feedback to the team.

DAD extends current agile strategies for addressing risk on IT delivery projects, but also adopts explicit, lightweight milestones to further reduce risk. At each of these milestones an explicit assessment as to the viability of the project is made by key stakeholders and a decision as to whether the project should proceed is made. These milestones, indicated on the DAD lifecycle depicted previously in Figure 1.3, are

- **Stakeholder consensus.** Held at the end of the Inception phase, the goal of this milestone is to ensure that the project stakeholders have come to a reasonable consensus as to the vision of the release. By coming to this agreement we reduce both functionality and delivery risk substantially even though little investment has been made to date in the development of a working solution. Note that the right outcome for the business may in fact be that stakeholder consensus cannot be reached for a given project vision. Our experience is that you should actually expect to cancel upwards to10% of your projects at this milestone, and potentially 25% of projects that find themselves in scaling situations (and are therefore higher risk).

- **Proven architecture.** In the early Construction phase iterations we are concerned with reducing most of the risk and uncertainty related to the project. Risk can be related to many things, such as requirements uncertainty, team productivity, business risk, and schedule risk. However, at this point in time much of the risk on an IT delivery project is typically related to technology, specifically at the architecture level. Although the high-level architecture models created during the Inception phase are helpful for thinking through the architecture, the only way to be truly sure that the architecture can support the requirements is by proving it with working code. This is a vertical slice through the software and hardware tiers that touches all points of the architecture from end to end. In the UP this is referred to as "architectural coverage" and in XP as a "steel thread" or "tracer bullet." By writing software to prove out the architecture DAD teams greatly reduce a large source of technical risk and uncertainty by discovering and then addressing any deficiencies in their architecture early in the project.

- **Continued viability.** In Scrum the idea is that at the end of each sprint (iteration) your stakeholders consider the viability of your project. In theory this is a great idea, but in practice it rarely seems to happen. The cause of this problem is varied—perhaps the stakeholders being asked to make this decision have too much political stake in the project to back out of it unless things get really bad, and perhaps psychologically people don't notice that a project gets into trouble in the small periods of time typical of agile iterations. The implication is that you need to have purposeful milestone reviews where the viability of the project is explicitly considered. We suggest that for a given release you want to do this at least twice, so for a six month project you would do it every second month, and for longer projects minimally once a quarter.

- **Sufficient functionality.** The Construction phase milestone is reached when enough functionality has been completed to justify the expense of transitioning the solution into production. The solution must meet the acceptance criteria agreed to earlier in the project, or be close enough that it is likely any critical quality issues will be addressed during the Transition phase.

- **Production ready.** At the end of the Transition phase your key stakeholders need to determine whether the solution should be released into production. At this milestone, the business stakeholders are satisfied with and accept the solution and the operations and support staff are satisfied with the relevant procedures and documentation.

- **Delighted stakeholders.** The solution is running in production and stakeholders have indicated they are delighted with it.

Scalable

The DAD process framework provides a scalable foundation for agile IT and is an important part of the IBM agility@scale[3] strategy. This strategy makes it explicit that there is more to scaling than team size and that there are multiple scaling factors a team may need to address. These scaling factors are

- **Geographical distribution.** A team may be located in a single room, on the same floor but in different offices or cubes, in the same building, in the same city, or even in different cities around the globe.

- **Team size.** Agile teams may range from as small as two people to hundreds and potentially thousands of people.

- **Regulatory compliance.** Some agile teams must conform to industry regulations such as the Dodd-Frank act, Sarbanes-Oxley, or Food and Drug Administration (FDA) regulations.

- **Domain complexity.** Some teams apply agile techniques in straightforward situations, such as building an informational Web site, to more complex situations such as building an internal business application, and even in life-critical health-care systems.

- **Technical complexity.** Some agile teams build brand-new, "greenfield systems" from scratch running on a single technology platform with no need to integrate with other systems. At the other end of the spectrum some agile teams are working with multiple technologies, evolving and integrating with legacy systems, and evolving and accessing legacy data sources.

- **Organizational distribution.** Some agile teams are comprised of people who work for the same group in the same company. Other teams have people from different groups of the same company. Some teams are made up of people from similar organizations working together as a consortium. Some team members may be consultants or contractors. Sometimes some of the work is outsourced to one or more external service provider(s).

- **Organizational complexity.** In some organizations people work to the same vision and collaborate effectively. Other organizations suffer from politics. Some organizations have competing visions for how people should work and worse yet have various subgroups following and promoting those visions.

- **Enterprise discipline.** Many organizations want their teams to work toward a common enterprise architecture, take advantage of strategic reuse opportunities, and reflect their overall portfolio strategy.

---

3. The term "agility@scale" was first coined by Scott in his IBM developerWorks blog by the same name. The full term is now IBM agility@scale™.

Each team will find itself in a unique situation and will need to tailor its strategy accordingly. For example a team of 7 collocated people in a regulatory environment works differently than a team of 40 people spread out across several locations in a non-regulatory environment. Each of the eight scaling factors just presented will potentially motivate tailoring to DAD practices. For example, although all DAD teams do some sort of initial requirements envisioning during the Inception phase, a small team does so differently than a large team, a collocated team uses different tools (such as whiteboards and paper) than a distributed team (who might use IBM Rational Requirements Composer in addition), and a team in a life-critical regulatory environment would invest significantly more effort capturing requirements than a team in a nonregulatory environment. Although it's the same fundamental practice, identifying initial requirements, the way in which you do so will be tailored to reflect the situation you face.

Concluding Thoughts

The good news is that evidence clearly shows that agile methods deliver superior results compared to traditional approaches and that the majority of organizations are either using agile techniques or plan to in the near future. The bad news is that the mainstream agile methods—including Scrum, Extreme Programming (XP), and Agile Modeling (AM)—each provide only a part of the overall picture for IT solution delivery. Disciplined Agile Delivery (DAD) is a hybrid process framework that pulls together common practices and strategies from these methods and supplements these with others, such as Agile Data and Kanban, to address the full delivery lifecycle. DAD puts people first, recognizing that individuals and the way that they work together are the primary determinants of success on IT projects. DAD is enterprise aware, motivating teams to leverage and enhance their existing organizational ecosystem, to follow enterprise development guidelines, and to work with enterprise administration teams. The DAD lifecycle includes explicit milestones to reduce project risk and increase external visibility of key issues to support appropriate governance activities by senior management.

Additional Resources

For more detailed discussions about several of the topics covered in this chapter:

- **The Agile Manifesto.** The four values of the Agile Manifesto are posted at http://www. agilemanifesto.org/ and the twelve principles behind it at http://www.agilemanifesto. org/principles.html. Chapter 2 explores both in greater detail.
- **Agile surveys.** Throughout the chapter we referenced several surveys. The Agile Journal Survey is posted at http://www.agilejournal.com/. The results from the Dr. Dobb's Journal (DDJ) and Ambysoft surveys are posted at http://www.ambysoft.com/surveys/, including the original source data, questions as they were asked, as well as slide decks summarizing Scott Ambler's analysis.

- **People first.** The Alistair Cockburn paper, "Characterizing people as non-linear, first-order components in software development" at http://alistair.cockburn.us/ Characterizing+people+as+non-linear%2c+first-order+components+in+software+ development argues that people are the primary determinant of success on IT projects. In "Generalizing Specialists: Improving Your IT Skills" at http://www.agilemodeling. com/essays/generalizingSpecialists.htm Scott argues for the need to move away from building teams of overly specialized people.

- **The Agile Scaling Model (ASM).** The ASM is described in detail in the IBM white-paper "The Agile Scaling Model (ASM): Adapting Agile Methods for Complex Environments" at ftp://ftp.software.ibm.com/common/ssi/sa/wh/n/raw14204usen/ RAW14204USEN.PDF.

- **Lean.** For more information about lean software development, Mary and Tom Poppendieck's *Implementing Lean Software Development: From Concept to Cash* (Addison Wesley, 2007) is the best place to start.

- **Hybrid processes.** In *SDLC 3.0: Beyond a Tacit Understanding of Agile* (Fourth Medium Press, 2010), Mark Kennaley summarizes the history of the software process movement and argues for the need for hybrid processes that combine the best ideas from the various process movements over the past few decades.

CHAPTER 2

Introduction to Agile and Lean

Important agile philosophy: If something is hard, do it more often so that you get good at it and thereby make it easy.

The first generation of software development methodologies has been described as "waterfall" or "traditional." They are plan-driven, serial processes that assume that software development is comprised of a series of tasks that are easily identified, predictable, and repeatable. History has shown that this is clearly not the case. Unlike other engineering disciplines, software is a creative science that requires some degree of invention and carries a material level of risk and uncertainty on almost every nontrivial project.

The second generation of software development methodologies has been described as "iterative." These methods acknowledge that breaking large projects into a series of time-boxed iterations allows opportunities to demonstrate progress to stakeholders, learn and adapt processes, and get an early insight into quality, among other benefits. Statistics show that iterative methods produce marked improvements in success over traditional approaches. However, project success level on iterative projects is still far from satisfactory.[1] We continue to miss deadlines, exceed budgets, and deliver solutions that do not meet the needs of our business stakeholders. Our productivity levels are poor and our processes and bureaucracies generate a phenomenal amount of waste in terms of unneeded documentation, meetings, signoffs, delayed feedback cycles, and handoffs. Additionally, we continue to have quality problems related to undetected defects and hard to maintain software.

In 2001, 17 thought leaders (self-described "organizational anarchists") got together in Snowbird, Utah, to brainstorm about a better way to work. What emerged was the Manifesto for

---

1. On a roughly annual basis Scott runs industry surveys that explore success rates by paradigm. The survey results are posted at www.ambysoft.com/surveys/.

Agile Software Development, published at www.agilemanifesto.org, often referred to simply as the Agile Manifesto. The Agile Manifesto defined four values that in turn are supported by twelve principles, and this concise publication has had a significant impact on the way IT professionals think about software development. This collection of ideas formed a rebellion of sorts against document-driven, heavyweight software development processes.

Some unfortunate consequences have resulted from the popularity of the Agile Manifesto. First, for a subset of the agile community the Agile Manifesto has become the equivalent of a religious document, from which one should not deviate. Second, biases captured in the manifesto toward software projects have narrowed the scope of the discussion within the agile community, hampering agile adoption in enterprise situations. (More on this bias later.) Third, although there have been many excellent suggestions over the years for improving the Agile Manifesto, the religious fervor surrounding it makes it all but impossible to change. Yet, as we argue below, changes to the Agile Manifesto are needed if we're to be truly effective at applying agile strategies in enterprise situations.

Figure 2.1 shows a mind map of the structure of this chapter. We describe each of the topics in the map in clockwise order, beginning at the top right.

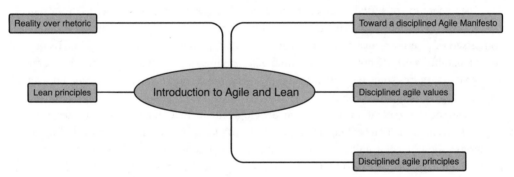

Figure 2.1   Outline of this chapter

THE BIG IDEAS IN THIS CHAPTER

- The values of, and principles behind, the Agile Manifesto provide an important philosophical foundation for agile.

- We have enhanced the Agile Manifesto to address the experiences of successful teams over the past 10 years taking a disciplined approach to agile delivery.

- The principles of lean software development are also an important part of the philosophical foundation for DAD.

- The rhetoric surrounding agile doesn't always reflect the realities of what people do on actual projects.

Toward a Disciplined Agile Manifesto

First of all, we are big fans of the ideas captured in the Agile Manifesto. Over the past decade we've applied the principles with great benefit for our customers and have learned from our experiences and from the experiences of other successful organizations doing so. However, what we've learned has motivated us to suggest enhancements to the manifesto to reflect the enterprise situations in which we have applied agile and lean strategies. These enhancements reflect the realities faced by most Disciplined Agile Delivery (DAD) teams.

We believe that the changes we're suggesting to the Agile Manifesto are straightforward:

1. Where the original manifesto focused on software development, a term that too many people have understood to mean *only* software development, we suggest that it should instead focus on solution delivery.

2. Where the original manifesto focused on customers, a word that for too many people appears to imply only the business stakeholders, we suggest that it focus on the full range of stakeholders instead.

3. Where the original manifesto focused on development teams, we suggest that the overall organizational ecosystem and its improvement be taken into consideration.

Furthermore, some interesting work has been done within the lean community since the Agile Manifesto was written, and we believe that it can benefit from these ideas. So let's explore what an updated Agile Manifesto might look like.

Disciplined Agile Values

Each of the four value statements of the Agile Manifesto is presented in the format X over Y. The important thing to understand about the statements is that while you should value the concepts on the right-hand side you should value the things on the left-hand side even more. A good way to think about the manifesto is that it defines preferences, not alternatives, encouraging a focus on certain areas but not eliminating others.

The four updated values—changes are indicated in italics—of the Agile Manifesto are as follows:

1. **Individuals and interactions over processes and tools.** Teams of people build software systems, and to do that they need to work together effectively. Who do you think would develop a better system: five skilled software developers with their own tools working together in a single room or ten low-skilled programmers with a well-defined process, the most sophisticated tools available, and each with their own best office money could buy? Our money would be on the smaller team of collocated software developers. Tools and processes are important; they're just not as important as working together effectively.

DAD differences: None. DAD whole-heartedly embraces individuals and interactions over processes and tools.

2. **Working *solutions* over comprehensive documentation.** When you ask someone whether they would want a 50-page document describing what you intend to build *or* the actual solution itself, what do you think they'll pick? Our guess is that 99 times out of 100 they'll choose the working solution. Doesn't working in such a manner that you produce a potentially consumable solution quickly and often make more sense? Furthermore, stakeholders will have a significantly easier time understanding any working solution that you produce rather than complex technical diagrams describing its internal workings or describing an abstraction of its usage, don't you think? Documentation has its place; deliverable documentation such as user manuals and operations manuals are in fact part of the overall solution, but it is only a small part. Never forget that the primary goal of IT delivery teams is to create solutions, not documents; otherwise it would be called documentation development wouldn't it? Note that the original Agile Manifesto used the term "software," not "solutions," for this value statement.

DAD differences: It's not enough to just have working software, but instead a consumable (usable) solution that includes software as well as potential changes to the hardware it runs on, the business process it supports, the documentation that should be produced with it, and even the organization of the people working with it.

3. *Stakeholder* **collaboration over contract negotiation.** Only your stakeholders can tell you what they want. Yes, they likely do not have the skills to exactly specify the solution. Yes, they likely won't get it right the first time. Yes, they'll likely change their minds once they see what your team produces. Yes, there is a wide range of stakeholders, including end users, their managers, senior IT managers, enterprise architects, operations staff, support staff, regulatory auditors, and many more (Chapter 4, "Roles, Rights, and Responsibilities," goes into greater detail). Working together with your stakeholders is hard, but that's the reality of the job. Having a contract with your stakeholders is important, but a contract isn't a substitute for effective communication. Successful teams work closely with their stakeholders, they invest the effort to discover what their stakeholders need, and they educate their stakeholders as to the implications of their decisions along the way. Mainstream methods suggest that the team should be able to create the solution in isolation, needing only to collaborate with each other and the "one voice of the customer" known as the product owner. This is seldom the case on nontrivial projects. The team will need to collaborate with many types of stakeholders such as those listed previously, not just the customer (representative). Note that the original Agile Manifesto used the term "customer" instead of "stakeholder" for this value statement.

DAD differences: Explicit recognition that there is a wide range of potential stakeholders for a solution, not just the business customer, and that you will need to interact with more than just a stakeholder representative to understand their true needs.

4. **Responding to change over following a plan.** People change their priorities for a variety of reasons. As work progresses, stakeholders' understanding of the problem domain and of your solution changes, as does the business environment and even the underlying technology. Change is a reality of software development, a reality that your delivery process must reflect. There is nothing wrong with having a project plan; in fact, we would be worried about any project that didn't have one. However, a project plan must be malleable and should only be detailed for the near term (a few weeks or less).

   DAD differences: None.

The interesting thing about these value statements is they are something that almost everyone instantly agrees to, yet rarely adheres to in practice. Senior management always claims that its employees are the most important aspect of an organization, yet we still see instances in industry where they treat their staff as replaceable assets. An even more damaging situation arises when management refuses to provide sufficient resources to comply with the processes that they insist project teams follow. Everyone will readily agree that the creation of a consumable solution is the fundamental goal of delivery, yet insist on spending months producing documentation describing what the solution is and how it is going to be built instead of simply rolling up their sleeves and building it. You get the idea—people say one thing and do another. This has to stop now. Disciplined agile developers do what they say and say what they do.

Disciplined Agile Principles

To help people to gain a better understanding of what agile software development is all about, the members of the Agile Alliance refined the philosophies captured in their manifesto into a collection of twelve principles. We have modified several of these principles—changes to the wording are shown in italics—and have added three new ones. The fifteen disciplined agile principles are the following:

1. **Our highest priority is to satisfy the stakeholder through early and continuous delivery of valuable *solutions*.** We must remember that the goal of solution delivery should be the delivery of an actual consumable solution—not only are we developing software, but we're often improving the hardware it runs on, evolving the business processes around the usage of the software, evolving the operations and support processes required to run the solution (an aspect of a "DevOps" approach to delivery), and even changing the organization structure of the people working with the solution. We need to move away from a strategy where we try to think through all the details up

front, thereby increasing both project risk and cost, and instead invest a bit of time thinking through the critical issues but allowing the details to evolve over time as we learn through incremental creation of the solution.

2. **Welcome changing requirements, even late in the *solution delivery lifecycle*.** Agile processes harness change for the *stakeholders'* competitive advantage. Like it or not, requirements will change throughout a project. Traditional software teams often adopt change management processes designed to prevent/reduce scope creep, but when you think about it these are really change prevention processes, not change management processes. Disciplined agilists follow an agile change management approach where functionality is worked on in priority order and requirements evolve to reflect stakeholders' improved understanding of what they actually need. Taking into consideration all of the aspects of delivering a solution, we recognize that we have to engage representatives from all stakeholder groups who are impacted—end users, end user managers, senior managers, operations, support, enterprise architects, IT governance personnel, finance, marketing, and more.

3. **Deliver working *solutions* frequently, from a couple of weeks to a couple of months, with a preference to the shorter time scale.** Frequent delivery of a consumable solution provides stakeholders with the opportunity to provide timely feedback, making the current status of your project transparent while at the same time providing an opportunity for stakeholders to provide improved direction for the development team.

4. ***Stakeholders* and developers must work together daily throughout the project.** Your project is in serious trouble if you don't have regular access to your project stakeholders, or at least their representatives. Disciplined agile teams adopt practices such as on-site customer and active stakeholder participation, and adopt inclusive tools and techniques that enable stakeholders to be actively involved with solution delivery.

5. **Build projects around motivated individuals.** Give them the environment and support they need, and trust them to get the job done. Too many organizations have a vision that they can hire hordes of relatively unskilled people, provide them with a CMMI/ISO/...-compliant process description, and they will successfully develop solutions. This doesn't seem to work all that well in practice. Disciplined agile teams, on the other hand, realize that you need to build teams from people who are willing to work together collaboratively and learn from each other. They have the humility to respect one another and realize that people are a primary success factor in solution delivery. We should allow them to create an environment in which they will thrive as a team. This includes allowing them to set up a work environment that fosters collaboration, use of tooling that they find most effective, and the freedom to customize and optimize their team's development process.

6. **The most efficient and effective method of conveying information to and within a** *delivery* **team is face-to-face conversation.** For a delivery team to succeed its members must communicate and collaborate effectively. There are many ways that people can communicate together, and face-to-face communication at a shared drawing environment (such as paper or a whiteboard) is often the most effective way to do so. Sending endless emails and creating exhaustive documents are far less effective than the immediate feedback of conversation. Distributed teams are not an excuse for reverting back to extensive documentation practices since video chat can be used for face-to-face conversations.

7. *Quantified business value* **is the primary measure of progress.** The primary measure of a solution delivery project should be the delivery of a consumable solution that provides actual value to your stakeholders. This solution should meet the changing needs of its stakeholders, not some form of "earned value" measure based on the delivery of documentation or the holding of meetings. Note we have replaced the phrase "Working software" with "Quantified Business Value." Demonstrable working solutions are indeed a key measure of progress but give a false measure of success if they do not provide the expected business value.

8. **Agile processes promote sustainable** *delivery*. The sponsors, developers, and users should be able to maintain a constant pace indefinitely. Just like you can't sprint for an entire marathon, you can't successfully produce a consumable solution by forcing people to work overtime for months at a time. Our experience is that you can only do high-quality, intellectual work for 5 to 6 hours a day before burning yourself out. The rest of the day can be filled up with email, meetings, water cooler discussions, and so on, but people's ability to do "real work" is limited. Yes, you might be able to do high-quality work for 12 hours a day, and do so for a few days straight, but after a while you become exhausted, and all you accomplish is 12 hours of mediocre work a day.

9. **Continuous attention to technical excellence and good design enhances agility.** It's much easier to understand, maintain, and evolve high-quality source code and data sources than it is to work with low-quality ones. Therefore, agilists know that they need to start with high-quality work products, to keep the quality high via refactoring, and to have a full regression test suite so that they know at all times that their solutions work. Disciplined agilists also adopt and follow organizational guidelines, such as programming standards, data guidelines, security guidelines, and user interface conventions (to name a few).

10. **Simplicity—the art of maximizing the amount of work not done—is essential.** Agile developers focus on high value activities, strive to maximize our stakeholders' return on investment and either cut out or automate the drudge work. From a lean point of view, simplicity is essential, so only the most important things are worked on and delays to them (e.g., by starting on less important work in parallel) are minimized.

11. **The best architectures, requirements, and designs emerge from self-organizing teams.** This is one of the most radical principles of the agile movement, one that we would love to see researched thoroughly by the academic community. The agile model driven development (AMDD) and test-driven design (TDD) methods are the primary approaches within the agile community to ensure the emergence of effective architectures, requirements, and designs.

12. **At regular intervals, the team reflects on how to become more effective, then tunes and adjusts its behavior accordingly.** Software process improvement (SPI) is a continual effort, and techniques such as retrospectives should be adopted to enable you to improve your approach to software development.

13. **NEW: Leverage and evolve the assets within your organizational ecosystem, and collaborate with the people responsible for those assets to do so.** Disciplined agile teams recognize that they are not working in a vacuum. Existing systems, data sources, frameworks, services, and other assets can and should be used and better yet improved as part of the delivery process of their new solution. These existing assets will constrain your solution architecture; much of the technical plumbing for your solution may have already been chosen for you. However, your productivity will potentially improve if you can focus on delivering new functionality and not on reinventing existing infrastructure.

14. **NEW: Visualize workflow to help achieve a smooth flow of delivery while keeping work in progress to a minimum.** DAD teams use status or dashboards to monitor their work in progress and to coordinate their activities, adjusting their approach to address bottlenecks or underutilization of people. This helps the team to maintain a consistent and sustainable delivery flow.

15. **NEW: The organizational ecosystem must evolve to reflect and enhance the efforts of agile teams, yet be sufficiently flexible to still support non-agile or hybrid teams.** Like it or not, organizations have a range of approaches when it comes to IT delivery. The overall IT strategy, including your governance strategy, must reflect this fact for the individual teams to work together effectively. Too many organizations run into trouble when they try to apply a repeatable, one-size-fits-all strategy to IT projects.

Stop for a moment and think about these principles. Is this the way that your IT delivery projects actually work? If not, is this the way that you think they should work? Read the principles once again. Are they radical and impossible goals as some people would claim, are they meaningless abstract principles, or are they simply common sense? Our belief is that these principles form a foundation of common sense upon which you can base successful DAD projects.

Lean Principles

In *Implementing Lean Software Development*, Mary and Tom Poppendieck show how the seven principles of lean manufacturing can be applied to optimize the whole IT value stream. We believe that these principles help to provide a foundation for effective agile development and also provide an explanation for why many of the agile techniques work in practice. The lean software development principles are the following:

- **Eliminate waste.** Lean thinking advocates regard any activity that does not directly add value to the finished product as waste. The three biggest sources of waste in software development are the addition of features that are not required, project churn, and crossing organizational boundaries (particularly between stakeholders and development teams). It is interesting to note that Walker Royce, chief software economist at IBM Rational, argues that the primary benefit of modern iterative/agile techniques is the reduction of scrap and rework late in the lifecycle. To reduce waste it is critical that DAD teams be allowed to self-organize and operate in a manner that reflects the work they're trying to accomplish.

- **Build in quality.** Your process should incorporate practices that minimize the number of defects that occur in the first place, but when this isn't possible you should work in such a way that you do a bit of work, validate it, fix any issues that you find, and then iterate. Inspecting after the fact, and queuing up defects to be fixed at some time in the future, isn't as effective. Agile practices that build quality into your process include refactoring, test-driven development (TDD), and non-solo development practices such as pair programming and modeling with others.

- **Create knowledge.** Planning is useful, but learning is essential. You want to promote strategies, such as iterative development, that help teams discover what stakeholders really want and act on that knowledge. It's also important for a team to regularly reflect on what they're doing and then act to improve their approach.

- **Defer commitment.** It's not necessary to start software development by defining a complete specification, and in fact we know it to be a questionable strategy at best. You can support the business effectively through flexible architectures that are change tolerant and by scheduling irreversible decisions to the last possible moment. Frequently, deferring commitment requires the ability to closely couple end-to-end business scenarios to capabilities developed in multiple applications by multiple projects. The DAD process framework adopts strategies from Agile Modeling that enable teams to think through issues and make commitments at appropriate points in time throughout the delivery lifecycle.

- **Deliver quickly.** Delivering high-quality solutions quickly is an achievable goal. By limiting the work of a team to its capacity, which is reflected by the team's velocity (this is the number of "points" of functionality a team delivers each iteration), you can establish a reliable and repeatable flow of work. An effective organization doesn't demand teams do more than they are capable of, but instead asks them to self-organize and determine what they can accomplish. Constraining these teams to delivering potentially consumable solutions on a regular basis motivates them to stay focused on continuously adding value. This strategy is reflected in the Disciplined Agile principle #14 described earlier.

- **Respect people.** The Poppendiecks also observe that sustainable advantage is gained from engaged, thinking people. The DAD "people first" tenet reflects this principle, the implication being that how you form and then support your delivery teams is critical to your success. Another implication is that you need a governance strategy that focuses on motivating and enabling IT teams, not on controlling them.

- **Optimize the whole.** If you want to be effective at a solution you must look at the bigger picture. You need to understand the high-level business processes that individual projects support—processes that often cross multiple systems. You need to manage programs of interrelated systems so you can deliver a complete solution to your stakeholders. This is a major difference from mainstream agile approaches, which tend to have a project focus and as a result will suboptimize around it. DAD avoids this problem by being enterprise aware and suggesting lean techniques such as value stream mapping, a stylized form of process modeling, to identify potential bottlenecks in the overall process so that they may be addressed. Measurements should address how well you're delivering business value, a motivation for the rewording of agile principle #7, because that is the sole reason for your IT department. A lean measurement system is one aspect of appropriate governance explicitly built into the DAD process framework.

The Kanban method, a lean methodology, describes several principles and techniques for improving your approach to software development. We want to share two Kanban principles that we believe are critical to your success. These principles are the following:

- **Visualize workflow.** Teams use a Kanban board, often a physical whiteboard or corkboard although electronic boards can also be used, that displays indications, called kanbans, of where in the process a piece of work is. The board is typically organized into columns, each of which represents a stage in the process or a work buffer or queue, and optionally rows indicating the allocation of capacity to classes of service. Each Kanban should have sufficient information, such as the name and ID of the work item and due date (if any), to enable decisions by the team without the direction of a manager. The goal is to visually communicate enough information to make the process self-organizing and self-expediting at the team level. The board is directly updated by team members throughout the day as the work proceeds, and blocking issues are identified during daily coordination meetings.

- **Limit work in progress (WIP).** Limiting work in progress reduces average lead time, which improves the quality of the work produced and thereby increases the overall productivity of your team. Reducing lead time also increases your ability to deliver valuable functionality frequently, which helps to build trust with your stakeholders. To limit work in progress you need to understand where your blocking issues are, address them quickly, and reduce queue and buffer sizes wherever you can. There are some interesting trade-offs: Although buffers and queues add WIP, and therefore increase lead time, they also smooth over the workflow and increase the predictability of lead time. The implication is that because every team is different, you will have different WIP limits that you'll need to set and then evolve yourself based on empirical results from experimentation.

Lean thinking is important for DAD teams, and particularly when you find yourself in a scaling situation, in several ways:

- **Lean provides an explanation for why many of the agile practices work.** For example, Agile Modeling's practices of lightweight, initial requirements envisioning followed by iteration modeling and just-in-time (JIT) model storming work because they reflect deferment of commitment regarding what needs to be built until it's actually needed, and the practices help eliminate waste because you're only modeling what needs to be built.

- **Lean offers insight into strategies for improving your software process.** For example, by understanding the source of waste in IT you can begin to identify it and then eliminate it.

- **Lean principles provide a philosophical foundation for scaling agile approaches.** Instead of optimizing software development, lean promotes optimizing the whole. That means that it's important to look at delivery of the overall solution to the customer, rather than suboptimizing by looking only at delivering software.

- **Lean provides techniques for identifying waste.** Value stream mapping, a technique common within the lean community, whereby you model a process and then identify how much time is spent on value-added work versus wait time, helps calculate overall time efficiency of what you're doing. Value stream maps are a straightforward way to illuminate your IT processes, providing insight into where significant problems exist. Scott has created value stream maps with several customers around the world where they analyzed their existing processes that some of their more traditional staff believed worked well only to discover they had efficiency ratings of 20% to 30%. You can't fix problems to which you are blind.

The implications of lean thinking are profound, and many organizations take some time to fully appreciate them. Think of everything that you do prior to delivering functionality to your customers as work in progress (WIP). This includes work products such as project plans, requirements, tests, defects, and designs. Lean properly adopted means that we vigorously reduce queues of any sort as they are sources of waste. Rather than *push* requirements to our developers, we *pull* requirements from a small queue of highest priorities and then deliver them quickly to the customer. Batching up a large inventory of requirements for delivery is not consistent with this lean approach. Most organizations currently consider it to be a normal practice to take months to gather a batch of requirements for the next release and then proceed with an elaborate plan to deliver these fixed requirements. Organizations that continue to use this approach risk becoming outdated by companies that release multiple versions of their solution in the time that they themselves release their first version.

While both agile and lean approaches consider writing detailed requirements up front to be unacceptable, lean is even more stringent than agile. Agile replaces detailed requirements with a requirement placeholder such as a user story in the work item list. The work item list represents a complete list of the backlog of all high level requirements currently known by the product owner (see Chapter 4 for a detailed discussion of this role). Lean advocates pruning this backlog to a few items only, and only adding new requirements to the list as items are delivered to the customer. An analogy might be a queue of pies on display at a bakery. The baker won't bake a week's worth of pies. Rather, as pies are removed from the displayed queue, he bakes more and replenishes the queue as needed. This is like pulling features from a queue and only then considering what might be a good replacement for the delivered feature.

You might consider the idea to have only a dozen or so features known at a time in advance (with no supporting details) a radical approach, and you would be right. Most organizations do not yet seem ready to adopt this just-in-time approach to eliciting and delivering functionality, which is adapted from just-in-time supply chains in manufacturing and retailing environments.

Perhaps in a few years, progressive organizations will feel more comfortable with supplementing their agile practices with ideas like these from lean thinking.

Reality over Rhetoric

There is a fair bit of rhetoric surrounding agile methods, some of which we subscribe to and some of which we don't. This section briefly examines the rhetoric we've found to be the most misleading for people trying to be effective at adopting agile techniques. The following list is in the format *X although Y*, where *X* is the rhetoric and *Y* is the strategy promoted by the DAD process framework. This includes

- **Requirements evolve throughout the lifecycle *although* the initial scope should still be agreed to at the beginning of the project.** You achieve this by formulating an initial vision for your project, a vision that your stakeholders should help define and then agree to. To come to that vision you need to perform some initial requirements envisioning—a list of high level features is part of this initial vision. Yes, the details are very likely to evolve over time, but the fundamental goals of your project and scope of your effort need to be defined early in your project. In a small minority of situations you may not be able to get the right people together, either physically or virtually, to define the initial vision—this should be seen as a significant project risk.

- **Simple designs are best** *although* **the architecture should be thought out early in the lifecycle.** Too many developers interpret the advice to focus on simple designs to mean that they should build everything from scratch. Yet more often than not the simplest design is to take advantage of what is already there, and the best way to do that is to work closely with people who understand your existing technical infrastructure. Investing in a little bit of architectural envisioning early in the lifecycle enables your team to identify existing enterprise assets that you can leverage, to identify your architectural options, and to select what appears to be the best option available to you. The details will still emerge over time, and some decisions will be deferred until a later date when it's more appropriate to make them, but the bottom line is that disciplined agilists think before they act.

- **Teams should be self-organizing** *although* **they are still constrained (and enhanced) by your organizational ecosystem.** Intellectual workers, including development professionals, are most effective when they have a say in what work they do and how they do it. Development professionals can improve their productivity by following common conventions, leveraging and building out a common "DevOps" infrastructure, and by working to common business and technical visions.

- **Delivery teams don't need prescriptive process definitions** *although* **they do need some high-level guidance to help organize their work.** Individual development professionals are typically highly skilled and highly educated people often with years of experience, and teams of such people clearly have a wide range of knowledge. As a result of this knowledge it is incredibly rare for such people to read detailed procedures for how to do their work. However, they often still require some high-level advice to help them organize their work effectively. Teams can often benefit from techniques and patterns used by other teams, and this knowledge sharing should be encouraged.

- **Development professionals know what to do** *although* **they're still not process experts.** A decade ago the strategy was to provide detailed process advice to teams, but recently the pendulum has swung the other way to provide little or no defined process at all. Over the last few years there's been a trend within the agile community to advise teams to define their own process so that it's tailored to their own unique situation. While this clearly strokes people's egos, it's relatively poor advice for several reasons. First, although every team is in a unique situation there is significant commonality, so having at least a high-level process framework from which to start makes sense. Having a baseline means that teams have a starting point that has delivered successful results for many other agile teams and can evolve beyond that baseline to optimize the value they are able to deliver. Second, although these teams have a wide range of knowledge it might not be complete, nor consistent, nor is it clear what the trade-offs are of combining all the really good techniques that people know about. There is significant benefit in having a flexible process framework such as DAD that shows how everything fits together.

- **Development professionals should validate their own work to the best of their ability** *although* **they likely aren't testing experts so therefore need help picking up the appropriate skills.** The mantra in the agile community is to test often and test early, and better yet to test first. As a result agile teams have adopted a "whole team" approach where the development team does its own testing. This works when there are people on the team with sufficient testing skills and more importantly can transfer those skills to others. Minimally you need to embed testers into your delivery teams, but you should also consider explicit training and mentoring of everyone on the team in testing and quality skills.

- **Disciplined agile teams work in an iterative manner** *although* **still follow a lifecycle that is serial[2] over time.** On any given day people on a DAD project team may be performing analysis, testing, design, programming, deployment, or a myriad of other activities and iterating back and forth between them. But, as you saw in Chapter 1, "Disciplined Agile Delivery in a Nutshell," the DAD lifecycle includes three distinct phases, which are performed in order. So, DAD is both iterative in the small but serial in the large.

Concluding Thoughts

Properly executed agile methods definitely deliver business value quicker, more frequently, and with higher quality and provide greater stakeholder satisfaction than traditional methods. Disciplined agile delivery teams produce solutions with features that are needed (not just wanted) with the highest return on investment in a timely just-in-time fashion. The solution is easy to maintain due to the greater focus on quality and has fewer defects than solutions produced with traditional methods. Most importantly, the solution delivered meets the expectations of the stakeholders since they participated actively in the development process, and what is delivered meets their conditions of satisfaction defined merely weeks ago.

As we show in subsequent chapters it is *unusual* to find defects for a feature in iterations subsequent to the feature being implemented when proper regression testing and better yet

---

2. We appreciate that "serial" is one of those agile swear words that cause some people a bit of heartburn.

test-driven development practices are used on agile projects. It is well known that the later in the lifecycle that defects are found, the more expensive it is to fix them. Addressing quality early to *prevent* defects reduces the need to find and fix them later.

Additional Resources

For more detailed discussions about several of the topics covered in this chapter:

- **Thoughts about the Agile Manifesto.** The values and principles of the Manifesto for Agile Software Development are published at www.agilemanifesto.org. The reasoning behind our extension to the manifesto, and detailed conversation around it, can be found in Scott's blog at https://www.ibm.com/developerworks/mydeveloperworks/blogs/ ambler/entry/reworking_the_agile_manifesto14. The Manifesto for Software Crafts- manship at manifesto.softwarecraftsmanship.org shares some interesting ideas for how to extend the Agile Manifesto to address issues around professionalism and craftsman- ship. Tom Gilb's presentation, "A Real Revolutionary Agile Manifesto: Value to Stake- holders, Not Working Code to Customers" at www.gilb.com/tiki-download_file. php?fileId=389 provides some insights into potential improvements to the Agile Manifesto.

- **Communication strategies.** Scott has a detailed article about various communica- tion strategies employed by agile project teams at www.agilemodeling.com/essays/ communication.htm. General research backs up the Agile Manifesto's claim that face- to-face communication is most effective, and surveys that Scott has run confirm this for agile software development teams.

- **Lean software development.** Mary and Tom Poppendieck have written three insightful books on this topic: *Lean Software Development* (Addison Wesley, 2003), *Implementing Lean Software Development* (Addison Wesley, 2006), and *Leading Lean Software Development* (Addison Wesley, 2010). David J. Anderson's *KANBAN: Successful Evo- lutionary Change for Your Technology Business* (Blue Hole Press, 2010) overviews Kanban, a methodology that applies lean principles.

- **Software economics.** Walker Royce's whitepaper, "Improving Software Economics: Top 10 Principles for Achieving Agility at Scale" (ftp://public.dhe.ibm.com/common/ ssi/ecm/en/raw14148usen/RAW14148USEN.PDF), provides a coherent argument for the quality-focused techniques adopted by agile teams and the quality-focused principles behind the Agile Manifesto.

CHAPTER 3

Foundations of Disciplined Agile Delivery

The explosion of "branded" agile methods has resulted in a jargon-filled confusion of siloed tribes made up of uncollaborative zealots. —Mark Kennaley, Author SDLC 3.0

Disciplined Agile Delivery (DAD) is a hybrid process framework that builds upon the solid foundation of many core agile methods. This includes many of the leading agile methods such as Scrum, Extreme Programming (XP), and Agile Modeling as well as others. These foundational sources are overviewed in this chapter.

Table 3.1 provides a brief summary of the core agile methods and the IBM Practices leveraged by the DAD process framework—each of them is described in detail later in the chapter. When considering the merits of various methods, we examine what guidance they provide and identify the critical practices adopted by DAD. While none of the mainstream methods provide end-to-end guidance, they each have certain strengths. DAD takes the strengths of these and other mainstream methods and consolidates them into a single hybrid process framework. The table lists the key contributors to DAD; however, other influences include Dynamic System Development Method (DSDM), the Scaled Agile Framework, Outside-In Development (OID), and Kanban.

Table 3.1   Sources of Agile Practices Adopted by Disciplined Agile Delivery

Agile Source	Strengths
Scrum	Project management framework; release, iteration and daily planning; prioritization/scope management; regular stakeholder reviews; retrospectives to help the team evolve; cross-functional team of generalizing specialists

(continued)

Table 3.1   Sources of Agile Practices Adopted by Disciplined Agile Delivery (continued)

Agile Source	Strengths
Extreme Programming (XP)	Technical aspects of software development with specific practices defined for fine-scale feedback, continuous integration, shared understanding, and programmer welfare
Agile Modeling	Lightweight requirements, architecture, and design modeling and documentation
Agile Data	Database architecture, design, and development
Lean software development	A collection of principles and strategies that help streamline software development and provide advice for scaling agile approaches
IBM Practices Library	A collection of practices, ranging from very traditional to very agile, documented by IBM
OpenUP	Full delivery lifecycle planning, modeling, development, testing, deployment, and governance

Fortunately, many aspects of mainstream agile are consistent across all methods. However, in many cases they have different terms for these common practices. In many cases DAD uses an existing term if it makes sense, and in some cases DAD uses a more generic term. The chapter begins by addressing the terminology issue and then overviews each method and its key practices in greater detail. The goal is to provide you with an overview of the wealth of agile practices available to you. Your team may not adopt all of these practices; some are mutually exclusive, and some would be adopted only in specific situations, but you will want to adopt many of them. Future chapters refer to the practices described in this chapter and provide advice for when you may want to apply them.

Figure 3.1 shows a mind map of the structure of this chapter. We describe each of the topics in the map in clockwise order, beginning at the top right.

THE BIG IDEAS IN THIS CHAPTER

- Mainstream agile methods focus on different portions of the agile delivery lifecycle. Most have some overlap and some gaps.
- The practices of each agile methodology are complementary and easily combined, although sometimes the terminology varies.
- Your project team will want to adopt and tailor a subset of the practices described in this chapter depending on the context you find yourself in.
- DAD combines common agile practices from various sources into a single, end-to-end delivery process.

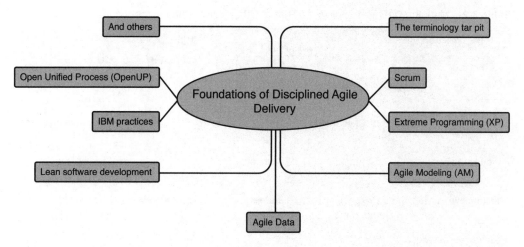

Figure 3.1   Outline of this chapter

The Terminology Tar Pit

In the early 1990s there were debates about object-oriented modeling notations and which ones were the best. Thankfully, the Unified Modeling Language (UML) became a de facto standard and ended the so called "notation wars." Unfortunately we now have the agile method wars—branded methods based on metaphors, unique terminology, and sometimes questionable certification programs.

To better understand the terminology tar pit in which we find ourselves, consider Table 3.2, which summarizes common terms from several agile sources. This table is a rough mapping of the terminology used in the DAD process framework to that of Scrum, XP, Agile Modeling, and other sources. It's important to note that the mapping isn't one-to-one; this is particularly true for the first row, which maps the differing concepts of lead/coach/master/manager to each other. Furthermore there is no consensus around official agile terminology, nor is there likely to be any time soon. In DAD we have avoided the proprietary branded terminology from the various methods and have instead adopted simple and intuitive terms wherever possible.

Table 3.2   Mapping DAD Terminology to That of Other Agile Methods

DAD	XP	Scrum	Agile Modeling	Other
Team lead	Coach	ScrumMaster	-	Project manager, project lead, facilitator
Iteration	Iteration	Sprint	Iteration	Timebox, cycle

(continued)

Table 3.2   Mapping DAD Terminology to That of Other Agile Methods (continued)

DAD	XP	Scrum	Agile Modeling	Other
Coordination meeting	Daily standup	Daily Scrum	-	Coordination meeting
Retrospective	Retrospective	Sprint retrospective	-	Reflection meeting
Product owner	Customer	Product owner	Product owner	Stakeholder representative
Team member	Extreme programmer	Team member	Team member	Developer, implementer
Architecture owner	-	-	Architecture owner	Architect, solution Architect, technical Architect, application Architect
Iteration review	-	Sprint review	Iteration review	Iteration assessment
Work item list	-	Product or sprint backlog	Work item list	
Spike	Spike	-	Architecture spike	Technical proof-of-concept

Now let's explore each of the primary sources of practices and strategies adopted by the DAD process framework.

Scrum

Scrum[1] is an example of a core agile method, and it captures some really great ideas that have become commonly adopted by agile teams. However, Scrum intentionally does not provide guidance on the practices that should be used within that framework. The idea is that teams may adopt those practices that they find to be valuable and helpful in combination with the framework. Additionally, the focus is primarily on Construction phase aspects of agile delivery. Figure 3.2 depicts the Scrum lifecycle, which focuses on the construction aspects of agile delivery, which if you remember from Chapter 1, "Disciplined Agile Delivery in a Nutshell," is an important part of

---

1. The Scrum community typically refers to Scrum as a process framework, not a method, because the idea is that you can expand on and tailor Scrum to meet your needs. The exact same thing can be said of the Extreme Programming, Agile Modeling, Open Unified Process, and other agile methods.

the DAD lifecycle. The following practices[2] are key to Scrum and are adopted by the DAD process framework:

- **Product backlog (work item list).** In Scrum the product backlog is a *uniquely ranked* stack of requirements, everything that might be needed in the product. Although Scrum does not mandate any specific requirements method, most Scrum practitioners recommend the use of user stories to encourage the team to focus on delivering valuable functionality. Rather than separately identifying work items related to implementing new technologies, configuring systems, setting up test automation tools, and so on, Scrum teams typically address those tasks as they are required to implement the functionality (or user stories). Ranking requirements forces stakeholders to decide which functionality is truly more valuable than the others. The product backlog may be changed or reprioritized at any time.

  Agile teams don't mind if requirements in the part of the stack that they are not currently working on change because the team hasn't gotten to them yet. This contrasts to a traditional approach where we force our stakeholders to decide up front what all their detailed requirements are and then enforce strict change management procedures (more like "change prevention") to restrict change. Radical changes to the product backlog need to be carefully managed, however. For larger enterprise efforts there may have been some substantial effort into assembling the backlog during release planning. The work items may include items requested by product owners from other projects as dependencies for them. Note that in the basic DAD lifecycle a work item list is a ranked stack of work items,[3] including requirements, defect reports, and any other activity performed by agile teams. Some of this work may be part of delivering the overall solution and not just related to building software, such as resourcing or communication activities. DAD explicitly recognizes the need to identify and prioritize other work related to the project, while providing a new level of transparency regarding the work that is required to deliver the project.

- **Value-driven lifecycle.** Deliver potentially shippable software at the end of each sprint (Scrum's term for an iteration, which they suggest to be one month or less). Scrum, like other agile methods, emphasizes prioritizing and implementing requirements that provide the greatest value to the customer. In addition to considering value, DAD adopts a risk-value-driven lifecycle, popularized by the Unified Process, which is discussed in detail later in the chapter.

---

2. In some cases the practice name is in the format *Scrum name (DAD name)* where *Scrum name* is the name of the Scrum concept and *DAD name* is its DAD equivalent. Throughout the rest of the book we use the DAD name, although where appropriate indicate the Scrum name for readers who are familiar with Scrum terminology.

3. With the advanced/lean version of the lifecycle, work items categorized, not prioritized, and are treated as if they're in a pool and pulled individually from the pool when the team has capacity to address them. More on this in Chapter 8.

- **Daily Scrum (coordination meeting).** Once a day, typically in the morning, the whole team gathers to coordinate their activities for the day. Scrum prescribes three questions for team members to answer: What did you do yesterday? What do you think you'll do today? What obstacles are in your way? This meeting should be no more than 15 minutes in length. DAD is a little more flexible, suggesting that the primary question people should address is whether they foresee any upcoming problems. The challenge with the first two Scrum questions is that they are basically status questions, albeit ones that help team members to communicate their commitments and then publicly stick to them, and the third question effectively waits until a problem occurs (far better to avoid the problem in the first place with a forward-looking question).

- **Release planning.** At the beginning of a project agile teams develop an initial high level plan and then throughout the lifecycle maintain it appropriately. Traditional methods often create overly detailed work breakdown structures extending far into the future. This is a flawed practice that makes no sense in modern software development projects. The tasks and durations are simply far too unpredictable to accurately plan more than a few weeks into the future. Also consistent with agile's principle of self-organization is that management really should not care about micromanaging the team to the task level. Instead, release planning suggests abstracting the project plan to a higher level that describes higher level milestones such as delivery of small increments of demonstrable functionality. These higher level plan items can then be allocated to a set of sprints (iterations) over the life of the project. It is important to understand that Scrum makes no promises as to what items from the backlog can actually be delivered over the life of the project. This can only be determined on an iteration-by-iteration basis as we move through the project. The project ends when the customer determines that they don't want to fund another iteration and are satisfied that they have sufficient functionality. Scrum no longer includes release planning as part of the official Scrum guide, which we find to be of concern. As we discuss in Chapter 6, "The Inception Phase," our research indicates that the vast majority of agile teams spend some time planning their release before starting development.

- **Sprint planning (iteration planning).** At the beginning of the sprint/iteration the team plans in detail what they will deliver and how they will do the work. This involves taking a set of highest priority requirements off the backlog and then decomposing these requirements into detailed tasks. The team estimates this work and commits to the product owner that they will deliver the work according to the plan that they have created themselves.

- **Sprint review and demonstration.** The team conducts a demonstration of what they have completed during the sprint/iteration to stakeholders. They also assess progress against the release plan. Periodically, this might be the logical time to review needs for additional funding.

- **Sprint retrospective (retrospective).** At the end of the sprint/iteration the team takes the opportunity to identify opportunities for improvements in process so that they may improve as the project progresses. The DAD process framework suggests that teams new to agile perform a retrospective at the end of each iteration and that experienced teams instead hold retrospectives whenever it makes sense to do so (perhaps in the middle of an iteration when a problem is actually occurring or perhaps once every few iterations for teams that are truly running smoothly). At minimum though, at some regular frequency DAD teams should explicitly consider whether they need to have a retrospective to review opportunities to improve.

- **User story driven development (usage-driven development).** A user story captures in one or two sentences what the user wants to achieve in the system. A collection of stories is listed and sized in the product backlog in priority order for development in subsequent sprints/iterations. Note that user stories aren't officially part of Scrum, but over the past few years they have become the de facto standard. DAD is less prescriptive in that it recommends a usage-driven approach where the primary requirements artifact is usage focused, such as a user story, usage scenario, or use case.

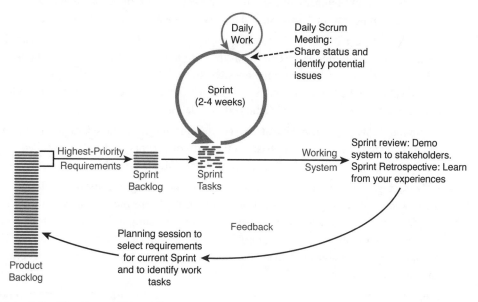

Figure 3.2   The Scrum lifecycle[4]

---

4. For comparison purposes, you may find it useful to compare this diagram to the basic DAD lifecycle diagram (refer to Figure 1.3 in Chapter 1). You will see how DAD draws much from Scrum.

Extreme Programming (XP)

Extreme Programming (XP) is a core agile method that focuses primarily on construction-oriented practices. Although XP's practices appear straightforward on the surface, many of them require not only technical skill but also significant discipline on the part of practitioners. The following XP practices[5] are adopted by the DAD process framework:

- **Coding standard (development guidelines).** Team members should follow established coding guidelines and standards. This includes recommended patterns and mechanisms to ensure consistency, reduce defects, and simplify readability and maintenance. DAD explicitly extends this to all types of development guidelines, including data guidelines, user interface standards, architectural guidelines, and security guidelines to name a few.

- **Collective ownership.** Every team member is allowed to view and edit another team member's code or any other project artifact. This encourages transparency and accountability for work quality. A shared understanding and ownership of the code base reduces the risks related to people leaving the team. All team members are better prepared to maintain or improve any code in the system and will speed up the development process because any team member can implement any new feature or fix any defect. Note that pair programming facilitates the shared understanding and ownership of the code.

- **Continuous integration.** Team members should check in changes to their code on a frequent basis, integrating the system to ensure that their changes work, so that the rest of the team is always working with the latest version of the system. The integration effort should validate whether the system still works via automated regression tests and potentially even through dynamic and static code validation.

- **Customer tests (acceptance test-driven development).** Detailed requirements are captured on a just-in-time (JIT) basis in the form of acceptance tests (also called story tests). See discussion of test-driven development (TDD) later in this section.

- **Refactoring.** A refactoring is a small change to something to improve its design and thereby make it easier to understand and to modify. Therefore a code refactoring is a simple change to your code, a database refactoring is a simple change to your database schema, a user interface (UI) refactoring is a simple change to your UI, and so on. The act of refactoring enables you to evolve your work slowly over time, to take an iterative and incremental approach to development.

- **Pair programming (non-solo work).** Pair programming is a practice where two programmers work together on the same artifact. One programmer types the code, while the other programmer looks at the bigger picture and provides real-time code review. Pair programming is an example of non-solo work, as is Agile Modeling's practice of model-

---

5. Once again, in some cases the practice name is in the format *XP name (DAD name)*.

ing with others, where two or more people work together to accomplish a task. Non-solo work provides opportunities for people to learn from one another, leads to higher quality as defects are often spotted as they're being injected into the work, and spreads knowledge of the work artifacts across a greater number of people (this is particularly true when you switch work partners regularly).

- **Planning game (release planning and iteration planning).** The purpose of the planning game is to guide the product into successful delivery. This includes high-level release planning to think through and monitor the "big issues" throughout the project as well as detailed just-in-time (JIT) iteration planning.

- **Simple design.** Programmers should seek the simplest way to write their code while still implementing the appropriate functionality. This increases productivity. Note that periodic refactoring may be required to ensure that the design remains simple and of high quality.

- **Small releases.** Frequent deployment of working software into production is encouraged. This functionality should be delivered in increments that provide the greatest value to the customer. Frequent deployments build confidence in the team and trust from the customer. DAD takes this one step further to focus on delivering working solutions, not just working software.

- **Sustainable pace.** Although overtime is sometimes needed on an irregular basis, it is not sustainable over long periods of time and can reduce morale, productivity, and quality substantially. The team should be able to sustain an energized approach to work at a constant and gradually improving velocity.

- **Test-driven development**. In TDD the first step is to quickly code a new test, basically just enough code for the test to fail. This could be either a high-level acceptance test or a more detailed developer test (often mistakenly referred to as a unit test). Next you run your tests, often the complete test suite although for sake of speed you may decide to run only a subset, to ensure that the new test does in fact fail. You then update your functional code to make it pass the new test. The fourth step is to run your tests again. If they fail you need to update your functional code and retest. Once the tests pass the next step is to start over (you may first need to refactor any duplication out of your design as needed). When you write a test before you write the code to fulfill that test, the test not only validates at a confirmatory level that your code works as it is expected it also effectively specifies your work in detail on a just-in-time (JIT) basis.

- **Whole team.** Team members should collectively have all the skills required to deliver the solution, although in Chapter 5, "Forming Disciplined Agile Delivery Teams," we'll see that sometimes agile teams need to bring specialists in for short periods to address specific and unique issues. Furthermore, the stakeholder(s), or their representatives such as product owners or business analysts should be available to answer questions and make decisions in a timely manner.

Agile Modeling (AM)

Agile Modeling (AM) is a practice-based methodology for effective modeling and documentation of software-based systems. At a more detailed level AM is a collection of values, principles, and practices for modeling software that can be applied on a software development project in an effective and lightweight manner. AM was purposely architected to be a source of strategies that can be tailored into other base processes, something the DAD process framework takes explicit advantage of.

With an Agile Model Driven Development (AMDD) (see Figure 3.3) approach you typically do just enough high-level modeling at the beginning of a project to understand the scope and potential architecture of the system. During construction iterations you do modeling as part of your iteration planning activities and then take a just-in-time (JIT) model storming approach where you model for several minutes as a precursor to several hours of coding. AMDD recommends that practitioners take a test-driven approach to development although does not insist on it (DAD takes the same stance).

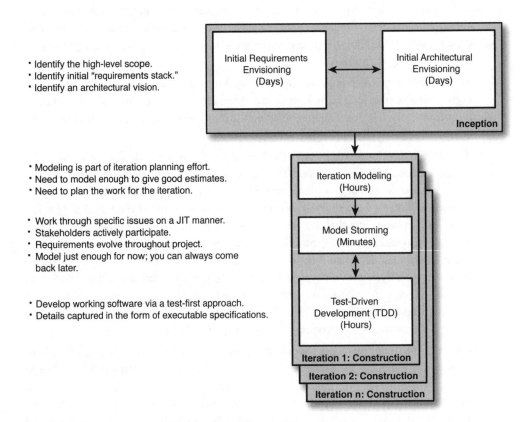

Figure 3.3   Agile Model Driven Development (AMDD)

The primary take-away point of Figure 3.3 is that modeling and documentation activities occur throughout the entire lifecycle. The practices map of Figure 3.4 overviews the modeling and documentation practices defined by AM. These practices are the following:

- **Active stakeholder participation.** Stakeholders (or their representatives) should provide information in a timely manner, make decisions in a timely manner, and be actively involved in the development process through the use of inclusive tools and techniques.

- **Architecture envisioning.** At the beginning of an agile project you need to do some initial, high-level architectural modeling to identify a viable technical strategy for your solution. This practice is performed iteratively in parallel with requirements envisioning.

- **Document continuously.** Write documentation for your deliverables throughout the lifecycle in parallel to the creation of the rest of the solution. Note that some teams choose to write the documentation one iteration behind to enable them to focus on capturing stable information.

- **Document late.** Write deliverable documentation as late as possible, avoiding speculative ideas that are likely to change in favor of stable information. This practice is in juxtaposition, on purpose, to document continuously—you need to adopt the approach that is best for your situation.

- **Executable specifications.** Specify detailed requirements in the form of executable "customer tests," and your detailed design as executable developer tests, instead of nonexecutable "static" documentation. Also, note that this works well for detailed information, but that high-level or conceptual information is likely better captured via diagrams and/or written prose. Note that sophisticated modeling tools such as IBM Rational Rhapsody® and IBM Rational Software Architect provide the ability to execute diagrams.

- **Iteration modeling.** At the beginning of each iteration you will do a bit of modeling as part of your iteration planning activities to help identify what needs to be built and how you'll do so.

- **Just barely good enough artifacts (sufficient artifacts).** A model or document needs to be sufficient for the situation at hand and no more.

- **Look-ahead modeling.** Sometimes requirements that are nearing the top of your work item list are fairly complex, motivating you to invest some effort to explore them before they're popped off the top of the work item stack so as to reduce overall risk.

- **Model storming.**[6] Throughout an iteration you will model storm on a just-in-time (JIT) basis for a few minutes to explore the details behind a requirement or to think through a design issue.

---

6. The term "model storming" is a variation of "brainstorming" where you brainstorm various candidate models.

- **Multiple models.** Each type of model has its strengths and weaknesses. Effective developers needs a range of models in their intellectual toolkit, enabling them to apply the right model in the most appropriate manner for the situation at hand. We discuss many types of models and how to apply them in Chapter 8, "Identifying the Initial Scope," and Chapter 9, "Identifying an Initial Technical Strategy."

- **Prioritized requirements (work item list).** Agile teams implement requirements in priority order, as defined by their stakeholders, so as to provide the greatest return on investment (ROI) possible.

- **Requirements envisioning.** At the beginning of an agile project you need to invest some time to identify the scope of the project and to create the initial prioritized stack of requirements.

- **Single source information.** Strive to capture information in one place and one place only.

- **Test-driven development (TDD).** Same as the XP practice described earlier in this chapter.

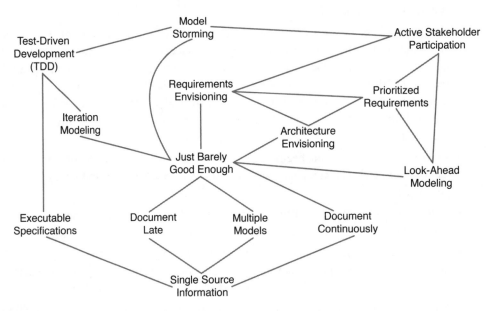

Figure 3.4   Agile Modeling practices

Agile Data

The Agile Data (AD) method defines a collection of strategies that IT professionals can apply in a wide variety of situations to work together effectively on the data aspects of software systems. This isn't to say that AD is a "one size fits all" method. Instead, consider AD as a collection of techniques and philosophies that enable IT professionals within your organization to work together effectively when it comes to the data aspects of software-based systems. Practices for evolutionary/agile database development are

- **Database refactoring.** A database refactoring is a small change to your database schema that improves its design without changing its semantics (e.g., you don't add anything nor do you break anything). The process of database refactoring is the evolutionary improvement of your database schema without changing its functionality so as to improve your ability to support the new needs of your customers.

- **Agile data modeling.** With an evolutionary approach to data modeling you model the data aspects of a system iteratively and incrementally. With an agile approach you do so in a highly collaborative manner. You envision the initial requirements and architecture early in the project at a high-level and then model storm the details on a just-in-time (JIT) basis when and if they're needed.

- **Database regression testing.** You should ensure that your database schema actually meets the requirements for it, and the best way to do that is via testing. Minimally this should be done via regression testing, but better yet via test-driven development (TDD). Agile testing provides the concrete feedback that you need to ensure data quality.

- **Configuration management.** Your data models, database tests, test data, and so on are important project artifacts that should be configuration managed just like any other artifact.

- **Developer sandboxes.** Developers need their own working environments, called sandboxes, where they can modify the portion of the system they are building and get it working before they integrate their work with that of their teammates.

- **Development guidelines.** Having a common, usable set of development standards that are easy to understand and to comply with can greatly improve the quality of the systems that you develop. These guidelines may include, but not be limited to, programming guidelines, modeling style guidelines, data naming conventions, and user interface conventions (including report design conventions).

Lean Software Development

Practitioners of agile development are increasingly looking to adapt ideas from lean thinking, which includes principles and practices adapted from the Toyota Production System. Lean software development includes the following seven principles:

- **Eliminate waste.** Everything not adding value to the customer is considered waste.
- **Amplify learning.** Improve software development by learning and adapting continuously.
- **Decide as late as possible.** Delay decisions as long as possible until they can be based on facts, not assumptions and predictions.
- **Deliver as fast as possible.** Customers value rapid and frequent delivery of a quality product.
- **Empower the team.** Find good people and let them do their job.
- **Build integrity in.** Structure your process to ensure integrity of the customer's experience and its architecture.
- **See the whole.** Think big but act small. We build a large system by breaking it into smaller parts, but attention needs to be given to the larger interactions with other components and systems.

We reference lean principles at various points in this book.

IBM Practices

IBM has made, and continues to make, a significant effort to identify and document development best practices, including ones focused on agile delivery. The IBM Practices are captured using Rational Method Composer (RMC) so that they can be easily tailored to address the situation in which your team finds itself. The goal of the IBM Practices is to provide the building blocks from which you can develop processes, and IBM has in fact defined processes such as OpenUP, Eclipse Way, and Harmony/ESW in exactly that manner. IBM customers are then taking these practices and methods and tailoring their own processes.

Some of the iterative and/or agile practices in the IBM Practice Library include the following:

- **Concurrent testing (whole team testing).** The development team should test their work to the best of their ability concurrently with other development activities.
- **Continuous integration.** Same as the XP practice described earlier in the chapter.
- **Evolutionary architecture.** Envision the architecture early in the lifecycle, prove the architecture early in the project via working code, and allow the details to evolve over time. The DAD process framework adopts more granular practices from Agile Modeling, which together form this practice.
- **Evolutionary design.** The design will evolve over time, and to explore it agile teams perform iteration modeling, just-in-time (JIT) model storming, test-driven development (TDD), and other activities to make and communicate design decisions. The DAD process framework adopts more granular practices from Agile Modeling, which together form this practice.

- **Iterative development.** Create a solution incrementally, where each increment is completed in a fixed period of time called an iteration. Each iteration is planned in detail at its start, work is performed, and at the end of the iteration the results are stabilized and demoed to key stakeholders. The DAD process framework adopts more granular practices from Scrum, which together form this practice.

- **Release planning.** At the beginning of a project a high-level plan showing major milestones, dependencies on other teams, and the timing of iterations is developed. This plan is updated throughout the project based on the actual progress and activities of the team.

- **Risk-value lifecycle.** With a value lifecycle you produce consumable solutions on a regular basis that could be potentially deployed into production. Using this approach the priorities for what is implemented first is based solely on the value of each feature. A risk-value lifecycle extends the value lifecycle to explicitly address common risks that aren't mitigated by a value-driven approach. These risks include obtaining stakeholder consensus early in the lifecycle regarding what should be delivered, proving the architecture with working code early in the lifecycle, waiting until there's a minimally marketable release but not much longer before deploying into production, and ensuring that the solution is in fact production ready before deploying it. The implication is that risk is taken into account when prioritizing work so as to increase the team's probability of success.

- **Shared vision.** An overall vision for the project should be defined, communicated, and agreed to early in the project.

- **Team change management (work item list).** Change requests, including reported defects, should be estimated by the team, prioritized by the stakeholders, and then addressed in priority order.

- **Test-driven development.** Same as the XP practice described earlier in this chapter.

- **Use case-driven development.** A use case is a sequence of actions that provide measurable value to a stakeholder (a person, organization, or even other system). Use cases are a way of writing requirements as workflows that describe the interactions between the users and the system being developed. Use case-driven development allocates usage scenarios to particular iterations for implementation.

- **User story-driven development.** A user story is a high-level depiction of a requirement, containing just enough information so that the developers can produce a reasonable estimate of the effort to implement it. User stories are not actually requirements per se, but rather a placeholder for a discussion with the product owner just before they are actually to be implemented. User story-driven development allocates user stories to particular iterations for implementation.

- **Whole team.** Same as the XP practice described earlier in this chapter.

WHY LARGER-GRAINED PRACTICES?

The IBM Practices are generally larger grained than many of the practices we've described so far. Where Scrum has practices such as Sprint demo, Sprint planning, and Sprint retrospective, IBM captures these as a single practice called iterative development. IBM did this because they noticed that many of the smaller practices are synergistic and typically deployed together, so as a result it makes sense to combine them. It's interesting to observe that many of the adherents of specific agile methods do insist that you need to adopt a core collection of practices to truly gain the benefit of that method.

Open Unified Process (OpenUP)

The Open Unified Process (OpenUP) is an open sourced method captured using the Eclipse Process Framework (EPF). As you can see in Figure 3.5, OpenUP has an iterative and incremental (evolutionary) lifecycle based on the four-phase approach of the Unified Process and supported by a kernel of agile practices. To help avoid using too much process, OpenUP was designed as a minimal kernel of practices, suitable for small agile projects. Practices can then be incrementally added to this simple set of core practices to add enterprise, governance, or technology related guidance where necessary. The concept is to scale up your process, seeking to use the minimum required for your organization or project, rather than trying to understand comprehensive bloated processes and then scaling down appropriately, which has been proven to be challenging in practice.

Personal effort on an OpenUP project is organized in micro-increments. These represent short units of work that produce a steady, measurable pace of project progress (typically measured in hours or a few days). The process applies intensive collaboration as the system is incrementally developed by a committed, self-organized team. These micro-increments provide an extremely short feedback loop that drives adaptive decisions within each iteration.

OpenUP divides the project into iterations: planned, time-boxed intervals typically measured in weeks. Iterations focus the team on delivering incremental value to stakeholders in a predictable manner. The iteration plan defines what should be delivered within the iteration, and the result is a demo-able or shippable build. OpenUP teams self-organize around how to accomplish iteration objectives and commit to delivering the results. They do that by defining and "pulling" fine-grained tasks from a work items list. OpenUP applies an iteration lifecycle that structures how micro-increments are applied to deliver stable, cohesive builds of the system that incrementally progresses toward the iteration objectives.

OpenUP structures the project lifecycle into four phases: Inception, Elaboration, Construction, and Transition. The project lifecycle provides stakeholders and team members with visibility and decision points throughout the project. This enables effective oversight, and allows you to make "go or no-go" decisions at appropriate times. A project plan defines the lifecycle, and the end result is a released application.

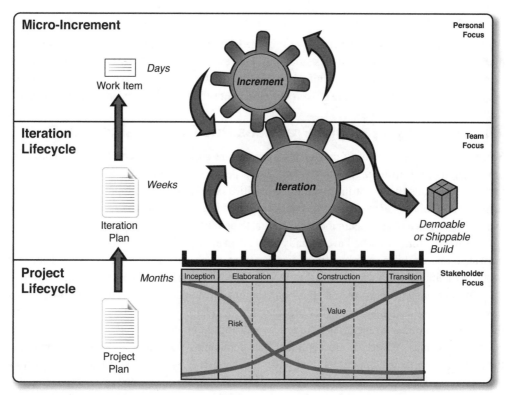

Figure 3.5   OpenUP layers: micro-increments, iteration lifecycle and project lifecycle

The lifecycle of OpenUP is similar to DAD. Both methods have an Inception phase, and a focus on reducing risk as early as possible by building the "tricky" bits first in the early iterations thereafter. Consistent with other Unified Process based methods, OpenUP has an explicit Elaboration phase to focus on the baselining of the architecture and reducing risks as much as possible. DAD has a similar focus (described in Chapter 13, "The Construction Phase," as the risk-value lifecycle practice) but does not have an explicit Elaboration phase to account for this focus.

WHAT ABOUT RUP?

OpenUP was developed as a lightweight, open source version of IBM's Rational Unified Process (RUP). Unfortunately, the manner in which many organizations have implemented RUP is not as agile as it was meant to be. RUP can certainly be instantiated as an agile process, and many organizations have in fact done so. 'Nuff said.

And Others

We have described the core concepts of four of the leading mainstream agile methods. DAD primarily leverages its content from these methods. However, DAD also draws supplementary ideas from other methods such as Agile Unified Process (AUP), Crystal Clear, Dynamic System Development Method (DSDM), Feature Driven Development (FDD) and the Scaled Agile Framework.

Those Who Ignore Agile Practices Put Their Business at Risk

Yes, this is a bold statement to make. However, we are amazed at the complacency that many organizations have to the agile movement. Some people have criticized the agile fanatics as immature hotshots that don't understand the realities of enterprise development. We agree that there is a level of arrogance in the agile community that is a bit disconcerting, especially since the average experience of agile team members seems to be fairly low.

However, for those who have actually worked on agile projects, it is easy to see where their arrogance and confidence comes from. For experienced agilists, it becomes crystal clear how obsolete traditional methods are, and they tend to view traditionalists as completely out of touch.

We encourage you as you read this book to think outside the box and consider how you can incorporate these techniques into your organization. As junior agilists achieve success and work their way up into management, agile practices will indeed be driven top-down throughout successful companies. While we are confident that companies that adopt agile will differentiate themselves from their competitors, this will only happen if agile is applied in an enterprise-appropriate, "disciplined" fashion. Many of agile's practices are disciplined by nature, but applying them appropriately in the context that makes sense is where the "disciplined" in DAD makes the difference between success and failure in your agile adoption.

Concluding Thoughts

This chapter described the fundamentals of the core agile methods upon which Disciplined Agile Delivery is based. There are many similarities, but each method has some differences. Ken Schwaber, the co-creator of Scrum, has compared agile methods to a game of chess. There are a small number of pieces and the basics are relatively easy to grasp. However, there are unlimited variations, and the path that you take depends on the situational dependencies of your project and organization. You can think of any application of agile in this way. Every project we have worked on has been different in some ways. But the unifying practices of agile steer us with a common goal of delivering high-value, high-quality software in a timely and predictable fashion.

A significant challenge with the material in this chapter is that it can seem overwhelming at first. Do you really need to adopt all of the management practices of Scrum, technical practices of Extreme Programming (XP), modeling and documentation practices of Agile Modeling (AM), database practices of Agile Data (AD), and governance practices of Unified Process (UP)? No, but you do need to adopt a large subset of them, and that subset is situationally dependent.

Throughout the rest of this book we provide advice for how and when to apply these practices and more importantly work through a concrete case study.

Additional Resources

For more detailed discussions about several of the topics covered in this chapter:

- **Scrum.** Our favorite resource is Mike Vizdos's Implementing Scrum site at www.implementingscrum.com because of his open and honest conversations about Scrum and his great cartoons. Mike Cohn's book *Succeeding with Agile: Software Development Using Scrum* is a good read as it shares a lot of real-world advice. The Scrum Guide from www.scrum.org is also a great introductory resource.

- **Extreme Programming (XP).** Kent Beck's book, *Extreme Programming Explained* is still the primary reference for XP practitioners. Ron Jeffries' site http://xprogramming.com provides blunt, experience-based advice about applying XP in practice.

- **Agile Modeling (AM).** Scott maintains www.agilemodeling.com, which shares advice about agile strategies for architecture, design, requirements, documentation, and roles.

- **Agile Data (AD).** Scott also maintains www.agiledata.org, which focuses on agile strategies for data-oriented activities both at the project and enterprise levels.

- **Lean Software Development.** Mary and Tom Poppendieck are the primary thought leaders in this space. Their book *Implementing Lean Software Development* (Addison-Wesley, 2007) describes how lean principles can be applied to software development.

- **IBM Practices.** The IBM Practices are summarized at www.ibm.com/developerworks/rational/practices/.

- **OpenUP.** OpenUP is developed and maintained as open source via the Eclipse Process Framework (EPF) http://epf.eclipse.org/wikis/openup/.

- **Outside-in Software Development.** Kessler and Sweitzer's book *Outside-in Software Development* (IBM Press, 2007) is the source for more information on this subject.

- **Scaled Agile Framework.** Dean Leffingwell, a former Rational employee, described this framework in his blog at scalingsoftwareagilityblog.com.

CHAPTER 4

Roles, Rights, and Responsibilities

Build projects around motivated individuals. Give them the environment and support they need, and trust them to get the job done. Principle #5 behind the Agile Manifesto

People build solutions—not processes, not tools, not practices—people. The first value of the Agile Manifesto is "individuals and interactions over processes and tools," indicating that people and the way that they work together are a primary determinant of success for an IT delivery project. This chapter also describes the rights and responsibilities that people have, as well as the roles they take, on Disciplined Agile Delivery (DAD) projects. These three things provide an organizational foundation for building DAD teams, for interactions within the team, and for interactions with people external to the team. In turn they are an important part of your overall governance strategy, the topic of Chapter 20, "Governing Disciplined Agile Teams." The structure of agile teams and how to form them are described in Chapter 5, "Forming Disciplined Agile Delivery Teams."

First, some definitions:

- A *role* is a part that you play within a given situation. In the case of a DAD project, this includes stakeholders, team leads, team members, and more.

- A *right* is something to which you have just claim. For example, anyone involved with a DAD project has the right to be respected.

- A *responsibility* is an obligation that you have to someone else; for example, DAD team members must show respect to the people with whom they are working.

Not long ago Scott had a conversation with an existing IT practitioner that went something like this:

Practitioner: We understand and are very interested in agile here but are struggling to see how it can fit into our environment.

Scott: This has to be one of the most common challenges I run into. What issues are you struggling with?

Practitioner: The first value of the Agile Manifesto talks about individuals and interactions over processes and tools, but we work in a completely opposite manner right now.

Scott: Yikes. Sounds like you're doomed with absolutely no hope of success.

Practitioner: What?

Scott: Just joking. Moving to an agile approach requires you move away from traditional project roles—such as business analyst, project manager, and programmer—to agile roles such as product owner, team lead, and team member.

Practitioner: Sounds like you're putting new labels on old wine.

Scott: On the surface it may look like that, but it would be a serious mistake to assume that. People in the roles on agile teams take on different responsibilities, and rights, than you're used to. Furthermore, they also work in different ways, and more importantly work together in different ways, than what you're used to.

Practitioner: But don't agile teams still do things like business analysis, project management, and in particular programming?

Scott: Yes we do, but that doesn't mean we have specific roles that focus on just those activities. For example, because business analysis is so important to the success of an agile team we do it every single day. It's something that the product owner will do so that he can represent the stakeholder community effectively, and it's something that team members will do, often on a just-in-time (JIT) basis, to understand the details of what they're developing. Similarly, the activities that a traditional project manager would be responsible for are performed in part by the product owner, in part by the team lead, and in part by team members.

Practitioner: Wow, sounds like we have some big changes coming our way.

Scott: It seems daunting at first, and the full cultural and organizational changes required may take several years for your organization to fully adopt, but many companies similar to your own have successfully done this. The good news is that individual teams have made this shift on the order of weeks, and I suspect you can too. First step is to understand what the new roles are, how people in those roles interact with one another, and what people's rights and responsibilities are.

This chapter begins with a discussion of the rights and responsibilities of everyone involved with a DAD team, including both people who are members of the team and stakeholders of the solution. It then describes the DAD roles, focusing on the five primary roles and introducing several secondary roles that are common in scaling situations.

Figure 4.1 shows a mind map of the structure of this chapter. We describe each of the topics in the map in clockwise order, beginning at the top right.

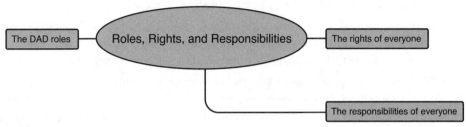

Figure 4.1 Outline of this chapter

THE BIG IDEAS IN THIS CHAPTER

- The DAD primary roles are stakeholder, team member, product owner, team lead, and architecture owner.
- DAD roles are named similarly to those in other agile methods, but there are important differences.
- The rights, roles, and responsibilities are an important aspect of DAD's governance strategy.
- DAD rights are counterbalanced by responsibilities.

The Rights of Everyone

Everyone involved with a DAD project, including stakeholders and people in secondary roles, has a collection of rights. These rights help to provide a philosophical foundation for both how people interact with one another and how to effectively govern DAD projects. The rights of everyone are the following:

- To be treated with respect.
- To have decisions made in a timely manner.
- To produce and receive quality work at all times based on agreed to project standards and principles.
- To estimate the activities you are actively involved with, and to have those estimates respected by others. These estimates should be as aggressive as possible yet still achievable.

- To be provided adequate resources, including but not limited to time and money, to do the job that's been asked of you.

- To have commitments made to you honored, and in the case where this is not possible to have alternatives negotiated with you in a timely manner.

- To determine how your resources will be invested. For the people funding the project this is how the funds will be spent, and for the people working on the project (and thereby investing their time), this is what tasks they choose to work on.

- To be given the opportunity to gain the knowledge and skills pertinent to making the project a success. For example, businesspeople will likely need to learn about the underlying technologies/techniques, and technical staff will likely need to learn about the business.

- To work in a "safe environment" where people have the opportunity to make mistakes, and better yet to have those mistakes recognized as valuable learning opportunities.

- To be commended, nurtured, and supported.

- To be provided good-faith information in a timely manner. Sometimes this is just the "best guess" at the time, and that's perfectly all right. This includes but is not limited to business information such as prioritized requirements and detailed domain concepts as well as technical information such as designs and detailed technical concepts.

- To own your organization's software processes, following and actively improving these processes when needed.

The Responsibilities of Everyone

Of course the rights described previously quickly translate into corresponding responsibilities. For example, if everyone involved with the project has the right to be respected there is an implied responsibility that you need to show respect to the people with whom you're interacting. Additionally, there are also some other important responsibilities that DAD team members have:

- To produce a solution that best meets your stakeholder needs with the degree of resources they are willing to invest.

- To optimize your organization's resources (time and money) invested in your team/ project.

- To be willing to collaborate extensively within your team as well as working with others outside your chosen specialties.

- To share all information, including "work in progress."

- To coach others in your skills and experiences.

- To validate your work to the best of your ability, as early as possible, working with others as needed to do so.

- To actively expand your knowledge and skillset and apply these skills in areas outside your specialty when needed.

- To attend coordination meetings in person if on-site or through other means if not collocated.

- To proactively look for ways to improve your or your team's performance throughout the project (kaizen).

- To avoid accepting work currently outside the current iteration without agreement by the team. Any new work should be prioritized and addressed accordingly, regardless of the source of the work request.

We are not suggesting that these responsibilities supersede your employment contracts. At the end of the day we are typically expected to take direction from our line manager when it is given. As Dean Leffingwell says, we work in companies, not democracies. However, we are suggesting that in a trusting relationship between management and the team where they have demonstrated a record of delivery, these holistic responsibilities make sense.

The DAD Roles

DAD adopts and extends several of the roles from core agile methods such as Scrum and Agile Modeling. On a DAD project any given person will be in one or more roles, an individual can change her role(s) over time, and any given role will have zero or more people performing it at any given time. For example, Peter may be in the role of team member and architecture owner right now but step into the role of team lead next month when Carol, the existing team lead, goes on vacation.

Roles are not positions, nor are they meant to be. For example, Jane may be in the role of stakeholder for your project but have the position of chief financial officer (CFO) within your organization. In fact, although there may be hundreds of stakeholders of your project none of them is likely to have a position of "stakeholder."

Figure 4.2 overviews the roles for people involved with DAD projects. An important thing to understand is that agile deemphasizes specialized roles and considers all team members equal—everyone pitches in to deliver a working solution regardless of their job description. An implication of this is that with the exception of stakeholder everyone is effectively in the role of team member. Consistent with the principle of "everyone is equal" on agile projects, in DAD we have a minimal set of roles that represent certain responsibilities, but do *not* exist in a hierarchy. These roles are organized into two main categories: primary roles, which are commonly found regardless of the level of scale, and secondary roles, which are often introduced (often on a temporary basis) to address scaling issues. Some of the roles are further partitioned into team roles to make them explicit.

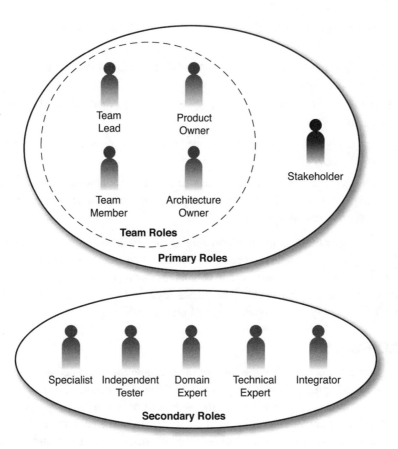

Figure 4.2   The roles of Disciplined Agile Delivery (DAD)

LESSONS FROM THE TRENCHES—DON'T LET ROLES GET IN THE WAY OF TEAMWORK

Elizabeth Woodward, coauthor of *A Practical Guide to Distributed Scrum* and a founder of the IBM Agile Community, has been actively involved with helping IBM teams learn and adopt agile strategies for several years. She has noticed that many team leads and architecture owners new to agile view these labels as higher in the hierarchy and, as a result, attempt to bring a command and control style to the team. For agile to work, team leads and architecture owners really need to view other team members as providing equal value to the effort, and they need to be able to take a truly collaborative approach to development. As a result, in 2008 we began a program within IBM to help our technical staff and others focus on collaborative leadership skills.

Stakeholder

In Chapter 2, "Introduction to Agile and Lean," you learned that DAD teams ideally work together with their stakeholders daily throughout the project. But who are your stakeholders? A stakeholder is someone who is materially impacted by the outcome of the solution. In this regard, the stakeholder is clearly more than an end user: A stakeholder could be a direct user, indirect user, manager of users, senior manager, operations staff member, the "gold owner" who funds the project, support (help desk) staff member, auditors, your program/portfolio manager, developers working on other systems that integrate or interact with the one under development, and maintenance professionals potentially affected by the development and/or deployment of a software project, to name a few. To simplify the definition of stakeholders, we've adopted Outside In Software Development's four stakeholder categories:

- **End users.** These are the people who will use your system, often to fulfill the goals of your principals. They typically want systems that are usable and enable them to do their jobs more effectively.
- **Principals.** These are the decision makers who ultimately pay for and then put your system to use. This includes gold owners, senior business management, and purchasers of the commercial systems.
- **Partners.** These people make the system work in production. This includes operations staff, support staff, trainers, legal experts, installers, application hosting companies, and application developers on external systems that integrate with yours.
- **Insiders.** These are members of the development team and people who provide technical and business services to your team. This includes enterprise architects, database administrators, security experts, network experts, toolsmiths, marketing experts, and sales staff.

So why does DAD use the term "stakeholder" instead of "customer"? Although customer is a perfectly good term and is popular with XP adherents, we've found that many agile teams inadvertently limit themselves to considering just end users and principals to be their customers and miss the partner stakeholders and sometimes even the insider stakeholders. Granted, you'll often work with some insider stakeholders as a matter of course throughout the project so it's hard to miss these people, although both of us have seen core agile teams neglect working with their organization's enterprise architects in the name of "having the courage to worry about tomorrow's problem tomorrow." Our experience is that although "stakeholder" is a bit more formal than "customer," in practice it seems to lead agile teams to a more mature strategy.

One challenge with the term "stakeholder," which "customer" also suffers from, is that it reinforces the "them vs. us" mentality prevalent in many IT departments. When we use terms such as "the stakeholders" or "the customers" or "the business," they imply that we see ourselves as a group set apart from them. The reality is that it isn't *the* business, it's *our* business; we're all in this together. So, be careful with your terminology.

Product Owner

In a system with hundreds or thousands of requirements it is often difficult to get answers to questions regarding the requirements. The product owner is the one individual on the team who speaks as the "one voice of the customer." She represents the needs and desires of the stakeholder community to the agile delivery team. As such, she clarifies any details regarding the solution and is also responsible for maintaining a prioritized list of work items that the team will implement to deliver the solution. While the product owner may not be able to answer all questions, it is her responsibility to track down the answer in a timely manner so that the team can stay focused on their tasks. Having a product owner working closely with the team to answer any questions about work items as they are being implemented substantially reduces the need for requirements, testing, and design documentation. You will of course still need deliverable documentation such as operations manuals, support manuals, and user guides to name a few. Each DAD team, or subteam in the case of large programmes organized into a team of teams, has a single product owner. A secondary goal for a product owner is to represent the work of the agile team to the stakeholder community. This includes arranging demonstrations of the solution as it evolves and communicating project status to key stakeholders.

As a stakeholder proxy, the product owner:

- Is the "go to" person for domain information and is typically collocated with the project team
- Provides timely information and makes timely decisions
- Prioritizes all work for the team, including but not limited to requirements and addressing defects, taking both stakeholder and team needs into account when doing so
- Continually reprioritizes and adjusts scope based on the evolving needs of the stakeholders
- Is an active participant in modeling and acceptance testing
- Helps the team gain access to expert stakeholders
- Facilitates requirements modeling sessions, including requirements envisioning
- Educates the team in the business domain
- Is the gateway to funding

When representing the agile team to the stakeholder community, the product owner:

- Is the public face of the team to project stakeholders
- Demos the solution to key stakeholders, typically principals such as senior managers, who are unable to attend the normal iteration demo (which is typically done by team members)
- Announces releases

- Monitors and communicates team status to interested stakeholders
- Organizes milestone reviews
- Educates stakeholders in the process followed by the delivery team
- Negotiates priorities, scope, funding, and schedule

Why do you need a product owner? Since the team can get timely answers to questions from one person, who is working daily with the project team, the customer is "speaking with one voice" from the point of view of team members. In this way inconsistencies of requirements are avoided, and the team can focus and be highly productive. Similarly, the stakeholders have a single person to approach who "speaks their language" when they want to provide feedback to the team. Having such a person in the role of product owner can greatly increase the chance that your team gets such feedback.

Although DAD adopts the product owner role from Scrum it takes a more realistic approach for larger projects. In Scrum the product owner role is the single person responsible for maintaining the list of work and the value of the work that the team performs. The product owner obtains input from a number of sources but is ultimately responsible for the decisions. In all but the simplest of domains no one single person can understand all the nuances of the requirements, something that should be obvious when you consider the full range of stakeholders described earlier. In traditional terms, a product owner is in many ways an empowered business analyst without the burden of the bureaucracy surrounding big requirements up front (BRUF).

DAD teams do more than simply implement requirements, so the "product backlog" evolves from being a stack of requirements to a stack of work items that include requirements, defects to be addressed, work to support other teams (such as reviews of their work), and activities to help support the team (such as deployment activities and training). The entire work item list needs to be prioritized, not just the backlog of requirements, implying greater responsibility for the product owner. This concept alone may be a significant change for Scrum teams moving to a DAD approach.

There are several potential challenges with the product owner role:

- **Product owners often "go native."** The more time that a product owner spends working with a DAD team the better he understands and can relate to the team's strategy for providing the solution. This is a good thing to a point, although it can decrease a product owner's ability to properly represent the stakeholders. This can be a hard problem to detect, something that your governance efforts should be on the lookout for (see Chapter 20), and often the solution is to rotate product owners into different teams.
- **The product owner can become a bottleneck.** Because the product owner is the one person that people go to for information and prioritization decisions, he can quickly become a bottleneck for the team. This is particularly true when the product owner isn't always available; both of us have seen organizations that split product owners between

two or more teams as well as teams where the product owner still has other responsibilities outside the delivery team. When the product owner becomes a bottleneck you need to consider offloading any nonteam responsibilities onto someone else or consider having more than one product owner (requiring coordination between them and delineation of responsibilities).

- **You have a "truck number" of one.** A team's truck number is the minimum number of people that if they left the team suddenly—for example, they were hit by a truck—that the team would be in serious trouble. Because you rely on the product owner for domain information and decisions, losing him would be deleterious for your team.

- **The product owner should not be the architecture owner.** Disciplined agile teams need a separation between the person with final say over the work prioritization decisions and the technical direction. When the same person is in both roles there is too much temptation to gold plate the solution with features that are technically interesting but of little or no value to the actual stakeholders.

- **The product owner should not be the team lead.** The product owner is a critical and time-consuming role on an agile team. While the product owner should be available to team members as much as possible, he is often away from the team negotiating with other stakeholders, communicating status, balancing multiple stakeholder priorities, and so on. Furthermore, the skillsets are different, with team leads requiring a solid understanding of solution delivery practices and product owners requiring a solid understanding of the domain and the needs of stakeholders. It is unusual in most organizations to find individuals with both sets of skills.

- **Product owners rarely represent the entire stakeholder community.** The stakeholder community can be wide ranging—there's no way a single person can be knowledgeable in the current, day-to-day details of what all the stakeholder types do and need. Worse yet, they may not even know what all the stakeholder types are, or if they do, who the key people are who represents each type. To address this problem product owners must be good networkers and must constantly strive to interact with the full range of the stakeholder community.

- **Product owners must be skilled negotiators.** For larger scale efforts the need for a product owner to be a good negotiator cannot be underestimated. Many projects often have competing and mutually exclusive needs, as well as differing views on the priorities of the work. There are additional challenges for product owners when scaling to large projects such as working with other product owners to manage requirements dependencies between subteams and to ensure that there is a consistent vision across subteams.

LESSONS FROM THE TRENCHES—BUSINESS ANALYSTS AND PRODUCT MANAGERS POTENTIALLY MAKE GREAT PRODUCT OWNERS

Existing, experienced business analysts, particularly those from the business side, are often good candidates for being product owners. The same is true of product managers in commercial software companies (such as IBM). People in these roles often understand the domain and have good contacts with businesspeople, increasing the chance that they will represent the majority of stakeholders reasonably well. Furthermore, they will have the requirements elicitation and negotiation skills required to be successful product owners. However, many business analysts or product managers will find that they need to break some of their "bad habits" around detailed requirements specification, and they may not yet have good contacts within the insider stakeholder community.

Be aware that some people in your organization may be sensitive about the product owner role name. Some cultures in organizations are very conscious of role names and associate them with job titles and hierarchies. The sponsor of your project may resent the idea that anyone on the project is the "owner" when he may see himself as the ultimate project authority. The name product owner or product manager is natural for product development companies, most of whom have had this role in place for years. However, for corporate IT departments, this role name may cause some grief. Be prepared to downplay the corporate significance of this role name so that your key stakeholders are not offended.

Team Member

The role of team member focuses on producing the actual solution for stakeholders. Team members perform testing, analysis, architecture, design, programming, planning, estimation, and many more activities as appropriate throughout the project. Note that *not* every team member will have every single one of these skills, at least not yet, but they will have a subset of them, and they will strive to gain more skills over time. Team members are sometimes described by core agile methods as "developers" or simply as programmers. However, in DAD we recognize that not every team member necessarily writes code.

Team members identify tasks, estimate tasks, "sign up" for tasks, perform the tasks, and track their status toward completion. Chapter 14, "Initiating a Construction Iteration," describes in detail how team members do this in a self-organizing, collaborative manner. In addition to the general responsibilities described earlier, team members have several additional responsibilities. They will

- **Go to the product owner (PO) for domain information and decisions.** Although team members provide input to the PO, in the end the PO is responsible for providing the requirements and prioritizing the work, not the team members. It requires significant discipline on the part of team members to respect this and to not add new features (known as "scope creep") or to guess at the details.

- **Work with the architecture owner (AO) to evolve the architecture.** The AO, described later, is responsible for the technical strategy followed by the team. Team members work closely and collaboratively with the AO to identify and evolve the technical strategy but must still respect the fact that the AO has the final say as to the technical direction that the project team takes.

- **Follow enterprise conventions and leverage and enhance the existing infrastructure.** As you learned in Chapter 1, "Disciplined Agile Delivery in a Nutshell," the DAD process framework is enterprise aware. An implication of this is that DAD team members will adopt and have the discipline to tailor where appropriate, any enterprise/corporate coding standards, user interface design conventions, database guidelines, and so on. They should also try to reuse and enhance existing, reusable assets such as common web services, frameworks, and, yes, even existing legacy data sources.[1]

- **Lead meetings.** Although other agile methods assign this responsibility to the team lead, the fact is that anyone on the team can lead or facilitate meetings. The team lead is merely responsible for ensuring this happens.

Here are some potential challenges of being a team member:

- **Overspecialization.** Traditional IT organizations often encourage career paths that lead to skill specialization at the expense of generalist knowledge. Effective agilists are "generalizing specialists" in that they have one or more technical specialties (e.g., Java™ programming) but also a general knowledge in other areas of software development. Agile-oriented organizations encourage individuals to work on tasks outside their specialty even if it means short-term lower productivity during the learning process.

- **Organizational resistance to cross-functional work.** Mark remembers a conversation with a senior manager wherein she suggested that having a tester do work normally done by a business analyst was unacceptable because the business analysts were in a higher pay grade. This is an example of an organizational impediment that is all too common in many companies.

- **Struggling to collaborate effectively.** Many technical experts prefer to work in isolation rather than working in a collaborative team environment. There are several potential reasons for this: Many organizations adopt office layouts (such as cubicles or doored offices) that promote this sort of behavior; many organizations promote Tayloristic cultures based on specialists focused on their own work handing off their results to other specialists; and, yes, some technical people are introverted and not comfortable with proactively collaborating and communicating. A good team lead is sensitive to these

---

1. In Chapter 7, Scott shares a poignant rant about the development community's blind spot when it comes to database issues, a problem exacerbated by the "simple design" strategies of core agile methods.

challenges and encourages team members to be more extroverted and to communicate proactively in a non-judgmental environment.

Note that the team lead and architecture owner are considered to be team members as well, albeit with additional responsibilities. The product owner is also a member of the team, although typically does not take on the team member responsibilities just described.

Team Lead

On agile projects the role of the traditional project manager changes substantially, and in fact the term "project manager" is now frowned upon. The agile community has focused on project or team leadership over team management, observing that the best "managers" prioritize leadership over technical management issues such as planning and estimation. An important aspect of self-organizing teams, see Chapter 14 for more information, is that the team lead facilitates or guides the team in performing technical management activities instead of taking on these responsibilities him- or herself. The team lead is a servant-leader to the team, creating and maintaining the conditions that allow the team to be successful.

The team lead is also an agile coach, helping to keep the team focused on delivering work items and fulfilling their iteration goals and commitments that they have made to the product owner. She acts as a true leader, facilitating communication, empowering the team to self-optimize their processes, ensuring that the team has the resources that it needs, and removes any impediments to the team (issue resolution) in a timely manner. When teams are self-organizing, effective leadership is crucial to your success.

While an experienced team lead brings these skills to a new team, it is unrealistic for this person to be a true coach if she has not had some mentoring. For teams new to agile, it often makes sense to have a part-time experienced coach working with the team for a few iterations.

A team lead's leadership responsibilities can be summarized as the following:

- Responsible for the effectiveness and continuous improvement of the process being followed by the team
- Facilitates close cooperation across all roles and functions
- Ensures that the team is fully functional and productive
- Keeps team focused within the context of the project vision and goals
- Is responsible for removal of team-based impediments and for the escalation of organizationwide impediments
- Protects the team from interruptions and external interferences
- Maintains open honest communication between everyone involved with the project
- Coaches others in the use and application of agile practices
- Prompts the team to discuss and think through issues when they're identified
- Facilitates decision making (does not make decisions or mandate internal team activity)

The agile community sometimes assumes that basic management related activities go away in the agile world. We have observed that certain responsibilities previously done by a project manager remain part of the ScrumMaster/coach/lead role, albeit going unsaid in many situations. In DAD we rectify this oversight by explicitly calling out the management responsibilities of the team lead role. These include the following:

- **Assessing team members.** Many of your organization's human resources policies, such as annual reviews, are still relevant in an agile environment. This may ultimately be the responsibility of the line manager, so the team lead needs to keep him appraised of the team members' performance.

- **Managing the project budget.** Although individual team members will be actively involved in detailed planning and estimating, the overall project budget still needs to be managed and reported to senior management. Sometimes this is done by a program or project administrator but typically requires input from the team lead as well.

- **Ensuring that someone on the team, perhaps themselves, keeps relevant records such as iteration burndowns, defect trend charts, taskboards, and other artifacts.** DAD teams must provide adequate visibility to senior management as part of the overall governance effort. Note that the creation of many of these records can be automated through the use of tools such as Jazz-based IBM Rational Team Concert (RTC).[2]

- Ensuring that the team keeps their focus on producing a potentially consumable solution each iteration.

- Ensuring that value-added practices and principles are used within the team, tailoring them accordingly.

- Ensuring that collaborative tools, such as taskboards for team coordination and whiteboards for modeling, are available to the team.

- Ensuring that someone on the team, often themselves, facilitates the various meetings (coordination meetings, iteration planning meetings, demos, modeling sessions, and retrospectives).

WHY DO WE NOT CALL THE TEAM LEAD A SCRUMMASTER?

The team lead is indeed similar to the ScrumMaster in Scrum, albeit with a greater focus on leadership. However, in DAD we prefer to use terminology that is clear and not tied to marketing a particular method. So we call "Scrum meetings" coordination meetings instead (which is what they were originally called before Scrum co-opted them), and we call "Scrum-Masters" team leads.

---

2. A live example of automated project dashboards can be found at www.jazz.net for the IBM Jazz project teams.

Here are some potential challenges of the team lead role:

- **The team lead should not be the product owner.** See the earlier discussion.

- **Smart team members "promoted" to the team lead role.** Within many IT organizations there often exists a career path hierarchy based on traditional human resources strategies. Career paths are often described as some starting out as a developer, then becoming systems analyst, and then eventually a project manager. Unfortunately, outstanding developers often make lousy project managers. People should be team leads because they're effective leaders who understand agile delivery, not simply because they're good at development.

- **Regression to "command and control" management.** It can be a difficult thing for traditional, classically trained project managers to transition to a style of leadership that allows the team members to self-organize. It requires a great degree of trust in your team that they have the competence and are motivated to deliver to their commitments effectively. We have both seen team leads that are new to agile start to regress to traditional project management behavior if they do not trust their teams. Those new to agile who become team leads often believe that "they know better" and start to hand out tasks with prescribed deadlines. This is a slippery slope and should be avoided at all costs. In point of fact, the project manager seldom knows better than the team members who actually do the work.

- **The team lead isn't fully utilized.** Being a team lead may not always be a full-time job. You need to lead the daily coordination meeting, participate in a program-level coordination meeting, facilitate retrospectives, coordinate team demos, capture and display key metrics, and perhaps spend some time helping to make things easier for your team. So what do you do with any free time during the day? Many team leads will also take on the role of team member and be active participants in development. Some will be the architecture owner of the team (who still develops), and some may even be in the role of product owner as well (although as we have said, we advise against this). A common anti-pattern that we see, particularly when traditionally trained project managers have recently moved into the role of team lead, is for the team lead to continue doing many of technical project management activities (such as detailed planning and estimating) that are better done by the team members themselves. When team leads do this they reduce the self-organization within the team and thereby run the risks of lower morale, lower productivity, and lower accuracy of the plans and estimates. It can be very hard, but all team members need to break old traditional habits and adopt new, disciplined agile habits, including people in leadership roles.

The team lead role is crucial to the success of a DAD team because the team lead implicitly drives the culture of the team. Team member energy levels, productivity, and even their attitude change to match the environment the team lead creates.

Architecture Owner

Architecture is a key source of project risk, and someone needs to be responsible for ensuring the team mitigates this risk. As a result the DAD process framework explicitly includes Agile Modeling's role of architecture owner. The architecture owner is the person who owns the architecture decisions for the team and who facilitates the creation and evolution of the overall solution design. As you see in the next chapter, it may not be necessary to formally designate a team member as an architecture owner on small teams. The person in the role of team lead often is also in the role of architecture owner. This isn't always the case, particularly at scale, but it is common for smaller agile teams.

Although the architecture owner is typically the senior developer on the team—and sometimes may be known as the technical architect, software architect, or solution architect—it should be noted that this is not a hierarchical position into which other team members report. She is just like any other team member and is expected to sign up and deliver work related to tasks like any other team member. Architecture owners should have a technical background and a solid understanding of the business domain.

The responsibilities of the architecture owner include the following:

- Guiding the creation and evolution of the architecture of the solution that the team is working on. Note that the architecture owner is not *solely* responsible for the architecture but leads the technical discussions.

- Mentoring and coaching other team members in architecture practices and issues.

- Understanding the architectural direction and standards of your organization and helping to ensure that the team adheres to them appropriately.

- Understanding existing enterprise assets such as frameworks, patterns, and subsystems, and ensuring that the team uses them where appropriate.

- Ensuring that the solution will be easy to support by encouraging good design and refactoring to minimize technical debt.

- Ensuring that the solution is integrated and tested on a regular basis, ideally via the practice of continuous integration (CI).

- Having the final say regarding technical decisions, but they try to avoid dictating the architectural direction in favor of a collaborative, team-based approach. The architecture owner should work closely with the team lead to identify and determine strategies to mitigate key project technical risks.[3]

- Leading the initial architecture envisioning effort at the beginning of the project and supporting the initial requirements envisioning effort (particularly when it comes to understanding and evolving the nonfunctional requirements for the solution). Chapter 8,

---

3. See the Risk-Value Lifecycle in Chapter 13 for more information on reducing risk early in the project.

"Identifying the Initial Scope," and Chapter 9, "Identifying an Initial Technical Strategy," address envisioning activities in greater detail.

Here are some potential challenges faced by the architecture owner role:

- **Traditional architects who don't make the transition to agile.** Old habits, particularly bad ones, die hard. Traditional approaches to architecture are typically documentation heavy, most of the work is performed "up front" in the lifecycle before any coding begins, and sometimes the architecture is even imposed upon the developers by the architects. Agile approaches to architecture are evolutionary and collaborative in nature, with some initial envisioning performed at the beginning of the project, but the details are identified throughout the lifecycle. Agile teams need architecture owners who lead and facilitate, not architects who command and control.

- **Architecture owners also code.** One key differentiator is that architecture owners know that the only way to validate any architecture is by demonstrating that it supports the nonfunctional requirements through working software. Some organizations have built a culture where their architects are senior IT people who no longer actively write code, which increases the risk that they don't fully understand the implications of the technologies that they're working with, which in turn increases the chance that the team(s) that they're supposedly supporting will ignore their advice.

- **Smart techie without the technical leadership skills.** Architecture owners require leadership skills. Sometimes the smartest developer on the team may not be the most effective leader, so choose your architecture owners wisely.

- **The architecture owner should not also be the product owner.** For many of the same reasons a team lead should not be a product owner, neither should the architecture owner be. The product owner role is typically a full-time role, leaving little capacity to do justice to the architect ownership role. The architecture owner specializes in solution delivery, rather than the business domain. The product owner has a completely different set of skills related to the business. Additionally, the architecture owner may skew the priorities of the work item list (backlog) toward technical priorities rather than on delivering value to the customers.

- **Neglecting enterprise assets in favor of building your own.** Assets are anything of value created on your project that may have value beyond completion of the project. Examples include code, patterns, templates, and standards. Unfortunately, many teams exhibit a "not invented here" syndrome whereby no code or design is any good unless it was done from scratch by the team—sadly the agile mantra of "simple design" is often used to justify writing everything from scratch. A crucial responsibility of the architecture owner is to be aware of enterprise assets that are available for reuse and then ensure that the team does so. Additionally, the architecture owner should be proactive in creating assets for reuse by other teams and publishing them so that other teams are aware of their existence and how to use them. Asset repositories such as IBM Rational Asset Manager can facilitate this reuse.

- **Dictating architecture vs. "self-organizing design."** Architecture owners must not assume that they understand the best designs for the team in all situations. Since the team members write most of the code, they often discover elegant designs that the architecture owner may not be aware of. A good architecture owner understands this and encourages team members to discover better designs and bring them to her attention so that they may be shared with other team members and potentially other teams.

- **Architecture gold-plating.** A huge source of waste in our industry is the perceived need for perfect work products of all types. Agile principle #12 "Simplicity—the art of maximizing the amount of work not done" is essential. There will always be a better architecture, but the time spent seeking perfection where often the users would not realize the improvements, could rather be used to deliver additional value or speed up delivery of the solution.

Potential Secondary Roles

We would like to be able to say that all you need are the five primary roles described previously to succeed. The fact is the primary roles don't cover the entire gambit—there's no way that your team will have all the technical expertise that it needs, your product owner couldn't possibly have expert knowledge in all aspects of the domain, and even if your organization had experts at all aspects of solution delivery it couldn't possibly staff every single team with the full range of expertise required. The bottom line is that your team needs to be supported by people in a variety of other secondary roles, something particularly true for agility at scale.

Your project may include the need to add some or all of the following roles:

- **Domain expert.** The product owner represents a wide range of stakeholders, not just end users, so it isn't reasonable to expect them to be experts in every nuance in your domain, something particularly true with complex domains. The product owner will sometimes bring in domain experts to work with the team, for example, a tax expert to explain the details of a requirement or the sponsoring executive to explain the vision for the project. Domain experts often fall into the stakeholder categories of either insiders or partners.

- **Specialist.** Although most agile team members are generalizing specialists, sometimes, particularly at scale, specialists are required. For example, on large teams or in complex domains one or more agile business analysts may join the team to help you explore the requirements for what you're building. On large teams a program manager may be required to coordinate the team leads on various subteams (more on this in Chapter 5). You will also see specialists on DAD teams when generalizing specialists aren't available—when your organization is new to agile it may be staffed primarily with specialists who haven't yet made the transition to generalizing specialists.

- **Technical expert.** Sometimes the team needs the help of technical experts, such as a build master to set up build scripts, an agile database administrator to help design and test a database, a user experience (UX) expert to help design a usable interface, or a security expert to provide advice about writing a secure system. Technical experts are brought in on an as-needed, temporary basis to help the team overcome a difficult problem and to transfer their skills to one or more developers on the team. Technical experts are often stakeholder insiders, working on other teams that are responsible for enterprise-level technical concerns or are simply specialists on loan to your team from other delivery teams.

- **Independent tester.** Although as you see in Chapter 15, "A Typical Day of Construction," the majority of testing is done by the people on the DAD team themselves, some DAD teams are supported by an independent test team working in parallel that validates their work throughout the lifecycle. This independent test team is typically needed for agility@scale situations within complex domains, using complex technology, or addressing regulatory compliance issues. Independent testers are effectively partner stakeholders who are outside the team.

- **Integrator.** For large DAD teams that have been organized into a team of subteams, the subteams are typically responsible for one or more subsystems or features. The larger the overall team, generally the larger and more complicated the system being built. In these situations, the overall team may require one or more people in the role of integrator responsible for building the entire system from its various subsystems. On smaller teams or in simpler situations the architecture owner is typically responsible for ensuing integration, a responsibility picked up by the integrator(s) for more complex environments. Integrators often work closely with the independent test team, if there is one, to perform system integration testing regularly throughout the project. This integrator role is typically only needed at scale for complex technical solutions.

Transitioning to DAD Roles

Traditional roles, such as business analyst and project manager, do not appear in DAD. The goals that people in traditional roles try to achieve, for example, in the case of a business analyst to understand and communicate the stakeholder needs/intent for the solution, are still addressed in DAD but in different ways by different roles. There isn't a perfect one-to-one match between any given traditional role and a DAD role, but, given an open mind and the willingness to learn new skills, people in traditional roles today can choose to transition to a new DAD role tomorrow. The critical thing for traditionalists to understand is that because the underlying paradigm and strategy has changed, they too must change to reflect the DAD approach. Figure 4.3 shows potential mappings of traditional roles to DAD roles. The thick lines between a traditional role and a DAD role indicate the most likely DAD role to transition to. The thin lines indicate other good options.

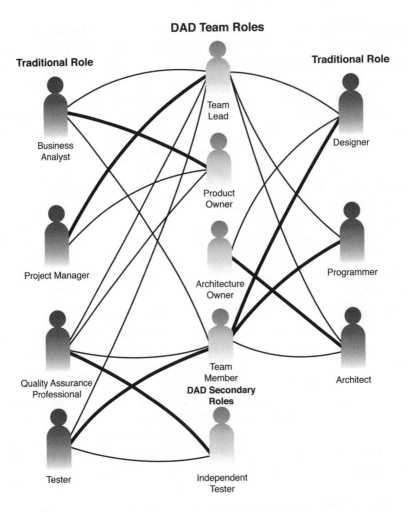

Figure 4.3   Mapping of traditional roles to potential DAD roles

For people with experience in other agile methodologies transitioning into a DAD role should be fairly easy. The important thing to remember is that the roles are often more robust. For example, where a product owner on a Scrum team prioritizes requirements, a product owner on a DAD team is responsible for prioritizing the full range of work items for a DAD team. Where people in the ScrumMaster role in Scrum may have been required to take on technical leadership responsibilities, in DAD these responsibilities are explicitly addressed by the architecture owner role. The roles are similar, but there are still important differences.

Concluding Thoughts

A crucial aspect to putting people first is to understand the rights, responsibilities, and roles they take on project teams. These three things provide a framework for how people interact with, and collaborate with, one another. The DAD process framework provides people with a collection of rights counterbalanced by a collection of responsibilities. Organizations should acknowledge that teams have certain rights if they are expected to fulfill their commitments to the stakeholders when delivering the solution. Teams should acknowledge that they have certain responsibilities to the organization in return for the trust and rights that they have been given.

There are five primary roles on DAD project teams (stakeholder, product owner, team member, team lead, and architecture owner), each of which has additional responsibilities that they must fulfill. You also learned about five secondary roles (domain expert, specialist, technical expert, independent tester, and integrator) that typically appear when DAD teams find themselves in scaling situations. These roles are not positions—any given person may find himself in one or more roles, and several people often are in the same role on a single DAD team.

The rights, responsibilities, and roles defined by the DAD process framework need to be tailored accordingly to reflect the unique situation your team finds itself in. Having said that, the more you deviate from the suggested framework defined in this chapter the greater the chance that your team will run into trouble due to unintended consequences of your changes. If you do choose to tailor these concepts, think it through first, try out your change, observe the effects, adjust accordingly, and then iterate.

Additional Resources

For more detailed discussions about several of the topics covered in this chapter:

- **Product owners.** Scott maintains an article titled "The Product Owner Role: A Stakeholder Proxy for Agile Teams" at www.agilemodeling.com/essays/productOwner.htm that provides a detailed overview about this role. Of particular interest is the discussion around how this role changes at scale.

- **Architecture owners.** The original article about the architecture owner role is posted at www.agilemodeling.com/essays/architectureOwner.htm.

- **Generalizing specialists.** A detailed overview of what it means to be a generalizing specialist, and how it is possible to become one, appears at www.agilemodeling.com/essays/generalizingSpecialists.htm.

- **Independent testing.** The article "Agile Testing and Quality Strategies" at www.ambysoft.com/essays/agileTesting.html presents a detailed overview of agile testing, including independent testing. Chapter 15 addresses this topic in greater detail as well.

- **Stakeholders.** The Outside-In method, described in the book *Outside-In Software Development* by Karl Kessler and John Sweitzer (IBM Press, 2007), has one of the most coherent descriptions of stakeholders that we've run across. Scott also maintains an article at www.agilemodeling.com/essays/stakeholders.htm exploring this role.

- **Leading agile teams.** Mary and Tom Poppendieck's book *Leading Lean Software Development* (Addison Wesley, 2010) provides insightful advice for leading development teams at both the team and organizational level. In *Leadership: 50 Points of Wisdom for Today's Leaders* (HarperCollins Publishers, 2010) General Rick Hillier describes a collection of people-focused principles for being an effective leader.

CHAPTER 5

Forming Disciplined Agile Delivery Teams

Great developers care deeply about the code. Great teams care deeply about each other.
—Declan Whelan via Twitter

A team is a set of individuals working together toward a collective goal, and without such a goal several people working together is merely a working group. Teams of developers and stakeholders working closely together are fundamental philosophies behind agile, philosophies captured by the fourth and fifth principles of the Agile Manifesto:

- Business people and developers must work together daily throughout the project.
- Build projects around motivated individuals. Give them the environment and support they need, and trust them to get the job done.

Disciplined Agile Delivery (DAD) teams are typically small-to-medium sized. We consider teams of 15 people or fewer to be small, teams between 10 and 40 people to be medium-sized, and teams of 30 or more people to be large. We've purposely overlapped these ranges because there are no agreed-to definitions in the industry and because people's perception of size varies based on their experience and situation. What we can tell you, though, is that the average agile team size is 10 members, and we're seeing successful agile programs with hundreds of people. We also know that the success rate of agile teams drops the larger the team; this is also true of traditional project teams, with average success rates of roughly 80% for small teams (1-10 people), 70% for medium-sized teams (11-25 people), and 55% for large teams (25 or more people).[1]

---

1. Your definition of small, medium, and large may vary. Scott chose these sizes based on results of previous surveys that explored team-size issues.

DAD teams are also typically collocated or near-located. The definition of collocation is straightforward—everyone, including primary stakeholders, is in the same work room. The definition for near-location is a bit nebulous as it includes people working on the same floor, same building, same campus (e.g., within walking distance), and same city/area. In short, if everyone on the team is close enough that they could drive in to attend a coordination meeting, then they're near-located. Far located teams may have some people who are not near-located. When it comes to collocation, roughly 50% of development teams are in the same room although less than 10% are collocated with their stakeholders. But, an additional one quarter of agile teams are near-located, and similarly one quarter of stakeholders are near-located to the team (therefore roughly three quarters of agile team members are at least near-located and 30% of stakeholders at least near-located). As you'd expect, collocated agile teams have a higher success rate than near-located teams, which in turn do better than far-located teams.

Not surprisingly, our advice is to reduce your project risk as much as possible by keeping your teams as small as you can and as geographically close as you can. The principles in this book are straightforward to apply with small teams but require some context-specific tailoring as you scale up.

Figure 5.1 shows a mind map of the structure of this chapter. We describe each of the topics in the map in clockwise order, beginning at the top right.

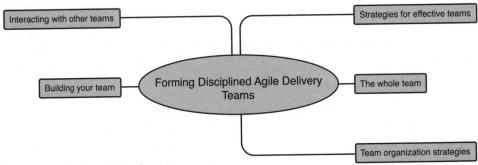

Figure 5.1   Outline of this chapter

THE BIG IDEAS IN THIS CHAPTER

- Ideally, DAD teams are "whole" in that together they have sufficient skills to achieve their goals without needing to collaborate with people outside the team.
- Realistically, DAD teams need to interact with people on other teams that are external to them to achieve their goals.
- Effective teams evolve over time; they are more than just a group of people cobbled together and given the moniker "team."
- The way that you organize a team varies based on its size and geographic distribution. No single strategy works for all situations.

Strategies for Effective Teams

Solution delivery is a team sport. Over the years, both of us have been involved with dozens of teams, ranging from successful to downright abysmal. As a result we've experienced first-hand many strategies that worked well and many that didn't. The following advice represents ideals— you won't achieve all of them fully, and unfortunately the further you stray from them, the greater the risk to your project. Effective DAD teams:

- **Are focused.** Fellow team members need to feel that each team member is dedicated to the successful outcome of the team, often referred to as "unity of purpose" or "positive interdependence." Show teams respect by asking them to identify the root problem to solve and to define measurable objectives against which their success can be judged. An important observation is that for people to do a good job, you must first give them a good job to do. Teams are most successful when distractions and external influences that remove focus from attaining their team goals are minimized and better yet eliminated.

- **Are tailored to the environment.** An important message of this chapter is that one team structure does not fit all, that you will form your team to reflect the situation that you face. The structure of a DAD team varies by size and geographical distribution as well as by needs driven by the problem and technical domains.

- **Are based on trust and respect.** When team members don't trust and respect one another they will be unwilling to share information, to share skills, to help one another, or in extreme cases to even interact with one another. The importance of trust and respect are built right into the rights and responsibilities described in Chapter 4, "Roles, Rights, and Responsibilities." Trust is built over time through ongoing interactions and conscious practices.

- **Are safe.** People must be free to share ideas with one another without fear of retribution and more importantly be allowed to try new ideas and even potentially fail at them. Yes, people can still criticize these new ideas but should do so in a frank and comfortable manner. However, recognize that disagreement is a good thing from which the team learns. Similarly, mistakes along the way, and sometimes even failures, are considered learning opportunities for the team. For teams to be safe, there must be open and honest communication between team members, a desire to learn together, and trust. Social interaction theory tells us that promotive interaction occurs when individuals encourage and facilitate each other's efforts to accomplish team goals.

- **Provide learning opportunities.** Mastery, or the opportunity to master something, is one of the key motivators of intellectual workers. Successful teams provide opportunities for people to learn from one another as they work together, to experiment, and to try new things (often with someone more experienced in that area providing guidance). Social interdependence theory has shown that cooperative learning is effective within teams that are positively interdependent.

- **Are as small as possible.** The larger the team the greater the overhead associated with coordination and communication. Sociology research isn't conclusive about optimal team size, giving a range of between five and twelve people depending on the types of tasks taken on by the team and the organizational culture. When a team gets to be ten people or more, a good heuristic is to reorganize this "large" team into smaller sub-teams, something discussed later in this chapter.

- **Have shared workspaces.** DAD teams need to be able to share and access information easily, ideally in an open and collaborative manner. Teams that are collocated or near-located (typically in the same building) often set up physical workspaces, including taskboards used to coordinate their activities, whiteboards to sketch on, and hopefully work tables and shared workstations. Electronic workspaces, including but not limited to version control systems, document management systems, and electronic collaboration tools, enable DAD teams to share information even when team members are geographically or temporally dispersed. Workspaces are discussed in detail in Chapter 11, "Forming the Work Environment."

- **Are "whole."** Ideally, DAD teams should have the sufficient skills and resources to accomplish their goals. The implication is that DAD teams are cross-functional in nature and ideally composed of "generalizing specialists" (multidisciplinary developers). However, as we'll see at scale, sometimes it isn't possible for teams to be completely whole and instead they will occasionally interact with specialists on a temporary basis to address thorny domain or technological issues.

- **Are self-organizing within the constraints of appropriate governance.** DAD teams are self-organizing in that they have the authority to choose how they perform the work and the responsibility to do that work in the best way. Chapter 20, "Governing Disciplined Agile Teams," describes agile governance strategies based on motivation and enablement, not command and control.

- **Have adequate resources to fulfill their remit.** Teams must have the resources, including money, time, equipment, tools, and skills required to achieve the goal(s) they've signed on to fulfill. Too few resources and you risk the tendency for teams to take short-cuts, and history has shown that shortcuts on delivery projects typically prove to be "longcuts" in practice. Conversely, too many resources leads to the tendency to be wasteful of those resources.

- **Are accountable.** An important part of appropriate governance is ensuring that teams are accountable for fulfilling the goal(s) they have taken on, or providing compelling reasons why they were unable to do so, and for investing the resources provided to them in an appropriate manner. Social interdependence theory shows that positive interdependence motivates the concept of "ought"—as a team member I ought to complete my share of the work, I ought to contribute positively, and I ought to help others learn and succeed.

- **Are self-aware.** What we mean by this is the team members understand what work they're supposed to perform, how it all fits together, and the current status of said work. Self-aware teams take time to reflect inwardly on their personal and team performance and take steps to improve continually as the project progresses. This self-awareness comes from open and honest communication, close collaboration, and shared coordination tools such as taskboards (either physical or electronic). Self-awareness is particularly important because it enables DAD teams to identify and address bottlenecks/problems when, or better yet before, they occur.

- **Are enterprise aware.** DAD teams recognize that they don't work in a vacuum, that what they do should reflect the overall vision and culture of their organization. They leverage and often enhance existing assets, they follow common guidelines, and work closely with enterprise professionals to do so. DAD teams also strive to share their learnings—perhaps achieved through experimentation, thoughtful reasoning during retrospectives, or even from failures—with the rest of the organization.

- **Include dedicated people.** Ideally any given individual should be on a single team so that they can focus on the goals of the team. Realistically many people aren't allowed this luxury, perhaps because they work in matrix organizations where they report to two or more managers or more often because they're assigned to multiple teams due to over-specialization of skills. For example, when you have seven teams requiring people with database skills, but only three people with those skills you're going to have those people assigned to multiple teams until they can transfer their skills to others. When individuals work on more than one team at a time their productivity decreases due to the overhead of task switching. Research shows that most people are capable of working on two major activities in parallel, but more than that and their effectiveness drops precipitously. Sadly many organizational cultures lead them to assign people to far more than just two activities or teams at the same time.

- **Are geographically close.** When people are collocated they are able to streamline the way they communicate and share information with one another, increasing overall productivity while reducing project risk. Close proximity enables teams to reduce the overall feedback cycle, providing opportunities to address problems quickly and cheaply and thereby increase quality. It is still possible to be agile when the team is geographically distributed, but they need to tailor their practices to reflect that reality and adopt tools that support distributed agile teams.

- **Follow a common strategy.** Effective teams have shared values, often based on a set of agreed-to principles, rights, and responsibilities. These shared values provide the foundation for a common process followed by team members, albeit on which the team will evolve over time based on their shared learnings.

- **Stay together.** It takes times for teams to gel, for team members to learn how they can work together successfully. An all-too-common mistake in traditional IT shops is to disband solution delivery teams at the end of a project, making the individuals available to become members of new project teams. The problem with this is that these new teams need to now suffer through the process of gelling again. A better approach is to keep effective teams together, or more realistically to keep a core portion of the team together to move on together either to the next release of the solution they just produced or to begin working on addressing a new opportunity.

The Whole Team

Let's start with the ideal, something to aim for in the long term if not the short term; later in the chapter we explore less-than-ideal situations. Ideally your team is cross-functional in that it includes people with sufficient skills to get the job done, and those people themselves are cross-functional "generalizing specialists." When teams have the skills and resources to achieve the goal(s) they've taken on they are much more able to work in a streamlined manner than teams that need to rely on outside resources to achieve their goals. When individuals are generalizing specialists,[2] people with one or more specialties (such as Java programming, testing, analysis, and so on), and at least a general knowledge of the overall solution delivery process and the domain that they're working in, they are better able to collaborate with others and to perform the work that needs to be done.

In many ways the whole team strategy is a critical success factor for DAD teams, as it is for teams following other agile methods such as Scrum or XP. Throughout the DAD lifecycle, the "whole team" collaborates together to successfully address the goal(s) they've taken on. For example, at the beginning of each iteration the team collectively identifies what work they can reasonably achieve that iteration, identifies the tasks to do so, and cooperatively distributes responsibility for tasks to people on the team. This practice is called iteration planning and is described in greater detail in Chapter 14, "Initiating a Construction Iteration." Throughout the iteration the team organizes their activities on a regular basis, typically at least once a day, via short coordination meetings. They work together to fulfil their tasks, helping each other as needed and learning from one another while doing so. Some teams decide to adopt non-solo development practices, such as pair programming or modeling with others, to fulfil their tasks and to share knowledge.

When team members work together collaboratively, when they choose to partner with team members with different skills to accomplish a task together, when they choose to share their skills with others and similarly pick up new skills from others, they quickly move away from being just specialists to generalizing specialists. Both of us have seen former specialists, such as someone who had previously focused just on testing or just on business analysis, transition to agile teams and within a few months be well on the way to being generalizing specialists with a wider range of skills. Specialists may still be needed at scale, but in the majority of cases people who are

---

2. Sometimes referred to as "T-skilled" people.

generalizing specialists are far more suitable for being agile team members. This philosophy can be uncomfortable at first, particularly in organizations that have promoted narrow specialization of roles for years, but it is one that leads not only to higher levels of project success but also to greater employability of individuals. There is a surprising lack of encouragement in many organizations for developing skills outside individuals' specialties, and in some cases it is even discouraged.

Team Organization Strategies

Chapter 4 described the potential roles people take on DAD teams. Any given person will be in one or more roles, and any given role may have zero or more people in them given certain restrictions (which will soon become clear). This section focuses on the differences between small teams (2 to 15 people), medium teams (10 to 40 people), and large teams (30 or more people). We purposely overlap the categories because there are no exact demarcation points—does it really make sense to claim that a team of 30 people is medium sized, whereas a team with 31 people is large? We also overview the implications of geographically distributed DAD teams.

Small Teams

Figure 5.2 depicts the typical structure of a small DAD team. On small DAD teams, the architecture owner and team lead are often the same person, but when there is significant technical complexity or organizational complexity you may need to have separate people in each role.

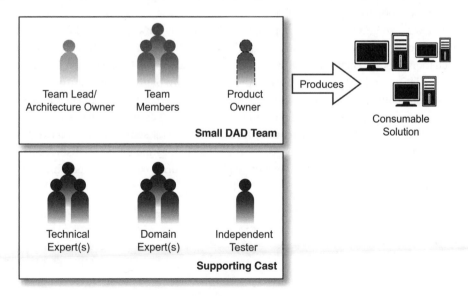

Figure 5.2   The structure of a small DAD team

What may be new to experienced agile practitioners is the explicit inclusion of the extended team members in the supporting cast, people who may be involved for short periods of time or in a part-time manner. These roles are optional and included on an as-needed, as-appropriate basis. For example, a technical specialist with deep database experience may be brought into your team for a few days to help you set up your database, configure it, and teach you basic administration tasks. Or a user experience (UX) specialist may be available to your team a few hours a week to help you with understanding and addressing usability concerns. Or your product owner may invite domain specialists to provide detailed information to your team on an as-needed basis throughout the project—remember, the product owner likely won't be an expert in all aspects of the problem domain. Or you may have an independent tester, who may be part of a larger test team, working in parallel to your team performing exploratory testing or other complex forms of testing in addition to your whole team testing efforts.

Medium-Sized Teams

Medium-sized teams of 10 to 40 people are typically organized as a team of small subteams as you see in Figure 5.3. For example, a team of 30 people may actually be comprised of four sub-teams of 8, 7, 10, and 5 people, respectively. Each subteam works on a portion of the overall solution each iteration, typically one or more features (or defects); the scope of each may be applicable to a single component or may affect several architectural components. The advantages and disadvantages of feature teams and component teams are discussed later in the chapter. Regardless of the tactic, the work of each subteam must be integrated together to form the entire consumable solution for your stakeholders.[3]

As team size grows, it's likely that the architecture owner(s) and team leads are different people—a primary reason to have a larger team is increased domain or technical complexity, each of which motivates a greater focus on architecture. You may have a single person as the architecture owner for several subteams. Similarly one person may be the team lead for two or more teams, and someone may be in the product owner role for two or more subteams. However, the more subteams a given individual is involved with, the lower their efficiency due to the overhead associated with task switching. Realistically it may be viable for someone to be on two or *maybe* three subteams and still be efficient. Also, a given subteam may include specialists on them—for example, a subteam working on the development of a security component may include one or more security specialists.

---

3. Figure 5.3 uses the UML notation for aggregation, a line with a diamond on it, to indicate that the work of the sub-teams is part of the overall consumable solution. The same notation is applied in Figure 5.4.

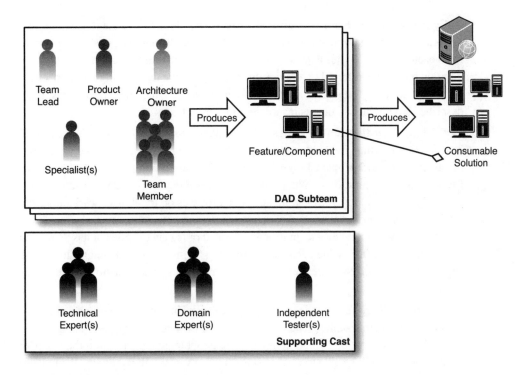

Figure 5.3   The structure of a medium-sized DAD team

There are several stratagems you may consider adopting to coordinate activities on medium-sized teams:

- **Increased envisioning and release planning efforts during Inception.** To ease coordination of your overall team throughout construction, one of the more valuable things you can do is ensure you're reasonably organized to begin with. The implication is that you'll need to invest a bit more time on initial requirements envisioning so that you have a better understanding of the scope, a bit more time on initial architecture envisioning so that you have a better understanding as to how you're going to build the solution, and a bit more effort on initial release planning so that everyone understands how the team is going to work together. Notice we said "a bit more" not "a lot more." Where a team of 10 people may need to spend three weeks in the Inception phase, a team of 30 people may require five weeks.[4]

---

4. These numbers are an off-the-cuff example, not prescriptive advice. The length of time Inception takes is driven more by experience of the people involved, domain complexity, technical complexity, access to stakeholders, willingness of stakeholders to be involved, and your organization's culture (specifically your ability to make decisions in a timely manner).

- **Daily subteam and team coordination meetings.** With this strategy each subteam holds a daily coordination meeting as they normally would, and then one or more people from each subteam attends a daily team coordination meeting. In Scrum the daily coordination meeting is referred to as a Scrum meeting and the team coordination meeting a "scrum of scrums." This tactic works reasonably well for medium-sized teams, but as described later, typically proves insufficient for larger teams.

- **Lean daily coordination meetings.** The Kanban community reports holding daily coordination meetings with 40 to 60 people in 10 to 15 minutes, compared with Scrum meetings of 10 to 15 people taking 15 minutes. The main difference is that where Scrum focuses on three questions—What did you do yesterday? What do you intend to do today? What's blocking you?—Kanban instead focuses on the flow of work rather than the individual team members and addresses any impediments to that flow. The Scrum approach works well when a team is newly formed or is new to agile but has an obvious scaling limitation (hence the need for a scrum of scrums on larger teams). The Kanban approach works well for gelled teams and is clearly well suited for a great range of team sizes.

- **Electronic tooling.** Team size and geographical distribution often go hand-in-hand— the greater the team size the greater the chance that the team will be geographically distributed. The implication is that the greater the geographical distribution the lower the chance the team will be able to easily get together physically to coordinate their efforts, requiring electronic support. A common approach to dealing with these challenges is to use techniques such as audio or video conference calls, email, or online chat to coordinate activities. Many teams also adopt tooling that supports these realities of geographically distributed development (GDD), such as IBM Rational Team Concert (RTC), which supports electronic work item management, task/Kanban/Scrum boards, integrated chat, and many more features that support collaboration. Having said that, it is still important for team members to meet face-to-face occasionally for key coordination activities.

Another interesting change as your team size grows is the need to support multilevel continuous integration (CI). CI is a common agile practice, described in greater detail in Chapter 15, "A Typical Day of Construction," where you regularly compile and test your work. Many agile teams use tools such as Cruise Control, the build manager in RTC, or in enterprise environments IBM Rational Build Forge® to automatically reintegrate whenever an updated code or configuration file is checked into your version control system. With small teams this is fairly straightforward, but as your team grows you may need to adopt a strategy where the work of an individual subteam is integrated within its own environment. When appropriate the subteam's work is promoted and made available so that it can be integrated into the overall solution. At the solution level there may be a test suite focused on solution-level issues, such as system integration, which aren't addressed fully within the test suites developed by the subteams. Furthermore, within the subteam each team member integrates her work within her own developer sandbox, promoting it to the subteam integration environment when appropriate. Where possible, system integration should be localized within the subteams as much as possible to reduce dependencies outside the teams.

An important observation about the previous discussion is how you need to tailor your process and tooling to reflect the situation in which you find yourself. Regardless of size, DAD teams perform initial requirements envisioning, regression testing, daily coordination meetings, and many other practices, but the way that they do so varies depending on which scaling factors apply. Similarly the tools they use to do so also need to reflect the situation they find themselves in—whiteboards are great for status tracking on small, collocated teams but are insufficient for large teams or geographically distributed teams, and instead electronic tooling will be needed.

Large Teams

When a disciplined agile team is 30 or more people it's considered large. Similar to medium-sized teams, a large team is organized as a team of subteams as depicted in Figure 5.4. What is different is the addition of explicit roles required for coordination, particularly those within the leadership team (which is sometimes called a coordination team) as well as an optional role of integrator.

The leadership team is typically headed up by someone in the role of program manager, sometimes referred to as a project manager, who is responsible for overall team coordination. As Figure 5.4 indicates, the leadership team is mainly comprised of the people in senior roles on the individual subteams. Together these people address critical aspects of overall team collaboration:

- **Project management coordination.** The individual team leads are each part of the project management team responsible for coordinating fundamental management issues, such as schedule dependencies, staffing, conflicts between subteams, and overall cost and schedule tracking. The program manager typically heads up the project management team.

- **Requirements coordination.** Because there are dependencies between requirements, and between work items in general, there is a need for product owners to coordinate the work item stacks between subteams. This includes ensuring that the same requirement isn't being worked on unknowingly by two or more subteams, and that the priorities of each subteam are consistent. For example, if requirement X being worked on by subteam A has a dependency on requirement Y being worked on by subteam B, you want to ensure that they have similar priorities. For example, if X is being implemented in the current iteration, Y should ideally be implemented this iteration if it isn't already in place; otherwise, the Y functionality will need to be mocked out until the point in time that subteam B implements Y (and removes the mocks). A mock is a simulation of something, so a mock of Y appears to be a working Y from the point of view of X, which interacts with it. Because of the dependency X isn't truly done until Y is also done, implying that if mocks are used the solution isn't shippable while Y is mocked out. The overall implication is that if requirement dependencies aren't coordinated between subteams the advantages associated with producing a potentially consumable solution each iteration are lost. The product owner team, often headed up by a chief product owner, is responsible for requirements coordination.

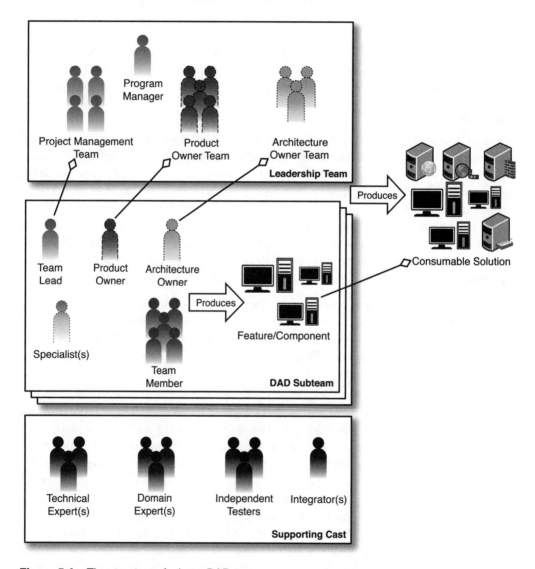

Figure 5.4   The structure of a large DAD team

- **Technical coordination.** There will also be technical dependencies between each subsystem/component or feature, resulting in the need to address those strategies effectively. Such technical dependencies include the need to invoke services or functions provided by another part of the solution, common nonfunctional requirements shared across components, and shared data sources to name a few. These technical dependencies require the appropriate subteams to coordinate with one another, work that is typically initiated by the architecture owners on each subteam but often involving other team members as needed. Another aspect of technical coordination is regular integration of the overall system. Very large or complex teams will have one or more people in the role of integrator—while the architecture owner is responsible for integration within his subteam, the integrator(s) is responsible for solution integration and will coordinate accordingly with the architecture owners and other team members of the subteams.

STILL NO PROJECT MANAGER?

The role of project manager has not been explicitly included in any of the team organization strategies. However, the program manager role on large agile teams is a specialized form of project manager (and some teams will call it that). Does this mean that small and medium-sized DAD teams don't do project management? Of course not, it just means they don't have someone focused solely on that. DAD teams are self-organizing, which means that many management activities are performed collaboratively by the team themselves, with facilitation by the team lead. Project management is so important on DAD teams that we don't leave those activities in the hands of a single person. Granted, some organizations choose to call the team lead role project manager, although this runs the risk of experienced traditional PMs not fully making the transition to agile because they don't recognize the changes in the agile form of the role.

This philosophy can provide significant heartburn for organizations new to agile who have strong Project Management Offices (PMOs) steeped in traditional project management thinking. In fact, the 2010 How Agile Are You survey revealed that nearly half of agile teams were not self-organizing, a strong indication of cultural dissonance within the project management teams of those organizations.

Can an existing project manager (PM) fit into a DAD team? Certainly. While, for small teams, we often see the architecture owner also fill the role of the team lead, for larger teams, a traditional project manager could be the team lead. This only works, however, if the PM clearly steps back from any resemblance of a command and control style in favor of self-organization. Since a DAD team lead does far less detailed planning and reporting than a traditional PM, project management is not a full-time job on a DAD project. So even as a team lead, a PM needs to roll up her sleeves and help out in other areas in a cross-functional style. For instance, PMs could do modeling, write user acceptance tests, or (gasp!) write some code.

How does the leadership team achieve these goals? As with medium-sized teams, there is a need for a bit more requirements and architecture envisioning during Inception. The leadership subteams (project management, product owners, architecture owners) need to coordinate any issues via team coordination meetings and electronic means as needed. Many teams discover that these coordination issues have different cadences; for example, requirements and technical coordination occurs daily at the beginning of an iteration but peters out later in the iteration, whereas project management coordination is needed daily throughout the iteration. There is a greater need for shared models, documentation, and plans, particularly if the team is geographically dispersed. Finally, use of integrated tooling that is instrumented to provide key measures, which in turn are displayed on project dashboards, can provide greater visibility of what is happening within the team and thereby aid coordination. We'll discuss such dashboards in greater detail in the chapters describing Construction iterations, but if you want to see actual live dashboards from several IBM agile development teams, visit www.jazz.net.

The need for roles in the supporting cast grows in proportion to the team size—scaling factors such as domain complexity and technical complexity are primary motivators of both greater team size and several of the supporting roles. Working with multiple technologies increases the need for people with experience in those technologies, potentially increasing team size. Multiple technologies may also increase the complexity surrounding issues such as application security, secure data access, performance, and integration potentially requiring specialists in those areas to work with your team. Similarly, increased domain complexity may require additional effort to explore the domain, thereby potentially requiring more people on your team and perhaps even specialists focused on business analysis.

Medium- and large-sized DAD teams are organized into a team of teams. Three fundamental strategies can be combined to organize subteams:

- **Feature teams.** Subteams are created that are responsible for delivering end-to-end slices of functionality throughout the entire subsystem. For example, in a banking system a feature team may take on a user story such as "As a loan officer, I want to transfer loan responsibility between two customers," which would potentially require work requiring updates to existing loan functionality, account functionality, and perhaps customer functionality as well. This work would need to occur in parallel to the work being performed by other feature teams who could also potentially be working in those codebases at the same time.

- **Component teams.** A given subteam is responsible for one or more components[5] within the overall solution being delivered. Services for the components need to be defined early in the lifecycle so that development of each component can occur in

---

5. Note that we are using the term "component" to refer to a variety of architectural strategies including components, large-scale components, frameworks, and subsystems.

parallel (a practice called "API First" in the Eclipse Way and an important aspect of Agile Modeling's Architecture Envisioning practice). One of the challenges with component teams is to deliver working solution increments at the end of each iteration. With components being developed by different teams, functionality for a particular story may not be ready in a particular component (unless the stories are written to reflect the underlying architecture). "Mocking" of incomplete components may be required for missing functionality so that the complete bits can still be tested and demonstrated to stakeholders. Components can be organized by tier, such as user interface components (applications), technical components (i.e., database services, security framework, and a message bus), and business services (i.e., in a bank, a loan component, an account component, and a customer component). Another line of attack is to identify fully functioning domain-driven subsystems (i.e., loan, account, and customer) that are standalone for the most part (they may share a common infrastructure and will be integrated somehow). For component teams to work, the requirements must also reflect the architectural strategy (and vice versa). For example, your user stories/scenarios would need to reflect the individual components. So, the "As a loan officer, I want to transfer loan responsibility between two customers" user story would need to be broken down into something like "As a customer, I accept responsibility for an existing loan," "As customer I drop responsibility for a loan," and "As a loan, I transfer ownership between two customers." (Note that we may still have needed to do something like this with a feature team approach to ensure the user stories could be implemented in a single iteration.)

- **Internal open source.** Also called private open source, this is a refinement of the component team approach where a component/framework is developed via open source tactics. Within IBM we've found this strategy to be useful when a component is mission critical to many other teams and is evolving at such a pace where a specific component team becomes overwhelmed with the rate of new requests coming in for it. In some cases we simply increased the size of the subteam, but in other cases we "open sourced" the component privately within IBM, requiring subteams that needed changes to the component to make them via open source practices (typically following something similar to the Eclipse Way, the process followed by the Eclipse team). With this approach, a small subteam, often a single individual, is required to oversee the open source process.

Our experience within IBM and with customers is that feature teams work best for the vast majority of situations. From what the two of us have seen working with customers, feature teams are used in about 80% to 90% of situations, component teams for another 10% to 20%, and internal open source for 1% to 4%. But no approach is perfect, and you need to organize your team according to your situation. Table 5.1 compares the three team organization strategies.

LESSONS FROM THE TRENCHES—COMPLEXITY MOTIVATES COMPONENT SUBTEAMS

It is my experience that the larger the number of components involved in the solution, the more difficult it is to have multiple teams touching multiple components in parallel, thus leading to a bias for component teams on larger projects. While projects with relatively few components work well with feature teams, I often work on larger teams facing greater complexity that tend to take a component team approach. —David L. Brown, IBM Rational's Chief Architect for Systems

Table 5.1   Comparing Large Team Organization Strategies

Strategy	Potential Advantages	Potential Disadvantages	Considerations
Feature team	End-to-end functionality implemented incrementally.	Sophisticated software configuration management (SCM) is required. Sophisticated system-level integration and regression testing is required.	Makes sense when product owners are able to define small "vertical slices" of your solution. Product owners should also be able to manage the dependencies between requirements.
Component team	Components are treated as black boxes that can potentially evolve on separate release schedules. Increases potential for reuse of components between development teams.[6]	Requires a clean architecture that is loosely coupled and highly cohesive. Requires a bit more architecture envisioning up front to identify components and their interfaces. Component teams may need to mock out functionality not yet implemented, implying that their components are not potentially consumable until the mocks are replaced with actual functionality. Can be difficult to demo technically oriented components. Can lead away from a stakeholder focus by the team toward a technical focus.	Applicable when product owners are able to define "horizontal slices" of your solution. You should have skilled architecture owners who are able to manage the technical dependencies between components. There should be an architecture-oriented culture within your organization.

6.   In this book we frequently refer to the benefits of reusing assets when building your solutions. You should, of course, make sure that you have the legal right to do so.

Strategy	Potential Advantages	Potential Disadvantages	Considerations
Internal open source	Enables co-development of a common component.	Many organizations worry about funding the development effort. Issues surrounding ownership and long-term maintenance need to be determined. Requires at least some developers who are experienced with open source development.	Makes sense when you have an existing open source culture within your organization. Also could be a good strategy if you have an identified component required by several teams. Appropriate when component teams aren't desirable.

An important observation about large DAD teams is that the challenges with them have less to do with coordination overhead and more to do with developing relationships between team members. To their peril, too many large teams overly focus on the coordination strategies described earlier, which are clearly important, and downplay the team building strategies we started the chapter with. The stronger the bonds between team members, the stronger the understanding of the overall vision, and the stronger the consensus around the roles and responsibilities of team members, the lower the need for coordination. A related observation is that most communication occurs between people within a subteam, which is why it is so important to ensure your team organization strategy aligns with your architecture and requirements approaches as Table 5.1 implies.

Large DAD teams require tailoring of some practices and tools. For example, they often require a bit more architectural envisioning during Inception, particularly if you have one or more component subteams. Because large teams are typically formed to address more complex problems, the implication is that your continuous integration (CI) procedures can be a lot more complex, often including an overall solution-level build and regression test suite. You may find that you need an independent testing effort focused on preproduction system integration testing (among other issues) to support the more complex situation your find yourself in. Larger teams often have longer iteration lengths, with four weeks being a common option for large teams (iteration length choices are discussed in detail in Chapter 10, "Initial Release Planning").

Geographically Distributed/Dispersed Teams

We make a distinction between geographically distributed and geographically dispersed teams (and combinations of the two). A team is geographically distributed when subteams are far from one another, but each subteam is either near-located or collocated in its own right. Sometimes a portion of the team members work individually at their own locations, either in offices/cubicles or from home. When there is a collocated subteam with a few people working from other locations we call this partially dispersed. When everyone is working from different locations it is referred to as fully dispersed. Figure 5.5 depicts these team configurations. In practice many geographically distributed teams often include several geographically dispersed members too.

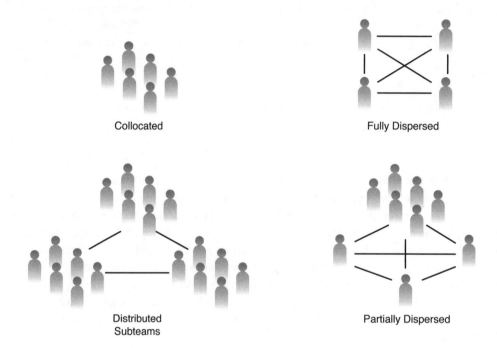

Figure 5.5   Different geographic distributions of team members

Geographically distributed teams have a similar organization structure to medium or large teams and need to be supported by electronic tooling. Geographically distributed teams experience greater communication challenges, caused by distance and potential cultural differences, than near-located teams. The Dr. Dobb's Journal 2008 Agile Adoption survey found that the more geographically distributed a delivery team is, regardless of paradigm, the lower the success rate. It also found that regardless of distribution level agile teams had as good or better success rates than similarly distributed traditional teams.

Some lessons we've learned with geographically distributed agile teams over the years:

- You'll need to invest a bit more time with Inception phase activities than you would with collocated teams.
- Consider performing the Inception phase in a collocated manner with key team members and stakeholders to help gel the team, reach agreement around the vision, and to increase the chance of starting off on the right foot.

- Identifying or developing common guidelines around enterprise infrastructure, development conventions, data conventions, and so on at the beginning of the project is absolutely critical.

- Adopt tooling, such as IBM Rational Asset Analyzer, which provides quality information regarding the work being produced by the various subteams so that you can monitor and guide the subteams based on accurate and timely information (see Chapter 20 for detailed advice about governing agile teams).

- Be prepared for the need to have people travel between locations. These people are often referred to as ambassadors because they share information between teams and often help settle differences between distributed team members. Although your organization may have travel restrictions in place, the reality is that it is often far more cost effective to pay for travel at key points in the project (particularly Inception) and for a handful of travelers throughout the project than it is to not do so. Regardless of tooling support, face-to-face communication is still a critical success factor.

- Getting the roles and responsibilities clear for those you need to collaborate with outside the project team is critical for large efforts. Misaligned expectations or gaps in responsibilities can be project killers.

- Maximize the independence of the subteams (see the large-team strategies described earlier) including outsourcing teams working for service providers. We've found that the greater control that the "home/main team" tries to inflict upon the external teams, such as creation of detailed specifications, the lower the overall success rate of the outsourcing effort. Having said that, lightweight monitoring is critical (see Chapter 20).

There is far more to dealing with geographically distributed teams than what we've discussed here. Luckily there is a great book on the subject, *A Practical Guide to Distributed Scrum* by Ganis, Surdek, and Woodward (IBM Press, 2010), which goes into the topic in much greater detail.

Building Your Team

Few project teams, regardless of paradigm or process framework, start out fully staffed. Instead there is a building up process where people are "onboarded" (added) throughout the lifecycle, with the majority of onboarding occurring early in the lifecycle. An exception to this might be mature product companies that maintain team continuity between product releases. At the beginning of the project you may start with the team lead, product owner, and if you're lucky a few key team members including the architecture owner (who is often the same person as the team lead). Depending on your level of funding, you may even onboard people during Inception, although more likely you'll add the majority of team members during the first few construction iterations as they become available. Toward the end of the lifecycle you may begin to offboard (remove) people from the team, a topic covered in greater detail in Chapter 18, "The Transition Phase."

Where you are in the overall product lifecycle will affect your team building strategy. If you are on release 1 of the solution you will often need to build your team from scratch, which is what the rest of this section deals with. When you're on release N of the solution you should already have a team in place, perhaps needing to add some new team members if the project is growing or if you need to replace people who left at the end of the previous release. In this case the team has gelled already and understands the problem space, so growing the team (if required) will be reasonably straightforward and can be accomplished using heuristics described later. However, if there's been a significant period of time between release N-1 and release N and you've disbanded the delivery team, you in effect find yourself in a situation similar to a release 1 team. One unusual exception occurs when you're lucky enough to find an existing team finishing up with another effort that is looking for a new challenge. In this case the team has gelled but is potentially not familiar with the problem space, so it's similar to the release N situation from a team building perspective.

Clearly an important part of building an effective DAD team is to attract the right people. Ideally a DAD team is comprised of generalizing specialists (refer to Chapter 4) with a range of agile-experienced people on the team (some novices, some mid-level experience, and some experts) who are all eager to work together and learn from one another. People are onboarded when they are needed and offboarded when no longer required. Sounds simple enough, but this is of course easier said than done. Unfortunately many organizations new to agile, and even some that aren't, suffer from cultural issues that prevent them from building agile teams this easily. In fact there are several common problems people run into when trying to build DAD teams:

- **You don't have adequate agile mentoring.** We commonly see agile adoptions fail due to inadequate coaching—figuring it out as you go is a risky approach. You want to demonstrate success on your initial agile initiatives so an investment in coaching is worthwhile.

- **You don't have team leads that are skilled coaches.** A traditional project manager is not always automatically a good agile coach. They can indeed be taught, but the transition from traditional style project management to servant-leadership is not always obvious.

- **You don't have (enough) generalizing specialists.** Until now most organizations have built up their IT departments following a Tayloristic strategy where people are motivated to become specialists. As a result it is incredibly difficult to create a cross-functional team because of the number of people required to make the team whole. To address this problem you need to initially build your team with specialists but make it clear to people that they need to work closely with others to pick up new skills. The easiest way to do so is to adopt a promiscuous pairing strategy where everyone pairs up to perform a task and they switch pairs on a regular basis (at least daily). This helps to spread skills and knowledge around the team and within a few months productivity will start to rise and people will be well on their way to becoming generalizing specialists. The only drawback with non-solo work is that productivity will drop at first because of the learning curve, but the time saved downstream not having to fix poor quality more than makes up for this investment. Another simple and effective way to encourage skills development is to encourage peer reviewing of work products.

- **You don't have skilled product owners.** Product owner is a tough role requiring people who are empowered to make immediate decisions for a wide range of stakeholders. The empowerment issue can be tough for organizations used to a command-and-control management strategy or a consensus decision making strategy, not to mention organizations that have built up a cultural wall between IT and business stakeholders. You need to identify stakeholders who are willing to take on a full-time role as product owners, who are able and willing to make decisions, and who have many of the skills previously associated with business analysts. The latter skills can be learned through training, mentoring, and hands-on experience. An implication is that you need to educate your stakeholders on the need to make such investment.

- **Your human resources (HR) department is geared toward staffing traditional teams.** Symptoms of this problem include assigning individuals to multiple teams (often because they're overly specialized), organizing the development around job functions (having a testing group, a project management group, a data management group, and so on), and assigning people to new teams once a project is completed (instead of keeping the team together). This is a problem that may take years to solve because your HR department still needs to support traditional as well as agile teams as your organization transitions to disciplined agile development. The first step is to work with your HR staff to help them understand the implications of agile delivery, including sharing with them the ideas presented in both this chapter and in Chapter 4.

- **You don't have (enough) agile-experienced people.** There are two fundamental ways to address this problem. First, you can augment your existing staff with outsiders experienced in agile, including new employees, contractors, consultants, and giving work to external service providers. Second, grow the required expertise within your existing staff through training, mentoring, and hands-on project experience.

- **You can't build a whole team.** Sometimes you simply don't have the right people available. For example, you may not have enough people with database expertise to support all the projects that you need to, or you may be entering a new market where you have no expertise at all. One solution is to delay the project until the right people are available and another is to augment your team with outside expertise.

- **Not everyone is an agile expert.** The good news is that they don't need to be nor is it desirable anyway. The typical DAD team has some novices, some mid-experienced people, and some very experienced people in leadership roles. A team of all "agile novices" is clearly a bad idea because they won't have the experience required to judge how much/little to do, what to do, or even when to do it and risk having traditional thinking inappropriately infect their agile processes. But a team of all agile experts is not realistic either unless you've reached the point where everyone in your organization truly is an agile expert—otherwise, spread your agile experts out so that they can share their skills and experiences with others.

- **You don't know how to identify agile-experienced people.** Agile people prefer to work collaboratively in groups, learning from one another as they go. They're "quality infected" in that they strive to test their work to the best of their ability, produce high quality artifacts at all times, and when they detect low quality they refactor it to improve it. They work closely with their stakeholders in an evolutionary (iterative and incremental) manner. Someone may have been trained and mentored in agile techniques, and better yet in DAD, and they may use agile terms, but that doesn't necessarily mean that they're agile.

- **Some of your staff want/need to be directed and not be self-organizing.** Self-organizing teams optimize their own process, identify and estimate their own tasks, and can be counted on to deliver to their iteration commitments of working software at the end of iteration. This is a beautiful part of agile delivery. However, not all teams are capable of self-organization. What if the teams are not familiar with agile practices, do not have a background of working with cross-functional teams, or have a strong command-and-control culture that they have not yet overcome? Perhaps they are not self-aware enough to determine good versus bad process or are not inclined to reduce waste and take a minimalist approach in the way that agile requires. Mark finds in his role as a team lead that he usually ends up also acting as a mentor to team members in basic solution delivery practices such as those related to project management, architecture, requirements, and testing. Many of the agile books out there assume that team members are experienced software developers that are familiar with best practices across the solution delivery lifecycle. This is not usually the case. Strive for self-organizing teams, but if your organization is new to agile methods an investment in coaching can speed up the journey to build the necessary capability.

Interacting with Other Teams

One aspect of enterprise awareness is the recognition that your team doesn't work in a vacuum; other teams are working in parallel to your own. Some teams are focused on solution delivery, whereas others focus on specialist aspects of development, such as data management, operations, and quality management. These other teams may work in an agile manner or a non-agile manner, and they may or may not need to interact with your team. Regardless, you need to find a way to work with them.

There are several general techniques to consider first. For specialist teams such as your enterprise architects or technical writers, the best strategy is to embed individuals on your team so that their expertise is added to your overall skills pool. Ideally these people will share their skills with others on the team, pick up new skills of their own, and become more versatile generalizing specialists. Some people may be embedded on your team on a part-time basis or for a short period of time and thereby take on specialist/expert roles as discussed in Chapter 4, and therefore may be less likely to become generalizing specialists. Another general strategy, particularly useful when you primarily need to coordinate with an external team, is to invite one of their representatives to your coordination meetings (and potentially send someone to theirs). You may also consider asking people from these other teams to be actively involved in your requirements and architecture efforts during Inception, as appropriate, to ensure you address their concerns in your overall vision. With external teams new to agile you may find it worthwhile to educate them about DAD so as to address any misunderstandings they may have about your approach, and to give them greater insight into how they can work with you effectively.

In addition to these general strategies, you may find that you need to adopt a few techniques specific to the category of team you're working with:

- **Other agile delivery teams.** There are several different versions of this situation, each requiring a slightly different strategy. When there are few dependencies between the teams you will need to collaborate on an as-needed basis to address any dependencies as they arise and to share improvement ideas with one another. When there are significant dependencies between two DAD teams, their release planning, requirements envisioning, and architectural envisioning efforts will have identified the dependencies between the teams and the implications thereof. The leaders of each team (the team leads, product owners, and architecture owners) should facilitate the communication between the teams in the same manner as described for medium-to-large sized DAD teams earlier. If you're interacting with a non-DAD agile team they may not have invested the effort to explore the bigger picture early in the lifecycle and may not have a good understanding of the risks and dependencies they face. Your team may have to help them work through these activities to help get them on a more successful path, and better yet introduce them to DAD.

- **Other non-agile development teams.** Due to the cultural impedance mismatch between the traditional and agile ways of working, this can be tough. Traditional teams typically perceive themselves as taking a lower risk, more effective approach and think that the agile teams are doing little more than hacking (and to be fair, there are a lot of ad-hoc teams out there who claim to be agile). In fact, traditional teams have lower success rates and are more likely to deliver late and over budget than agile teams, making them higher risk. The detailed plans, specifications, and models being produced by traditional teams aren't living up to their promises of risk reduction. The implication for your team if you have dependencies on traditional teams, perhaps some new Web services or an update to your organization's security framework are being developed in a traditional manner, is that you must be prepared for these assets to be delivered behind schedule (if at all). Your team will also need to mock out the assets until they are available, which due to the serial nature of traditional non-iterative methods will be delivered in whole at the end of that team's lifecycle (and yet astoundingly this is still perceived as low risk).

- **Quality assurance (QA) and testing.** In many organizations the QA and testing efforts are addressed by a single team, even though they are in fact two different albeit related activities—testing verifies whether you delivered what was asked for, and QA validates whether you delivered it the proper way. Testers and QA professionals should be embedded with agile teams so as to support whole team verification and validation throughout the lifecycle, and teams in agility at scale situations may have a parallel independent testing effort as well (see Chapter 15). Indeed all team members should have a good grasp of agile testing and quality assurance principles. The challenge is that quality teams in many organizations still follow traditional methods driven by detailed specifications, not the more collaborative and evolutionary approach followed by agile teams. You need to educate your quality team in these ideas and work with them closely to help them adopt more successful, disciplined agile ways of work.

- **Technical writers.** Agile teams are just as likely to create deliverable documentation, such as user manuals, operations manuals, and support manuals, as traditional teams and need help doing so. People with technical writing skills have value to add on agile teams, following practices from Agile Modeling (AM) such as Continuous Documentation and Document Late, described in Chapters 15 and 18, respectively.

- **User Experience (UX) experts.** It is common for organizations to have specialists that focus on a "global" user interface design. One of the problems with traditional approaches where user interface designs are done up front is the lack of constant collaboration with agile teams since they are building software so early and continuously throughout the project.

- **Enterprise architects.** The 2010 Enterprise Architecture (EA) survey, www.ambysoft.com/surveys/stateOfITUnion201001.html, found that the EA teams that were successful had adopted strategies that were collaborative and lightweight in manner, and that the ones who struggled typically focused on heavier, documentation and review-based (e.g., traditional) methods. It is certainly the case that for EA teams to work well with agile teams they must be willing to get actively involved with the team, providing advice in person and helping the team to understand and leverage the existing infrastructure and long-term EA vision. For critical project teams one of the enterprise architects may even take on the role of architecture owner on the DAD team.

- **Governance body.** Your organization's existing development governance group, if one exists, is likely to be steeped in traditional methods often based on a serial, documentation-centric waterfall approach. Sadly, this will be very different than the collaborative and enablement focused strategy actually required to govern agile teams effectively. Chapter 20 describes agile governance in detail.

- **Project management office (PMO).** Although the PMO in some organizations still clings to traditional, command-and-control strategies, many are now experimenting with more effective, agile practices. The good news is that PMOs can still be an invaluable part of any large enterprise because many corporate initiatives, including any significant agile project, should be treated with the necessary rigor to monitor and guide the execution of the project. Smart PMOs recognize that solution delivery projects exhibit situationally dependent characteristics and do not lend well to a linear predictive approach—as a result mandating how and what should be done is often counterproductive. Therefore they allow delivery teams to self-adapt using self-organizing techniques, enabling them to quickly learn as they move from iteration to iteration and deliver solutions that add greater value with higher quality more quickly. PMOs can also add value by harvesting both good and bad practices based on learnings within the teams and socialize them throughout the organization. Harvesting of processes, practices, patterns, and other assets can facilitate enterprise alignment and knowledge management in the organization. Modern PMOs *encourage* nonconformist techniques if it saves money and is consistent with delivering working solutions to the customer in a timely manner, without increasing organizational or project risk.

- **Data management/administration.** Many if not most data groups today believe that databases must be designed up front before development begins, regardless of the overwhelming evidence that shows otherwise. In fact, both relational and hierarchical databases are suited to evolutionary design, and agile database techniques exist (described in Chapter 15) that enable you to do exactly that. The primary challenge is that many existing data professionals have not yet been trained in agile philosophies or techniques and in fact often strongly believe in very non-agile strategies that are counterproductive at best. You may find that you need to invest significant time helping your data group to both learn these new techniques as well as understand the need to abandon many of their existing traditional strategies.

- **Reuse engineers.** There are two ways that reuse engineers can work effectively with DAD teams. First, they should actively help them to understand and then integrate existing reusable assets into the team's build. Second, they should do the work to harvest, refactor, and reintegrate potentially reusable assets that the team created. The basic strategy is that your organization must make it as easy as possible for teams to reuse assets and to produce reusable assets, and the best way to do so is to fund those efforts separately via an independent reuse team so that the cost isn't borne by the project teams (clearly a major disincentive to reuse). Note that in many organizations the reuse engineers and enterprise architects work closely together, and you may not even distinguish between them.

Concluding Thoughts

Disciplined agile delivery is a team sport. People, and the way they work together, are the primary determinant of success for your solution delivery efforts. This chapter provided advice on the aspects of effective teams, how to organize a DAD team given its size and geographic distribution, and how to overcome common problems that you may run into. Unfortunately, the culture in many IT departments is still geared toward supporting traditional software development teams, not agile solution delivery teams. Organizational complexities such as this are always the most difficult and time consuming to overcome, yet you must do so if you are to set your DAD teams up for success.

Additional Resources

For more detailed discussions about several of the topics covered in this chapter:

- **Agile statistics.** Several times throughout the chapter we quoted statistics from Scott's industry surveys, the details of which are available at www.ambysoft.com/surveys/. Team size and location data came from the May 2011 Agile mini-survey; success rates by project size from the Dr. Dobb's Journal (DDJ) July 2010 State of the IT Union survey; and success rates by geographic distribution from the DDJ 2008 IT Project Success rate survey.

- **Motivating people.** The best book that we know of to understand how to motivate people is *Drive* by Dan Pink. He shows that motivation, particularly for intellectual works, comes from autonomy, mastery, and purpose, three aspects built into the DAD process framework.

- **Teams.** The book *Beautiful Teams* (O'Reilly Media, 2009) by Andrew Stellman and Jennifer Greene provides insights from a collection of IT teams over the years, and *The Wisdom of Teams* (Collins Business, 2003) by Jon R. Katzenbach and Douglas K. Smith argues for, and shows how to create, effective teams. For understanding agile teams at scale, the book *A Practical Guide to Distributed Scrum* (IBM Press, 2010) by Elizabeth Woodward, Steffan Surdek, and Mathew Ganis provides proven advice from teams both within IBM and from our customers. If you want to take a component team approach you should read *Domain Driven Design: Tackling Complexity in the Heart of Software* (Addison-Wesley Professional, 2003) by Eric Evans to learn strategies for architecting your solution effectively.

- **Internal open source.** Scott's article "Reuse Through Internal Open Source" at http://drdobbs.com/architecture-and-design/184414685 for the December 1, 2000, issue of Dr. Dobb's Journal overviews the internal OSS strategy.

- **Helping traditional teams become more agile.** Over the years Scott has written a collection of articles on this topic, including "Agile Enterprise Architecture" and "Agile Architecture Strategies" at http://www.agiledata.org/essays/enterpriseArchitecture.html; for data professionals a large collection of articles at www.agiledata.org; for quality assurance (QA) and testers Agile Testing and Quality Strategies at www.ambysoft.com/essays/agileTesting.html; for reuse engineers "Reuse Patterns and Antipatterns" at http://drdobbs.com/architecture-and-design/184414576 for the February 1, 2000, issue of Dr. Dobb's Journal; and for technical writers several articles at www.agilemodeling.com.

The Inception Phase

Our stakeholders are our best friends, whether we like it or not.

The Disciplined Agile Delivery (DAD) process framework includes an explicit Inception phase—sometimes called a project initiation phase, startup phase, or iteration zero—that is conducted before actually starting to build a solution. The goals of this phase include clarifying the business problem that needs to be solved, identifying a viable technical solution, planning your approach, setting up your work environment and team, and gaining stakeholder concurrence that it makes sense to proceed with investing in the implementation of the chosen strategy.

According to the 2009 Agile Project Initiation survey, the average agile team invests about four weeks performing project initiation activities, including initial requirements envisioning, initial architecture envisioning, forming the team, initial release planning, and so on. Of course this is just an average; some respondents reported investing less than a week to do so, and some reported investing more than two months. The amount of time required varies depending on the complexity of the effort, your stakeholders' understanding of their requirements, your team's understanding of the solution architecture, whether this is a new solution or merely a new release of an existing solution, and many other reasons.

One goal of this book is to provide practical guidance for your agile project. DAD is not a prescriptive method with step-by-step guidance. It is rather a process framework that you can adapt to the unique aspects of your project and organization. As you soon see, DAD provides options and a decision framework to help you choose the best options for your situation, but we don't prescribe a single one-size-fits-all strategy that you must follow to the letter if you're to succeed. Your team is in a unique situation; therefore, you must tailor your strategy to address that situation. We do, however, make suggestions, and we work through a case study based on an actual project that shows one potential way that a DAD project may run.

This chapter overviews the Inception phase. Chapters 7 through 11 explore important activities in detail, and Chapter 12 works through the Inception phase portion of the case study. Although this part of the book contains a lot of material, that doesn't mean you should spend a lot of time in this phase. It certainly doesn't imply that you should take a "water-scrum-fall" approach, where you have lengthy Inception and Transition phases and take a mostly traditional, documentation heavy approach with an agile construction effort in between. We believe that there has been too little writing about agile project initiation activities—sometimes downright hostility toward them—and we hope to address this problem in this book. At the same time a significant amount has been written elsewhere about agile construction activities, so we're not investing as much effort on that phase.

Figure 6.1 shows a mind map of the structure of this chapter. We describe each of the topics in the map in clockwise order, beginning at the top right.

THE BIG IDEAS IN THIS CHAPTER

- The team leadership initially gains agreement from the project sponsor to create an initial vision for the proposed solution.

- The fundamental goal of Inception is to build a foundation from which the project can be successful in as lightweight and quick manner as possible.

- DAD teams strive to align themselves with the rest of the organization as best they can, leveraging resources such as the existing technical infrastructure, development conventions, and your overall enterprise vision.

- During the Inception phase you should come to a relative consensus with your stakeholders as to the scope of the project, the timeline, relevant constraints, key risks, and the architectural strategy. The details will still evolve throughout the project.

- In some situations the DAD team may start activities normally deferred to the Construction phase such as setting up the tooling environment or coding parts of the architecture.

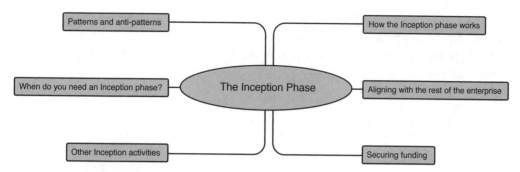

Figure 6.1 Outline of this chapter

How the Inception Phase Works

In addition to the usual ongoing project goals, the Inception phase has several specific goals all of which are indicated in Figure 6.2. Figure 6.3 depicts a high-level timeline for a typical configuration of agile practices that address the goals of the Inception phase, but you need to tailor and perform these activities to the extent they make sense for your situation. These practices are described in detail in Chapters 7 through 11.

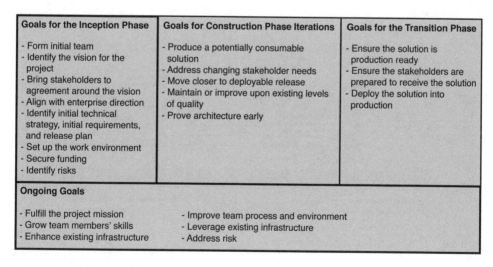

Figure 6.2 DAD lifecycle goals

An interesting aspect of Figure 6.3 is that it starts with the Project Selected milestone. This milestone reflects the idea that your organization likely has a portfolio management process that identifies and selects potential projects among other activities. This is implied in the DAD lifecycle of Figure 6.4. In this case the project has been selected to enter the Inception phase where sufficient work will occur to either put the project on a successful track or potentially cancel the project because it isn't considered viable at this time. Your portfolio management process may have produced a very high-level vision for the project that your team can leverage to initiate their Inception phase activities. You will also have been provided sufficient funding for the Inception phase at this point in time, but not for the rest of the project.

Figure 6.3   Overview of a typical approach to the Inception phase

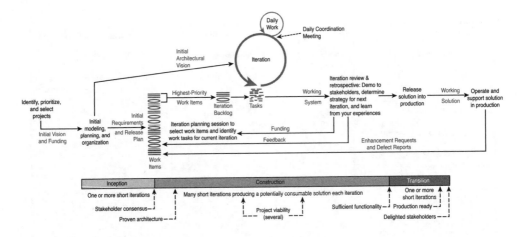

Figure 6.4   The basic DAD lifecycle

Table 6.1 presents an example schedule for a three-week Inception phase. In that example the logistical issues of getting access to stakeholders and team members and then having them invest their valuable time with your project team goes very smoothly. On most projects it rarely works this well because stakeholders have their normal day jobs to focus on, and potential team members may be working on other projects and aren't yet available (or at least not full time). The schedule is also fairly steady, with requirements activities occurring in the morning and then architecture and planning activities occurring in the afternoon. Once again logistical issues will get in the way on actual projects and motivate you to organize activities when the right people are available to perform them. Regardless, let's explore how each of the goals indicated in Figure 6.2 is addressed in Table 6.1:

- **Form the initial team.** You begin to form your project team on the first day of the project. Your team will evolve throughout the project; not everyone will be needed on the first day nor would they be available anyway. You will form your team so that you have the skills required to get the job done, or minimally you're in a position to gain the requisite skills, and have enough people to achieve your project goals in a reasonable amount of time. A typical initial team for your Inception phase might consist of the product owner, architecture owner, and the team lead. Whatever the initial team is, they should collectively have the cross-functional skills required to understand all aspects of the candidate solutions and what it would require to implement them. They also need to have access to your project's stakeholders. For individual team members an important reason to join the team is to have an opportunity to grow their skills. Chapter 5, "Forming Disciplined Agile Delivery Teams," addresses team building in greater detail. Normally you form a small team for the Inception phase and then staff up to begin Construction iterations. Since this takes time, as the vision starts to crystallize and you start to realize what size of team(s) that you require, it is important during Inception to start finding new team members that will join your team should the project continue into the Construction phase.

- **Align with enterprise direction.** From the beginning of your project you should strive to align your team's efforts with the rest of your organization. This helps get you started on the long-term goal of enhancing the existing infrastructure, a topic covered later in this chapter.

- **Identify initial requirements.** An understanding of the scope of what your team will deliver is often required for initial planning and governance. The degree of detail for your initial requirements artifacts, if any, as well as what type of modeling you do and even how you do it will vary based on your situation. One size does not fit all. Initial requirements modeling is explored in detail in Chapter 8, "Identifying the Initial Scope."

- **Identify initial technical strategy.** Your team is also likely to invest time with some initial architecture modeling during the Inception phase to aid in initial planning and to help you to get going in the right direction for the Construction phase. Chapter 9, "Identifying an Initial Technical Strategy," explores the issues around initial architecture envisioning. In most situations you are likely to capture your diagrams and architectural decisions in an architecture handbook.

- **Develop initial release plan.** To secure funding for your project, and to organize how you will work together to achieve your project goals, your team will likely invest some time in initial release planning. This planning effort addresses both schedule and financial concerns. Chapter 10, "Initial Release Planning," explores initial release planning in greater detail.

- **Identify the vision for the project and bring stakeholders to agreement around it.** An easy way to increase your team's chance of success is to identify and then come to agreement around the vision for what you're hoping to accomplish. Your team's vision reflects the high-level requirements, technical strategy, and release plan, each of which evolves to reflect one another throughout Inception (and your project in general). The long-term goal of fulfilling the project mission depends on you understanding, agreeing to, and working toward your project vision. How to develop and evolve your project vision is discussed in Chapter 7, "Identifying a Project Vision," as is how to hold an effective milestone review. Some organizations like to bundle the vision statement with the release plan and call it an "agile charter," which is similar to a lightweight traditional project charter.

- **Secure funding.** A key goal of Inception is to secure sufficient funding to move into the Construction phase. This is discussed later in this chapter.

- **Identify and address risks.** An important strategy for increasing your team's chance of success is to understand and then mitigate the risks that you face as early as possible. Chapter 10 discusses how to go about identifying potential project risks, and later in this chapter we argue for the need to address functional risk by coming to a common consensus around the vision for the project.

- **Set up the environment.** Should you obtain stakeholder consensus to proceed with implementing a solution, your team will need a workspace, or workspaces in the case of a distributed delivery team, development tools, workstations, integration environments, testing environments, an agreed-to process (in this case DAD), and other things that make up their overall environment. Many of these things will already exist, although you may need to purchase or lease some of them. Chapter 11, "Forming the Work Environment," addresses setting up your environment. In some organizations you will be allowed to start organizing some aspects of your environment before receiving the actual funding for Construction. This is particularly true in organizations with strong portfolio management practices that consider feasibility, at least at a high level, before funding Inception phase efforts. In other organizations you will set up the environment at the beginning of Construction. Either way it happens early in the project.

As you can see in Table 6.1, our example of an Inception schedule indicates that we might spend some time on Monday and Tuesday of the last week of the phase setting up the environment. This assumes that we feel comfortable that at the milestone review we will obtain approval to move ahead with implementing the suggested solution, which will require a work environment to locate the team. We are often asked, should we be creating a work environment and staffing up the team in advance of starting the Construction phase when we haven't yet reached the milestone review to approve continuation of the project into Construction? Well, technically we shouldn't, but practically we do. By collaborating with our stakeholders during the phase and investigating candidate solutions we form a plan that supports a good business case. Usually we have verbal commitment that the project will continue into Construction well in advance of the milestone review so it makes sense to invest time in setting up the work area, procuring the development environments, and beginning to staff up the team.

If you are using a disciplined agile approach, it is important to time box this phase to be as short as possible. Detail is typically not required at this time, except perhaps in some regulatory situations, as we are merely trying to understand enough about the project to determine that it makes sense and to obtain general consensus for the approach. You want just enough information to determine whether to continue to fund the project into the Construction phase, to pursue alternatives such as packaged solutions, to consider an alternative solution, or to abandon the idea entirely. In the previous timeline we showed a simple example for a project where the business case for potential solutions is well known and therefore the Inception team jumped into modeling the requirements and solution. For larger enterprise projects your Inception phase may be longer and include activities such as competitive analysis, business process improvement, return on investment analysis, and other research. This may differ from a mainstream agile approach but may be necessary due diligence before investing in a given solution.

The inclusion of the Inception phase is considered controversial by some agilists. Their primary concern seems to be that because you invest time in Inception phase activities you are losing out on the short-term gains that could have been derived by jumping into construction activities. Yes, this is definitely true. Our experience is that these short-term losses are more than made up for by long-term gain of reducing project risk by coming to agreement around a common vision for what needs to be delivered and how it will be accomplished.

Aligning with the Rest of the Enterprise

There are two critical aspects to being enterprise aware. The first is to recognize that you need to work with other teams and groups within your organization. As discussed in Chapter 5, this potentially includes your data administration group, your technical writers,[1] your enterprise

---

1. Technical writers in IBM are known as information developers. This is a perfect example of an organization having its own specific terminology to describe a concept for which we use a different term in this book. You may need to translate between your terminology and our terminology as you read this book.

Table 6.1   An Example Three-Week Inception Phase Schedule

	Monday	Tuesday	Wednesday	Thursday	Friday
Week 1 Morning	Initial meeting with project sponsors. Identify key stakeholders. Form team.	Set up environment for Inception work. Form Inception team.	Requirements envisioning.	Requirements envisioning.	Requirements envisioning.
Week 1 Afternoon	Schedule requirements sessions. Set up environment. Form team.	Set up environment. Form team.	Architecture envisioning.	Architecture envisioning. Set up environment.	Architecture envisioning. Set up environment. Release planning.
Week 2 Morning	Requirements envisioning. Add team members.	Review UI prototype. Requirements envisioning.	Review UI prototype. Requirements envisioning.	Review UI prototype. Requirements envisioning.	Review UI prototype. Requirements envisioning. Schedule milestone review.
Week 2 Afternoon	Architecture envisioning. User interface (UI) prototyping. Set up environment. Release planning. Document vision.	Architecture envisioning. UI prototyping. Set up environment. Release planning. Document vision.	Architecture envisioning. UI prototyping. Architecture spike. Release planning. Document vision.	Architecture envisioning. UI prototyping. Architecture spike. Release planning. Document vision.	Architecture envisioning. UI prototyping. Architecture spike. Release planning. Document vision.

	Monday	Tuesday	Wednesday	Thursday	Friday
Week 3 Morning	Review UI prototype. Requirements envisioning. Add team members.	Review UI prototype. Document architecture. Requirements envisioning.	Document architecture.	Free time.	Prepare for review.
Week 3 Afternoon	Architecture envisioning. UI prototyping. Set up environment. Release planning. Document vision.	Architecture envisioning. UI prototyping. Set up environment. Release planning. Document vision. Distribute vision document for review.	Free time.	Update vision document. Update architecture handbook.	Milestone review.

architecture team, your operations release team, your project steering committee, other delivery teams that yours has dependencies on, and other delivery teams that have dependencies on what you're working on. These groups and teams may or may not work in an agile manner, yet you will still need to interact with them to be successful.

Second, the DAD process framework explicitly recognizes your solution needs to be aligned with both the business and technical directions of your organization. During Inception there are several ways you can begin to do so:

- **Adopt common development guidelines.** As you identify the technologies that you'll be working with via architectural envisioning, you are able to start identifying the coding conventions, data conventions, user interface (UI) conventions, and so on that are appropriate to your project. Which guidelines to follow will be driven by your architectural decisions (e.g., if you decide on a J2EE-based architecture, then Java coding guidelines over Ruby coding guidelines should be followed).

- **Adopt common templates.** Yes, you'll still be writing some supporting documentation such as user manuals, operations manuals, and help desk manuals, so consider making them consistent. Good templates are concise, addressing just the critical information that must be captured. If more information is required than what is captured by the template, it can be added as appropriate. The goal is reasonable consistency between teams, not identical documentation.

- **Reuse existing infrastructure.** Unless there is no precedent of well-executed projects in your organization, existing software assets probably are available to reuse. Reusable assets could include existing components and services, patterns and mechanisms (techniques such as how to persist data, or design security, or distribution, for example), sample source code, or even a working reference architecture showing how to implement a specific architectural aspect. We recommend that you work closely with your enterprise architects and reuse engineers, if any are available, during your initial architectural modeling efforts (see Chapter 9) and throughout the project where appropriate.

- **Understand your IT governance approach.** Unless you have the luxury of working on a project where the team does not need to work with anyone outside your immediate team, or report status to management, or deal with project management offices (PMOs), enterprise database groups, other project teams, government, or your own organization's regulatory bodies, you will need some degree of governance of your team. It is a good idea to know what needs to be reviewed, by whom, and when. You should also know what information needs to be provided—perhaps via a combination of automated project dashboards, project taskboards, and status reports—to whom, to what extent, and when. These reviews and reports should be identified either as work items or constraints (as appropriate) so that they can be incorporated into your release planning activities. We discuss the considerations for governing agile projects in Chapter 20, "Governing Disciplined Agile Teams."

LESSONS FROM THE TRENCHES—WORKING WITH A NONAGILE GROUP

One development organization that I worked with outsourced translation of their simulations content into several languages. The translation company required that all files for translation be provided to them at once, rather than in small chunks throughout the project. We aligned our efforts to work within the constraints of the existing translation system, while simultaneously working to convince the translation company to take a more agile approach. By our second project, we had worked with the translation company to test a new process by which we delivered content in small chunks to be translated with a due date of two weeks after submission. This effectively allowed the translation company to become a more agile organization and enabled the development organization to take a more agile approach. —Elizabeth Woodward, coauthor of *A Practical Guide to Distributed Scrum* (IBM Press, 2010).

The strategies described previously will likely be used in combination. Table 6.2 summarizes the potential trade-offs that you're making when adopting them.

Teams require support at the organization level if they are to be truly enterprise aware, and there are several ways to do so. With a formal approach the delivery team creates specific artifacts, such as architectural diagrams or documents, reuse plans, or technology platform plans and submits them to an architectural review board for feedback and guidance. With a collaborative approach the enterprise professionals—potentially including architects, reuse engineers, data administrators, and more—work closely with the team to help them identify how they can best leverage and enhance the existing enterprise assets. A third strategy, often combined with the first two, is to have an enterprise repository of shared artifacts. A simple approach, which works well in smaller organizations, is to have shared folders where the available artifacts are maintained. A more robust strategy uses a tool such as IBM Rational Asset Manager (RAM) to streamline the overall reuse process. Table 6.3 compares these strategies.

We suggest the collaborative interaction approach to enterprise support. This should be further enhanced by a shared artifact strategy that is appropriate to your organization.

Table 6.2 Understanding the Trade-offs of Each Enterprise Strategy

Strategy	Potential Advantages	Potential Disadvantages	Considerations
Adopt common development guidelines	Consistency between IT projects, resulting in overall increase in quality. Increase in velocity/productivity due to better understanding between team members. Project continuity across releases and new team members.	Agreed-to guidelines may not exist, requiring your team to develop them. Team members may have to slow down to speed up. There will likely be something of a learning curve. Some of your team members may think that they have better guidelines.	Overly complex guidelines are less likely to be followed. An onerous effort to share your newly created guidelines with the rest of the organization may decrease the motivation to develop them in the first place. You may find that you need to work with the enterprise team responsible for shared guidance to help streamline their submission processes. Political battles regarding whose guidelines are best rarely work out well. There is often more value in consistently applying imperfect guidelines than inconsistent application of different "perfect" guidelines.
Adopt common templates	Documentation consistency between projects, increasing the overall consumability for downstream teams. Increase in velocity/productivity due to better understanding between team members. Templates can provide reminders of issues to consider.	Existence of a template may motivate creation of a document that doesn't add actual value in your situation.	All-encompassing templates that strive to capture all possibly required information often result in needless bureaucracy and extraneous documentation. Good templates focus on the minimal required information.

Strategy	Potential Advantages	Potential Disadvantages	Considerations
Reuse existing infrastructure	Increased return on investment (ROI). Increased quality. Improved time to value. Lowered operating costs.	Requires investment in creation and maintenance of reusable assets. Inability to easily find assets could result in unnecessary duplicates and wasted effort.	Onerous architectural reviews to ensure that the infrastructure is being leveraged motivates delivery teams to avoid working with the architecture team. Charge back schemes to pay for the assets will motivate teams to not reuse them. Existing infrastructure, such as an existing messaging service, may be far more than what is required and may be more expensive to use than it is to create a specific strategy for your application.
Understand your IT governance approach	You can plan for, and streamline, your strategy to comply to your governance scheme. You can identify how your organization's governance strategy can help your project team.	You may need to educate senior management on appropriate strategies for governing agile teams as your existing strategy likely reflects traditional thinking.	Traditional governance strategies, including Earned Value Management (EVM) schemes, are documentation based instead of value based. Agile teams must be governed in an agile manner. See Chapter 20.

Table 6.3 Comparing Enterprise Support Strategies

Strategy	Potential Advantages	Potential Disadvantages	Considerations
Formal enterprise support	Helps to align team to enterprise direction.	Draws out your Inception phase efforts waiting for review results. Often motivates heavier, overly detailed architectural approaches. Suboptimizations to the enterprise support process, which decrease the overall efficiency of your IT process.	Avoid needless overhead inflicted by enterprise teams simply to justify their own existence—always ask what real value is being provided to the organization, and whether that value can be achieved more effectively. Delivery teams that ignore enterprise considerations because they believe they don't have the time to work through the enterprise support processes are a clear indicator that either the delivery team is in serious trouble or the enterprise processes are onerous.
Collaborative interaction	Helps align team to enterprise direction. Enterprise professionals get direct feedback on their own strategies. Skills transferred to the team from the enterprise professionals (and potentially vice versa).	Enterprise professionals required to have a more robust, "hands on" skillset. Enterprise professionals must be sufficiently flexible to support both traditional and agile teams in a variety of manners.	Enterprise professionals who don't want to get actively involved with delivery teams may be doing more harm than good.

Strategy	Potential Advantages	Potential Disadvantages	Considerations
Shared artifacts	Provides a single source for reusable artifacts, guidelines, and other enterprise assets.	Requires an asset management strategy around versioning, grooming (removal of old or unused assets), and support.	Charge back schemes to fund reuse programs often motivate delivery teams to avoid reusing existing assets. Complex strategies to gain permission to reuse existing artifacts also reduces reuse rates. For reuse programs to be successful it must be as easy as possible for people to reuse things.
None	Reduces Inception phase efforts.	Delivery teams are unlikely to work to a common enterprise strategy.	Beware of delivery teams that believe they're in a special situation and therefore don't need to interact with the rest of your organization or leverage existing assets—this is a common sign of a team in trouble.

Securing Funding

Your funding strategy, although not the level of funding, will likely be set for you long before your project even begins. For example, most organizations have policies regarding how projects are funded, often regardless of the paradigm followed. There are three basic strategies, compared in Table 6.4, for funding agile projects:

- **"Fixed price."** At the beginning of the project you should develop, and then commit to, an initial estimate that is based on your up-front requirements and architecture modeling efforts. Hopefully this estimate is given as a range, as studies have shown that up-front estimating techniques such as COCOMO II or function points are accurate within +/- 30% most of the time. However the July 2009 State of the IT Union survey found that on average organizations are aiming for +/- 11% (their actual results come in at +/- 19% on average, but only after doing things such as dropping scope, changing the estimated cost, or changing the delivery date).

- **Stage gate.** With this strategy you estimate and then fund the project for a given period of time before going back for more funding. For example, you may be allocated sufficient money to fund the project for a three-month period at which point you must evaluate the viability of the project to receive further funding. Note that stages don't have to be based on specific time periods; they could instead be based on goals such as the DAD milestones of reaching stakeholder consensus, proving the architecture with working code, or building a portion of the system.

- **Time and materials (T&M).** With this approach you pay as you go, requiring your management team to actually govern the project effectively. Many organizations believe a T&M strategy to be risky, which it often is when your IT governance strategy isn't very effective. An interesting variation, particularly in a situation where a service provider is doing the development, is an approach where a low rate is paid for their time, which covers their basic costs, the cost of materials is paid out directly, and delivery bonuses are paid for working software. This spreads the risk between the customer/ stakeholder and the service provider. The service provider has their costs covered but won't make a profit unless they consistently deliver quality software.

Table 6.4 Comparing Project Funding Strategies

Strategy	Potential Advantages	Potential Disadvantages	Considerations
Fixed price (nonranged)	Provides stakeholders with an exact cost to hope for.	Doesn't communicate the actual uncertainty faced by the project team. Sets false expectations about accuracy and your ability to plan. When scope and schedule are also fixed it motivates questionable behavior on the part of IT professionals.[2]	Works well when the scope of what you need to deliver is allowed to vary. Stakeholders have caught on to the fact that most IT teams are padding the budget, so will do their best to negotiate that padding away. High probability that you will need to go back and negotiate for more funding, which in turn can lower stakeholder trust in your ability to get the job done.
Fixed with range	Provides stakeholders with a more realistic assessment of the uncertainty faced by the team.	Many stakeholders will focus on the lower end of the estimate range. Many stakeholders don't understand the need for ranged estimates (see Chapter 10 for a detailed discussion).	You will likely need to educate some of your stakeholders regarding the desirability of a ranged estimate.
Staged	Lowers financial risk of project. Provides stakeholders with financial leverage over your project.	Some organizations have an onerous project funding process, so requiring teams to obtain funding in stages can increase their bureaucratic overhead and increase risk of delivering late.	Align your funding gates with lifecycle milestones to hopefully reduce overall overhead and to focus both stakeholders and the teams on the importance of the milestone reviews.

(continued)

2. Scott has done extensive research into these behaviors, which include preventing requirements change; lying about cost, schedule, or scope; and extorting additional funds late in the project lifecycle. Several articles are published on drdobbs.com summarizing this work.

Table 6.4   Comparing Project Funding Strategies (continued)

Strategy	Potential Advantages	Potential Disadvantages	Considerations
Time and materials (T&M)	Significantly lower financial risk when projects are governed appropriately (see Chapter 20).	Requires stakeholders to actively monitor the project.	Some organizations have mistakenly concluded that a T&M approach is a risky way to fund IT projects. Invariably these organizations prove to have ineffective governance strategies where stakeholders take a "hands off" approach to IT.
T&M with performance bonus	Low financial risk for both the project team and for stakeholders.	Requires active monitoring by stakeholders and a clear definition of how to determine whether the project team has met their service level agreement (SLA) and therefore has earned their performance bonus.	Works very well for outsourced projects.

The point is that there are several strategies for funding agile software development projects, just as there are several strategies for funding traditional software development projects. Our experience is that fixed-price funding strategies are incredibly poor practice, which greatly increases the risk of your software development projects. We recognize how hard it can be to change this desire on the part of our business stakeholders, but have also had success changing their minds. If you choose to persevere, which is a difficult decision to make, you can help your organization's decision makers to adopt more effective strategies. Like you they want to improve the effectiveness of your IT efforts but may not understand the implications of what they ask for sometimes. We prefer a time and materials approach, although we have been successful with staged-gate strategies.

LESSONS FROM THE TRENCHES—FIXED PRICE ESTIMATES INCREASE PROJECT RISK

Having been a partner of a large IT services firm, Mark can tell you that agreeing to deliver software based on a fixed priced is risky and has the potential to seriously cripple the successful bidder financially. It is common in the business to bid low to win the contract, and then make the required profit by issuing change requests when the requirements inevitably change. An alternative to this approach is for the vendor to build a huge contingency into the bid. To be frank, customers that pay for projects based on fixed-price are wasting a huge amount of money.

Mark helped move an organization from a fixed price, offshore model to a better approach. The key was to fix the cost (budget), the schedule (with quarterly releases), but allow for variable scope. Business goals for the program and project streams were agreed to at a very high level. What this agile approach promised was that while detailed achievable scope could not be promised in advance, the budget invested would result in the best use of the funds with an optimized development process, and the highest value features being delivered, on time and on budget. With a history of going over budget, missing deadlines, and solutions that failed to deliver expected results, this was a huge improvement. This large company is now in the process of adopting DAD organization wide.

Other Inception Activities

For those familiar with the Unified Process Inception phase, there is some debate regarding whether any coding is done before Construction iterations. Our response is, as usual, it depends. Since we recommend using a goals-driven approach throughout the DAD lifecycle we suggest deferring any work that is not part of achieving stakeholder consensus until the Construction phase. Some people such as Dean Leffingwell suggest investing some time in the "starter" iteration building an architectural runway, which others might call an architectural spike. With this in place before Construction starts, the team has something upon which to implement their functionality allowing them to deliver value quicker in the early iterations. Other similar pre-Construction activities might include setting up the developers' build and testing tools as well as establishing the continuous integration environment (we discuss tooling in Chapter 11). Brad Appleton calls this "greasing the skids" for the development team. We agree that if the framework of the architecture and tooling to support continuous integration are not in place it will take a bit of time in the first iteration or two of Construction for the team to get this established. However, the investment made in Inception writing code or setting up environments may be premature for the following reasons:

- This work that is being done in parallel with creating the vision for the solution may need to be redone if the vision changes before Inception is completed.

- This effort is wasted if a decision is made at the conclusion of Inception to cancel the project or pursue an alternative such as implementing a packaged solution.

- Team members or funding may not be available to start development or setup of the environment.

As usual, DAD is not prescriptive about which approach to use. If doing preparatory work in Inception makes sense for you, then do it.

When Do You Need an Inception Phase?

There are several reasons why you need to run an Inception phase. Most obviously is when you are working on the first release of a product, you need to invest some time to organize your team. In these situations your Inception efforts could be several months in length, particularly when there isn't a firm understanding as to the scope of what you're trying to achieve. You are likely also going to need to invest some time getting organized for the second release. Hopefully you'll be quicker; this should certainly be the case if you keep your team together and if the first release was successful. The third release should have an even shorter initiation effort, and so on.

Figure 6.5 depicts two versions of a product lifecycle showing a series of ongoing releases. The agile product lifecycle is typical of a DAD team that is following a basic/agile version of the lifecycle, the focus of this book. The lean product lifecycle is typical of a DAD team that has tailored their lifecycle to be closer to the advanced/lean version overviewed in Chapter 1, "Disciplined Agile Delivery in a Nutshell," and discussed in greater detail in Chapter 21, "Got Discipline?" With the agile approach notice how the overall release cycle continues to have both Inception and Transition phases (depicted as "I" and "T" in the diagram), albeit ones that are shorter over time—the Inception phase shortens because an existing team (hopefully) is building on an existing solution, the implication being that the majority of the effort is to define the intended scope of the next release. It may even shorten to nothing, particularly with experienced teams with great relationships with their stakeholders. With the lean approach you still need an initial effort to get the team underway, and you will likely have a nontrivial transition effort because you will not yet have automated all transition activities. The next release you may not have an inception effort at all; you simply keep working on existing work items, and the transition effort will shorten as you automate more and more. Eventually your team will have a continuous stream of construction with releases into production on a fairly regular basis. In Chapter 10 release cadences are discussed in detail.

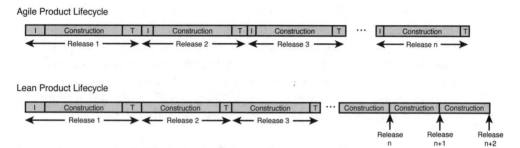

Figure 6.5   Agile and lean product lifecycles

From the previous discussion you can see that several issues determine how long your Inception phase will be:

- Your understanding of the problem domain and stakeholder agreement around it
- The existence of previous releases of the solution, your team's understanding of the architecture, and its ability to support the desired functionality of the new release
- The existence of a delivery team for this solution
- Your organization's governance process, in particular the overhead that it requires to initiate a new release of a system

Inception Phase Patterns

Several common strategies applied during the Inception phase seem to work well in practice, and several seem to work rather poorly in practice. The success of this phase is determined by your ability to understand and adopt the successful patterns appropriately and avoid the anti-patterns when you can. Let's begin with some patterns for success:

- **Short and sufficient.** With the exception of research or truly groundbreaking projects, the Inception phase should not take more than a month and ideally can be completed in two weeks or less. Having said that, in Scott's 2009 Agile Project Initiation survey the average agile team reported an Inception phase of four weeks, an indication that many teams still haven't squeezed some of the bureaucratic tendencies out of their organizational culture yet.

- **Ranged estimates.** The project management iron triangle tells us that it isn't possible to "set" all three of schedule, cost, and scope without negatively impacting quality—in other words if the business insists on a defined (nonranged) delivery date, defined cost, and specific scope, that will result in either a poor quality solution delivered or one or more of the three "set" factors changing negatively at some point. As we discuss in Chapter 10, it is highly desirable to provide ranged cost and schedule estimates to provide sufficient flexibility for the development team to deliver a good solution.

- **Minimal but sufficient documentation.** Your documentation should include some basic models (pictures) of the envisioned architecture and other views of the solution, UML-based or otherwise. In addition, you are likely to have a concise vision statement and a work item list. There will also be other critical diagrams resulting from your requirements and architecture envisioning efforts that weren't included in your vision statement but are actively used by the team to guide their efforts.

FOCUS ON GOALS, NOT WORK PRODUCTS

Why haven't we listed a set of work products that you need to produce in this phase? Well, we are not sure what work products you need to produce to fulfill the milestone goals for this phase. Ask yourself, "for this goal (such as determining scope), what documentation do I truly need (if any), and at what degree of detail does it need to be?" Remember Agile Principle #10 Simplicity—the art of maximizing the amount of work not done—is essential!

Inception Phase Anti-Patterns

There are several common *anti-patterns* that we've seen agile teams exhibit during this phase (and beyond):

- **No support for skills development.** Your organization needs to invest in mentoring, training, and education. Taking an agile course is a great start. Utilizing an experienced DAD coach/mentor is even better for ensuring that your team's adoption of agile is accelerated and supported with guidance related to actual hands-on experience.

- **No support for dedicated facilities.** As we discuss in Chapter 11, there are periodic tests of your management's resolve regarding support of your agile approach. Requesting a dedicated room or work area, with supporting logistics such as whiteboards, projectors, and other shared facilities will demonstrate their support. Being denied these facilities is a sure sign that they are not totally bought in. At scale with larger teams you need dedicated facilities for the individual subteams. With geographically distributed teams you need access to collaboration technologies such as team environments (such as a Jazz server), audio conferencing, and even video conferencing.

- **Autocratic project management practices.** Pressure from project management offices (PMOs) or middle management who are more comfortable with traditional/formal project management techniques can cause frustration for agile teams. Warning signs include requests for detailed work breakdown structures (WBS), earned value reports, detailed Gantt charts, detailed status reports, and onerous sign-off procedures. Often micromanagement of teams and their leaders stems from a lack of trust, which is inconsistent with self-organization. Now is the time to reinforce the principle that teams own their process, which includes how they meet, communicate, and report their progress. Chapter 20 explores agile governance strategies in detail.

- **Jumping into Construction.** "Just do it" is a catchy phrase, but DAD teams realize that a ready-fire-aim approach to solution delivery is risky. Successful agile teams spend some time at the beginning of the project working toward concurrence regarding their overall strategy for the project.

- **Overly detailed work products.** You should do just enough work to gain agreement that it makes sense to fund and proceed with the project into the Construction phase. Resist the urge to create long and detailed documents such as plans and requirements in this phase. In Chapters 8 and 9 we discuss the risks involved with detailed specifications written early in a project.

- **Analysis paralysis.** This occurs when your team strives to get the perfect answer before moving on. Delaying the completion of documents in Inception may often be an indication that either the team or your stakeholders fear moving forward into Construction.

Concluding Thoughts

During the Inception phase your team puts the foundation for success in place for your project. This includes identifying and leading your key stakeholders to agreement around the initial scope, cost, and schedule for the effort. Your team must also identify and agree to a technical strategy for providing a solution to your stakeholders. Because people are not good at defining in detail what they need, and because your business environment and understanding of it will change during the project anyway, these ideas are likely to be fuzzy at this point—exactness will come later. You will have reasonable, but still high-level, definitions of these things, agreed to and captured in your vision statement, release plan, and an architecture handbook. The goal is to get your team going in an effective direction even though you may not know your exact destination yet. This reduces project risk because you're making strategically important decisions now, deferring the smaller, tactical decisions for later in the project when it makes better sense to make them.

The following four chapters present alternatives for completing your Inception work in the goal of achieving stakeholder consensus for the path forward. While some of the approaches described are clearly more formal and less agile than others, it is important to keep in mind that you should take a minimalist and agile approach to reaching your Inception goal. If you want to get a clear idea of how an Inception phase can be run quickly with low formality you may want to jump ahead to the case study in Chapter 12, "Case Study: Inception Phase," and then return to these chapters for a thorough description of alternative approaches with their associated pros and cons.

Additional Resources

For more detailed discussions about several of the topics covered in this chapter:

- **Agile surveys.** Some statistics were quoted from the 2009 Agile Project Initiation survey at ambysoft.com/surveys/projectInitiation2009.html and from the July 2009 State of the IT Union survey at www.ambysoft.com/surveys/stateOfITUnion200907.html.

- **Project initiation.** Karl Wiegers' book *Practical Project Initiation* (Microsoft Press, 2007) provides a range of advice for successful IT project starts.

- **Water-scrum-fall.** This term was coined by Dave West of Forrester Research in his whitepaper "Water-Scrum-Fall Is the Reality of Agile for Most Organizations Today," available at www.forrester.com.

- **Iron triangle.** Scott describes the project management iron triangle and the implications of breaking it in his article "The Broken Iron Triangle Anti-Pattern" at ambysoft. com/essays/brokenTriangle.html.

- **Enterprise agile.** For strategies describing how enterprise professionals can work in an agile manner, enterpriseunifiedprocess.com has a collection of articles. Agile strategies for enterprise architects are described at agiledata.org/essays/enterpriseArchitecture. html and for enterprise data administrators at agiledata.org/essays/enterpriseAdministration. html.

- **Agile funding strategies.** Scott has written extensively about the issues surrounding how to fund agile projects. The article "Strategies for Funding Software Development Projects" expands on the strategies presented in this chapter and can be found at drdobbs.com/architecture-and-design/212200803. Scott has also written about how to deal with the challenges surrounding fixed budgets on agile projects in "Agile on a Fixed Budget" at drdobbs.com/architecture-and-design/201202925.

- **Other Inception Activities.** If your strategy includes preparing your architecture in advance of your Construction iterations, Dean Leffingwell describes the "architectural runway" in his book *Scaling Software Agility* (Addison-Wesley, 2007).

Identifying a Project Vision

Good business leaders create a vision, articulate the vision, passionately own the vision, and relentlessly drive it to completion. —Jack Welch

In many organizations a project officially begins when the team leadership gains agreement and funding from the project sponsor to create an initial vision for the proposed solution. Minimally the vision should answer what are the goals of the project team and who is on it. More robust vision statements also indicate the desired scope of the current release, overview the likely technical strategy to address that scope, and outline the plan to do the required work. When a feasibility study has occurred, the vision statement also summarizes its results. Project teams develop a vision statement to help guide their efforts throughout the rest of the project and to secure funding for the project.

A vision statement, or in more formal environments a project charter or business case, can be used by the project team to guide their efforts in several ways. First, it can be used as criteria for determining when a team has developed sufficient functionality so that it makes sense to release into production.[1] Second, it can be used to help the team keep on track. One of the dangers of evolutionary (iterative and incremental) approaches to delivery is the gradual "death by 1000 requirements changes," where the solution slowly morphs into something that nobody actually wants. This risk can be avoided by having an agreed-to vision (which may also evolve over time), by working closely with a wide range of stakeholders, and through the visibility provided by the regular production of a potentially consumable solution. Third, it often proves to be a key asset in the effort to secure funding for your project team because it summarizes your team's strategy, a

---

1. Chapter 10 discusses the various release rhythms and their trade-offs.

strategy that your key stakeholders should understand and support. Stakeholders need to agree on the business problem within the context of the larger organizational goals, and how the proposed solution addresses the problem. Your project sponsors need to understand the approach, the constraints, and their satisfaction criteria for the project. All this information is captured by your vision statement.

Figure 7.1 shows a mind map of the structure of this chapter. We describe each of the topics in the map in clockwise order, beginning at the top right.

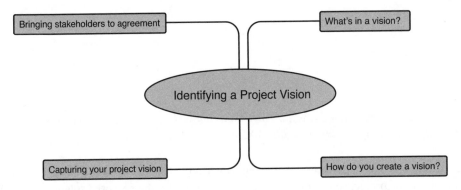

Figure 7.1   Outline of this chapter

THE BIG IDEAS IN THIS CHAPTER

- The team leadership initially gains agreement from the project sponsor to create an initial vision for the proposed solution.

- During the Inception phase you should come to a relative consensus with your stakeholders as to the scope of the project, the timeline, relevant constraints, and the architectural strategy. The details will still evolve throughout the project.

- A key challenge of creating a vision is to obtain enough information to gain stakeholder consensus to proceed with the project without producing too much documentation.

- Different aspects of your vision are documented in parallel as you learn more information about your stakeholder needs.

What's in a Vision?

Vision statements answer several fundamental questions, including: What are you going to produce? How long will it take? What will it cost? How are you going to build it? Do you understand the risks?

To answer these questions, the vision statement may contain the following information:

- The business problem that is being addressed and the value to your organization of doing so.

- High-level technical architecture being followed, and, if appropriate, any alternatives considered and why they weren't chosen.

- A summary of the scope, potentially including a list of the major stakeholder goals to be addressed. A scope overview diagram is often useful, such as a use case diagram or a business process diagram.

- The estimated cost of the project, presented as a range, and an indication of the funding approach for the project.

- The project schedule showing number of iterations, their durations, and expected release dates. This is often a high-level Gantt chart.

- A list of the critical project risks, mitigation strategies, and contingency plans.

- A list of key assumptions and decisions, if any.

- An indication of the process being followed, in this case DAD.

- Other project details such as team makeup (resourcing plan), budget constraints, communication plans, escalation procedures, and governance strategy.

Chapter 12, "Case Study: Inception Phase," includes examples of many of the items listed here. Although we have listed many potential topics for a vision statement, you will want to address only the topics appropriate to your situation. This risk of lists such as the one just presented is that some people think they need to fully address them, but our advice is to address an issue only if it adds actual value.

How Do You Create a Vision?

Your strategy will evolve throughout your project, but it is initially defined in an evolutionary manner throughout the Inception phase. Your strategy will reflect the desired scope for your solution, your technical strategy/architecture for addressing that scope, the amount of resources your organization, or your customer, is willing to invest, the amount of time you have to do so, and the ability of the team that you assemble to do the work. These individual components will themselves evolve over time to reflect your growing understanding of what needs to be done and how you will go about doing so. This evolutionary approach to defining your project strategy is overviewed in Figure 7.2. This strategy information is summarized by your project vision.

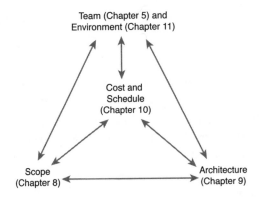

Figure 7.2   Evolving your initial project strategy

Capturing Your Project Vision

Effective vision statements are written using economic terms and the language of your business domain, although technical terms will still creep in at times when describing the proposed solution. The vision statement could be as little as three to four pages capturing a bulleted list of critical decisions and several key diagrams overviewing the scope, schedule, and technical strategy. Or it could be more detailed, often a requirement in regulatory environments or organizations with cultures still in the process of transitioning to agile, running to ten to fifteen pages. As with other artifacts, we recommend the agile principle of keeping the vision statement as concise as possible and just good enough to achieve its goals.

There are several approaches that you can take, which are compared in Table 7.1, when formulating the vision for your project:

- **Detailed vision document/project charter/business case.** This can be a document of up to 50 pages or more, although 20 to 30 pages are far more common. It describes in detail your financial analysis regarding the projected costs and benefits of your solution; the technical strategy, the trade-offs associated with it, and the validity of the direction you've chosen; a detailed project timeline, often captured as a Gantt chart; and a description of the business problem being addressed. If a detailed vision is required, you may choose to split the vision document into more traditional documents such as vision, project plan, business case, risk list, or architecture document. However, our preference is fewer, smaller documents are better, with separate sections for each area of concern. The primary difference between a vision document and a project charter or business case may be the inclusion of the results of a feasibility assessment. Good feasibility assessments address the economic feasibility (will we make/save money?), technical feasibility (do we think we can build it?), operational feasibility (can we run it once delivered?), and political feasibility (will our stakeholder community accept it)? Having said that, many vision documents also address feasibility to some extent so the line between charters, visions, and business cases is often blurred.

- **Lightweight vision statement.** A lightweight vision statement is a short document of roughly 1-4 pages that describes what you are doing and why you are doing it. It could include in short form descriptions of key project information such as the business problem to be solved, key features, stakeholders, and constraints—for example, financial, schedule, and technology alternatives. It should answer a question like "why are we spending $100,000 on this project?" Think of your vision statement as a sales brochure that is a compelling and concise description of the value of the project. Examples of the content of a lightweight vision statement can be found in Chapter 12.

- **Vision radiators.** Critical information about your project is captured on whiteboards or flipchart paper and posted on the walls of your team's work area so that it is visible to all team members. The practice of displaying information on all things related to the project is known as visual management, big visible charts, and information radiators (by Alistair Cockburn).

- **No investment in a shared vision.** Some teams decide to jump straight into construction without spending the time to formulate a shared vision to guide their efforts.

We suggest that you invest in a lightweight vision statement and combine it where possible with vision radiators. Having a document that provides an overview of what your project team intends to deliver will help to build trust with your stakeholders and help guide your decisions later in the project.

LESSONS FROM THE TRENCHES—VISION STATEMENTS HELP YOU TO STEER

Darren Blyth is a talented business analyst whom Mark has worked with for many years. Sometimes as a project proceeds teams find themselves doing more work than was initially envisioned at the beginning of the project. It is easy to fall for the temptation for changing scope in an uncontrolled fashion. At times Darren has helped avoid this by asking the teams "Why are we doing this? Does this support our approved business case and vision?" This is where it is useful to have a vision produced at the time the project was initially approved and funded in the Inception phase. The vision serves as the beacon to keep the team on track rather than trying to produce a solution that solves an unrelated business problem, or worse, solves no problem at all.

Table 7.1 Comparing Vision Strategies

Strategy	Potential Advantages	Potential Disadvantages	Considerations
Detailed vision document, project charter, or business case	Satisfies organizational or regulatory documentation requirements for project initiation.	Detailed descriptions can put a "scientific façade" over something that is inherently artful at this point in your project. Senior management may expect this document as a firm commitment. Requires extensive modeling and planning, thereby increasing the Inception phase effort.	Beware of aggressive, quantified benefits that often result in dysfunctional or myopic behavior that sacrifices holistic enterprise goals for short-sighted project goals.[2]
Lightweight vision statement	Satisfies organizational or regulatory documentation requirements for project initiation. Provides the team with a consumable description of their overall business and technical direction. Builds trust with your stakeholders.	Senior managers with significant traditional experience may see lightweight documentation as a project risk.	You still need to do some serious thinking. Don't allow sloppy thinking around the scope, architecture strategy, and overall planning to be excused through adoption of this practice.
Vision radiators	Provides the team with very consumable guidance.	Will not be easily accessible to any distributed team members or stakeholders. You may still need to document the vision at some point.	You may still have missing or poorly understood issues. Just because the information is in front of everyone it doesn't imply that they understand or agree to it. In addition, the information can be easily changed without governance. That might be an advantage, but could also lead to a situation where resources are working to different versions of the vision.

2. Galinsky & Bazerman have found that aggressive goal setting within an organization will foster an organizational climate ripe for unethical behavior. In the December 2010 State of the IT Union survey Scott found that unethical behavior is far too common on IT delivery projects, although agile teams were least likely to exhibit such behavior.

Strategy	Potential Advantages	Potential Disadvantages	Considerations
No shared vision	Enables the team to get going with construction efforts quickly. Appropriate for very small, straightforward efforts.	Potential for wasting several construction iterations, or more, going down false paths because of insufficient up-front thinking.	This could be a symptom indicating that you have an ad-hoc program claiming to be agile because they believe they don't need to do any initial up-front work.

Bringing Stakeholders to Agreement Around the Vision

The fundamental purpose of the Inception phase is to come to an agreement within your team and with your stakeholders regarding a strategy for the rest of the project. For some teams this may be lightweight, with a few goals, a rough target date, and a good group of people who have come together to get the job done. For other teams this may be a collection of detailed specifications and plans that have been reviewed and "signed off." For most teams this will be somewhere in between. As a result near the end of the Inception phase your team should meet with your stakeholder representatives to ensure that everyone agrees to the vision.

Whatever strategy you identify must be acceptable to your stakeholders, hence the "stakeholder consensus" milestone that you learned about in Chapter 2, "Introduction to Agile and Lean." You should strive to determine as quickly as possible whether the strategy is worthwhile and feasible, and if not to cancel the project so that no more resources are expended on it. It is safe to declare the Inception phase over, and thereby begin the Construction phase, when:

- Your stakeholders agree that it makes sense to proceed with this project based on your initial agreement on the achievable scope, schedule, budget, constraints, and other criteria related to the business case of your project.

- The identified risks seem tolerable and there is agreement on using a minimalist and agile process of developing the software.

- The team and environment have been set up that foster agile principles of collaborative teamwork.

- The process and governance strategies have been agreed to by both the team and your project stakeholders.

There are several techniques for working toward stakeholder consensus, compared in Table 7.2, several of which may be combined. They are the following:

- **Active stakeholder participation formulating the vision.** The easiest way to gain consensus among your key stakeholders is to have them be actively involved with its development. Stakeholders can clearly be involved with modeling sessions, particularly those exploring scope, as well as your high-level planning efforts. By actively working on the vision, and more importantly its components, they understand the trade-offs made and the overall priorities driving the project.

- **Distribute the vision statement to reviewers.** Many project teams opt to develop the vision for the project and then make it available to a wide range of stakeholders to get their feedback. This documentation review can not only help the team to improve the vision based on the feedback, it also helps stakeholders improve their understanding of the team's strategy and to even help evolve it.

- **Informal review.** In an informal review a group of people is gathered, either physically in the same room or virtually via electronic means, to discuss and provide feedback regarding an artifact (in this case the project vision). Informal reviews are often facilitated, and may roughly adhere to a simple set of procedures. A decision regarding the acceptability of the vision, and even to (not) continue funding the project, may be made as the result of this informal review meeting.

- **Formal review.** DAD teams working in regulatory environments may find that their organization requires them to hold formal reviews of key artifacts, including the project vision statement. These formal reviews are typically facilitated by a professional facilitator outside the team, follow a predetermined procedure, and often produce a written assessment of the artifact being reviewed. In the case of a project vision review the decision whether to move forward or not with the project may be a part of the assessment.

Our advice is to have active stakeholder participation throughout your entire project, including the Inception phase. We prefer informal reviews over formal ones when given the choice. We also avoid sharing information via documents in favor of face-to-face communication when we can, although we recognize that this isn't always viable.

Getting teams in that space called "shared vision" is one of the most powerful ways a DAD team lead or product owner can help the team and its stakeholders. A second type of buy-in that you should try to get at this time is related to the DAD approach itself. If you are getting questions from your stakeholders about needing detailed plans, requirements, and designs at this point, they have clearly not adopted an agile mindset in lieu of the flawed traditional approaches. This is a good time to set expectations regarding continual evolution of the vision and the expected continuous change of requirements and priorities as the project progresses.

LESSONS FROM THE TRENCHES—PREPARING FOR CONSTRUCTION ITERATIONS

Recently Mark led the Inception activities for a large program with six project streams, during which the director asked, "How many people do you need for the year?" Mark cheekily replied, "I don't know; what do you want done?" He was then given a one-page program overview for the year listing the six initiatives. Mark used this as the basis for the vision and started documenting the vision on the program's wiki.

As the sections of the vision started to be completed, Mark could then use this information as the basis for discussions on how the project teams needed to be structured. Once we had an idea of what the high-level goals for the solution were for the year, and keeping the budget constraints in mind, we could then start the process of procuring team members, structuring the teams, and setting up the work environments. Obtaining new team members, workstations, and space takes time, so we have found that this process needs to start in the Inception phase, before formal sign-off of the vision has taken place. Fortunately, with active stakeholder participation, verbal buy-in to the vision and permission to staff up the team(s) is usually easy to obtain.

Table 7.2   Comparing Agreement-Building Strategies

Strategy	Potential Advantages	Potential Disadvantages	Considerations
Active stakeholder participation formulating the vision	Increased chance of acceptance by the stakeholders because their concerns were heard and because they heard the concerns of others. Increased chance of higher quality vision due to greater range of input during its creation.	Increased risk of analysis paralysis due to involvement of too many people. Increased risk of a low-quality vision if too many concessions are given in the name of consensus.	In most situations only a handful of your stakeholder community will be available for active involvement, so you need to ensure that they represent the full range of stakeholders as best as possible.
Distribute the vision statement to reviewers	Easy way to gain feedback from a wide range of people.	Documentation is the least effective way to communicate information, increasing the chance that your stakeholders won't understand what the vision actually is. Feedback can be difficult to process when coming from multiple sources at different times. Several rounds of feedback are likely needed, yet reviewer fatigue quickly sets in.	Keep the material to be reviewed as concise as possible—the larger it is the less chance it will be thoroughly reviewed. Useful when some or all stakeholders are geographically distributed. Useful toward end of Inception after active stakeholder participation earlier in the phase.
Informal review meeting	Easy way to stimulate discussion and obtain feedback from multiple people simultaneously. Typically much lower overhead than formal reviews.	Reviews can get off track due to feedback of one or more strong-willed people.	Very useful before emailing a vision statement to a wider audience. Useful when earlier active stakeholder participation was done individually or with smaller groups.
Formal document review	Effective strategy when there is a risk of strong-willed stakeholders hijacking the review for their own purposes.	Risk of unnecessary overhead when the formality focuses on bureaucratic activities rather than on preparation, facilitation of the review, and acting on the results.	May be required in some regulatory situations. Consider hiring a professional meeting facilitator to run your formal reviews.

Concluding Thoughts

A key goal of the Inception phase on a DAD project is to obtain stakeholder consensus that the proposed solution makes sense for the identified business problems. To get everyone on the same page to obtain this consensus we create a project vision. Is this one document, or several? It is up to you. You could have one vision document that summarizes your Inception work, or package it into several small documents such as vision, project plan, risk list, architecture handbook, and work item list. Our preference is for fewer and lighter documents that are evolved in tools such as IBM Rational Team Concert and wikis.

Some projects mistake the Inception phase for a big up-front documentation exercise, which it definitely is not. For your vision, strive for total documentation of no more than ten printed pages (regulatory environments may require more). Time boxing your Inception phase and working closely with your stakeholders help you to stay agile.

The following chapters describe how to capture the information summarized in your vision. We cover how to describe your scope, plot your technical strategy, staff your team, plan your releases, and establish your work environment. The order of the chapters does not indicate that you should capture this information in this sequential order. Rather, you document each of these decisions iteratively in parallel as you learn more about your stakeholder needs, opportunities, and constraints.

Additional Resources

Dean Leffingwell describes how to create a vision in his book *Scaling Software Agility* (Addison-Wesley, 2007).

CHAPTER 8

Identifying the Initial Scope

It isn't the size that matters; it's what you deliver that really counts.

During the Inception phase Disciplined Agile Delivery (DAD) teams explore the initial requirements to arrive at a common understanding as to the scope of what they're trying to accomplish. This is an important aspect of your overall project vision (see Chapter 7, "Identifying a Project Vision") and is a key input into release planning (see Chapter 10, "Initial Release Planning"). Furthermore it is necessary to prime the Construction phase with work to do—without at least an understanding of the goals to accomplish your delivery team will flounder.

Some people will tell you that you don't need to do any initial requirements modeling at all, yet the Agile Project Initiation survey found that close to 90% of respondents indicated that their agile teams were in fact doing so. Our experience is that doing some initial requirements modeling offers several potential benefits:

- **You can answer fundamental business questions.** Like it or not, people are always going to ask you what the vision is for what you are going to build (what's the scope), how long do you think it's going to take (the schedule), and how much is it going to cost (the expected budget). You often don't need to answer these questions in detail, but you do need to convince the people who are funding and supporting your project that you understand the fundamental business issues that your project team is going to address.

- **Improved productivity.** You can identify and think through some of the critical business issues facing your project. Asking fundamental questions such as "What gets in the way of your work?" and "How do you currently get things done?" can lead to significant insights for what your team needs to actually do.

- **Reduced business risk.** Your team gains the advantage of having a guiding business vision without the disadvantages associated with big requirements up front (BRUF). In fact, the primary goal of the Inception phase is to drive to scope concurrence with your stakeholders. Not only do you identify the scope of the effort, you also help to make the relevant stakeholders aware that there is a range of needs being met by your system, not just theirs, and that they are going to have to compromise sometimes.

- **Increased scalability.** Your initial requirements model will be a key work product in any "agile at scale" effort because it provides the business direction required for your initial architectural envisioning efforts (typically done in parallel with initial requirements modeling) and by subteams to define and guide their efforts within the overall project. Furthermore, teams in regulatory situations often find that they need to include explicit requirements modeling activities in their process.

Figure 8.1 shows a mind map of the structure of this chapter. We describe each of the topics in the map in clockwise order, beginning at the top right.

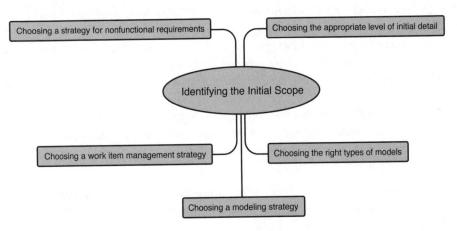

Figure 8.1   Outline of this chapter

THE BIG IDEAS IN THIS CHAPTER

- DAD teams typically explore the initial requirements for their solution before beginning construction.
- The level of requirements detail should vary based on your team's proximity to one another, access to stakeholders, need for regulatory compliance, and skill.
- You need to consider a range of views, including how people will use and interact with your system, the domain supported by your solution, and the business process that it supports.

- There are several work item management strategies—formal change management, a product backlog, a work item stack, or a work item pool—to choose from.
- Nonfunctional requirements for your solution should be addressed throughout your project—starting from the very beginning.

Choosing the Appropriate Level of Initial Detail

The objectives at this point in the project are to identify the business goals for the effort, develop a common vision, and as swiftly as possible identify the initial requirements for the system (in Scrum they refer to this as populating the backlog, but there's more to it than that). A critical issue is the level of detail that you choose to capture. At one extreme is the traditional strategy of writing a detailed requirements specification, often referred to as "big requirements up front (BRUF)," and at the other extreme is capturing nothing at all. The Standish Group's Chaos Report reveals that when a BRUF approach is taken on average 45% of the functionality delivered is never used by the end users of the solution, and an additional 19% is rarely used, a significant amount of potential wastage. This wastage likely occurs because of human behavior—people are simply not good at defining things up front, although they are good at iteratively exploring what they need; onerous change management processes that often focus on motivating stakeholders to not change their requirements and thereby avoid scope/feature creep prevent change and thereby prevent the team from delivering functionality stakeholders actually need; stakeholders are motivated to make up as many requirements as possible early in the lifecycle, thereby identifying many things that aren't actually needed, knowing that they won't be able to change their minds after the requirements are frozen due to the change prevention efforts of the delivery team. This indicates that many of the benefits described previously are being counteracted by the resulting human behavior around BRUF.

In the middle ground there's Agile Modeling's requirements envisioning approach, where just enough requirements elicitation and capture occurs to understand the scope and help bring your stakeholders to consensus as to what is to be delivered. Often this initial requirements envisioning effort is on the order of hours or days, not weeks or months as we see on traditional projects. An even leaner approach is to identify a handful of high-level goals for your project and then let all the details emerge over time. The lean philosophy is that requirements details are in practice high-level design constraints, and as such should be left until later in the lifecycle when it is most appropriate to finalize those design decisions—the Inception phase is rarely the right time for this. The levels of detail are compared in Table 8.1.

Table 8.1   Comparing Levels of Initial Requirement Detail

Strategy	Potential Advantages	Potential Disadvantages	Considerations
BRUF (detailed specification)	Very effective when the requirements are in fact well defined and unlikely to change, such as with government legislated changes. Traditional oriented stakeholders will be comfortable with this strategy. Supports systems engineering environments, particularly life critical regulatory systems such as medical device or automobile control system development.	Identify many "requirements" that aren't needed at all. Lose significant time getting to construction activities. Motivate stakeholders to not be involved with construction activities, where they are desperately needed, because the requirements are already defined. Slowly and expensively achieve the benefits of initial requirements modeling. Increase the time required for Inception activities, thereby increasing both schedule and political risk.	Watch out for situations where the requirements would in fact change if it wasn't for the onerous "change management" process inflicted upon stakeholders. Experienced development professionals who are new to agile are often at risk of wasting time trying to write a perfect specification before proceeding with construction. Scaling situations, such as larger or geographically distributed teams, may be mistakenly used as an excuse to justify detailed specification (yes, you may need a little more specification, but not much more).
Requirements envisioning (lightweight specification)	Quickly and inexpensively achieve the benefits of initial requirements modeling.	Stakeholders and IT professionals used to BRUF need to be educated and even coached in this lighter-weight method. Requires stakeholders, or minimally a stakeholder representative, to actively participate throughout construction. Can be difficult to judge when the requirements are "just good enough" as suggested by Agile Modeling, which requires experience.	Too little robustness in your requirements approach, e.g., "We only need to write up some user stories on a stack of index cards," often results in delivery teams having to scrap a lot of their initial work once they discover they've misunderstood the scope of what they need to produce.

Strategy	Potential Advantages	Potential Disadvantages	Considerations
Goals driven	Provides the team with significant flexibility as to how they approach providing a solution. Can and should be used with the more detailed approaches.	Requires significant discipline on the part of the delivery team. Requires significant trust between stakeholders and the delivery team.	This is a very lean/advanced approach that is appropriate for experienced DAD teams. Goals are typically captured as a simple list that is easily available to anyone involved with the project.
No modeling at all	You can quickly jump to construction.	You are likely to start producing inappropriate functionality early in the project.	When no initial modeling occurs the team risks building what they want instead of what their stakeholders need. Just because it is difficult to identify or access stakeholders, which can be the case with commercial product development and green-field development, this isn't an excuse to not define the initial scope.

Our suggestion for teams new to DAD is to do some lightweight requirements envisioning during Inception, with the exception of regulatory situations where detailed specifications are actually mandated. Experienced DAD teams, with several successful projects to their name, should consider the lean strategy of taking a goals-driven strategy. For most agile teams the objective is not to write a detailed requirements specification because the details will be explored later during construction in a just-in-time (JIT) manner.

An important philosophy to adopt is to recognize that the real value is in the modeling itself, not the models that are produced. Too many teams get focused on the outputs of requirements modeling instead of the act of doing it, and thereby lose track of the requirements forest due to the specification trees. Figure 8.2, used with permission from www.agilemodeling.com, overviews the value of modeling activities, comparing the traditional belief in the value (the dashed line) versus the observed value in practice (the full line). The times given are for effort, not calendar time. For example your team may put in 40 hours of effort, a full week, into requirements envisioning but spread it out over several weeks of calendar time. The fundamental point is that modeling quickly provides value because it enables you to explore ideas, but it quickly starts to lose value when you begin to overthink things or overdocument them. Iteration modeling is described in Chapter 14, "Initiating a Construction Iteration," and model storming in Chapter 15, "A Typical Day of Construction."

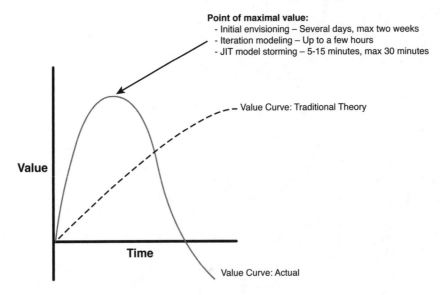

Figure 8.2 The value of modeling

Choosing the Right Types of Models

Today's business domain is complex, and most IT solutions that support this complexity may address a wide range of issues surrounding the business process, the overall business environment, usage of the solution, and consumability of the solution. The implication is that you need a varied, multiview approach to your requirements elicitation strategy. This doesn't imply that your strategy needs to be onerous, just multiviewed. In general, you should consider the following requirements views:

- **Usage model.** The goal of usage modeling is to explore how people work with the solution and gain value from doing so. There are several common ways to do so, including user story modeling, usage scenario modeling, and use case modeling. Your usage requirements are used to initially populate your work item list; more on this later. Good sources for usage information are your business stakeholders, particularly end users and their management, as well as enterprise modelers (if you have any) and of course the product owner.

- **Domain modeling.** The goal of domain modeling is to identify the major business entities and the relationships between them, thereby providing a common business language for your project team. This terminology will be used on other models, in your solution's user interface, and in conversations with stakeholders. Types of conceptual models vary based on the notation used, common choices being entity-relationship diagram (ERD), Unified Modeling Language (UML), or Barker/crow's feet. Good sources for this information are the same as for usage modeling.

- **Process modeling.** The goal of process modeling is to identify how something currently works or to think through how it should work. Where usage models explore how people interact with a solution, process models are different in that they explore the business processes and either the control flow or the data flow between them. Common choices are UML activity diagrams, data flow diagrams, and flow charts. Good sources for this information are the same as for usage modeling as well as operations and support people. Working closely with your operations staff early in the lifecycle like this to understand their requirements is an important part of your development and operations (DevOps) strategy, which in turn is an important part of enterprise awareness in the DAD process framework.

- **User interface modeling.** For many people the user interface (UI) is "the solution," and they will often talk in terms of screens/pages and reports in conversations with you. You will often find that you need to sketch the layout of major screens or reports early in the project so that everyone understands what you intend to build. Note that some people consider a UI flow diagram to be a critical architectural view—regardless of how you categorize it, only create it if it adds value. The best sources of this information are your actual end users and any user experience (UX) experts that you have available to you.

- **Nonfunctional requirements.** Nonfunctional requirements, also known as quality of service (QoS) or technical requirements, are typically systemwide, thus they apply to many and sometimes all of your functional requirements. Part of ensuring that your solution is potentially consumable each iteration is ensuring that it fulfills its overall quality goals, including applicable NFRs. This is particularly true with life-critical and mission-critical solutions. Good sources for NFRs include your enterprise architects and operations staff, although any stakeholder is a potential source for NFRs.

There are several ways that each of the five requirements views may be addressed. In some cases, such as usage modeling, the strategies are exclusive in that you should choose only one of user stories or use cases or usage scenarios. For user interface (UI) modeling the options are mostly complementary; it makes sense to create both UI sketches as well as UI flow diagrams in many situations. Table 8.2 lists some potential model types that you want to create, many of which are described in greater detail at www.agilemodeling.com/artifacts/, and the case study in Chapter 12, "Case Study: Inception Phase," shows some examples for some of them. A common challenge with several of the model types is that the existing culture surrounding them may motivate overmodeling on your team. For example, if you have people on the team who have deep experience in data modeling, and that experience was mostly on detailed up-front data modeling, their old habits may creep into your agile project and they may spend too much time data modeling as a result. Old modeling habits die hard.

Table 8.2 Comparing Requirements Modeling Options

Model Type	View	Use	Potential Advantages	Potential Disadvantages
Business process/data flow diagram	Process	Identify business processes, data sources, and data flow between them. Common notation option is Business Process Modeling Notation (BPMN).	Explore existing or potential process supported by the solution. When sketched collaboratively process diagrams can be an effective way to communicate with business stakeholders.	Complex BPMN notation can motivate overmodeling.
Business rule	General	Define a domain-oriented constraint on your solution, often part of the "done" criteria for functional requirements.	Defines critical business logic. Often acceptance criteria for one or more usage requirements. Well-defined body of knowledge around business rule identification.	Can promote overmodeling at beginning of the project due to BRUF culture among business rule experts.
Constraint	Non-functional	Identify some of the "done" criteria for functional requirements.	Understanding constraints can often speed up your development efforts because you have few options to consider.	Too many constraints can put you in a position where there is no viable solution.
Context diagram	General	Overview the primary users of a solution and their main interactions as well as any critical systems that the solution interacts with.	Overview how the solution fits into the overall organizational ecosystem. Often a key diagram for a vision statement (see Chapter 7), system overview documentation, and presentations to management.	Context diagrams are often created early in a project and then allowed to go stale and get out of sync with the actual implementation.

(continued)

Table 8.2   Comparing Requirements Modeling Options (continued)

Model Type	View	Use	Potential Advantages	Potential Disadvantages
Domain/conceptual model	Domain	Identify major business entities and their relationships. Typically captured using data models, entity relationship diagrams (ERDs), or Unified Modeling Language (UML) class diagrams.	Promotes a common understanding of domain terminology. Provides a high-level layout of your data schema and business class schema.	Can motivate overmodeling by people with a traditional data background.
Epic	Usage	Define a complex usage scenario that strings together a collection of related user stories.	Captures minimally marketable feature (MMF) for stakeholders. Provides higher-level view of requirements to stakeholders, making it easier to communicate scope.	Requires several iterations to complete, belying the claim that your solution is potentially consumable every iteration.
Feature statements	General	Capture a high-level list of the solution's key capabilities and benefits.	Straightforward approach to capturing functional requirements at a level your key stakeholders can easily understand. Generally small and easy to implement.	Value is less clear if feature isn't specific to a type of stakeholder. Since they are written at such an abstract level, they are as such ambiguous and can oversimplify what is required.
Flow chart	Process	Explore process logic.	Easy to teach stakeholders a simple form of flowcharting that in turn can be used to explore complex logic.	It can be difficult to depict complex scenarios in a comprehensible manner.

Model Type	View	Use	Potential Advantages	Potential Disadvantages
Mind map	General	Brainstorm and organize ideas and concepts.	Very visual and easy to understand. Structure similar ideas during a conversation. Supports collaborative idea generation, particularly when used with inclusive tools such as whiteboards or sticky notes.	Can be difficult to grow them past three or four levels of idea categorization.
Nonfunctional requirement (NFR)	Non-functional	Identify some of the "done" criteria for functional requirement. Address quality related requirements such as usability, reliability, performance, and supportability.	Captures aspects of your system that are critical to stakeholders, particularly IT stakeholders such as operations people. Explicitly identifies technical/quality aspects of your solution early in the lifecycles. Drive critical aspects of your architecture.	Desire to exactly specify NFRs can motivate "analysis paralysis" and lead to longer Inception efforts.
Persona	Usage	Describe a typical type of user, or person potentially affected by the solution.	Enables you to put other types of usage requirements into context by describing them from the point of view of a specific persona. Good option to put a human face on what you're doing when you don't have access to actual end users.	Can be used as an excuse to not work with actual end users.

(continued)

Table 8.2   Comparing Requirements Modeling Options (continued)

Model Type	View	Use	Potential Advantages	Potential Disadvantages
Shall statement	General	Formally identify functional or nonfunctional requirements in a Software Requirements Specification (SRS).	Supports contractual documentation requirements in some government and defense environments.	Can motivate overdocumentation by traditionally experienced modelers.
UI flow diagram/navigation map/storyboard	User interface	Explore how the various screens and reports all fit together.	Provide a high-level view of how major UI elements fit together to support one or more scenarios. Provide insight into potential consumability problems long before the UI is built.	Very few disadvantages to mocking up UI flows, as long as it is done in a low fidelity, efficient fashion, such as on a whiteboard.
UI prototype (high fidelity)	User interface	Identify the user-facing design of screens and reports and potentially the flow between them.	Concrete way to quickly explore what people want your solution to do. Identify a more consumable solution early in the lifecycle. Provide a mechanism to stakeholders to take portions of the solution for a "test drive" long before they're coded.	Desire to exactly define the UI, or to explore how all major UI elements work, can result in lengthy prototyping efforts. Prototyping tools may not exist for your platform, requiring potentially slower coding of the prototype. Some users believe that the system is "almost done" when they see high-fidelity screen prototypes.
UI prototype (low fidelity)/hand-drawn sketch	User interface	Identify requirements for screens and reports using inclusive tools such as paper and whiteboards.	Easily explore requirements for the UI in a platform-independent manner. Quickly explore potential UI design options without the overhead of high-fidelity UI prototyping.	Some stakeholders find low-fidelity UI prototyping too abstract.

Model Type	View	Use	Potential Advantages	Potential Disadvantages
UI specification	User interface	Define exactly how a screen or report is to be built by the development team.	Specify part of the solution to contract out to an external organization. Supports contractual or regulatory documentation requirements. Can help to ensure UI standards are met.	High potential to jump into design long before it's appropriate. Motivates overdocumentation of the UI, lengthening the Inception phase and increasing project cost. Evidence suggests that one of the highest rates of churn on new systems is related to UI changes. This can make it difficult if not impossible to keep UI specification up to date.
UML activity diagram	Process	Explore processes or activities and the control flow between them.	Allows for more sophisticated process modeling than flow charts, such as parallel processes and nested processes. Appropriate as an alternative for those who standardize on the UML notation.	Notation is not as rich for modeling business processes as BPMN.
UML use case diagram	Usage	Provide high-level overview of usage requirements, showing the key goals that the system fulfills, the roles of the users of the system, and the external systems with which the system needs to interact.	Simple, one or two page overview of the system. Explore usage requirements for missing, extraneous, or contradictory ideas. Organized detailed usage requirements such as user stories or shall statements. Provides the basis for organizing outlined or detailed requirements into specific documents.	Improperly applied, can lead to overspecification of the system. Not suitable for describing sophisticated user interactions such as geographic mapping software or real-time systems such as air traffic control systems.

(continued)

Table 8.2   Comparing Requirements Modeling Options (continued)

Model Type	View	Use	Potential Advantages	Potential Disadvantages
Usage scenarios	Usage	Describe a single end-to-end activity of someone working with the system.	Describes real business value to a collection of stakeholders. Puts the requirements of the system into the context of a workflow.	Usage scenarios can take several iterations to implement fully but have the advantage that they capture true business value to one or more stakeholders.
Use case specifications	Usage	Explore a coarse-grained, comprehensive view of a business activity. Capture the logic of a collection of related usage scenarios or user stories.	Describes real business value to a collection of stakeholders. Provides a more "whole system" view of related functionality, helping you to avoid inconsistencies and missing functionality. Puts the requirements of the system into the context of a workflow. Reuse by helping to identify test case scenarios.	Use cases are typically implemented in several iterations, requiring them to be split up (disaggregated). May promote overdocumentation when approached in an overly formal way.
State diagram	Process	Describe the lifecycle of the key entity states of the solution.	Suitable for modeling complex behaviors and states in real-time systems.	Not required for simplistic states of basic systems.

Model Type	View	Use	Potential Advantages	Potential Disadvantages
User stories	Usage	Describe small solution features that provide value to someone (or some organization).	Implementable in a single iteration. The favored approach of most agile teams. Not really true requirements, but rather placeholders for discussions with the stakeholders in lieu of requirements.	Often need to be combined into a collection to provide real business value to stakeholders, requiring organizational mechanisms such as themes or epics. Due to less structured elicitation, can result in material gaps in desired functionality, unless supplemented with other modeling techniques.
Value stream map	Process	Depict processes, the time spent performing them, and the time taken between them.	Identify potential inefficiencies in a process. Suitable when the focus on the solution is on improving the business flow rather than on building a solution to an existing business process.	This is an advanced lean technique that requires some in-depth sessions with stakeholders who have the authority to change their organization's business processes. It can take some time to do.

LESSONS FROM THE TRENCHES—INITIAL REQUIREMENTS ON AN ACTUAL
PROJECT

Tony Grout of IBM Rational UK recently coached a team through the latter stages of their
second major release using agile. This team still had challenges with the level of requirements detail, the granularity of their requirements, the format of their requirements, the definition of done, and their traceability to test cases and subsequent results. All of the
requirements were entered in to the team's work item management tool as simple text in the
description attribute of the user story work item, and there we no visual models at all. This
resulted in end of iteration reviews where it was challenging to understand what user stories
were left to do, in what order, and even what they meant.

To address this in the current release the team now has a clear definition of requirement
types starting with themes, then features followed by epics, and then user stories. Alongside
this they capture nonfunctional requirements (NFRs) when they span user stories. Each
user story can be complete within an iteration, and the team has decided that their granularity of epic should also fit in to a three-week iteration. They now use IBM Rational Requirements Composer (RRC) to describe the different requirement types, using simple text,
process models, glossaries, and storyboards. Links to corresponding test cases are also
captured. The team also developed a formal definition of done. This level of formality would
have felt alien to the "hard core agilists" had the team not experienced the pains of not knowing where they were or what they had left to build in any coherent way. The crisp definition
around the levels of granularity of requirements artifacts and their elements make tracking
progress, estimating, prioritizing, and traceability for impact analysis and quality management purposes straightforward.

The types of modeling you need to do varies based on your situation; one size does not fit
all. We suggest that you address each of the requirements views (usage, domain, process, user
interface, and nonfunctional) via the simplest techniques and tools most appropriate for your situation. A common selection to do so is the combination of user stories, a high-level domain
model (sketched), a high-level data flow diagram or use case diagram, sketches of several of the
key screens or reports, and a list of nonfunctional constraints.

Choosing a Modeling Strategy

During Inception you need to go about the actual work of eliciting and exploring requirements
with your stakeholders. There are several ways that you can do this, compared in Table 8.3:

- **Formal modeling sessions.** Formal modeling sessions typically have a professional
  facilitator, a predetermined set of rules and protocols for how people will interact, and
  often a predetermined schedule. A Joint Application Requirements (JAR) meeting is an

example of a formal modeling session strategy. Formal modeling sessions are often scheduled days if not weeks in advance and typically last for several hours at a time, and sometimes even several days.

- **Informal modeling sessions.** Informal modeling sessions are often led by someone, usually the product owner in the case of requirements modeling sessions, but there are no rules per se. Several people may talk at once, and if inclusive modeling tools such as whiteboards and paper are being used there may even be several people modeling at the same time (we consider sketching to be a form of modeling). Informal modeling sessions work well in rooms with lots of whiteboard space and shared table space for paper-based modeling.

- **Interviews.** The product owner, or someone else on the team, may choose to directly interview one or more stakeholders at a time. Interviews are most effective when they are face-to-face, although geographic dispersion may force you to hold them over the phone or even via email. Successful interviews are planned in advance—they are scheduled with the interviewees, reconfirmed if more than a few days have passed between the time they are scheduled and when they're held, and most importantly initial questions are prepared in advance.

LESSONS FROM THE TRENCHES—EVEN HARD-CORE AGILISTS GET FORMAL SOMETIMES

Scott was a participant in February 2011 in the tenth anniversary workshop of the Agile Manifesto (http://10yearsagile.org/). The goal of the workshop was to explore where the agile community has been and more importantly identify where it should be going in the next few years. Before the workshop many of us were concerned that we wouldn't achieve anything due to the range of strong personalities and contrasting strategies for making a living. To address these challenges Alistair Cockburn hired two professional facilitators to lead us through the discussion, and although they gave us inclusive tools (flipcharts and sticky notes) to capture information it was in effect a formal modeling session. Without the formality it was doubtful we would have achieved anything.

Table 8.3   Comparing Requirements Elicitation Strategies

Strategy	Potential Advantages	Potential Disadvantages	Considerations
Formal modeling sessions	Scales to dozens of people. Many people may get their opinions known during the session, enabling a wide range of stakeholders to be heard. Works well in regulatory environments.	Requires someone with solid facilitation skills (professional facilitators may need to be brought in). Can require significant overhead to organize. Can require significant lead time to schedule due to busy schedules of participants.	Your stakeholders likely need to do more than simply attend these formal modeling session(s), so make them aware of that early. Formal modeling sessions often devolve into ensuring that the specification (if any) is properly written. Instead the session(s) should focus on communication and collaboration.
Informal modeling sessions	Works well with groups of up to seven or eight stakeholders. Potential for collaborative and active modeling with stakeholders.	Requires some facilitation to ensure that a range of issues are addressed. Can require significant lead time to schedule.	Some stakeholders may see informal modeling sessions as unprofessional or a waste of their time, belying the need to communicate the value that you're getting from the sessions.
Interviews	Works well with groups of one to three stakeholders. May be only option with dispersed stakeholders. Much easier to schedule. Good way to begin understanding the needs of specific stakeholders before involving them in larger modeling sessions. Good way to follow up with specific stakeholders after modeling sessions.	Doesn't provide much opportunity for disparate stakeholders to interact with one another. Interviews are an expensive and time-consuming elicitation technique. Interviewees may have their own agendas, be politically motivated, and their opinions may not represent the larger group of stakeholders.	Interviewees often speak faster than you can write, so having a pair of interviewers, both of whom take notes, reduces this risk. You need to gain interviewing skills, so consider pairing with an experienced interviewer to help do so. Interview-only approaches may devolve into divide and conquer strategies for dealing with stakeholders in situations where it isn't easy to come to agreement.

Our advice is to keep your initial modeling sessions as informal as possible, supplementing with interviews where you need to when individual stakeholders aren't available for group work. The Agile Modeling (AM) method provides some valuable insights for ensuring that your initial requirements modeling efforts are successful. First, involve the full range of your stakeholders as best you can to ensure that you identify the true scope of your effort. Second, motivate them to participate as actively as possible. What we mean by that is find ways to get them involved with the actual modeling. Use inclusive modeling tools such as whiteboards and paper for working with them because those are tools that they know how to use. Don't try to force them to learn the complicated "standard" notations that technical professionals may prefer (if appropriate, intro-duce standard notations later in the lifecycle). Third, be prepared to invest the money to get people together. This can be particularly difficult when your stakeholders are geographically dis-tributed as many organizations are overly frugal when it comes to travel expenses. Getting your key stakeholders together in a single room to discuss the scope and vision for what your team needs to produce enables them to hear one another and make the trade-offs necessary for your team to be successful, thereby lowering your project risk. Not investing in travel can be a signifi-cantly more expensive proposition in the long run. Fourth, involve the other team members. Early in the project you may not have the entire team formed, in fact you're unlikely to have done so, but some team members will be identified. So invite them to any requirements modeling sessions or interviews so that they may hear what the stakeholders want, meet the people they'll hopefully be collaborating with later in the project, learn requirements elicitation skills, and most impor-tantly ask questions of and interact with your stakeholders.

Initial requirements modeling should consider ideal, constraint-free, out-of-the-box think-ing, but it is also constrained by the financial, technical, and schedule realities of your situation. Remember that initial requirements modeling occurs in parallel with other Inception activities. Both Mark and Scott have worked in organizations where for several days requirements were explored in the morning and architecture explored in the afternoon (often by many of the same people). We've also been involved in projects where the two concerns were addressed at the same time, a potentially dangerous proposition because stakeholders can feel their time is being wasted discussing technical issues better left to the technical people or worse yet business stakeholders who think they should be making key technical decisions based on their extensive knowledge gained by reading a few magazine articles. Similarly, initial requirements modeling will also occur in parallel to your release planning efforts. The scope that you're able to deliver will be constrained by both your budget and desired delivery date. The implication is that scope, budget, and schedule need to be negotiated with your stakeholders while remaining as flexible as pos-sible. Smart organizations know that they should build solutions that meet their stakeholders' needs over something to specification, that they should spend the money wisely over aiming for a specified budget, that they should release the solution when it is most appropriate and not neces-sarily to a specified delivery date, and that they should do so while producing the requisite quality.

Choosing a Work Item Management Strategy

The initial requirements that you identify during Inception will evolve throughout your project—details will emerge, new requirements will be identified, and existing requirements will be dropped—resulting from close collaboration with stakeholders. You may also have potential defects and enhancement requests being reported from your operations and support teams who are working with existing versions of your solution, or in complex situations potential defects from an independent test team working in parallel to your delivery team (more on this in Chapter 13, "The Construction Phase"). Because your team is likely one of many within your organizational ecosystem, you may receive requests to review the work of other teams, to collaborate with them to ensure that your solution works well with what they're producing, and other similar requests. Individual team members will have personal requests to attend training classes, take vacations, attend conferences, and a variety of other matters. All these work items should be managed and acted on by your team accordingly, and the strategy that you choose is determined in part by the level of initial requirements detail that you've chosen to support.

There are several common strategies, compared in Table 8.4, for managing work items:

- **Formal change management.** The work to be performed is typically defined in detail and agreed to early in the project, and any changes to that planned work are then managed throughout the lifecycle. In simple situations the product owner is responsible for considering and acting on change requests for requirements or defect reports, although at scale a change control board (CCB) may exist who would meet regularly (hopefully at least once an iteration) to manage any change requests. The team lead is typically responsible for making decisions pertaining to requests from other teams or personal requests. Part of deciding whether to accept a change may include analysis to determine the impact/cost of the change versus the priority and business value for the customer.

- **Scrum product backlog.** A foundational concept in Scrum is that requirements, and optionally defect reports, should be managed as a prioritized stack called a product backlog. The contents of the product backlog vary to reflect evolving requirements, with the product owner responsible for prioritizing work on the backlog based on the business value of the work item. Just enough work to fit into the current iteration is taken off the top of the stack by the team at the start of each iteration as part of the iteration planning activity (see Chapter 14).

- **Work item stack.** This is an extension to Scrum's product backlog to include all types of work items (requirements, defects, technical items, team collaboration requests, and personal requests). Work items are prioritized based on a variety of considerations, including both stakeholder value (an extension of business value to address all stakeholder concerns, not just business ones) and team health considerations. To reduce technical risk on your project a DAD team will prove that their architectural strategy works by creating a working, end-to-end skeleton that implements several high-risk requirements. Although risk and value often go hand-in-hand the relationship isn't perfect, the end result being that the product owner pushes a few requirements to the top of the stack that may not be the highest business value ones. More on this in Chapters 13 and 14. Figure 8.3 depicts the work item stack strategy.

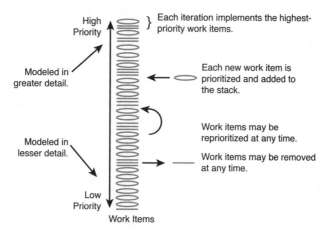

Figure 8.3 An agile work item stack

- **Work item pool.** A lean approach to work item management is depicted in Figure 8.4. This strategy explicitly recognizes that there are different ways to prioritize work items—the "standard way" based on stakeholder value, time-dependent strategies that reflect defined delivery dates, the occasional emergency/high-priority work item that must be expedited, and the intangible team health work items captured in personal requests. Anyone can identify work items and place them in the pool, although the product owner (if one exists) is most likely to focus on doing so. The entire team, including the product owner, is responsible for pulling work from the work item pool appropriately. The work item to pull is determined at the point in time that the team has capacity to pull a new work item into their process.

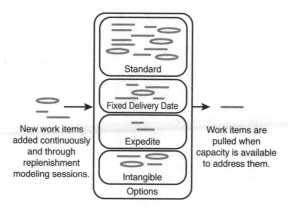

Figure 8.4 A lean work item pool

Table 8.4   Comparing Work Item Management Strategies

Strategy	Potential Advantages	Potential Disadvantages	Considerations
Formal change management	Can work well in some regulatory situations where it is mandated that changes are managed this way. Works well for environments where the requirements seldom change.	Motivates stakeholders to follow a BRUF approach and thereby take on all the disadvantages of that strategy. Can motivate onerous requirements traceability efforts to aid impact analysis efforts of the CCB. Can add significant overhead to the project team, particularly when requirements do in fact change. Work item prioritization strategy is still required.	Strict "change management" strategies can often devolve into change prevention strategies. For small changes, the overhead of considering the change may be greater than the cost of actually implementing it.
Scrum product backlog	Simple to understand and implement. Stakeholders allowed to define new requirements and evolve existing ones. Requires additional strategy to manage other work item types.	Must be groomed throughout the project lifecycle to maintain priority order. Requires supporting strategy to address nonfunctional requirements (NFRs).	Practitioners new to agile often adopt an overly simplistic approach that focuses only on managing functional requirements.
Work item stack	See Scrum product backlog benefits. Explicitly manages all work item types in a single, consistent manner. Addresses high risk work earlier as compared to above strategies.	Increases responsibilities of product owner to address team health and collaboration considerations. Must be groomed throughout the project lifecycle. Requires NFR strategy. See below.	Team health may erode because personal requests are ignored in favor of function-oriented work items (requirements and defects).

Strategy	Potential Advantages	Potential Disadvantages	Considerations
Work item pool	Addresses several prioritization schemes.	Requires teams to be responsible and disciplined. Requires teams to consider a variety of issues, including stakeholder value, risk, team health, and enterprise issues. Can be threatening to traditional organizations used to telling teams what their priorities are. Requires strict control over the number of work items to be expedited.	You need to be strict as to which requests are marked expedite; otherwise, requests in other categories are never addressed. Teams new to agile/lean may prioritize team health considerations or infrastructure work over delivering stakeholder value.
No strategy	No overhead. Works for very small or simple projects or research projects.	Significant potential for low value work to be implemented in favor of high value work.	This could be a sign of an ad-hoc project team posing as an agile team.

In most situations our advice is to first adopt the work item stack approach, and after you become comfortable with it, and if your organizational culture allows it, move toward the lean work item pool strategy.

Choosing a Strategy for Nonfunctional Requirements

As your stakeholders tell you about functional requirements they will also describe nonfunctional requirements (NFRs). These NFRs may describe security access rights, availability requirements, performance concerns, or a host of other issues as you see in Figure 8.5. (This diagram is used with permission from www.agilemodeling.com.) There are three basic strategies, compared in Table 8.5, for capturing NFRs:

- **Technical stories.** A technical story is a documentation strategy where the NFR is captured as a separate entity that is meant to be addressed in a single iteration. Technical stories are in effect the NFR equivalent of a user story. For example, "The system will be unavailable to end users no more than 30 seconds a week" and "Only the employee, their direct manager, and manager-level human resource people have access to salary information about said employee" are both examples of technical stories.

- **Acceptance criteria for individual functional requirements.** Part of the strategy of ensuring that a work item is done at the end of an iteration is to verify that it meets all of its acceptance criteria. Many of these acceptance criteria will reflect NFRs specific to an individual usage requirement, such as "Salary information read-only accessible by the employee," "Salary information read-only accessible by their direct manager," "Salary information read/write accessible by HR managers," and "Salary information is not accessible to anyone without specific access rights."

- **Explicit list.** Capture NFRs separately from your work item list in a separate artifact. This provides you with a reminder for the issues to consider when formulating acceptance criteria for your functional requirements. In the Unified Process this artifact was called a supplementary specification.

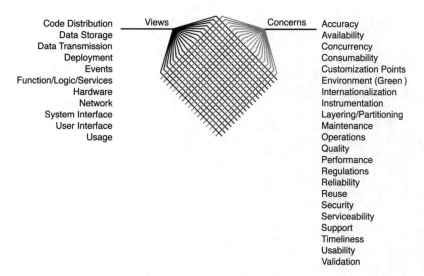

Figure 8.5 Potential architectural views and concerns

Our advice in most situations is to have the explicit list and then use that to drive identification of acceptance criteria as we've found that it's more efficient and lower risk in the long run. Of course capturing NFRs is only one part of the overall process of addressing them. You also need to implement and validate them during construction, as well as address them in your architecture.

Table 8.5   Comparing NFR Capture Strategies

Strategy	Potential Advantages	Potential Disadvantages	Considerations
Technical stories	Simple strategy for capturing NFRs. Works well for solutions with a few simple NFRs.	Many NFRs are cross-cutting aspects to several functional stories, so cannot be implemented within a single iteration.	Beware of leaving NFRs to the end of the construction phase because this effectively pushes technical risk to the end of the lifecycle.
Acceptance criteria	Quality focused approach that makes the complexity of an individual functional requirement apparent. Works well with test-driven approaches to development (see Chapter 15). NFR details are typically identified on a just-in-time (JIT) basis during construction.	Because many NFRs are cross-cutting, the same NFR will be captured for many functional requirements. Requires the team to remember and consider all potential NFR issues (refer to Figure 8.4) for each functional requirement.	You should still consider NFRs as part of your initial architecture efforts; otherwise, you risk a major rework effort during the Construction phase because you missed a critical cross-cutting concern.
Explicit list	Enables you to explore NFRs early in the lifecycle and then address them in your architecture. List can be used to drive identification of acceptance criteria on a JIT basis.	NFR documents can become long for complex systems. Some NFRs are specific to a small number of functional requirements.	Some teams will not write down the nonfunctional requirements and trust that they will remember to address them when they're identifying acceptance criteria for individual stories.
No strategy	Works well in very simple situations.	Significant risk of building a solution that doesn't meet the operational needs of the stakeholders.	This is often a symptom of teams only working with a small subset of their stakeholder types (e.g., only working with end users but not operations staff, senior managers, and so on).

Concluding Thoughts

In general it is common for agile teams to perform some initial requirements modeling at the beginning of a project. The goal to identify the initial scope for your project—it may evolve later in the project—is explicitly included in the Inception phase. As you learned in this chapter you need to consider several critical issues as you tailor your strategy to reflect the situation that you face. This chapter described these issues, the options that you have available to you, and the trade-offs associated with each. We also described our preferred strategies, which are the following:

- **Level of initial detail.** Do some lightweight requirements envisioning during Inception, with the exception of regulatory situations where detailed specifications are actually mandated, and explore the details later during construction in a just-in-time (JIT) manner.

- **Model types.** Address each of the requirements views (usage, domain, process, user interface, and nonfunctional) via the simplest techniques and tools most appropriate for your situation. A common selection to do so is the combination of user stories, a high-level domain model (sketched), a high-level data flow diagram or use case diagram, sketches of several of the key screens or reports, and a list of nonfunctional constraints.

- **Modeling strategy.** Keep your initial modeling sessions as informal as possible, supplementing with interviews when individual stakeholders aren't available for group work.

- **Work item management strategy.** Treat all work items—including requirements, reported defects, training requests, requests for assistance from other teams, and so on—as a prioritized stack.

- **Nonfunctional requirements (NFRs) strategy.** Identify and maintain a list of NFRs and use them to drive identification of acceptance criteria for functional requirements.

Additional Resources

For more detailed discussions about several of the topics covered in this chapter:

- **Agile surveys.** Throughout the chapter we referenced several surveys. The results from the Dr. Dobb's Journal (DDJ) and Ambysoft surveys are posted at ambysoft.com/surveys/, including the original source data, questions as they were asked, as well as slide decks summarizing Scott Ambler's analysis. Project initiation stats were taken from the 2009 Project Initiation survey.

- **Agile requirements modeling.** Several detailed articles are posted at agilemodeling. com about agile requirements practices, including initial requirements envisioning, active stakeholder participation, agile requirements best practices, and the importance of inclusive modeling.

- **The value of modeling.** The issues surrounding the value of modeling are discussed in detail by Scott at agilemodeling.com/essays/barelyGoodEnough.html.
- **Requirements by collaboration.** Ellen Gottesdiener's *Requirements by Collaboration: Workshops for Defining Needs* (Addison-Wesley, 2002) is a great book that describes fundamental requirements elicitation workshop techniques.
- **Big requirements up front (BRUF).** The BRUF approach, and the impact of following it, is discussed in detail at agilemodeling.com/essays/examiningBRUF.htm.
- **Work item management.** The work item management strategies discussed in this chapter are described in greater detail at agilemodeling.com/essays/prioritizedRequirements.htm.

CHAPTER 9

Identifying an Initial Technical Strategy

The most effective way to deal with technical debt is to avoid it in the first place.

Early in a Disciplined Agile Delivery (DAD) project you need to have at least a general idea of how you're going to build the system, or in some cases several good options to proceed. Is it a mainframe COBOL application, a .Net application, enterprise Java, something else, or combinations thereof? During the Inception phase the key developers on the team, ideally everyone on the team at that point, identify one or more potential architectural strategies that supports the stakeholder goals for the solution. Despite what some core agilists suggest, surveys show that most teams spend some time modeling their envisioned architectures before committing their ideas to code. The 2009 Agile Project Initiation survey found that 86% of respondents indicated that their agile teams did some sort of up-front architectural modeling.

It is important to observe that there is always a solution architecture. Always. It may not be documented well, a strategy may not have been identified before work began on the solution, and it may not be the best architecture for the situation at hand, but the architecture exists nonetheless. From the point of view of DAD, a solution architecture strategy is the set of guidelines, patterns, and constraints that guide a development effort. This strategy often explains desired partitioning and partitioning patterns, and often names layers or indicates some other organizational approach to be taken with the system under construction. Additional elements of a solution architecture strategy might include other viewpoints, common patterns to be instantiated whenever appropriate, and constraints.

There are several benefits to doing some initial architectural modeling at the beginning of an agile project:

- **Improved productivity.** You can think through some of the critical technical issues facing your project and potentially avoid going down fruitless technical paths.

- **Reduced technical risk.** Your team gains the advantage of having a guiding vision without the disadvantage of having to overbuild your system—just because you've modeled it doesn't mean you have to build it.

- **Technical debt avoidance.** By thinking through critical technical issues before you implement your solution you have the opportunity to avoid a technical strategy that needs to be reworked at a future date. The most effective way to deal with technical debt is to avoid it in the first place.

- **Improved enterprise awareness.** Looking at the big picture provides a systems perspective, supporting the lean concept of optimizing the whole. DAD teams work closely with your organization's enterprise architects, if you have any, to ensure that their strategy reflects your organization's overall long-term strategy. An important consideration is whether your team should enhance, rework, or even replace part of your existing infrastructure as part of your overall enterprise modernization goals.

- **Improved development/operations (DevOps) integration.** Because DAD teams are enterprise aware they understand the importance of the overall system lifecycle, which includes the delivery activities that are a focus of this book and the operations activities involved with operating and supporting the solution once it has been deployed. During architecture envisioning DAD teams work closely with operations staff to ensure that their solution addresses their needs. This potentially includes mundane issues such as backup and restore of data and version control of delivered assets as well as more complex issues, such as instrumentation of your solution so that operations may monitor it effectively and even control it remotely as needed. DAD teams strive to address DevOps issues throughout the entire lifecycle, starting with initial envisioning efforts.

- **Reduced development time.** Initial agile architecture envisioning gets you on a viable technical strategy from the very start, enabling you to avoid lost time due to major rework.

- **Address the nonfunctional "ilities" early.** An important part of ensuring that your solution conforms to the nonfunctional requirements—ilities such as availability, reliability, security, consumability, and others—is to identify an architectural vision that addresses them.

- **Improved communication.** Having a high-level architecture model helps you to communicate what you think you're going to build and how you think that you'll build it, two more critical pieces of information desired by management.

- **Scaling agile software development.** Your initial architecture model will be a key work product in any "agile at scale" efforts because it provides the technical direction required by subteams to define and guide their efforts within the overall project. This was discussed in greater detail in Chapter 5, "Forming Disciplined Agile Delivery Teams."

The goal of this chapter is to overview the critical process trade-offs that your team will make regarding your initial architecture efforts. It is not to go into detail about exactly how to go about architecting your solution (resources for that are provided at the end of the chapter). Figure 9.1 shows a mind map of the structure of this chapter. We describe each of the topics in the map in clockwise order, beginning at the top right.

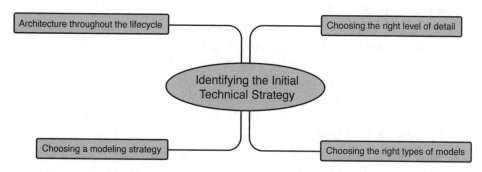

Figure 9.1   Outline of this chapter

THE BIG IDEAS IN THIS CHAPTER

- DAD teams typically explore the potential architecture for their solution before beginning construction.

- DAD teams work closely with your organization's enterprise architects, when they exist, to ensure that they leverage as much of the existing infrastructure as possible and to ensure their solution evolves the infrastructure in a manner that reflects your organization's technical strategy.

- DAD teams defer architecture and design decisions to the most appropriate point in the project to make them. For some decisions this is during the Inception phase, for many others this is during the Construction phase.

- DAD teams explore the technical strategy to the solution from several viewpoints.

Choosing the Right Level of Detail

When it comes to architectural modeling, the primary goal at the beginning of the project is to identify what you believe to be a viable technical strategy for your solution. There are several levels of architectural specification detail, compared in Table 9.1, for you to choose from:

- **Detailed end-to-end.** You can specify your architecture in a detailed manner through all architectural layers. For a business application this would include detailed specification of the mechanisms for how the various components/subsystems (user interface, business, persistence, security, messaging, and so on) work. This includes a detailed specification of the interfaces of these components and their subcomponents as well as details about how these components are to be built. This level of detail often proves to be a medium-to-highly detailed design.

- **Detailed interface.** With this approach you identify the main components/subsystems of your architecture and define in detail the interfaces to the components. Depending on the underlying technologies, these interfaces may be Web service definitions, Java interface definitions, application programming interfaces (APIs), or even business entity definitions to be implemented by your persistence framework. This technique of defining the interface is called API First in the Eclipse Way (the agile process followed by the Eclipse team) and Contract Model in Agile Modeling.

- **High-level overview.** In the middle ground there are lightweight, high-level agile models that are sufficient (but no more)[1] for your needs at the time. These agile architectural models are created following a practice called Architecture Envisioning adopted from Agile Modeling, which is performed over several hours or days as appropriate, not several weeks or months as seen in traditional environments. To do this the developers on the project typically get together in a room, often around a whiteboard, discuss and then sketch out a potential architecture for the solution. With architectural envisioning the strategy at this point is to identify an architectural strategy, not create detailed architectural models. The detailed design will be thought through during construction on a just-in-time (JIT) basis via techniques such as model storming and test-driven development (TDD), both of which are described in Chapter 8, "Identifying the Initial Scope."

- **None.** Some teams in fact do not do any up-front architectural envisioning at all.

---

1. Many agilists prefer the term *just barely good enough (JBGE)*.

Table 9.1 Comparing Levels of Initial Architecture Detail

Strategy	Potential Advantages	Potential Disadvantages	Considerations
Detailed end-to-end specification	Define exactly how you intend to have the solution built. Enables multiple subteams to work on components/subsystems in parallel. Meets the legal requirements of some industry regulations.	Details can deceive people into believing that the architecture will actually work (when it still hasn't been proven to), thereby increasing project risk. Important decisions are made early in the project based on information that is likely to evolve, thereby increasing project risk. Decreases morale of developers by taking away the challenges associated with architectural work. Increases overhead to evolve the architecture when the requirements change or the chosen technologies evolve. Supports a documentation-based governance strategy, increasing organizational risk. Increases length of time spent on Inception. Potentially increases the chance that you will overbuild your solution, which increases both cost and delivery time.	Detailed specifications will not alleviate fundamental staffing problems. For example, providing a detailed technical specification to low-skilled developers will likely lead to a low-quality implementation. Beware of "required" specifications solely needed to justify the existence of the people reviewing them.

(continued)

Table 9.1   Comparing Levels of Initial Architecture Detail (continued)

Strategy	Potential Advantages	Potential Disadvantages	Considerations
Detailed interfaces	Enables multiple subteams to work on components/subsystems in parallel. Enables you to mock or stub out the interfaces to components early.	The interface will still need to evolve throughout the project, although hopefully not much, requiring negotiation between the owning subteam and customers of the evolving component. Increases length of time spent on Inception. Potentially increases the chance that you will overbuild your solution, which increases both cost and delivery time.	Overly detailed interface definitions run the risk of specifying the internal design of the components. Too little specification of an interface risks implementations with unexpected side effects.
Light/high-level overview	Reduces project risk because critical technical issues are thought through. Enables team to coalesce around a technical vision. Enables flexibility, particularly when architectural options are left open. Detailed design decisions can be deferred to when they can be most appropriately made.	Requires greater collaboration between team members. Requires team members to have greater design and architecture skills. Team members making deferred decisions must be aware of enterprise architectural direction and guidelines. Can motivate overbuilding your solution early in the lifecycle.	Avoid deferring high-risk technical decisions that should be made at the beginning of the delivery lifecycle—sometimes the best time to make a decision is early in the project.
No modeling at all	Works well for very simple solutions produced by very small teams. Shortens the Inception effort.	Team members don't have a common vision to work to, resulting in confusion and wasted effort. Too many decisions are deferred to Construction, resulting in rework.	This can be a symptom of ad-hoc teams posing as agile teams by claiming they don't need to model or write documentation.

LESSONS FROM THE TRENCHES—IDENTIFY AND STUB OUT SYSTEM INTERFACES EARLY

Andy Pittaway is an Executive Project Manager in IBM Global Services in the U.K., having applied agile techniques at scale for many years. "A key area of risk that we find is the integration of the solution we are writing with other systems. This is particularly true when the other systems and interfaces are also being changed in parallel to our project. We identify those systems during initial architecture modeling so that we understand the potential risks we face regarding overall system integration. In these instances we ask for (or develop) a testing stub in one of our early iterations and then look to replace it with either a better stub or the final system as early as we can later in the project. It is true that this introduces all sorts of new risks, as often the stub will not fully represent the final solution developed and so a lot of attention is required around these. A critical point is that both the interfaces and also integrating the solution with other components (internal and external) are major sources of risk that we want to address early in the project."

How much detail you require to describe your chosen strategy depends on your team culture, your organizational culture, whether any external regulations apply, and the organizational strategy if your team is large. Some teams have cultures that lean toward detailed architectural specifications, whereas other teams are comfortable with high-level diagrams or sketches. Similarly some organizations prefer detailed specifications, although as agile strategies gain greater acceptance we're seeing a move toward less architectural specification in favor of greater collaboration. Some industry regulations, particularly when it comes to safety-critical or life-critical systems, motivate the creation of detailed specifications early in a project. Finally, as you saw in Chapter 5, when a large DAD team is organized into smaller component subteams you will not only want to define what those components are but also a detailed definition of the interface to each one.

Our advice is to keep your initial architectural modeling effort as light as possible and when possible keep your options open. So, instead of deciding on a farm of IBM Websphere® application servers, instead decide that you use a Websphere-based approach with certain performance characteristics. You can decide later whether you'll run it on a single large machine, a server farm, in an internal cloud that your organization hosts, or even in a cloud hosted by an external provider. Identify the decisions that you need to make now and make them, and defer other decisions until the latest responsible moment to do so (a lean strategy).

We also recommend that you consider starting an architecture handbook at this time. This "handbook," which is often captured via a wiki, contains the main architectural diagrams that you choose to maintain. It also captures your key architectural decisions, and relevant thinking behind them, to support future maintenance and enhancement efforts. The architecture handbook is the key component of your solution overview documentation.

Lessons from the Trenches—Architect Early, but Defer Details

Jim Densmore, a technical solution architect at IBM Rational, has found that even on small projects there's value in initial architecture modeling. "In the late '90s we worked on a proto-type telephone call routing system for a major telecommunications firm which needed to be responsive to rapid, chaotic changes in the telephony government regulations environment. My team built a GUI to permit the legislative analysts a vehicle for teaching our call routing platform how to route calls legally. A significant architectural question was how to persist the object data, and someone on the team suggested using a commercial object database at the start of the project so we could all gain experience with this emerging technology. The only problem is that the technology, while mature today and extremely useful, was really still prototypical then, and we incurred significant delays and expense just getting it to work. During Construction we learned a lot about the actual requirements pertaining to the data store. We also realized that much of this information were requirements we understood reasonably well at the start of the project. Too late we realized that our learnings made it obvious that a standard relational database, or even a file-based storage mechanism, would have been better choices for persistence."

What this team should have done is identify an architectural need for a persistence mechanism to address persistence requirements such as access speed, write speed, typical size or granularity of reads and writes, patterns for reading and writing, and so on. The actual choice for how to implement this mechanism should have been left until enough information was present to make those choices well, and it shouldn't have been driven by the resume-building desires of some of the team members. "Had we waited until we knew what we needed instead of prematurely assigning an object database for persistence we would have saved ourselves a ton of development dollars. We would have completely avoided the need to train support and maintenance personnel on a new database system with which they had no prior experience," believes Jim.

Choosing the Right Types of Models

Regardless of the level of detail, your architectural modeling efforts typically focus on several major views:

- **Technology.** The primary goal of technology diagrams is to explore the high-level structure of the hardware or software (or both) and how they fit together. This includes free-form diagrams, technology stack diagrams, network diagrams, and UML component diagrams.

- **Business architecture.** These models explore how business concepts and activities are implemented by the solution, including several "requirements models" described previously as well as diagrams also used for more technical purposes.

- **User interface (UI).** Many of the UI models discussed previously for requirements modeling are also used to explore architecture and design issues, too. For example, is the UI flow of your system a requirements issue, a user experience (UX) architectural issue, or a usability/consumability design issue? The answer is yes to all three concerns, the implication being UI flow diagrams could be applied for requirements, architecture, or design purposes. The categorization doesn't matter; the critical issue is whether the creation of the diagram adds value.

Common types of models that can be used to explore these architectural modeling views are described in Table 9.2. Figure 9.2 depicts the range of detailed views and concerns that should be considered when you are addressing the major views listed previously. Many of these views and concerns address potential categories of nonfunctional requirements for your solution, discussed in Chapter 8. Examples of many of these model types can be found at agilemodeling.com/artifacts/.

As with initial requirements modeling the types of models that you will create vary on your situation. We've found that it is common for teams to create some sort of architectural overview diagram, usually a stack diagram or a free-form diagram, and a diagram that explores hardware topology issues, such as a deployment diagram or network diagram. Not as common, and often to their detriment, is a mechanism such as a wiki page or a shared text file, where the team captures their important architectural decisions.

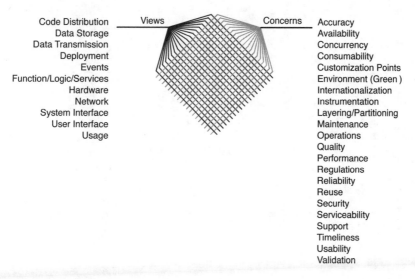

Figure 9.2 Potential architectural views and concerns

Table 9.2 Comparing Architecture Modeling Options

Model Type	View	Use	Potential Advantages	Potential Disadvantages
Architectural stack diagram	Technology	Describe a high-level, layered view, of the hardware or software (or both) of your solution.	Explores fundamental issues around architectural organization. Best suited for layered architectures. Well understood by most IT and systems professionals.	Sometimes used to describe architectures based on a network of components or services for which it is not well suited.
Business process/data flow diagram	Business architecture	Identify business processes, data sources, and data flow between them. Common notation option is Business Process Modeling Notation (BPMN).	Explore existing or potential process supported by the solution. When sketched collaboratively process diagrams can be an effective way to communicate with business stakeholders.	Complex BPMN notation can motivate over modeling.
Change cases	General	Change cases explore what could change, either from a tech or a business point of view.	Drives many important architectural decisions. Often sufficient to discuss them informally while modeling; they don't always need to be captured.	Significant potential for analysis paralysis when discussions of "what if" get too detailed.
Critical decisions	General	Capture the reasons behind important or potentially unclear aspects of your architecture or design.	Provides reminders to the team as to why they made the decisions that they made months or years earlier. Can help to avoid arguments about the trade-offs that you purposefully made earlier in the project.	Document can become cluttered and difficult to use when too many low-level design decisions are captured.

Model Type	View	Use	Potential Advantages	Potential Disadvantages
Deployment diagram	Technology	Explore how the major hardware components work together and map major software components to them (solution topology).	Well understood by most IT and systems professionals.	Diagrams can become large in complex environments.
Domain/ conceptual model	Business architecture	Identify major business entities and their relationships. Typically captured using data models, entity relationship diagrams (ERDs), or Unified Modeling Language (UML) class diagrams.	Promotes a common understanding of domain terminology. Provides a high level layout of your data schema and business class schema.	Can motivate overmodeling by people with a traditional data background.
Free-form diagram	General	Explore any architectural aspect.	Very flexible and likely the most common form of architecture diagram. Very inclusive strategy when several people are modeling together around a whiteboard or paper.	–
Network diagram	Technology	Model the layout of major hardware elements and their interconnections (network topology).	Well understood by most IT and systems professionals.	Can become very large.

(continued)

Table 9.2   Comparing Architecture Modeling Options (continued)

Model Type	View	Use	Potential Advantages	Potential Disadvantages
Threat model	Technology	Consider security threats via a form of deployment/network diagram.	Straightforward way to explore security threats to your solution long before you build/buy it. Threat boundaries can be indicated on almost any type of architecture diagram, although a specific diagram is often useful.	Can be used by the team to mask a lack of security expertise by making it appear that they've considered the issues.
UI flow diagram/ navigation map/storyboard	User interface	Explore how the various screens and reports all fit together.	Provide a high-level view of how major UI elements will fit together to support one or more scenarios. Provide insight into potential consumability problems long before the UI is built.	Very few disadvantages to mocking up UI flows, as long as it is done in a low fidelity, efficient fashion, such as on a whiteboard.
UI prototype (high fidelity)	User interface	Concrete way to quickly explore what people want your solution to do. Identify a more consumable solution early in the lifecycle. Provide a mechanism to stakeholders to take portions of the solution for a "test drive" long before they're coded. Identify the user-facing design of screens and reports and potentially the flow between them.	Desire to exactly define the UI, or to explore how all major UI elements work, can result in lengthy prototyping efforts. Prototyping tools may not exist for your platform, requiring potentially slower coding of the prototype. Some users believe that the system is "almost done" when they see high-fidelity screen prototypes.	Identify the user-facing design of screens and reports and potentially the flow between them.
UML component diagram	Technical, business architecture	Describe software components or subsystems, and their interrelationships (software topology).	Can be used to explore either technical or business architecture issues.	Can easily become overly complex.

LESSONS FROM THE TRENCHES—APPLICATION INSTRUMENTATION TO SUPPORT DEVOPS

A few years ago Scott was the team lead for an application at a large Canadian financial institution. One of the cross-cutting requirements was to instrument the application to enable support staff to provide better service to end users. The basic idea was that when an error was detected by the application, such as a database connection being lost, it would first do its best to recover from the problem. Failing that the application displayed an appropriate message to the end user, logged the issue into the help desk system, and displayed the problem along with contact information for the end user on the screen of the appropriate support person if someone was currently available. This in turn enabled the support person to immediately call the end user and help them through the problem, dramatically improving overall service.

Choosing a Modeling Strategy

There are four critical issues you must consider when modeling your solution's architecture during the Inception phase:

- **Identify how much modeling you need to do.** For a large majority of project teams many of the technical architecture decisions have already been made for them years earlier. Your organization will have already chosen a network infrastructure, an application server platform, a database platform, and so on. In these situations your team needs to invest the time to understand those decisions and to consider whether the existing infrastructure build-out is sufficient (and if not identify potential improvements). These teams find that they need to do little architectural modeling at all, other than perhaps to identify the aspects of the infrastructure that they intend to leverage and enhance—the logistics of getting everyone together aside, this should be hours of work and days at most, certainly not weeks or months. Occasionally a team finds itself in a situation where they are in fact building a truly new solution and are formulating a new architectural strategy to support it. This is often the case when your solution supports entering a new market or is purposefully replacing an antiquated legacy solution; both of these are risky endeavors requiring a bit more thinking. These situations are likely to require several days of initial architecture modeling, logistics aside.

- **Get the right people involved.** Architectural modeling is inherently a team sport, often requiring a range of people and viewpoints for it to be successful. For small and medium-sized teams you should have all team members who are currently available involved with your modeling effort to improve the quality of what is produced as well as to increase buy-in to the overall vision. For large teams this may not be viable, with your likely architecture owners and other key team members involved. You should also invite some of your technical-leaning stakeholders, in particular the enterprise architects (if any) that will be supporting your team and knowledgeable operations staff. The enterprise architects will provide guidance as to the desired technical direction of your organization and should be able to suggest potentially reusable assets that your team can leverage as well as applicable development guidelines. Your operations staff will provide insight into current and forecast loads within your production environment, potential limits regarding your production environment, and strategies to address any challenges.

- **Choose the right level of formality.** The level of formality for your architectural modeling efforts typically reflects the level of formality of your requirements modeling efforts—formal architectural modeling goes with formal requirements modeling, informal architectural modeling goes with informal requirements modeling, and no requirements or architectural modeling at all tend to go together. Table 9.3 compares the two approaches to initial architecture modeling.

- **One initial strategy or several?** In some situations, particularly when you're building something completely new for your organization, it makes sense to identify several potential technical strategies and work on them in parallel until one clear winner emerges. Table 9.4 compares and contrasts these two approaches.

We've found that informal architecture modeling sessions work best in most situations, although occasionally there is the need for formal sessions due to the inclusion of a few strong-willed people. Most applications need only to have a single solution architecture strategy identified for them, although multiple strategies are likely to be considered in the process of driving to that single candidate.

Table 9.3 Comparing Architectural Modeling Strategies

Strategy	Potential Advantages	Potential Disadvantages	Considerations
Formal modeling sessions	Scales to dozens of people. Many people may get their opinions known during the session, enabling a wide range of people to be heard. Works well in regulatory environments. Works well in contentious situations where extra effort is required to keep the conversation civil or to avoid someone dominating the conversation.	Requires someone with solid facilitation skills (professional facilitators may need to be brought in). Can require significant overhead to organize. Can require significant lead time to schedule due to busy schedules of participants.	"Architecture by consensus" often results in a mediocre technical vision. Formal modeling sessions risk devolving into specification focused, instead of communication focused, efforts.
Informal modeling sessions	Works well with groups of up to seven or eight people. Potential for very collaborative and active modeling with stakeholders.	Requires some facilitation to ensure that a range of issues are addressed. Can require significant lead time to schedule.	Experienced architects, including enterprise architects that your team relies on, may not be comfortable with informal modeling.

Table 9.4 Single Versus Multiple Architecture Strategies

Strategy	Potential Advantages	Potential Disadvantages	Considerations
Single candidate architecture	Works very well when the technical environment is (mostly) known.	Can be expensive if your initial architectural strategy proves wrong late in the lifecycle.	Prove your architecture early in Construction with working code; see Chapter 14, "Initiating a Construction Iteration."
Multiple candidate architectures	Viable strategy for new product development when time-to-market is critical. Increases chance that the best architectural strategy is taken. Several candidate architectures explored, reducing technical arguments later.	Can initially be expensive.	Few organizations will adopt this strategy due to the increased initial expense, so be prepared to justify this approach.

Architecture Throughout the Lifecycle

Defining the technical strategy at the beginning of the project is just the start. As you see in Part 4, "Building a Consumable Solution Incrementally," of this book, which focuses on the Construction phase, architecture is so important for DAD teams we continue to evolve it throughout the project. The architecture owner guides the team through understanding and evolving the architecture, mentoring people in architecture, and other skills as appropriate. Early in Construction the team proves the architecture with working code, a strategy described in greater detail in Chapter 15, "A Typical Day of Construction," to help reduce the technical risk on the project. The architecture owner ensures that the architecture handbook is kept up to date throughout the Construction phase. Your team should also work closely with your organization's enterprise architects and operations staff, if they are available, to ensure that you are leveraging and enhancing the existing infrastructure whenever possible.

Concluding Thoughts

It is common for DAD teams to invest some effort in identifying what they believe to be a viable technical strategy before beginning Construction. This architectural vision is likely to evolve throughout your project, like it or not and regardless of how much effort you put into initially defining it, because your understanding of both the problem domain and the implementation technologies will evolve. As Martha Stewart is wont to say, this is a good thing. In following chapters you see how architectural evolution can occur in a safe and effective manner. This chapter explored three key process decisions you need to make pertaining to initial architectural modeling:

- **Level of initial detail.** Our advice is to keep your initial architectural modeling effort as light as possible and when possible to keep your options open. Identify the decisions that you need to make now and make them; defer other decisions until the latest responsible moment to do so (a lean strategy).

- **Right types of models.** The types of models that you will create vary on your situation. It is common for teams to create some sort of architectural overview diagram, usually a stack diagram or a free-form diagram, and a diagram that explores hardware topology issues, such as a deployment diagram or network diagram. We also suggest capturing important architectural decisions and the reasons behind them.

- **Modeling strategy.** Informal architecture modeling sessions work best in the majority of situations. Most applications need only to have a single solution architecture strategy identified for them, although multiple strategies are likely to be considered in the process of driving to that single candidate.

Additional Resources

For more detailed discussions about several of the topics covered in this chapter:

- **Project initiation statistics.** Initial architecture modeling statistics were taken from the 2009 Agile Project Initiation survey (ambysoft.com/surveys/projectInitiation2009.html).

- **Agile architecture modeling.** Scott has written several articles over the years about agile architecture strategies, which are posted at the Agile Modeling (agilemodeling.com) site.

- **Online architecture resources.** There are some great IT architecture resource sites: Grady Booch's Handbook of Software Architecture site (handbookofsoftwarearchitecture.com), the International Association of Software Architects (IASA) site (iasaglobal.org), and the TOGAF information site (www.togaf.info).

- **Architecture modeling books.** There is a wealth of software architecture books available, but two exceptional ones that come to mind are *The Process of Software Architecting* by Peter Eeles and Peter Cripps (Addison-Wesley, 2009) and *Lean Architecture for Agile Software Development* by James O. Coplien and Gertrud Bjornvig (Wiley, 2010).

- **Agile architecture at the enterprise level.** For agile architecture at the enterprise level, we suggest looking at the Enterprise Unified Process (EUP) site (enterpriseunifiedprocess.com) and the enterprise architecture and enterprise administration articles at the Agile Data site (agiledata.org). It is not only possible but highly desirable for enterprise professionals to work in an agile manner.

CHAPTER 10

Initial Release Planning

It is always wise to look ahead, but difficult to look further than you can see. —*Winston Churchill*

In all but the most trivial of situations some sort of initial planning will be involved on a Disciplined Agile Delivery (DAD) project. When that planning occurs, the level of detail involved and who does it varies depending on your situation. An important philosophy is that the value is in the planning itself, not in the actual plan that gets produced. Your primary goal should be to think things through before you do them, not to produce documentation describing what you think you're going to do. In general, your planning efforts should address schedule, cost, and work allocations. Naturally these issues are affected by the scope of what you're trying to achieve and your strategy for doing so, hence your initial plan, initial requirements, and initial architectural strategy will evolve in step with one another.

Scott has shown via his agile surveys that despite claims to the contrary most teams do some up-front planning of their release prior to construction. Agile release planning typically entails organizing the project into a set of iterations within which potentially consumable increments of the solution are built and demonstrated, although advanced teams following a lean approach may forgo the cadence of a regular iteration and simply release a working build whenever they deem appropriate. More on this later. These pieces of the solution can potentially be deployed to your end users at any time that it makes sense to do so. Typically most iterations result in an internal release into a demo or testing environment, with external releases into production or the market place occurring less frequently. For example, you may have two-week long iterations but release into production once every three months. Or six months. Or twelve months. Setting expectations for these regular milestones that show progress toward delivering the complete solution is an important step for disciplined agile projects.

Figure 10.1 shows a mind map of the structure of this chapter. We describe each of the topics in the map in clockwise order, beginning at the top right.

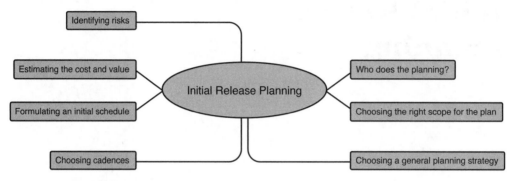

Figure 10.1   Outline of this chapter

THE BIG IDEAS IN THIS CHAPTER

- DAD teams invest some time at the beginning of a project in release planning to help them organize their work efforts.

- The initial release plan evolves in step with the initial requirements (see Chapter 8, "Identifying the Initial Scope") and potential architecture for their solution (see Chapter 9, "Identifying an Initial Technical Strategy").

- DAD teams often need to provide initial ranged cost and delivery date estimates for their project before beginning construction.

- Your schedule should address key milestones and external dependencies, if any. It should also indicate your iteration and release cadences.

Who Does the Planning?

The eleventh principle behind the Agile Manifesto is "The best architectures, requirements, and designs emerge from self-organizing teams." On a self-organizing team everyone is involved with the planning effort, including estimating the cost, allocating the work among themselves, and estimating the time it will take to perform the work. This is different from traditional approaches, where the project manager is primarily responsible for the planning effort. There are two flavors to traditional planning—a manager-driven approach where the manager(s) develops the plan in relative isolation and then dictates it to the team, or a manager-facilitated one where the manager gets input from team members about critical issues and puts the plan together based on that input. Planning responsibility options are compared and contrasted in Table 10.1.

Table 10.1 Comparing Planning Responsibility Options

Strategy	Potential Advantages	Potential Disadvantages	Considerations
Manager driven	Produces a plan that is acceptable to senior management and stakeholders.	The plan is overly optimistic due to aggressive goals, increasing the risk that the team won't deliver on plan. The team may not accept the plan given to them, decreasing motivation. The plan doesn't reflect the realities faced by the team. Significant effort invested throughout the project tracking actual results against the plan.	Plans based on generic positions/people are often not very accurate as the productivity of developers has been shown to range by more than an order of magnitude between individuals. Also, this is a symptom of project teams that risk not being adequately staffed. Watch out for plans that make unrealistic assumptions about staff availability, dependencies on deliveries by other teams, or implementation technologies.
Manager facilitated	Produces a plan that is acceptable to senior management and stakeholders.	The plan is overly optimistic due to aggressive goals.	Beware of manager-driven plans with a façade of being manager facilitated.
Self-organizing team	Produces a realistic plan that is acceptable to the people who have to follow it.	The plan may not be what senior management and stakeholders want to hear. The plan may be overly pessimistic in an attempt to be conservative. Still needs someone in a team lead role to facilitate the planning effort. Team members may need some coaching in the various planning techniques (this is typically on the order of hours for most people).	Teams new to agile run the risk of insufficient planning at the beginning of the project—detailed planning during construction supports initial release planning; it doesn't replace it.

Regardless of the obvious downsides to the approach, manager-driven planning is still alive and well in the IT community, and even on agile projects. Far too often teams have the cost of the project, the delivery date, and even the scope dictated to them by senior management. This is particularly common when outsourcing is involved in an effort to decrease project risk by defining exactly what the terms of the contract are. It also occurs on internal projects in a misguided effort to decrease project risk or to motivate staff to be more productive. More often than not project risk increases and motivation decreases as the result.

We recommend a self-organizing approach, tempered by an appropriate governance strategy as described in Chapter 20, "Governing Disciplined Agile Teams." Unfortunately self-organizing teams aren't as common as we're being led to believe by agile pundits. In the 2010 How Agile Are You? Survey Scott found that about 60% of people claiming to be on an agile team were actually working in a self-organizing manner. This is a symptom of organizational cultures that haven't yet fully shifted to agile ways of thinking, particularly when it comes to project management and governance.

Choosing the Right Scope for the Plan

We have been using the term *project plan* fairly loosely until now. The reality, however, is that the scope of plans varies, with a "project plan" being only one of several common scopes as you see in Figure 10.2.[1] There are several levels of scope to consider for your planning efforts:

- **The portfolio plan.** Large organizations typically maintain a portfolio plan that identifies potential new projects, and more importantly the ongoing projects and the dependencies between them. Portfolio planning is beyond the scope of this book.

- **The solution plan.** This plan captures the number of projected production releases there will be (or at least the next few releases) and what the expected business goal(s) are for each release. Most solutions plans look forward two to three releases at most because of shifting priorities. Solution planning, also known as product planning or program planning, is also beyond the scope of this book.

- **The release plan.** An agile release plan (sometimes called a project plan or in the case of large teams a program plan) reflects the major parts of the lifecycle including the Inception effort, the Construction phase organized into iterations, and the Transition phase. They also capture the major milestone reviews; project constraints such as legislated delivery dates; any external dependencies on other teams, perhaps your team relies on the release of another system to be in production before you can ship; the target release date(s) if any; and any blackout windows (periods when you aren't able to release into production) if any. Your release plan provides an evolving baseline providing guidance to your team and provides a mechanism through which you can collaborate with your stakeholders to help make decisions about change.

1. This is adapted from Mike Cohn's *Agile Estimating and Planning*, Addison-Wesley, 2006.

- **The iteration plan.** With this approach detailed planning is performed on a just-in-time basis at the beginning of an iteration (some teams do look ahead planning in the previous iteration to get started on the detailed plan for the next iteration). During this planning effort work items are decomposed into a lightweight detailed task list. These practices are discussed in detail in Chapter 14, "Initiating a Construction Iteration."
- **The daily plan.** Detailed planning and coordination also occur on a daily basis in a daily coordination meeting that the team conducts in their common work area. These coordination meetings are covered in detail in Chapter 15, "A Typical Day of Construction."

Figure 10.2   The agile planning onion

An important implication of Figure 10.2 is that these planning efforts are interconnected. For example, your iteration planning efforts must reflect any issues for that iteration called out in the release plan, such as a milestone review or a dependency on an external team. In this case you may have to plan to prepare for and hold a milestone review during the current iteration and work with the external team to accept whatever they're producing for you (perhaps they're releasing a system that yours needs to integrate with). In turn your iteration planning efforts could motivate changes to the release plan—perhaps it's more appropriate to hold the milestone review next iteration, for example. You are likely to evolve your plans as you adapt to the actual situation that you face throughout the project.

Choosing a General Planning Strategy

Your DAD team needs to make two fundamental decisions regarding their approach to planning. First, how much up-front planning will you do? Second, how much planning do you intend to do throughout the project? These questions lead to several different planning strategies (discussed further in Table 10.2):

- **Predictive (detailed).** The idea is that you invest significant effort, often on the order of several weeks, at the beginning of the project speculating what needs to be done, how you're going to do these things, how long it will take, and how much it will cost. The result of this work is usually a detailed work breakdown structure and often one or more Gantt charts. This level of planning typically requires a detailed approach to initial requirements specification and architectural modeling. This is often referred to as big up-front project planning in the agile community.

- **Predictive (light).** The idea is that you put together a high-level plan indicating the target delivery date of the project, target dates for major milestones (see Chapter 20), the iterations (if you're working with iterations), and any dependencies that you may have on other teams (such as releases of other systems). This effort should take hours or a few days, and is often referred to as release planning or agile release planning by agilists.

- **Predictive (none).** With this approach there is no up-front planning, and all planning is performed on a just-in-time (JIT) basis.

- **Adaptive (detailed).** Planning occurs throughout the project on a just-in-time (JIT) basis. Details are identified at the task level (e.g., update screen, update business logic, update db schema) whenever a work item is pulled off the stack or out of the pool. This planning occurs either as iteration planning or daily planning.

- **Adaptive (light).** Light planning occurs throughout the project on a JIT basis, with just enough performed so that team members may coordinate their work, but the details of what each person is doing are left up to the individuals.

- **Adaptive (none).** Although this is theoretically possible, neither of us have ever seen this in practice nor heard of an example. Even the most detailed up-front plans require some adaptation later in the lifecycle.

Our experience is that DAD teams benefit from the risk reduction advantages of agile release planning combined with some sort of adaptive planning throughout the project. Our recommendation is to combine agile release planning (predictive light) with adaptive detailed if your team is relatively new to agile; otherwise, agile release planning and adaptive light with an experienced team. As teams become more experienced working together they find that they need to identify fewer planning details throughout the project. For example, at the beginning of the project you may be identifying the need to develop the user interface (UI), write UI tests, develop the business logic, write business tests, develop the database schema, and test the database logic. Later in the project you may identify the need to develop the UI, the business logic, and the database because corresponding testing by the developer(s) is assumed. Even later you may just identify the need to implement the functionality, the UI and database work being assumed, and focus in on any potentially unusual aspects of that work that needs to be thoroughly thought through. DAD teams plan, but do so in such a way that they maximize the value in doing so.

Table 10.2 Comparing Planning Strategies

Strategy	Potential Advantages	Potential Disadvantages	Considerations
Predictive (detailed)	Enables you to identify and think through critical issues before they occur. Supports the requirements of some life/safety-critical regulations. Stakeholders see that you are considering major risks early in the project.	Time is often lost early in the project in an attempt to think through everything. You are likely to need to invest significant effort reworking the plan to reflect the actual situation. The high ceremony gives stakeholders the false impression of how things will unfold on the project. Milestone dates are likely to vary in practice, potentially giving the impression of a troubled project.	This could be a symptom of a traditional team claiming to be agile. Detailed up-front project planning does not result in greater cost or schedule predictability, although it does provide the foundation for a façade for such.
Predictive (light)	Enables you to identify and think through critical issues before they occur. Often supports the requirements of some life/safety-critical regulations. Stakeholders see that you are considering major risks early in the project.	Milestone dates are likely to vary in practice, potentially giving the impression of a troubled project.	There is still a risk of too much up-front planning because people haven't yet abandoned some of their traditional habits.
Predictive (none)	Jump into the construction effort quickly.	Difficult for team members to coordinate their activities, increasing the chance of several people doing the same thing. Major dependencies likely to be ignored at first, increasing project risk.	This may be a symptom of an ad-hoc team claiming to be agile.

(continued)

Table 10.2   Comparing Planning Strategies (continued)

Strategy	Potential Advantages	Potential Disadvantages	Considerations
Adaptive (detailed)	The plan is more accurate because it is easier to think through immediate issues. Greater acceptance of the plan due to the increased accuracy. It is clear what each person should be doing. It is easier to adjust the plan to reflect the current situation because people are used to doing so. Much less overhead required to formulate and maintain the detailed plan.	Traditionally experienced people will at first be uncomfortable with the idea of not thinking through everything ahead of time.	Teams new to agile may invest significant time maintaining planning documentation, such as a detailed Gantt chart, simply because that's what they used to do. However, just because you're doing detailed planning it doesn't necessarily mean you need to officially document it.
Adaptive (light)	The plan is more accurate because it is easier to think through immediate issues. Greater acceptance of the plan due to the increased accuracy. It is clear what each person should be doing. It is easier to adjust the plan to reflect the current situation because people are used to doing so.	Inexperienced people may need more details, requiring some flexibility.	Needs considerable management trust, which may need to be earned first.
Adaptive (none)	Appropriate for simple and straightforward projects that you are experienced at. Removes planning overhead throughout the project.	Significant chance of waste resulting from lack of coordination of team members.	This may be a symptom of traditional or ad-hoc teams claiming to be agile.

Figure 10.3 depicts how the various paradigms approach planning. Ad-hoc teams do little planning at all, DAD teams do a bit of up-front planning and a lot of JIT planning, and traditional teams do a lot of up-front planning and hope that they don't have much JIT planning to do. Iterative teams often take a middle-ground approach, with some up-front planning and some JIT planning throughout the project. At scale, often with large or geographically distributed teams but also potentially with teams facing regulatory constraints or deep complexity, the approaches start to converge (although don't). DAD teams will find they need to do a bit more up-front planning to address the complexities of the situation that they face, iterative teams will do more up-front and JIT planning, and traditional teams will find that they need to do more JIT planning.

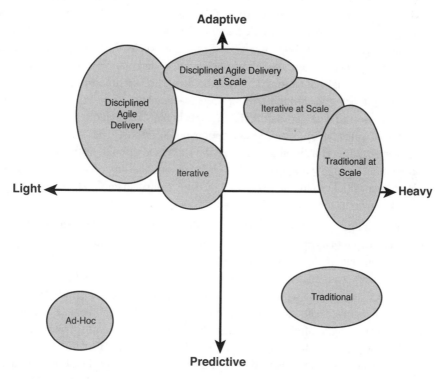

Figure 10.3   Comparing planning strategies

Choosing Cadences

An important planning decision that you need to make at the beginning of the project is to choose your management cadences, in this case:

- **Phase duration.** Most DAD teams follow the Inception-Construction-Transition lifecycle, although experienced teams may take a leaner approach and adopt the leaner "advanced" lifecycle without phases and iterations. Assuming you're taking a phased approach, you want to keep your Inception and Transition efforts as short as possible to focus your efforts on Construction where most real business value is being added. Scott's 2009 Agile Project Initiation Survey found that agile teams take an average of about four weeks to initiate agile projects, and his November 2010 Agile State of the Art survey found that experienced agile teams had Transition phases of several hours to several months, with an average of a bit less than five weeks. The Inception phase can be kept short by keeping your modeling, specification, and planning efforts as streamlined as possible through motivating key stakeholders to make time to be actively involved with the project, and through freeing up team members to be actively involved—the logistics involved with getting the right people in the room can often add weeks or even months of calendar time to your Inception phase efforts. The Transition phase, see Chapter 18, "The Transition Phase," may be shortened through testing and deployment automation, through working closely with operations and support staff during Construction iterations (a DevOps strategy), and by continuous and comprehensive testing practices throughout Construction.

- **Iteration length.** Iterations—DAD teams that have also adopted lean strategies (see Chapter 21, "Got Discipline?") may not have iterations—should be as short as possible. The fundamental trade-off is between the length of the learning feedback cycle of making your work available and your ability to add sufficient functionality to your consumable solution to make it worthwhile to seek that feedback. This depends on the skills of your team members and their ability to collaborate with one another seamlessly—teams that are new to agile often find they need longer iterations than experienced teams that have already gelled effectively. In fact, Scott's November 2010 Agile State of the Art survey found that inexperienced agile teams had an average iteration length of 2.6 weeks, whereas experienced teams had an average of 2.3 weeks. A contributing factor is the overhead from your iteration coordination activities, particularly iteration planning and modeling, and potential iteration conclusion activities such as demos and retrospectives (process learning sessions). The coordination activities vary based on your iteration length, perhaps two hours for a one week iteration, three to four hours for a two week iteration, and up to a day for a four week iteration, yet the concluding activities may still take roughly two hours. So, unless you're unable to streamline your initial coordination efforts, which is easier said than done, short iterations have significant overhead built into them. Note that the length of your iterations, if you have iterations, must be shorter than or equal to the time between production releases. Table 10.3 summarizes the iteration length options and trade-offs available to you.

- **Frequency of internal releases.** Many agile teams produce internal releases of their potentially consumable solution on a regular basis for the purposes of obtaining feedback, perhaps via demos or from an independent test team working in parallel to development (see Chapter 13, "The Construction Phase"). This is particularly important when the period between production releases is greater than the length of an iteration, which is commonly the case. Table 10.4 summarizes the trade-offs between internal release strategies.

- **Frequency of production releases.** Production releases should be as often as possible, with the primary decision being whether the team has produced sufficient business value to be of interest to your stakeholders and that value is greater than the cost to release it. You need to negotiate with your organization's release team, if there is one, otherwise, your operations team to identify a potential release schedule. Production release strategies are compared in Table 10.5.

LESSONS FROM THE TRENCHES—CADENCE AT SCALE

The IBM Rational Team Concert (RTC) team is currently about 100 people globally dispersed around the world. They work in three week iterations, which they've gotten down from six weeks several years ago. They have an internal release at the end of each iteration, with several hundred internal IBM users picking up these releases. A working release is made available to the public every second iteration (tens of thousands of users within IBM in addition to customers pick up these releases). The RTC general availability (GA) release occurs once a year in June.

Table 10.3 Comparing Iteration Length Strategies

Strategy	Potential Advantages	Potential Disadvantages	Considerations
Long iterations (six or more weeks)	Good starting point when initially transitioning to iterative approaches.	Long iterations typically devolve into mini-waterfalls where early in the iteration the focus is on modeling, then later on development, and then toward the end on hardening (testing and fixing). This is less risky than large waterfalls but still far riskier than working in a truly iterative manner.	Both of us run into teams that are new to agile development who believe that they're in a special situation requiring longer iterations. The real problem is that they haven't made the effort to squeeze out the low value activities or they still suffer from too many handoffs between overly specialized staff. Look for handoffs.
Medium-length iterations (three to six weeks)	Good starting point for teams new to agile.	Still likely to fall into mini-waterfalls. Very likely you're still doing low value/wasteful activities.	Common for teams at scale. You want to adopt better team structures and practices.
Short iterations (one to three weeks)	Forces team to focus. Especially valuable on distributed or large projects to help highlight communication challenges through regular integration.	Overhead of coordinating and concluding the iteration very high. Overhead is particularly high on distributed or large projects.	This is where agile teams want to be, and most are.
No iterations	Avoids organizational overhead of iterations.	Lack of iteration cadence can be disconcerting at first. Requires significant discipline.	This typically reflects a lean strategy that an experienced DAD team has evolved to.

Table 10.4 Comparing Internal Release Cadences

Strategy	Potential Advantages	Potential Disadvantages	Considerations
Every X iterations	Good starting point because it gets you thinking about deployment issues.	Increases risk due to longer feedback cycle with external team(s). Increases integration risk for other development teams that rely on the work that your team is producing.	Keep X small, ideally no more than three.
At the end of each iteration	Aligns with major team cadence.	Increases overhead associated with concluding the iteration. May not be often enough for some external teams, particularly if your iterations are long. Requires automated deployment between sandboxes.	Natural strategy for many teams, particularly those with short iterations.
Several times an iteration	Shortens feedback cycle with other external teams. Potentially improves support for external teams because it enables them to pull your current solution into their environments whenever they need it.	Requires automated deployment between sandboxes. Requires your team to accept feedback from external teams on a regular basis.	Overloading whoever is validating the builds with too many releases.
No internal releases	No internal release process overhead required.	Very risky if release cadence is long (say greater than 4 iterations or 3 months, whichever is longer).	Works well with very short production release cadences.

Table 10.5 Comparing Production Release Cadences

Strategy	Potential Advantages	Potential Disadvantages	Considerations
More than annual	Appropriate for low priority systems or for high-risk deployments (e.g., embedded software).	Very risky. Requires internal releases to obtain some feedback.	This is common for infrastructure systems, such as a database or transaction managers, that have many other systems highly dependent upon them.
Annual	Appropriate for low-to-medium priority systems or medium-to-high risk deployments.	Requires internal releases.	Don't include the year in the name of the release, for example, ProductX 2014, if the ongoing release cadence is going to change.
Bi-annual	Good starting point for agile teams because it motivates adoption of disciplined strategies.	Can be difficult for stakeholders who are used to less frequent releases.	
Quarterly	Enables simpler requirements management practices due to lower impact of a feature moving to the next release.	Requires disciplined continuous integration (CI) strategies.	CI refers to the practice of regularly, at least daily, building/compiling and regression testing your solution. CI is described in Chapter 15.\n\nThis is a major milestone for teams moving toward an "advanced" lean-agile strategy as it motivates greater discipline.
Monthly	Enables teams to respond to quickly changing environments.	Requires disciplined continuous deployment (CD) strategies.	CD is CI plus automated deployment of working builds to nondevelopment environments/sandboxes.

Strategy	Potential Advantages	Potential Disadvantages	Considerations
Weekly	Enables quicker response to stakeholders.		Effective for high-use systems, particularly e-commerce or BI/reporting systems.
Daily	Enables teams to adapt very quickly.	Requires extensive deployment automation. Requires high discipline to maintain quality.	
Variable	Teams need to be able to judge when their work reaches the minimally marketable release (MMR) stage and the business value added exceeds cost of transition.	Stakeholders, or their representatives, need to be a good judge of MMR. Politics can hamper this decision point.	You should put an upper limit on the acceptable time between releases. This decision point is captured in the DAD lifecycle by the "sufficient functionality" milestone. The less expensive the transition effort the easier it is to make this decision.

We recommend aiming for a release cadence of no more than six months, with a goal of getting it down to three months or shorter. We recognize that organizations new to agile may find the concept of releasing every six months difficult at first, particularly when length release processes during the Transition phase still exist (see Chapter 18 for a discussion of how to shorten this process). Strive to keep your Inception phase to two weeks or less, which can be hard if key stakeholders are unavailable or your organization still has lengthy milestone review processes. During Construction, we recommend aiming for iterations of two weeks for collocated teams and of no more than four weeks for DAD teams working at scale. We also recommend that construction iteration lengths remain the same, although if you're a team new to agile you should consider longer iterations at first and then as you gain experience with agile techniques and learn to collaborate effectively, you should shorten your iterations over time. We prefer having an internal release at the end of each iteration, although once you've fully adopted the practice of continuous deployment (CD) we recommend making your builds available to others whenever they're successful. Finally, strive to keep the Transition phase to be less than or equal to the length of a single Construction iteration, ideally shorter.

Formulating an Initial Schedule

In most organizations your team will also be asked to provide an estimate of the schedule, the amount of time required to complete the work. This is driven primarily by the amount of work to be accomplished, the availability of people to do the work, the skills of said people, and the way that they work together. Other factors that affect the schedule include dependencies on other teams, the available release windows, and any desired or legislated release date requested by your stakeholders. More on this later in the chapter.

Murray Cantor has shown that cost and schedule estimates are in effect probability distributions that narrow over time, as shown in Figure 10.3.[2] Unfortunately, far too many managers and other stakeholders still ask for an exact delivery date, the top schedule line. The reality is that at the beginning of the project the range of your schedule estimate should be wide to reflect the uncertainty of the information, the requested scope (Chapter 8) and initial technical strategy (Chapter 9). As your understanding of your stakeholders' needs evolves, and as the solution that addresses those needs evolves, you can tighten up the ranges of your cost and schedule estimates. As you see in Figure 10.4, the probability distribution, and hence the range of your estimate, narrows as you learn throughout the project. The numbers along each time line stand for months.

Therefore, your goal shouldn't be to produce a precise estimate, such as $1.2M or 10 months but instead present a reasonable range in which you believe the cost will come in, such as $700,000 to $1.5M or 8 months to 13 months. Whereas you might have a 40% chance of delivering within 10 months, you might have a 90% chance of your delivering within the given range. Which schedule criterion would you rather be judged against? Clearly the ranged estimate. If you

---

2. This example shows a schedule estimate, but the concept also holds for cost estimates.

were in senior management, which gives you a better basis from which to make reasonable governance decisions? Once again, clearly the ranged estimate.

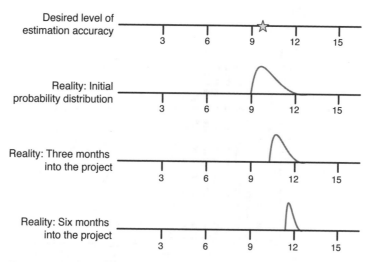

Figure 10.4 Time estimates as probability distributions varying throughout the project

As Figure 10.4 implies, you should update your estimates throughout your project as you learn. A simple way to improve your estimates is to create a burndown chart, an example of which is shown in Figure 10.5. This chart shows the amount of work remaining on the vertical axis and time on the horizontal axis. Up to the current point in the project, the chart shows the amount of work the team has accepted for the current release (burndown charts are also used to track work at the iteration level), and the projected time to complete the release past the current iteration. This projected number of remaining iterations is calculated by taking the amount of work remaining and dividing it by the team's current velocity (the amount of work completed in the previous iteration). In Figure 10.5 during iteration 10 the team had completed 16 points of work, and 176 points of work are remaining. Therefore, at the end of iteration 10 it appears that it will take another 11 iterations to complete that work (176 divided by 16 rounded up), for an estimated 21 iterations for the total schedule.

A more sophisticated approach is to create what we call a ranged burndown chart. The basic observation is that there are really two velocities exhibited by a team, the gross and net velocity. The gross velocity is the amount of work completed in an iteration, which is what a regular burndown chart shows. The net velocity is the change in the amount of work still to do, which is the amount of work completed in an iteration less the added amount of functionality that iteration. So, as Figure 10.6 depicts if a team completes 20 points of work in an iteration but 5 extra points of work was added by the stakeholders, the gross velocity is 20 points, whereas the net velocity is 15 points. If there's 230 points on the stack then the gross velocity implies that there are 12 iterations left and the net velocity 16 iterations, providing you with a ranged estimate as discussed previously.

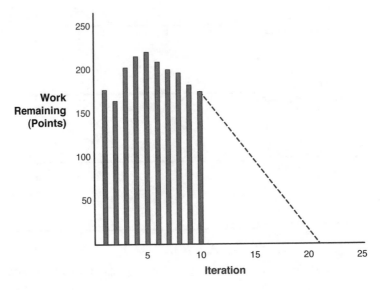

Figure 10.5   A burndown chart

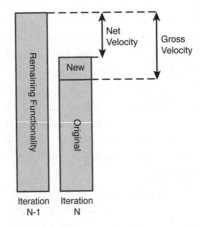

Figure 10.6   Gross versus net velocity

An example of a ranged burndown chart is shown in Figure 10.7, based on the data in Table 10.6. An interesting thing about Table 10.6 is the Net Velocity (applied) column, which is needed because things don't always work as smoothly as what Figure 10.6 implies. Several things can happen. First, the net velocity may be the same as the gross velocity because no new functionality was added that iteration, which is what happened during the first two iterations. Second, the actual net velocity may be negative because more functionality was added than implemented that iteration, which is what happened during iterations three through five. This is a common occurrence early in a project because the first few times your stakeholders see a working solution they will realize they had missed or misunderstood what they originally believed they wanted. This early in the project we applied the heuristic of setting the applied net velocity to be half of the gross velocity, although had we been later in the project we would have simply used the net velocity of the previous iteration, as requirements surges at that point are typically the result of unusual events such as other organizations releasing competing products into the marketplace. Third, because it's possible that functionality can be dropped from a release part way through a project, perhaps because of a major shift in strategy or in an effort to hit a desired date, the net velocity will exceed the gross velocity that iteration. In this case our advice is to use the gross velocity that iteration.

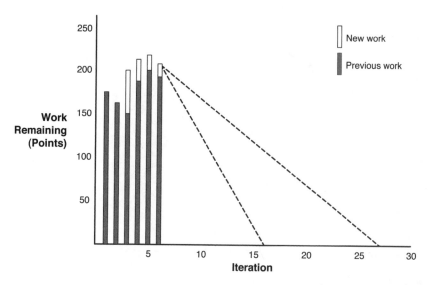

Figure 10.7   Ranged burndown chart at iteration 6

Figure 10.8 depicts the ranged burndown chart at the end of iteration 10. Notice how the range has clearly narrowed as compared with Figure 10.7, which is generally what you'd expect later in the project. As you can see in Table 10.6, the range narrows even further in iterations 12 and 13 where the estimated schedule seems to stabilize around 21 or 22 iterations for the current release.

Table 10.6 Ranged Estimate Example

Iteration	Work Remaining	Gross Velocity	Work Added	Net Velocity (actual)	Net Velocity (applied)	Estimated Iterations Remaining	Estimated Schedule
Initial	187	15					13
1	174	13	0	13	13	14	15
2	160	14	0	14	14	12	14
3	200	12	52	-40	6	17-34	20-37
4	213	13	26	-13	7	17-31	21-35
5	218	12	17	-5	6	19-37	24-42
6	208	22	12	10	10	10-21	16-27
7	198	20	10	10	10	10-20	17-27
8	195	16	13	3	3	13-65	21-73
9	182	17	4	13	13	11-14	20-33
10	172	16	6	10	10	11-18	21-28
11	159	16	3	13	13	10-13	21-24
12	144	17	2	14	14	9-11	21-23
13	129	17	2	15	15	8-9	21-22

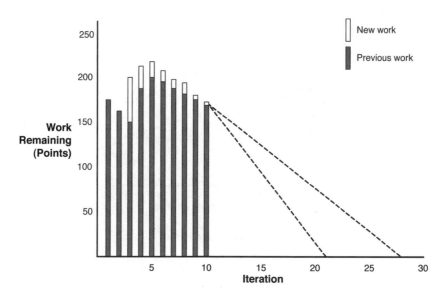

Figure 10.8   Ranged burndown chart at iteration 10

On the one hand gross velocity is the best-case situation and therefore overly optimistic. Net velocity, on the other hand, is often the worst-case scenario and therefore overly pessimistic. Interestingly, if you track the ranges over time you end up with a chart such as Figure 10.9, which corresponds to the estimate convergence path (depicted by the dashed lines). It's interesting to note that this example includes two common occurrences that you'll see. First, during iterations 1 and 2 the gross and net velocities were the same because no new functionality had been identified yet, resulting in an unranged estimate. Second, iteration 8 had a very small net velocity because the amount of new functionality was almost as much as the amount implemented, giving a huge estimation range due to the small net velocity.

There's a good chance that you're still going to be asked for a visual representation of your release schedule such as a Gantt chart—Scott's January 2012 Agile Planning survey found that one quarter of agile teams created a high-level Gantt chart at the beginning of the project. Figure 10.10 presents an example of a Gantt chart for a high-level release schedule. Major activities, in this case phases and iterations, are shown as horizontal rectangles, milestone reviews are depicted as solid diamonds on the end of an activity, and dependencies are indicated with hollow diamonds at the beginning of an activity. Along the right the major milestones, dependencies, and associated dates are listed. Notice how the focus is on the schedule, not on the details of what is being implemented—this is a high-level release schedule; the details will be identified on a JIT manner throughout the project. A detailed version might list subactivities within each of the major activities, a detailed predictive strategy discussed in Table 10.2. Although the notation used is a bit simpler than that implemented by most project management tools, the concepts captured in the example are what matters.

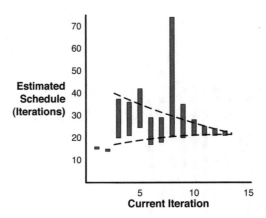

Figure 10.9   Trend tracking the ranged burndown over time

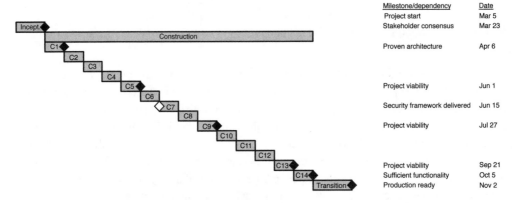

Figure 10.10   Example high-level Gantt chart

One challenge is that it isn't easy to depict ranges on a Gantt chart. For example, although Figure 10.10 indicates that Inception is expected to be three weeks in length it may prove to be four or five in practice. We currently show 14 construction iterations, but it may prove to be 20 or more, or only 11, in the end. We expect Transition to take four weeks, but it may only take two weeks. Or seven weeks—we won't know until we get closer to actual deployment. Another issue is that we don't know how long it will take to determine if our stakeholders are delighted, so that milestone was left off the Gantt chart for now. There are three basic strategies to get around this challenge: you can abandon the use of Gantt charts, you can create a single Gantt chart that presents an average, or you can maintain two Gantt charts (one for each extreme). Table 10.7 compares and contrasts these approaches. Our recommendation is to have a single Gantt chart only if your organization requires it or if your team finds value in creating and then maintaining it.

Table 10.7 Comparing Gantt Chart Strategies

Strategy	Potential Advantages	Potential Disadvantages	Considerations
No Gantt charts	One less artifact to create and maintain.	The project management culture in many organizations expects Gantt charts.	Be prepared to justify the use of an alternative, such a taskboard or simple list of milestones and dependencies and associated date ranges.
Single chart	Single chart conforms to management expectations.	Whatever you show is likely to be perceived as the expected schedule against which your team will be judged. Doesn't provide much value to the team nor to stakeholders due to inaccurate portrayal of key dates.	To protect yourself show a chart that is as close to the worst-case scenario as is politically acceptable. This will likely prove to be little more than status reporting overhead throughout the project.
Two charts	Greater opportunity to portray the schedule in an honest manner.	You have two charts to maintain.	This approach is rarely taken and is likely to prove confusing to your stakeholders and any teams dependent on yours. One way to make this coherent is to have a single file with two separate work streams, one for the best-case scenario and one for the worst case, so that it's clear that you're maintaining both scenarios in parallel.

When developing a release schedule there are several important considerations to take into account:

- **Team members.** The primary determinant of the schedule will be the people who make up the project team, their skills, and the way that they work together. Studies have shown that there is more than an order of magnitude difference in developer productivity, belying the idea that you can create viable plans based on generic "resources"—you need to know who will be on the team, their level of availability, and their commitment to the success of your project. More on team building in Chapter 11, "Forming the Work Environment."

- **Milestones.** DAD teams typically address several common milestones throughout a project. These milestones include coming to stakeholder consensus early in your project (the end of the Inception phase); proving that your architecture works early in Construction; identifying when you have sufficient functionality to justify releasing a new version of your solution; identifying when your solution is ready to be released; confirming that your stakeholders are delighted with the solution; and in the case of long-running projects you should regularly determine whether the project is still viable. The implication is that milestone reviews, ideally lightweight ones, should be included in your project schedule as you saw in Figure 10.9. Milestone reviews are an important part of agile project governance, the topic of Chapter 20.

- **Dependencies with other teams.** Delivery teams often have dependencies with other teams. For example, perhaps your solution requires the release of some new infrastructure services, or perhaps another team relies on your team to deliver functionality that they intend to reuse. Furthermore, your team will find that you need to work closely with enterprise teams such as your database administration group, your operations group, your enterprise architects, and so on to leverage and enhance your technical infrastructure.

- **Available release windows.** Many organizations have release slots/windows, such as every Sunday morning from 1 a.m. to 5 a.m. or the third Saturday of each month, that delivery teams must aim for to transition their solution into production. Some organizations may have blackout periods, such as November 1 to January 15 for retail organizations, during which teams should not deploy due to peaks in the business cycle. If these release windows or blackout periods exist they will affect your choice of target end date.

- **Desired or legislated release dates.** Your team may have an end date that they must aim for. Sometimes this is a hard end date due to government legislation or contractual promises made to a customer that you must meet. Some requested dates are flexible, although they may not be initially presented that way, motivated by the goals of some of your stakeholders.

- **When to start iterations.** Although many iterations are multiples of a week, they do not need to start on a Monday, and for some teams it's better that they don't. By starting an iteration in the middle of the week you avoid Monday morning energy lulls, the tendency of people to be tired after a weekend, when you're doing iteration planning. Granted, some people come in energized after the weekend, so it depends on who is on your team. Similarly Friday afternoon energy lulls, the tendency of people to be exhausted at the end of the week, aren't good times to be doing demos or holding retrospectives. Furthermore, many local holidays, such as Labor Day in the United States or Victoria Day in Canada, are held on either Mondays or Fridays further complicating starting or ending iterations that begin on Mondays.

Our advice is to list any critical assumptions that you've made when formulating a schedule. For example, the Gantt chart shown previously in Figure 10.10 indicates that you assume that the security infrastructure will be available on or before the middle of June. If the team delivering this functionality was to slip their schedule, and if it would then cause you to slip yours, then you should at least capture this as a risk somewhere. You should also have your schedule reviewed by someone, ideally anyone responsible for governing your team, to get feedback on the viability of your plan. Better to find out that you're off track early in the project when it's easy to correct than later when it may not be.

Our advice is to avoid Gantt charts on simpler projects and instead educate your stakeholders on the virtues of a taskboard for detailed planning, a ranked risk list (discussed later in the chapter) for longer term issues, and ranged burndown charts for identifying the potential delivery date. Teams in more complex situations, or in situations with release cycles of several months or more, will likely need at least one Gantt chart, the risk list, and a ranged burndown chart for at least their own team management efforts.

LESSONS FROM THE TRENCHES—SHORT RELEASE CYCLES REQUIRE LESS PLANNING

It's important to note that the scheduling issues explored in this section are the result of long release cycles—you need to invest some time in initial release planning when your releases are many months, say six or more, apart. As you tailor your process to become leaner, shortening your release cycle to quarterly to monthly and even more often, the need to do any release planning goes away. Scott once worked on an agile team where they released weekly. "The plan is to release every Friday morning" was the level of detail that they needed by the time they got down to weekly releases (they started at bi-annual releases). We found that by releasing that regularly the team got into a rhythm, the plan effectively became the process equivalent of "body memory"—we worked through the entire release cycle so often that everyone involved, including stakeholders, knew what the plan was without having to write it down.

Estimating the Cost and Value

Every single project team that either of us has been involved with had to provide some sort of financial estimate at the beginning of the project as part of the overall process of securing funding. Every. Single. One. The implication is that your team needs to invest some time developing an initial financial estimate, an important part of which is the initial cost estimate. There are several strategies for cost estimating, compared in Table 10.8, commonly employed by agile teams:

- **Formal point counting.** With this strategy you take the information captured within your detailed requirements and architecture/design specifications and identify the size points of the potential solution. There are several strategies for identifying these points, with function point counting being the most popular. Using this technique a count is taken of all the outputs, inquiries, inputs, internal files, and external interfaces for a particular system being built. Because these size points are identified using a consistent strategy, it's possible for organizations with historical sizing databases to then produce what they believe to be a realistic cost estimate for their project.

- **Planning poker.** This technique, formally called Wideband Delphi, was popularized by Mike Cohn within the agile community. In addition to any available team members, the product owner and possibly a domain expert should be present for this estimating session, which usually lasts a couple of hours (or days for larger projects). It entails going through each item on the work item list (mainly user stories) and assigning a "relative" point value to the item according to the overall effort and relative complexity. The candidate point values then can be assigned to each item corresponding roughly to the Fibonacci sequence, such as 0, 1, 2, 3, 5, 8, 13, with higher numbers added such as 20 and 40. Figure 10.11 shows an example of planning poker cards. Each requirement is considered one at a time, and the team "votes" on what they believe the relative size to be. If there is a range in individual votes, differences are discussed and voting occurs again (this is repeated until consensus is reached). Once all work items have been estimated, add up all the point values. This number represents the total work item list estimate.

  Let's say for example that the total is 240 points. In the first iteration of the Construction phase, we would pull off the work item list a set of work items that the team feels they can deliver in the timebox of the iteration. If this were, for example, 24 points, and the team did indeed deliver the selected work items, you might conclude that your progress is 10% complete. The project may then require an additional 9 iterations to finish, assuming the same team pace, commonly referred to as "velocity." As each Construction iteration is complete, we consider the number of points delivered and adjust average velocity accordingly to refine the estimate to completion based on the number of remaining points on the work item list. The expected total points for a release can be plotted on a release burndown chart. This tracks team progress on an iteration by iteration basis to track whether the team is delivering the expected functionality points. This method of tracking productivity and using it to extrapolate an expected time to complete the remaining work has been shown to be accurate, within normal estimation tolerances and is an efficient way of getting an estimate quickly. Additionally, the velocity is specific to the particular team doing the estimating, which of course makes it more applicable than more generic and stereotypical estimation techniques.

Figure 10.11   Planning poker cards

- **Educated guess by the team.** Another, even less formal approach is to have the team get together and discuss what they think it will cost. This conversation will likely focus first on identifying what work needs to be accomplished and how much time, in person months, it will likely take. Knowing the amount of time, say 135 person months, and the fully loaded rate per person month, say $14,000, it enables you to give a rough cost estimate of the work component, in this case $1,890,000. You would still need to account for any hardware and software purchases required to support the solution once it is deployed to production. This guess is typically made several times throughout Inception as your understanding of the scope and technical strategy evolves. Educated guesses such as this are sometimes referred to as guesstimates.

- **Educated guess by an experienced individual.** A good guess by an experienced person, particularly one who will be involved in the project and therefore is motivated to "get it right," often proves to be effective in practice. On DAD teams this experienced person is often the team lead or other senior team member such as the architecture owner. The fact is that both formal point counting and planning poker are just ways of making a bunch of little guesses that are then added up to a larger guess. Once the person creating the estimate is familiarized with the requirements and architectural strategies, these educated guesses can often be made in short order.

- **Cost set by the stakeholders.** Some projects have the cost set for them by the stakeholders, often a reflection of how much they're willing to spend on the solution or simply how much they have to spend. What this amount actually implies is situational. This may be an actual upper limit on what you can spend. It may be the initial amount your stakeholders are willing to spend, but they're prepared to spend more if you're providing good return on investment (ROI). It may be an amount that is meant to motivate you to spend the money wisely, and that you still need to produce a serious cost estimate on your own.

LESSONS FROM THE TRENCHES—MODERN ESTIMATION TOOLING WORKS

Jim Densmore, a technical solution architect at IBM Rational, has found with customers that a bit of advanced tooling support can go a long way toward quick yet accurate and more honest estimates—estimates that include variances so that customers are comfortable with accountability for them. Experts can be supported in their efforts to estimate the yield of projects (and other investments) by products such as IBM Rational Focal Point, which includes investment analysis functionality. The investment analysis component helps you to identify likely, best-case, and worst-case potential cost accrual curves over time for a project, and do the same for the potential revenues and savings. It then statistically analyzes these inputs to produce an estimate of the ROI for your project as a *distribution*, which therefore includes both a mean (a likely outcome) and variance (project risk or uncertainty). The interesting thing about this component is that it enables you to visually, explicitly, and quickly do what experts were previously doing as spreadsheet ROI calculations, which were never well trusted.

Our advice is to stay away from formal point counting whenever you can. We prefer collaborative approaches such as planning poker and educated guesses by the team as they are often more realistic and lead to greater acceptance by the team—the demotivational power of an unrealistic estimate can put your team on a path to failure from the start of the project.

Table 10.8 Comparing Estimation Techniques

Strategy	Potential Advantages	Potential Disadvantages	Considerations
Formal point counting	Fulfills contractual obligations in some situations—for example, the U.S. government often requires function-point based estimates. Provides a consistent way to compare projects and team productivity. Often increases the political acceptability of the estimate due to the complexity of the effort to create it.	Extends the Inception phase effort. Provides a scientific façade over the estimation activity, even though estimation is often more of an art in practice. Reduces team acceptance of the estimate because the estimate is typically produced by a professional estimator. Historical data won't exist for new technology platforms or development techniques, requiring you to guess the value of some complexity factors. Provides a mechanism to compare the productivity of development teams, which can motivate them to overestimate and thereby decrease comparability and the value of your historical database. Total cost of ownership (TCO) is high as it motivates questionable specification practices, which in turn motivate change prevention and other poor behaviors by the development team.	Overly long estimation efforts in an effort to get the "right answer" often prove to be far more costly than the actual benefit provided. Beware of misguided desires for "accurate" or "consistent" estimates that prove costly to produce in practice yet don't improve the decision making ability of senior management to any great extent.

(continued)

Table 10.8   Comparing Estimation Techniques (continued)

Strategy	Potential Advantages	Potential Disadvantages	Considerations
Planning poker	Simple, collaborative and relatively inexpensive strategy. Greater acceptance by the team because they produced it. Greater accuracy because the people responsible for implementing are the ones producing the estimate. If your productivity differs from expectations (e.g., your velocity proves to be different in practice), re-estimating is not required because the relative values remain constant.	The points are unitless, making it difficult to compare teams using them (also an advantage). Explicitly reveals to stakeholders that estimating is often more art than science.	The desire to have a single point system across your organization (typically for comparison purposes) typically proves to be expensive and less accurate than a unitless approach.
Educated guesstimate by team	Greater acceptance by the team because they produced it. Simple, collaborative, and inexpensive strategy. Greater accuracy because the people responsible for implementing are the ones producing the estimate.	Some stakeholders may be uncomfortable with the fact that you're guessing. Explicitly reveals to stakeholders that estimating is often more art than science.	A common problem is overly conservative estimates by the team to provide a safety margin. Conversely, overly aggressive estimates by the team that placates unrealistic demands by stakeholders is also common.
Educated guesstimate by experienced individual	Quick and inexpensive way to get a reasonable estimate.	Requires that you have an experienced person involved with your project (if you don't, then you should consider this a serious risk). Explicitly reveals to stakeholders that estimating is often more art than science. Some stakeholders may be uncomfortable with the fact that you're guessing.	Beware of estimates by people who are inexperienced with the platform or domain or who do not know the abilities of the team.
Cost set by stakeholders	Potentially reflects the cost constraints faced by the team.	Often doesn't reflect the real costs of delivering the desired functionality within the desired timeframe.	-

There are several easy ways to improve the quality of your estimates. First, small things are easier to estimate than large things, motivating you to identify smaller work items. Second, people who have experience in the domain and the proposed architectural strategy are better at estimating than people without that background, so build your team wisely. Third, people who are responsible for committing to an estimate are more motivated to provide an accurate estimate than people who are not. Fourth, the best estimates are presented as ranges. Scott has found via surveys that on average initial cost estimates are given within a +/-10% range. The surveys also found that the actual costs where within a range of +/-20% on average, often after dropping scope, reworking the schedule, or reducing delivered quality.

LESSONS FROM THE TRENCHES—USING POINTS FOR ESTIMATING VERSUS ACTUAL VALUES

Some people prefer release estimating with hours, and others prefer points. Mark's preference is points (as is Scott's). Mark's experience is that his teams can estimate much quicker once they grasp the concept of "relative" estimates. When Mark has used actual hours for estimating, the session has typically been slow and painful as team members tend to decompose the work item into actual tasks, with the idea of then rolling up the totals into one estimate. They also seem to want a complete and detailed understanding of the requirement, as well as their design before they commit to an estimate number. This is a traditional estimating technique that actually ends up not being accurate since the details often change when the team starts to truly understand how to implement the story. Mark has found that once the team understands that we are expecting a high-level estimate, with one estimate for the team (rather than many estimates for each task), the process is simpler and more efficient.

However, at some point Mark is usually still asked to translate the total point estimates into a dollar figure. It is actually not that difficult to translate your points into a dollar figure. Your organization's financial people can give you an estimate for the burn rate (dollars expended on your team per day), which you can easily map to points delivered per iteration and number of iterations remaining to deliver remaining points on the work item list.

Although the focus of your financial estimating efforts is typically around development costs, there are several other issues that your team may be asked to address (or at least understand when discussed with them):

- **Quantitative benefits and costs.** Quantitative things can be measured numerically, preferably converted to a monetary amount. For example, you may expect a project to take eight staff years to complete (the equivalent of eight people working for one year). If your fully burdened cost for each staff member (the average salary plus benefits plus operational costs per person of your environment) is $14,000 per month, the development cost for that project is $1,344,000 ($14K * 12 * 8).

- **Qualitative benefits and costs.** Qualitative issues cannot be easily converted to a monetary value. For example, the consumability of your solution is a qualitative issue as is being environmentally neutral. Yes, solutions that are easier to use are likely to promote greater productivity, and those that are "green" may be more likely to be purchased than those that are not, but it is difficult to put an exact monetary value on these benefits. Qualitative issues are important, they are often the ones that are the deciding factor when justifying a project, and you will often find that you need to at least acknowledge them in your overall project vision (see Chapter 7, "Identifying a Project Vision").

- **Projected revenue or savings.** This is the amount of money that you estimate you will either earn or save, or perhaps a combination of both, as the result of releasing your solution to your stakeholders.

- **Present value (PV).** The present value of an amount is the amount adjusted for the cost of money over time. For example, if it would cost you 5% a year to borrow money, $1,000 four years from now would be $1000/(1.05)^4 = 822.70. The implication is that you would need to invest $822.70 today at an interest rate of 5% to have $1,000 four years from now. Present values are used to compare amounts of money that are either invested or earned at different points in time. An outgoing amount that is spent will have a negative PV; an incoming amount that you earn or is saved has a positive PV.

- **Net present value (NPV).** The net present value (NPV) of collection of amounts, either positive or negative, is the sum of the present values (PVs). For example, if the PV of the cost of your solution is $700,000 and the PV of the savings from the solution is $400,000 in the first year, $600,000 in the second, $650,000 in the third, $350,000 in the fourth, and then $200,000 in its fifth and final year for a total PV of $2.2 million, then your project has an NPV of $1.5 million (-$700K + $2.2 million).

- **Total cost of ownership (TCO).** The TCO is the sum of all the expected costs, both quantitative (the ones you can add up) and qualitative (the ones you list), over the life of your solution. This includes the costs to identify and justify the need for the solution, to develop or purchase it, to release it into production, to operate and support it over time, and to decommission it once it is no longer needed.

- **Total value of ownership (TVO).** The TVO is the sum of all the expected quantitative and qualitative benefits of owning a solution over its lifetime.

- **Return on investment (ROI).** This is the quantitative aspect of the TVO divided by the TCO. For example, if the NPV of the savings from your solution is $1.5 million and the cost $700,000, the expected ROI over its lifetime is 47%. If that ROI is earned over a five year period, the annual ROI is 9.3%.

- **Payback period.** The period of time required for the return on an investment to "repay" the sum of the original investment. For example, a solution that cost $1,000,000 that produced $300,000 a year in savings would have a payback period of 3.33 years.

Your stakeholders should understand that the purpose of the initial estimates—schedule, cost, and value—is to simply act as input into the go/no-go decision at the end of Inception. You can assure them that you will be able to provide increasingly accurate estimates on what can be achieved for a given budget and schedule once you have had the opportunity to deliver a few increments of functionality over several short iterations in Construction. As the project progresses the "cone of uncertainty" of your estimates will converge on the actual cost in step with your improved understanding of your stakeholder needs domain and your solution.

LESSONS FROM THE TRENCHES—SURVIVING A "FIXED EVERYTHING" PROJECT

Some organizations still insist on having a defined scope, defined schedule, and defined cost estimate at the beginning of a project. Although this strategy has been known for several decades to significantly increase the risk to a project team, some agile teams find they cannot avoid these situations. Scott has helped several customers commit to a fixed but still flexible scope definition by applying Agile Modeling's flexible features split strategy. The basic idea is that the team commits to a percentage, often 70% or 80%, of the "required" functionality but not to the remainder. With this approach the stakeholders get most of what they want in the defined time and budget, and if possible will get some or all of the rest. This provides stakeholders with the desired predictability while enabling the team to take a flexible approach to scope management and thereby reduce project risk.

Identifying Risks

An important aspect of taking a disciplined approach to agile delivery is to identify and address risks early in the project. In fact, as you learned in Chapter 1, "Disciplined Agile Delivery in a Nutshell," the DAD lifecycle explicitly includes milestones that address common risks faced by most DAD teams. This practice is referred to as following a Risk-Value Lifecycle and is described in more detail in Chapter 13, which focuses on mitigating the highest outstanding project risks. At this phase of the project, however, we first are concerned with *identifying* likely risks.

Project management theory suggests that risk management is a critical part of successful project delivery. The DAD process framework adopts this premise and suggests that a risk list should be created in the Inception phase and used as part of the prioritization criteria for work items. Consideration of risk is also a criterion for determining whether to proceed with the project into Construction. If the risk level is too high, it may be worthwhile considering alternatives such as buying a package, adjusting scope, taking a different approach, or canceling the project outright. Canceling a troubled project early is healthy behavior.

We suggest that you create a simple itemized risk list—some agile teams refer to this as a risk backlog and project managers may call this a risk register—ranked by risk magnitude.

Calculation of the magnitude is done by multiplying the probability of occurrence by the impact if it actually occurs, as you see in Table 10.9. The risk list includes technical risks (such as insufficient response time), organizational risks (such as lack of access to stakeholders), and project risks (late delivery of the security framework by another team). This list is initially created during Inception as part of your team's release planning efforts and then maintained throughout the project. The risk list could be itemized on a whiteboard or flip chart and posted for all to see. If you were to take a more formal approach to creating your risk list, you could add more information to this list, such as steps to mitigate and contingency should the risk manifest itself. You may also choose to link a risk to any work item(s) in particular requirements that mitigate the risk.

Table 10.9   Example of a Ranked Risk List

Risk	Probability (%)	Impact (1-10)	Magnitude
We will not have sufficient access to key stakeholders.	80%	10	8
The security framework will not be available on or before June 15.	40%	10	4
The continuous connection to Head Office for inventory management will not be sufficiently fault tolerant.	70%	5	3.5
We are not sure if we can get 3 second response time on credit transactions.	60%	4	2.4
The users are not sure what kind of operational reports they need.	50%	2	1

You should make this list highly visible once completed in the Inception iteration and ensure that you select work items in the early iterations that, by implementing them, help to mitigate these risks. Although we can identify an initial list of risks in the Inception phase and take specific actions to mitigate them by implementing related features, risks will continue to surface throughout the project. The implication is that you will evolve your risk list throughout the project, removing risks from the list as they are mitigated, and adding new ones as they arise.

Concluding Thoughts

Your initial release plan potentially addresses two important facets of your project: its schedule and its financial aspects. The schedule should indicate the expected delivery date—ideally expressed as a range of dates, any important dependencies on external teams or events, and key milestones in the project. The financial aspects of your plan should address the expected costs and benefits, also ideally expressed as a range. Your release plan will evolve throughout your project as you learn more about what your stakeholders actually need, how you can fulfil those needs, how well your team works together, and how well your overall environment is conducive to allowing you to successfully deliver a solution. Your release plan is an important part of your project vision (Chapter 7). As described in that chapter, some people prefer to call the vision an "Agile Charter."

In this chapter we indicated our suggestions for several key issues pertaining to release planning:

- **Who should do the planning.** We recommend a self-organizing approach to planning, tempered by an appropriate governance strategy as described in Chapter 20.

- **General planning strategy.** Our recommendation is to combine agile release planning with adaptive detailed if your team is relatively new to agile; otherwise, agile release planning and adaptive light with an experienced team. As teams become more experienced working together they find that they need to identify fewer planning details throughout the project.

- **Release cadence.** We recommend aiming for a release cadence of no more than six months, with a goal of getting it down to three months or shorter.

- **Phase lengths.** Strive to keep your Inception phase to two weeks or less, which can be hard if key stakeholders are unavailable or your organization has a lengthy milestone review processes. Try to keep the Transition phase less than or equal to the length of a single Construction iteration, and ideally much shorter than adoption of a continuous deployment (CD) approach (see Chapter 15).

- **Construction iteration length.** We recommend aiming for iterations of two weeks for collocated teams and of no more than four weeks for DAD teams working at scale. We also recommend that Construction iteration lengths remain the same.

- **Internal release cadence.** Minimally, we prefer having an internal release at the end of each iteration. Once you've fully adopted the CD practice we recommend making your builds available to others whenever they're successful.

- **Initial scheduling.** Our advice is to avoid Gantt charts on simpler projects and instead educate your stakeholders on the virtues of a taskboard for detailed planning, a ranked risk list (see later in this list) for longer term issues, and ranged burndown charts for identifying the potential delivery date. For teams in more complex situations, or in situations with release cycles of several months or more, they will likely need at least one Gantt chart, the risk list, and a ranged burndown chart for at least their own team management efforts.

- **Cost and value estimates.** We prefer collaborative approaches such as planning poker and educated guesses by the team as they are often more realistic and lead to greater acceptance by the team. Stay away from formal point counting whenever you can.

- **Risk identification.** Create a simple itemized risk list ranked by risk magnitude.

Additional Resources

For more detailed discussions about several of the topics covered in this chapter:

- **Agile surveys.** In this chapter we referenced results from several surveys. Statistics regarding the proclivity for agile teams to perform initial release planning were taken from the 2009 Agile Project Initiation survey at ambysoft.com/surveys/ projectInitiation2009.html. Iteration lengths were explored in the November 2010 Agile State of the Art Survey at ambysoft.com/surveys/agileStateOfArt201011.html. The 2010 How Agile Are You? survey at ambysoft.com/surveys/howAgileAreYou2010 .html explored how agile teams are in practice. Planning practices, including both cost and schedule practices, were explored in the Dr. Dobb's Journal December 2010 State of the IT Union survey at ambysoft.com/surveys/stateOfITUnion201012.html. The January 2012 Agile Planning survey at ambysoft.com/surveys/agilePlanning2012.html explored how agile teams approach planning throughout the lifecyle.

- **Planning poker.** Planning poker was first described by James Greening in 2002 at http://renaissancesoftware.net/files/articles/PlanningPoker-v1.1.pdf. It is a variation of another estimating technique called Wideband Delphi, and planning poker card decks can be obtained by contacting UPMentors at contact@UPMentors.com.

- **Agile project planning.** Mike Cohn's *Agile Estimating and Planning* (Prentice Hall, 2005) is a great book describing the fundamentals of agile project planning. Kevin Aguanno's *Managing Agile Projects* (Multi-Media Publications, 2005) is a collection of articles by agile luminaries that provide a range of viewpoints about fundamental agile management issues.

- **Project financials.** Steve Tockey's *Return on Software* (Addison-Wesley, 2005) provides a detailed discussion of fundamental management accounting practices as they are applied to software development projects.

- **Fixed everything projects.** Scott has written extensively about the risks involved with "fixed bid" and "fixed everything" projects in various articles posted at www.drdobbs. com.

Forming the Work Environment

"Get a room"—Mark, among others

During the Inception phase the team lead needs to work with the project sponsors to secure a work environment that will maximize the effectiveness of the team. This chapter describes various work environments and tooling alternatives that you should consider adopting. Note that some of the activities described in this chapter may be performed early in the Construction phase. This depends on your organization's funding rules; you may not be allowed to start organizing your physical or virtual environments until funding has been secured, or your Inception phase may be so short that you simply don't have time to get to some of this work.

Figure 11.1 shows a mind map of the structure of this chapter. We describe each of the topics in the map in clockwise order, beginning at the top right.

THE BIG IDEAS IN THIS CHAPTER

- Team planning should take place in the Inception phase to prepare to scale up the team for beginning to build the solution in the Construction iterations.
- Ideally the team should be set up in a common work area to optimize collaboration.
- Tooling strategies are likely to include manual tools, open source tools, and commercial tools.
- The need for sophisticated tooling increases as the team scales beyond small, collocated efforts.

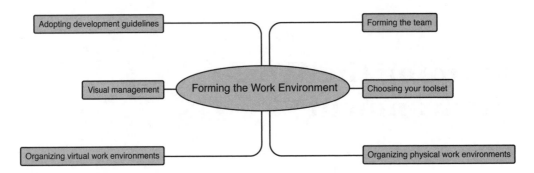

Figure 11.1   Outline of this chapter

Forming the Team

Strategies for organizing your DAD team were discussed in detail in Chapter 5, "Forming Disciplined Agile Delivery Teams." Teams are typically small during Inception, often consisting of just the product owner, team lead, and perhaps the architecture owner (lead developer). This of course is just a guideline, and for larger projects the initial team could include more people such as domain experts and specialists.

As part of framing the project during Inception, you will start thinking about what kind of team you will require to scale up for your Construction iterations. We are often asked how large the team needs to be for a given project, and this is not an easy question to answer. Early in the project, there are many unknowns regarding scope, technical challenges, team productivity, and project risks. Our recommendation is to staff the team for what seems realistic for the project at hand, keeping the team as small as possible. We then set expectations with our customers that we will deliver work for a couple of Construction iterations according to our capacity. After completing these iterations and based on the velocity of the team and work remaining, we can scale the team up (or down) accordingly. If increasing the team is not feasible, then the stakeholders need to adjust their expectations regarding what is possible to be delivered in the first release of the project.

Table 11.1 compares the various methods for resourcing your teams. These team formation strategies include the following:

- **Existing product team.** Product teams typically keep the team intact from release to release to maintain continuity. The team is responsible for building new functionality but also is responsible for fixing defects for prior releases.

- **Existing team from another product.** Well-functioning teams sometimes move from one product to another.

- **New team.** New teams are often created to deliver a solution that is perceived as a one-time project rather than a stream of regular releases. Organizations following this approach often use contractors or external service providers to deliver solutions.
- **Full-time team members.** Full-time team members are dedicated to only one project at a time. They have few work responsibilities, if any, outside the team and thus are not distracted by other priorities.
- **Part-time team members.** Part-time team members have significant work commitments outside the project team. Although discouraged on agile projects, some team members may be assigned to several teams due to a lack of expertise within your organization in a certain area. It is common for business team members to insist that they need to spend some of their time away from the project supporting their normal business functions. Some organizations have a matrix organization where people temporarily belong to one or more project teams but are permanently assigned to a specialty group of people (such as a developer group, an architecture group, a testing group, and so on).

Our recommendation is to keep the team intact as much as possible from release to release. New teams comprised of individuals who have not worked together before or are unfamiliar with the product domain always take some time to achieve good momentum. We also suggest that the people on teams be full-time committed members.

Choosing Your Toolset

As indicated in Chapter 6, "The Inception Phase," you may choose to start organizing your tooling environment before the Construction phase begins. This is particularly true if you believe that your project will in fact get funding, and if you currently have people available to do this work who aren't needed for critical Inception activities such as getting quickly to a shared vision. You'll also want to wait until later in the Inception phase until your vision has stabilized; otherwise, you risk having to scrap some of your environment when the vision shifts in a different direction.

At a minimum, tooling needs to be set up for the development environment, configuration management, automated unit testing, and build generation. You definitely need separate sandboxes for each developer, a central repository that supports multiple source code streams, and preferably a dedicated build machine. For straightforward projects, such minimal tooling may be adequate. DAD teams working at scale will find they need more sophisticated tooling to help address the challenges that they face. Many DAD teams are in organizations where many tools have already been selected for them by their enterprise teams—one aspect of enterprise awareness is to leverage common tooling whenever appropriate.

Table 11.1   Comparing Team Formation Strategies

Strategy	Potential Advantages	Potential Disadvantages	Considerations
Existing product team	Continuity of team. An agile team will already be benefitting from an optimized process of working together.	May be complacent with their process and not realize that they can improve. Being on one product team for long periods of time can lead to tunnel vision and not learning about other parts of the business.	Utilizing an existing team reduces the time to come up to speed about the problem domain and for the team to gel.
Existing team from another product	Having worked together, their collaboration effectiveness should be good.	They still need time to learn new business domain. Need to build a trusting relationship with a new product owner.	Keeping the team together as they move to another product can be an effective strategy when the team works well together.
New team	No baggage from prior projects.	Takes time to develop an optimized collaborative team and learn the domain.	Forming a new team has an element of risk that the team may not work well together. Additionally there is a delay and associated costs as the team learns to work effectively together.
Full-time team members	Focused on the goals of the project without distractions.	Requires additional strategies to pollinate ideas across teams.	An agile coach who works with multiple teams can help socialize practices that are effective across teams.
Part-time team members	May have conflicting priorities.	Diversity of experience from multiple projects.	This is seldom a good strategy and inconsistent with agile's philosophy of team commitment and focus on one product owner's goals. May be useful for larger projects where two subteams have functionality dependencies on each other.

Table 11.2 compares various tooling strategies that you may consider. They are

- **Commercial tools.** Vendors such as IBM offer suites of tools that support agile development.

- **Open source tools.** A number of open source software (OSS) tools support agile development and can be downloaded free of charge.

- **Integrated tool suites.** Using integrated suites is a strategy whereby a set of individual tools are integrated and sold by one company or could be available as open source.

- **Point-specific tools.** A point-specific tools strategy seeks to use best-of-breed tooling for specific purposes such as agile planning, testing, building, or deployment. Integration between these separate tools may be difficult or not possible.

- **Automated tools.** An automated tooling approach is often used for optimizing agile practices for large or distributed teams in the areas such as release planning, work item management, and dashboards.

- **Manual tools.** Manual tools include paper, sticky notes, index cards, corkboards, and whiteboards. These tools are commonly used by collocated or near-located teams and by individuals in general.

LESSONS FROM THE TRENCHES—COMMERCIAL AND OPEN SOURCE GO HAND-IN-HAND

Lauren Schaefer is a test automation specialist working on the independent test team supporting the Jazz Collaborative Lifecycle Management product suite. This geographically distributed team was struggling to fulfill its test commitments as the first line of testing for the entire product development team. Such circumstances ultimately led this team to develop a complete quality management solution to overcome its challenges. This quality management solution has drastically reduced the resources and manpower needed from the team to fulfill its commitments. The solution provided functionality to automatically provision test environments in different topologies on a wide range of platforms by utilizing various application servers, database management systems, and LDAP providers. The solution also allowed executing various types of tests such as GUI tests, install tests, update tests, and others on software products.

We use a combination of Rational tools and open source tools to manage our work. We use IBM Rational Team Concert (RTC) work items to track defects. Because the team is distributed they rely on dashboards to quickly relay information about the status of our work items. They use the RTC build system to automatically kick off our test automation after every successful build, which is a huge time saver—when they arrive in the morning the tests have already been run so they can just focus on analyzing the results. They use OSS tools such as Selenium and JUnit. Commercial testing tools include IBM Rational Functional Tester and IBM Rational Quality Manager (RQM) for tracking test results and provisioning test environments.

Table 11.2   Comparing Tooling Strategies

Strategy	Potential Advantages	Potential Disadvantages	Considerations
Commercial tools	Vendors typically provide support for their tools. Often have a consistent look and feel and are well integrated with other tools provided by the same vendor.	Reliance on one vendor for a specific tool.	Often appropriate for organizations with a good relationship with the vendor beyond the set of tools (such as services, hardware, operating systems, and so on).
Open source tools	Initial adoption is free.	Total cost of ownership (TCO) may be greater than similar commercial tools.	Appropriate for cost sensitive customers that need very little support.
Integrated tooling	More integrated than point solutions. Single vendor support for all (or at least many) of your tools. Potentially less expensive than a set of point solutions. All features upgraded in one regular release.	Some tools in the suite may not be best-of-breed or be appropriate for the project.	Features integrated into one product should have a unified user experience and seamless integration. Any support required can be through one vendor rather than finger pointing between vendors.
Point-specific tools	Opportunity to seek best-of-breed point solutions.	Integration may be clumsy or nonexistent. Inconsistent user experiences for tool users. Locally optimized tooling choices in one area of the process may suboptimize other parts of the process at any scale.	Releases that are not synchronized and maintenance agreements across multiple vendors can make integration difficult. There is a potential to integrate point-specific tools using standard approaches such as Open Services for Lifecycle Collaboration (OSLC).

Strategy	Potential Advantages	Potential Disadvantages	Considerations
Automated tools	Simple and cost effective to use manual big visible charts in combination with tools that support practices such as continuous integration.	More expensive than manual approaches. Learning curve and setup time. Benefits of live status and issues may not be visible unless dashboards are projected visually.	The need for tooling increases for larger more complex projects.
Manual tools	Cheaper than alternatives. Sometimes the simplest approach is the most effective.	Doesn't scale well. Not good for distributed teams.	May be suitable for very small collocated teams and trivial solutions. Often a good strategy to supplement some automated tooling.

We suggest that you keep an open mind to tool selection and consider a combination of both commercial and OSS tools. A real challenge that we see in the marketplace is that there is sometimes too much focus on adopting point-specific OSS tools. They clearly have their place. A significant problem is that teams lose the benefits associated with integrated tools, which share artifacts smoothly and better yet generate data that can be used for automated reporting. Of course there are drawbacks from integrated tools as you see in Table 11.2. We do, however, consider IBM Rational Team Concert (RTC) to be the most complete, integrated, and extendable tooling for DAD development that we are aware of at the time of this writing. We are impressed with its out-of-the-box support for continuous integration, build, deployment, integrated work item management, group chat, release iteration planning, and automated metrics dashboards.

There are several categories of tools that you will need to consider adopting:

- **Build management.** These tools support compilation of source code, packaging binary code, dependency management, and running tests. Many tools do this in a distributed manner across several machines or within a cloud. These tools are often used in combination with deployment management tools.

- **Code analysis (dynamic).** These tools perform tasks such as analyzing security vulnerability, looking for memory leaks, and verifying test coverage.

- **Code analysis (static).** These tools may support adherence to coding guidelines, test coverage, complexity analysis, and some forms of security analysis.

- **Code review.** Code review tools enable people to capture review comments inline with the source code and often capture code review coverage metrics.

- **Collaboration tools.** When your team has members who are distributed in some manner, or when you need to interact with stakeholders who are, you need support for distributed collaboration. This includes functionality such as online chat, audioconferencing, videoconferencing, and webcast software. Some teams choose to adopt tools that support distributed documentation, drawing, and even modeling.

- **Configuration management (CM).** Sometimes referred to as version control tools or software configuration management (SCM) tools. You need to be able to manage your electronic project artifacts including source code, documents, plans, models, and so on. For source code consider tooling that supports branching and change set management.

- **Continuous integration (CI).** CI, described in detail in Chapter 15, "A Typical Day of Construction," is supported by several categories of tools, including testing frameworks, build management, and code/schema analysis tools.

- **Dashboards.** These tools display metrics based on data generated by, or captured in, other tools. You may need tools that support reporting at the subteam/project, program, and portfolio levels. Manual tools include corkboards and whiteboards.

- **Deployment management.** These tools support automatic deployment of working builds between environments (such as from your project integration sandbox to your demo environment) and validation that the deployment was successful. These tools are often used in combination with build management tools.

- **Documentation.** Your team needs documentation tools such as a word processor, a drawing tool, a presentation tool, a wiki, and even documentation generation tools such as Javadoc.

- **Estimating.** Automated tools include support for planning poker (Wideband Delphi) and ranged-based estimating. Manual tools include planning poker cards.[1]

- **Modeling.** Software-based modeling tools support notations such as Unified Modeling Language (UML), Business Process Modeling Notation (BPMN), and freeform diagrams. Sophisticated modeling tools support full round-trip engineering where code is generated and reverse-engineered. Some modeling tools support collaborative modeling where the modelers may be geographically distributed. Manual tools include whiteboards and flipcharts. Manual models are often captured using digital cameras.

- **Planning (agile).** Automated tools should provide features such as work item management, task planning, estimating, burndown charting, and task boards. Manual tools utilize corkboards with index cards or task boards and whiteboards with sticky notes for task boards.

- **Planning (classic).** Traditional planning tools are potentially useful for release planning. They include support for high-level work breakdown structures and Gantt charts, features that some agile planning tools are starting to include, too.

- **Schema analysis.** Schema analysis tools may validate that a data source conforms to data design conventions, perform data value validation, and code analysis of any functionality implemented in the data source such as triggers and stored procedures.

- **Test data management.** These tools enable you to create test data and potentially load it into your data source. These tools are particularly important for load/stress testing.

- **Test planning and management.** Independent test teams need tools that enable them to plan their testing efforts, particularly if they support multiple delivery teams, and to manage their test infrastructure.

- **Testing (acceptance).** These testing frameworks enable you to create and run acceptance tests (also known as customer tests or story tests) in a regression manner.

- **Testing (other).** This category includes a range of different tools, including tools for record-playback testing for user interface (UI) testing, defect tracking and management, security testing, database testing, and load and performance testing.

- **Testing (unit).** These testing frameworks, such as xUnit, enable you to write unit/developer tests.

---

1. Planning poker cards can be obtained via contact@UPMentors.com.

When writing this section we struggled with whether we should list example tools. The challenge is that the tool market is dynamic, with new tools being introduced, existing tools disappearing, and in the case of some OSS tools the code base splitting into competing products. We chose instead to focus on the categories of tools that you need and trust in your ability to find appropriate tools for your environment. One complicating factor to remember when you're doing this is that sometimes a single tool supports multiple categories, making it difficult to compare tools. For example, some build management tools include deployment functionality. As described earlier, an integrated tool such as RTC may support many tool categories.

LESSONS FROM THE TRENCHES—PROCURE YOUR HARDWARE EARLY

Traditionally organizations tend to purchase production hardware late in the project lifecycle. This is when they expect to do testing of nonfunctional requirements such as performance and load testing. DAD suggests that we test our increments of software in production-like environments early in the project. One of the key sources of risk on any project is related to these nonfunctional requirements. DAD projects mitigate these types of risks by implementing functionality early to test these requirements. To do this you need to have the relevant bits of your hardware infrastructure in place. This issue is another test of your organization's acceptance of agile approaches since it may require purchase testing environments early in the project.

Organizing Physical Work Environments

A number of logistical items need to be addressed at the beginning of the project that will quickly determine the degree of acceptance by your organization of agile development. One of these is to obtain a common work area.[2] We recommend that all team members, including the product owner and ideally key stakeholders as well, relocate to this central area *full time for the duration of the project*. This room or work area should have plenty of whiteboards to sketch on and some corkboard space if you intend to use non-sticky paper such as index cards for modeling and planning. Much of the modeling and documentation on agile projects is transitory in nature to fulfill a short-term communication need. Collaborative agile modeling around a whiteboard is effective for exploring requirements and technical details, and for supporting conversations in general. If you are using sticky notes for your taskboards, you will want to dedicate some whiteboard space for that, so plan accordingly.

If your team members have large dual monitors, you may not need data projectors. However, if teams are using laptops, it is common to have multiple data projectors running simultaneously

---

2. Scott refers to the willingness or lack thereof to set up a common work area as an "interior decorating decision."

for creating and reviewing all sorts of work products. If you have electronic taskboards, such as those provided by RTC, you may want to project the taskboard during coordination meetings.

Table 11.3 compares various strategies for organizing your team's physical workspace. For the sake of definition, a team is collocated if everyone is in the same room, near-located if team members are within driving distance, and far-located if one or more team members would need to take an airplane to physically attend a meeting. With the caves and common approach there is an open work area, the commons, in combination with one or more offices or cubicles, the caves. More on distributed teams later in the chapter.

In our experience the following factors, presented in priority order, are critical for creating an effective work area:

1. **Dedicated space.** The most effective teams have their own working areas. Even if space is at a premium in your organization, senior management needs to provide your team with the resources that you need if they want you to succeed. You don't want to have to wait to find a meeting room that's available to get some modeling done. You don't want to have to worry about somebody erasing your whiteboards or throwing your index cards in the garbage. We have both worked in several companies where there was a severe shortage of space, and we would have to wait for days to find meeting rooms. Progress ground to a halt. If you really are short on space, consider alternatives such as renting more office space for your team, moving other people elsewhere to make room for your team (this rarely goes over well with them), or even renting non-office space. Scott once worked on a project where they rented a house for a year so that the team could collocate.

2. **Significant whiteboard space.** As far as we are concerned you can never have too much whiteboard space, and luckily whiteboards are incredibly inexpensive. Our preference is for having whiteboards floor to ceiling wherever empty wall exists, even on support pillars if they're more than a foot (30 cm) or so in width. Developers should have their own private whiteboard space so they can sketch diagrams on them, either alone or with co-workers. If you don't have this level of whiteboard space, talk to your facilities people and whoever needs to approve such changes and tell them that it's a priority for your team.

3. **Digital camera.** Most of your team members will likely have smart phones with built-in digital cameras that can be used to take snapshots of your modeling artifacts. Common uses of digital cameras are to take pictures of critical whiteboard diagrams or paper-based models to include them in documentation.

4. **Agile modeling supplies.** You need a supply of whiteboard markers, sticky notes (have different colors and different sizes), index cards, writing paper, flip-charts, tape, stick pins, and even string.

5. **A bookshelf or storage cabinet.** You need somewhere to store your modeling supplies, reference books, and food.

6. **Large table.** Some modeling techniques, such as class responsibility collaborator (CRC) modeling, require a large table on which to work. Other times you need a table to place your notebooks on or more importantly somewhere to put food when you get lunch delivered. Mark recently worked on a team comprised of coffee connoisseurs that set up a coffee making station for their eclectic brews.

7. **Wall space to attach paper.** It's good to have some non-whiteboard wall space so you have somewhere to attach paper artifacts. If possible have a corkboard installed or simply leave some wall space empty.

8. **Projector.** Your work area should ideally have a built-in projector for on-demand projection of anything project related or for demonstrations. Some teams have a large flat panel for a "wallboard" that displays rotating views of key project dashboard and taskboard information.

9. **Reference books.** There is in fact some useful information in printed books. Hopefully *this* book is within easy reach of your team.

10. **Food.** Having food available in your working area is often appreciated by all and helps to build camaraderie. A selection is a good idea as not everyone has the same tastes or eating habits.

11. **Toys.** Having something to play with in your hands can help you to get "unstuck" when you're working. Many teams also enforce politeness rules by allowing people to throw a foam ball at someone else when they're being rude or inconsiderate.

Other features for your team room could include the following:

- A printer
- Electrical outlets for laptops (with adequate power supply to those outlets)
- A wireless network (within your corporate security constraints of course)
- Teleconferencing or videoconferencing capability to support dispersed team members or stakeholders
- Mobile whiteboards to supplement existing whiteboard space and to support impromptu model storming sessions
- Toll-free access to the tele/videoconferencing to encourage people to participate

Table 11.3 Comparing Work Area Strategies

Strategy	Potential Advantages	Potential Disadvantages	Considerations
Work room	Maximizes close collaboration between team members. Everyone can see the big visible charts and taskboard posted in the room.	Can become loud when multiple conversations are going on simultaneously. Some consider it claustrophobic. There is often a lack of whiteboard space (an interior decorating decision). There is a potential for hygiene issues. There is seldom an opportunity for personalization of individuals' workspace although great opportunity to do so for the team. Some team members may not be comfortable with the lack of privacy.	To address noise concerns team members sometimes wear ear plugs or listen to music. This prevents them from collaborating effectively and monitoring what is happening around them. If you are using a work room, sometimes called a war room, rather than an open work area, ensure that the room has adequate ventilation. These rooms typically have lots of equipment, projectors, and people that can cause the room to quickly heat up without adequate cooling. You don't want the team to use this as an excuse for not working in a collocated manner.
Open work area	More space than a work room. Supports teams greater than 20 people.	Potential lack of whiteboard space. If nonteam members are in the same open space they may not appreciate the noise level.	Consider going one step further and adopting a caves and commons approach.
Caves and commons	The commons provide the benefits of open work areas, listed previously. The caves provide privacy for team members when required.	Can often be difficult to obtain this much space, particularly in organizations new to agile.	–

(continued)

Table 11.3   Comparing Work Area Strategies (continued)

Strategy	Potential Advantages	Potential Disadvantages	Considerations
Near-located cubicles	Team members can personalize their space. More privacy for team members. Team members can still attend the daily meeting.	It is harder to collaborate due to the distance between people. Team members may forget or neglect updating the physical taskboard if it is not nearby. Reduced effectiveness of the physical taskboard.	Scott has found in surveys that the success rates of agile teams that are near-located is lower on average than teams that are collocated, even though the distribution of the team is minimal.
Near-located offices	Same as near-located cubicles. The ability to close the door increases the opportunity for privacy.	Team members will use low-collaboration styles of communication such as email.	Consider using online chat so that team members can see when team members are at their desks and be ready for instant answers.
Far-located members	Possibility for follow-the-sun development around the clock.	Potential time zone differences. Reduces effectiveness of the daily meeting.	—

Figure 11.2 depicts the layout of an agile work area at one of Capgemini's Accelerated Delivery Centres (ADC) in the UK. Both Mark and Scott have visited the ADC to observe the purpose-built workspaces, known as "pods," and how they aid the use of agile practices. The pods are open areas but are separated by walls to help give some privacy to the (sub)teams in each pod. The small round tables in the middle of each pod have a whiteboard surface, which allows the teams to regularly turn and face the center of the pod to model on the table. Another interesting feature of the Capgemini work area is that the lighting is slightly lower than normal and faintly blue in color. Software delivery can be stressful at times and even little things like the lighting can help address this challenge.

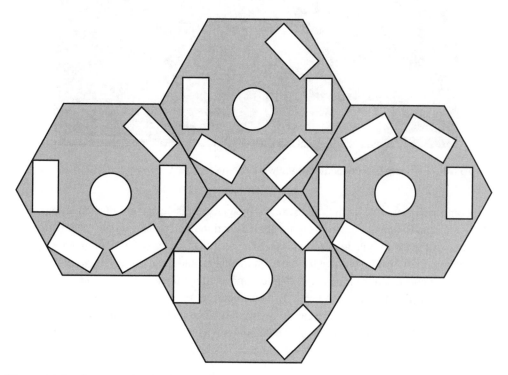

Figure 11.2 An example of agile team work areas. Picture courtesy of Capgemini's Advanced Delivery Centre UK.

Figure 11.3 shows a work room for one of Mark's projects where the team consisted of more than 20 team members. This picture was not staged and shows the team collaborating together. In the middle two team members are working to solve a problem. On the far left the infrastructure team is discussing the deployment process. Also on the left is a deep discussion between the infrastructure lead and the architecture owner. On the right-hand side a team member is reviewing a possible defect with the product owner to get clarification of the expected behavior.

Figure 11.3   Example of a collocated team work room

Comparing these two layouts there are advantages and disadvantages of each. Capgemini's approach is ideal for smaller teams as it has some isolation in its pods from the other teams. The work room of Figure 11.3 is good for a larger team as it maximizes collaboration among everyone. However, there was no privacy for the team members, and the noise level was high at times when multiple conversations took place. While some team members were comfortable with this, others were sensitive to the noise level. To help focus some team members listened to music while working, and some even wore ear plugs at times when they needed intense concentration. This in turn had the side effect of reducing collaboration a bit. It is worthwhile considering these factors and the makeup of your team when you design your work area.

Organizing Virtual Work Environments

Not all DAD teams are collocated with their stakeholders in a single room. In fact many agile teams in general are near-located, which means that people are reasonably close to one another, perhaps working in cubes in the same building and even with some people working from home. Roughly one in five agile teams are far located, which means that one or more team members are in different cities or even different continents. The physical work room strategy is appropriate for collocated teams, but something else is needed for distributed teams.

You may in fact have one or more physical work environments in different locations. Scott once worked with a team that was made up of three subteams in different cities. With this distributed subteam approach each subteam was collocated in their own right and communicated with other teams as needed. Sometimes a portion of the team members work individually at their own locations, either in offices/cubicles or from home. When there is a collocated subteam with a few people working from other locations we call this partially dispersed. When everyone is working from different locations, it is referred to as fully dispersed. For example, Scott is currently involved with a dispersed team of seven people with everyone working from home. Figure 11.4 depicts various possible team configurations. You can of course have the combination of several distributed subteams with one or more dispersed people.

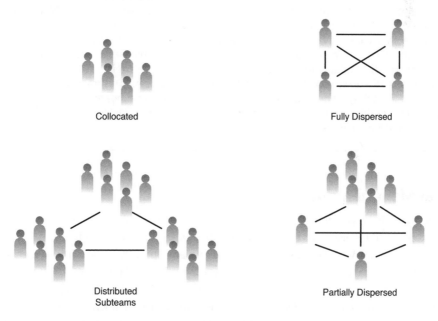

Collocated   Fully Dispersed

Distributed   Partially Dispersed
Subteams

Figure 11.4   Different geographic distributions of team members

The greater the level of geographical distribution the greater the need for tooling to address the collaboration challenges that result. For example, whiteboards and paper are incredibly effective modeling tools for collocated teams and for dispersed individuals who need to think something through on their own. But they're not that effective on their own to communicate in a distributed manner. Minimally you at least need to share images of the whiteboards and paper, either via digital snapshots or scans, or even use software-based modeling tools for anything that needs to be shared across locations. The point is that tools that work perfectly fine for collocated teams may not work so well for distributed ones. Similarly using a corkboard with paper pinned to it is a great way to implement a taskboard when the team is collocated or near-located enough that everyone has direct access to the board. But, this strategy quickly runs into problems when the team is distributed in any way, large, or working in a regulatory environment requiring proof of the process followed. As the result of the challenges associated with geographic distribution many distributed agile teams have adopted Jazz-based tools; see www.jazz.net, in particular RTC.

LESSONS FROM THE TRENCHES—FULLY DISPERSED TEAM

Lauren Schaefer is part of an independent test team in IBM Software Group, which is fully dispersed. The team has two people in North Carolina, two in Canada, one in Massachusetts, one in Maryland, and one in France. They rely on Jazz-based tools to manage their work, all of which is captured electronically. They use automated dashboards to manage their tasks and track defects. Once they started really tracking all of their work in work items they were able to customize the dashboards so they could easily tell what work was highest priority and what was in progress. They use these dashboards to make their daily meetings go faster. The build status for the entire Jazz development team is tracked in a work item where they all comment on blocking defects and build problems. This tracking work item is a huge benefit as they all get notifications when the work item is updated, enabling everyone to be aware of the status of the build and work to keep it in a stable state. The team also records all of their test results in RQM for easy traceability.

Visual Management

The practice of displaying information on all things related to the project is known as visual management, big visible charts, and information radiators (by Alistair Cockburn). The displayed information includes whiteboard sketches, iteration plans on taskboards, burndown charts, and often examples of screen or report designs. The status of the build might be indicated via a light (if the light is on, the build is broken); vacation schedules and a listing of highest outstanding risks may also be posted. Mark likes to display cartoons such as "Dilbert" that poke fun at traditional development methods and corporate bureaucracy, which remind the team that they are fortunate to be working on an agile team. Teams using instrumented tooling such as RTC may have a large monitor present displaying real-time metrics in a dashboard fashion. On this team daily coordination meetings are held in this common area so that team members can reference the displayed project information. They also have an electronic taskboard, an example of which is shown in Figure 11.5, which they reference and update as well.

One benefit of a visual management approach is that with so much project information available on view by anyone, including people wandering by from outside the project team, the need for written status reports disappears. In fact the need for status information that is stored somewhere else that is not as easily viewed is discouraged as a needless overhead. During coordination meetings and work throughout the day such information radiators speed things up considerably and reduce delays because everyone has the information they want about the project. The primary disadvantages are that you'll share both good and bad information about the project, something that can be challenging in politically charged environments.

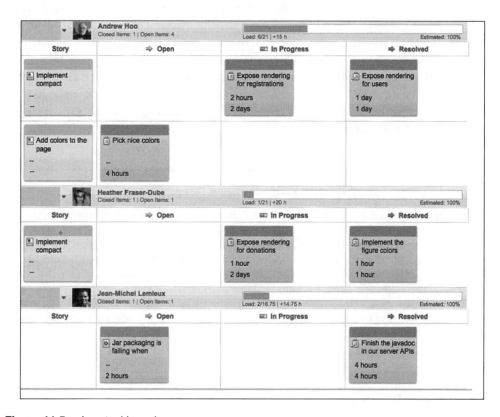

Figure 11.5   Jazz taskboard

Another benefit of visual management is that it promotes "swarming behavior" just as just-in-time (JIT) model storming to explore the details of a requirement or group discussion about how to address a blocking item identified during a coordination meeting. The basic idea is that team members swarm around the visual picture or taskboard and collaborate to address a problem or issue.

Adopting Development Guidelines

Part of being enterprise aware is following common guidelines, and these guidelines should be identified and agreed to early in the project. These guidelines should of course be appropriate for your situation. Potential guidelines include language-specific coding guidelines, user interface

(UI) conventions/standards, data naming conventions, security guidelines, and so on. Having such guidelines can accelerate your team's productivity because they encourage consistency, potentially avoid delays thinking through certain technical issues, and potentially increase quality.

One challenge that you may find at the beginning of a new project is that your organization doesn't have such guidelines. Perhaps one or more guidelines haven't been developed yet. In this case the onus may be on your team to start work on them or at least to agitate for someone to do so. Regardless of who does this work, they should first do a bit of research to discover whether existing guidelines are available externally to your organization. In general we believe that it is better to follow industry-level guidelines than organizational-level guidelines. In turn guidelines specific to your organization are typically more effective than those specific only to your project team. This level of guidance is better than individual guidelines, which in turn are better than no guidelines at all.

LESSONS FROM THE TRENCHES—AMBYSOFT GUIDELINES FOR JAVA

In the late 1990s Scott published the Ambysoft Java Coding Guidelines at www.ambysoft.com and made a PDF file available free of charge for anyone looking for comprehensive coding guidelines. Although these guidelines are a bit long in the tooth now since Scott hasn't updated the document for several years, many organizations licensed it from him because they realized it was much less expensive than writing a similar document from scratch. In fact one such company was Rational in the early 2000s for inclusion into the Rational Unified Process (RUP) at the time. Scott still runs into people who thank him for that set of guidelines and the time it saved them. These guidelines are still available and are downloaded regularly.

Concluding Thoughts

During the Inception phase you begin to build your team, or at least begin thinking about who you want on the team. This leads to considerations about providing them an environment in which to work. As such you need to secure both physical and virtual workspaces. While you may need to wait until the Construction phase begins, often teams set up the work area during Inception in preparation for staffing the team. Hardware may be installed in the room, and perhaps a virtual or cloud image might be created with the stack of development tools so that environments can be quickly "spun up" for newly onboarded team members.

Setting up a work environment that is conducive to seamless team collaboration is critical to the success of your DAD projects. Teams of fewer than 20 people should be collocated if possible to reduce overall project risk. However in many situations this is not realistic, especially for large or distributed teams. In these situations many types of tools can be helpful in maximizing collaboration effectiveness.

Additional Resources

For more detailed discussions about several of the topics covered in this chapter:

- **Surveys.** The effect of geographic distribution on the success rate of agile teams, and of other types of teams, was explored by Dr. Dobb's Journal 2008 IT Project Success Rates survey. The results of this survey are available at ambysoft.com/surveys/success2008. html.
- **Communication effectiveness.** In an article posted at agilemodeling.com/essays/ communication.htm Scott compares and contrasts the effectiveness of various communication techniques.
- **Distributed agile teams.** The book *A Practical Guide to Distributed Scrum* (IBM Press, 2010) by Elizabeth Woodward, Steffan Surdek, and Matthew Ganis is an incredible source of information about applying agile strategies successfully on geographically distributed teams.

Case Study: Inception Phase

To better understand how to successfully initiate a Disciplined Agile Delivery (DAD) project we're going to work through a fictitious case study—the AgileGrocers[1] Point of Sale (PoS) system. This case study is based on a similar project Mark was involved with although the names and details have been changed to protect everyone's privacy. The focus of this chapter is the Inception phase for the PoS system; later chapters explore the rest of the project in detail. Note that this is only one potential way to initiate a DAD project—tailor your approach to reflect the realities of your situation.

Introducing the AgileGrocers POS Case Study

On a Wednesday, Mark meets with Dean, the VP of Store Operations for AgileGrocers International, a retailing company that has 250 grocery stores across Canada.

Dean: Our store managers have been complaining about the fact that our point of sale systems are old. They also mention that customers have been complaining about long checkout lines. I have some money in my budget to upgrade the store systems, but I am not sure whether the investment would be worthwhile. I am not sure what they really need and what I will get for my money.

Mark: Why don't you give me a week to outline a solution for you? You will then have a better understanding of what the real problem is, what the solution alternatives are, and what it would take to implement the best solution.

Dean: Just a week! Surely that is not enough time. Traditionally we have spent three to six months doing planning and writing detailed requirements documents. I have usually ended up

---

1. This is based on a real project. However, "AgileGrocers" is a fictional name. Any resemblance to any similarly named enterprise is entirely coincidental.

spending a good portion of my budget on these documents while not seeing anything of real value in the meantime.

Mark: Well we are going to use a more modern approach to building solutions that does away with unnecessary work that delays delivering value to you, the stakeholder. This approach is called Disciplined Agile Delivery. It is a process framework that we use to guide our team in an efficient, yet disciplined fashion. Using this approach, there are very few surprises for you. You will quickly see your solution evolve before your eyes and have the opportunity to adjust what you want as we go.

Dean: Sounds interesting. Okay. Let's see what you can get done in a week.

Mark: Great. I need to spend some quality time with someone who can properly represent your business needs. He or she should understand the challenges you currently face and can help articulate what a good solution would look like. I also need to spend some time with an expert on the company's architecture.

Dean: I know just the people. Louise knows our business very well and is available to your project. If she does not have the answers, she can definitely get them quickly. Terry is our enterprise architect who could free up some time to spend with you next week. Bob understands the systems ops side.... *But*, they'll only be available 3 hours a day because....

Mark: Okay, I didn't expect them to be available full time anyway. We have project-related things such as envisioning the architecture, getting the workspace set up, and so on. We'll be doing that stuff when your people aren't available to work with us. But when they are with us they need to be prepared to be focused, to make decisions, and make trade-offs all in a timely manner. One more thing. We should assemble a cross-functional team of developers to set up their work environment and do some estimating.

Dean: Doesn't the project manager do the estimating?

Mark: Actually, modern agile methods understand that the best estimates come from those committed to actually doing the work.

Dean: That seems a bit strange to me; I'll have to see it work. I'll assemble your development team immediately. But I don't think they've heard about this agile thing before. Maybe we should just do things the old way.

Mark: Well part of my job as the agile team lead is to act as an agile coach. I will spend some time with them this week bringing them up to speed with key aspects of the DAD framework. Dean, you are a busy man, so as soon as I get back to my desk I am going to book some time with you for next week to review the results of this phase and determine next steps.

Dean: Okay, well don't get carried away. I am not sure whether it makes sense to change any systems in the stores at this time. I really don't know how a new system is going to fix our problems. So we'll see what kind of business case you can come up with in a week, before I commit to funding anything further.

The next day (Thursday) we decide to run a one week effort (the Inception phase) starting next Monday. Mark and the team need to create a business case and plan for implementing a solution for Dean's business problem. We also need to set up the environment and get the commitment of people and resources. This is not trivial and is a challenge to finish quickly. To get ready to start on Monday, Mark meets with the product and architecture owners to get buy-in to the approach.

Mark meets with Louise, the candidate product owner to discuss her involvement in the project.

Mark: Hi Louise. I am very pleased that you have decided to join our project.

Louise: Actually, I was "volunteered" to join this project. I have a lot of work to do already. I have training sessions with new store managers and need to prepare some new materials for these sessions. Hopefully this project won't take much of my time.

Mark: Well, Louise, we *do* need you full-time on this project if we are going to be successful.

Louise: That is not possible. Can I send someone in my place for these meetings this week? Since we are just doing planning this week, the project hasn't really started yet.

Mark: While we are not starting to build the solution until the week after next, the decisions on the scope and vision of the solutions are extremely important. Dean says that you have the best understanding of the current problems in the stores and already have expressed some ideas for the new point-of-sales systems. How about we hold the visioning sessions from 10:00 a.m. to 1:00 p.m. each day next week and I bring lunch in?

Louise: I hate to give up my lunch time, but if you limit it from 11:00 a.m. to 1:00 p.m. I suppose I could adjust my schedule.

Mark: I guess that is a reasonable compromise. This way we can minimize your time initially and have time to summarize your feedback and create some minimal documentation to describe the vision for what we are going to build.

The discussion turns to setting up a work environment:

Mark: Louise, we need a common work area. Our small team of eight people should all relocate to a common room and work there side-by-side. Can we have room E for this?

Louise: I don't think that is possible. The business analysts use that room for meetings with the users. We do lots of slide presentations, process diagramming, and discuss requirements and issues. The analysts then go back to their cubicles where they can work in peace and quiet to document the results of the meetings. They then schedule more meetings to review the documents. I know that the analysts would not want to work together in the same room.

Mark: I know that this is a new approach, but we know from experience that if our customer representatives such as yourself work together with the development team, the need for these meetings and the extensive related documentation is reduced dramatically. Let's try it. If it is not working, we can discuss alternatives.

Louise: Okay, but I don't think this will work.

Mark: I understand your skepticism, but let me promise to show you a new way of working next week when we get into developing your solution. Rather than trying to explain it now, it will make more sense when you see it in action.

Louise: Should we start your planning sessions on Monday?

Mark: Yes, let's. I will also invite Terry, the architect, to these meetings. It will be fun.
Later that day, Mark meets with Terry, the enterprise architect:

Terry: I understand that you are moving our developers for this project into one room. They won't like that! What are your requirements for the room and workstations?

Mark: Ideally the team should have notebook computers with wireless access to the network. They should have tooling that supports instant messaging. This will allow us to get instant answers to questions in the event that a team member is working outside the work area or offsite.

Terry: Our new tooling allows us to run constant builds and automated tests as we craft your solution. It allows us to also plan and track our work. Do we need a separate defect tracking tool?

Mark: For the approach that we plan to use, surprisingly no. Our development tool supports the ability to track defects as work items and that is all we need for now. I will explain when we get into the next iteration.

Terry, we are going to designate one of the developers on the team as the architecture owner. They represent your enterprise architectural vision on the project. This needs to be someone familiar with your organization's standards as well as what other enterprise assets are available to leverage or reuse.

Terry: Pete would be ideal for this role. I have worked with him closely for the last couple of years. I will make sure that I touch base with him regularly to ensure that he gets everything he needs.

Developing a Shared Vision

The following Monday Mark (team lead), Louise (product owner), and Pete (architecture owner) get together with Dean (project sponsor) to outline the business problem to be solved and to envision a candidate solution.

As a facilitator, Mark helps the assembled team put together a snapshot for the business case of this project.

Mark: Dean, what information do you need to help you make a decision on whether to invest in this project?

Dean: I suppose I would like a basic understanding of the following before I can dedicate more dollars to this project:

- What is the business problem? The symptoms and root causes? What happens if we don't change?

- What is the suggested solution? How does it address the business problem?

- What are the key needs and benefits (features) of the proposed solution?

- How long should the project last? At what point is the solution provided to the end users?

- What does the architecture of the solution look like?
- How long will this solution last? Will it need new features or an upgrade to a newer technology soon?

Mark: Wouldn't it also be useful to capture a list of the project's highest risks that could jeopardize delivery so that we can proactively take steps to mitigate them before they arise?

Dean: Yes, I suppose that would be useful. This seems like a lot of information. So I don't know how you can possibly do this in one week!

Mark: This may look like a daunting list. However, we are not looking for exhausting descriptions of the above. No amount of documentation written up front will accurately represent what our stakeholders want. The truth is, they will not know exactly what they want until they see it. Likewise, the delivery team will not know how long it will take to deliver the system until they get some experience building increments of the solution. So this is why we are spending a time-boxed week to get enough information to justify pushing the boat out to sea. We will quickly begin to steer as we get into the Construction phase iterations and form a common understanding of our true destination.

Dean: Okay, let's give it a shot, but it sure sounds like lots of meetings and documentation to me.

The team decides to jump in and create some work products to answer the above questions. To describe the business problem and outline a proposed solution with a list of features, they choose to create a short vision statement. The vision statement has been a popular work product of the Unified Process for many years. However, on our DAD project, we choose to capture the same information in a more streamlined fashion. Following is a summary of the key vision information that the team captured.

Vision for AgileGrocers' New Point of Sale (POS) System

AgileGrocers is a grocery chain with 250 stores across Canada. Thee stores have not had any updates to their store cash register equipment and software for more than ten years. The cash registers are continually breaking down and frustrating the cashiers. Lines are unacceptably long because each purchase transaction takes too long.

In the grocery industry, there is a trend to allow customers to check out their own grocery purchases. This reduces the need for cashiers and the cost saving can allow us to open up more checkout lanes. This vision statement describes the need for the new system as well as the proposed new functionality.

The team spends some time on the whiteboard mind mapping symptoms and root causes for the pain that the stores are experiencing with their current system. The salient points from the mind map, see Figure 12.1, were then captured as part of the vision statement (see Figure 12.2).

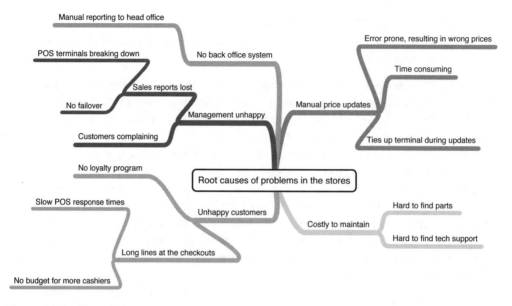

Figure 12.1   The mind map

AgileGrocers' sales are falling, largely due to

   Old cash registers that frequently break down

   Cannot find replacement parts

   No back office system for administering the store

   No connection to the head office

   Resulting in pricing errors and lost business to competitors

The best solution would entail replacing our old outdated POS system with a modern grocery store management solution that integrates with a back office system and allows us to exchange pricing and inventory information with our head office.

Figure 12.2   Capturing the business problem in the vision statement

   The team decides that as they proceed with implementing the solution they need to ensure that key stakeholders are kept informed and allowed the opportunity to guide the team toward the most effective solution. They therefore quickly list their key stakeholders in the vision statement, as shown in Table 12.1.

Table 12.1 Listing Key Stakeholders as Part of the Vision Statement

Stakeholder	Representative	Description	Responsibilities
Business sponsor	Dean	The business sponsor funds the projects and is the ultimate decision maker regarding project issues and requirements.	Provides funding, approves project plans and change requests.
Product owner	Louise	The voice of the customer, representing stakeholder needs to the team.	Determines and prioritizes scope for the solution. Acts as conduit to all stakeholders to clarify any information needed by the team.
Customer	TBD	Customer will use the system to self-check out groceries. Also receives service from cashiers.	A customer representative (TBD) will participate in usability testing of the new system.
Cashier	TBD	Cashier will use the new POS terminals for the system.	A cashier representative (TBD) will participate in usability testing of the new system.
Store manager	TBD	Store manager will use the back office portion of the new system.	A store manager representative (TBD) will participate in usability testing of the new system. He or she will also review requirements documents and provide feedback.

The team next does a brainstorming exercise to determine the business needs related to the problem. During the session, Louise says, "we need to track average cashier transaction time!" Mark suggests that this may be a good feature, but let's first concentrate on the business needs, before we start to identify system requirements. Mark suggests that perhaps the business need in this case is to track cashier productivity. We can decide how exactly later. Figure 12.3 depicts the list of needs identified by the team during their brainstorming session.

Now that we have a list of business needs that would address our business problem, Mark leads the team through an exercise to brainstorm stories and features that would address these needs. They associate each story with a need that it fulfills. This helps us to avoid dreaming up features that are not related to a basic need of the solution. By doing this we can avoid scope creep with "wants" versus true "needs."

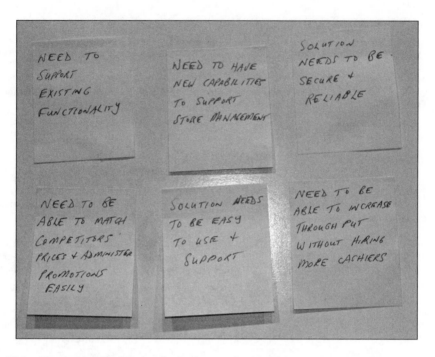

Figure12.3   Needs identified during the brainstorming session

The architecture owner Pete reminds Mark and Louise that we need to remember to capture the quality aspects of the solution (also known as nonfunctional requirements), such as expected system performance. Some of these ideas become sticky notes. Figure 12.4 shows a picture of the stickies from the brainstorming session that have been posted on the whiteboard, organized with their related needs from the previous exercise.

The needs and features from the sticky notes are quickly added as a list in the vision statement and are summarized in Figure 12.5. While a classic vision statement captures the key capabilities as features, we chose to write most of them in user story format. Notice that one of the features on a sticky note is "user friendly," which is a famously popular but ambiguous requirement. We captured the request from Louise during the brainstorming, but knowing that this is not testable as written, we made it a testable feature as shown in the list of needs and features in Figure 12.5.

Figure 12.4   User stories/features to satisfy the needs

DON'T WORRY ABOUT CONSISTENCY OF THE WORDING

The feature list in Figure 12.5 isn't worded consistently. Sometimes it talks about a solution and sometimes a system. Sometimes a feature is worded as a formal shall statement, and sometimes it's merely a statement. Sometimes "The system shall . . . " and sometimes "System shall . . . ." The important thing is that the information is being sufficiently captured so that it can be understood. Both Mark and Scott have been involved with projects where incredible amounts of effort were wasted to ensure dubious levels of consistency within the documentation, which added no practical value to the organization.

Product Overview

The new system will include software running on each new POS terminal as well as software running on a back office system. There will also be a connection to the head office system for the purposes of sharing inventory pricing information.

List of Needs and Features

The new system will include all the expected features of a modern POS system including

ID	Need	User Stories/Features

Need to be able to increase throughput without hiring more cashiers.

1. A cashier can transact a purchase of groceries on behalf of the customer in the traditional manner.

2. A customer can self-check out their grocery purchases without the assistance of a cashier.

3. Solution must support up to 10 POS terminals.

4. Groceries being scanned must return and display prices to the POS terminal within 2 seconds.

Solution needs to be easy to use and support.

5. Any user can choose to use English or French languages.

6. A user manual will be provided for cashiers, customers, and store managers in both English and French.

7. A cashier with no experience can use the POS terminal with 1 hour of training.

Need to be able to match competitors' prices and administer promotions easily.

8. A store manager can update electronic stock inventory and prices from the back office system.

9. Suggested prices of groceries are retrieved automatically from head office when maintaining inventory stock levels and prices.

10. A store manager can schedule store promotion sales in advance that will discount prices for the effective sales dates.

11. Price changes done via the back office system will be propagated to all POS terminals in real-time.

Solution needs to be secure and reliable.

12. System shall automatically failover to a backup system in the event of failure of the system to ensure no disruption in service.

13. Any user can log on securely to use the system.

Need to have new capabilities to support store management.

14. The system shall produce a number of sales reports and automatically distribute them to the store manager every night.

15. Each POS terminal tracks the time required to process each transaction on average as a measure of productivity.

16. A summary report is printed by each POS terminal when it is closed out.

17. The new back office system will have a Web-based interface that can be used remotely from outside the store.

Needs to support existing functionality

18. A customer can pay using credit and debit cards.

Figure 12.5   Product overview within the vision statement

After creating this initial list of stories, the following dialogue occurs among the team:

Louise: This looks like a great list of stories for our new system. However, Dean has asked me to remind you that we only have a staff budget of $400,000 for developing this system. Hardware and software are in addition to this amount, and naturally we need to be smart about that too.

Mark: Thanks for letting us know, Louise. This is a constraint on the solution and is useful to know.

Pete: We will have to make some compromises on the architecture to bring this in on budget. I don't believe that 2 second response time is possible given the hardware that we will have to use. I think that 3 second response time is a more reasonable expectation.

Louise: Well, I don't like it, but I suppose we all have to make compromises.

Story 4 is then adjusted to 3 second response time as a result of this conversation.

A key point is that constraints are useful to identify at the beginning of the project so that expectations are reasonable about what is achievable given the constraints. Table 12.2 shows the constraints that the team identified and listed in the vision statement.

DAD recognizes that agile project teams seldom work in a vacuum. At times they may be constrained by organizational standards such as those defined by architecture and database authorities. The table of constraints includes a requirement of the team to collaborate with the enterprise architect to ensure that opportunities for reuse are identified. These types of constraints are a good thing.

Table 12.2 Constraints for the AgileGrocers PoS

	Constraint
CON1	The costs of services to produce the system must not exceed $400,000.
CON2	The new system must use Java technologies and our existing standard tooling.
CON3	Designs for each story must be reviewed with the enterprise architect to ensure reuse of available services.
CON4	The system cannot go live during the months of November or December due to the holiday season.

Louise: I am pleased to hear that we will be conducting demonstrations of the solution at the end of each iteration. Will sign-offs be required for these demonstrations? Perhaps we should note that in the vision?

Mark: That is a good point, Louise. While we are indeed conducting demos, we try to minimize sign-off as much as possible as they can slow down the team. However, what we should talk about now is quality of service requirements related to the solution. We need to determine what your criteria are for accepting stories implemented in an iteration as "complete."

Louise: That is easy. All the requirements need to be implemented for each story, and they need to have zero defects.

Mark: I would suggest that if we wait for all defects, no matter how trivial, to be fixed, we will not be able to complete the stories at the end of each iteration. We will continue to discover and fix minor defects from all stories as we move through the iterations, so let's compromise on the quality expected at the end of the iteration for the stories that are developed.

After further discussion, the team agrees on conditions of satisfaction for the stories, documents them in Table 12.3, and adds it as a section in the vision.

Table 12.3   Conditions of Satisfaction for Work Delivered at the End of Each Iteration

ID	Acceptance Condition
AC1	Each story will have no priority 1 (Urgent) or 2 (High) defects.
AC2	Each story will have passed the acceptance tests as defined by the product owner before the end of the iteration in which the story is implemented.
AC3	Each story will be accessible only by those defined in the security model at http://internal.AgileGrocers.com/security/guidelines/.
AC4	Each story will be demonstrated to be recoverable in the event of a system failure—all database updates will be ACID transactions.
AC5	The user interface will conform to the user interface standards described at http://internal.AgileGrocers.com/dev/ux/.

We produced the preceding information for a brief vision statement over the course of two sessions over lunch, for a total of 4 hours.

VISION STATEMENTS AND PORTFOLIO MANAGEMENT

For our case study, we chose to enter the Inception phase with nothing more than a conversation and understanding that we should do something about a perceived business problem. This is of course from our point of view—long before our project began Dean had lobbied the CIO for a better solution, they discussed several strategies, and then the CIO initiated this project. Some organizations, though, go into Inception with some business case or document like the vision already completed. In fact, they may use these documents as the method to select projects using a portfolio management approach. If you indeed have this information going into Inception, that is great! It will greatly speed up this iteration.

Requirements Envisioning

A vision statement is useful for ensuring that all parties agree on what the business problem is and what a candidate solution could provide. Now, we need to elicit some requirements for the solution. There are many different ways to visually elicit requirements, including prototypes, storyboards, brainstorming, and mind mapping. Other ways of eliciting requirements include traditional techniques such as questionnaires and interviews.

For the AgileGrocers System we decided to create a use case diagram, shown in Figure 12.6, to help us derive user stories from our list of features. We gathered the team and our domain expert, Louise, around one of our whiteboards, and spent 20 minutes determining the key goals (use cases) and users (actors) for our system.[2] Tip: It is easy to create a use case diagram from a list of stories or features that you have already created.

Figure 12.6 AgileGrocers' use case diagram

---

2. For a discussion on why and when we use use cases as a modeling technique to supplement user stories, see Chapter 8.

This diagram shows the five key goals of the new system as well as the actors (cashier, customer, and store manager) that use the system. The new system will support the traditional model of asking the cashier to process the sale of groceries for the customer. However, we are adding the capability for the customer to self-check out via a Buy Groceries use case. The diagram also shows that we need to interact with three other systems (payment authorization, head office, and scheduler for running nightly jobs).

Mark facilitated the diagramming of this use case on the whiteboard. When everyone agreed it looked complete, he pulled out his phone camera and took a picture of it.[3]

Louise: What are you doing? That is not exactly a work of art!

Mark: Agreed. However, I am going to paste this into our vision statement.

Louise: Shouldn't you do it up nice in our McDrawing tool?

Mark: That could take an hour or two to make it look pretty. I think we can all read it, so let's be agile and use what we have done already and move on.

IS A USE CASE DIAGRAM AGILE?

A use case model is typically composed of both a diagram like the one shown previously in Figure 12.6, as well as a textural specification of the workflow for each of the use cases. These workflows can be written at various levels of detail depending on your preference. However, to be as agile as possible, we chose to do the diagram only for the purpose of clarifying the key users and goals of the solution. Mark finds that such a diagram can help to ensure that we have proper "coverage" of user stories such that we have stories to deliver each of the required goals. He has found that without this diagram, stories representing key functionality can easily be missed. Scott has found that business process diagrams and data flow diagrams (DFDs) are also good options for viewing the overall usage of your solution, depending on what your team and stakeholders are familiar with. Use whatever agile modeling technique you prefer to help flesh out your stories.

Creating the Ranked Work Item List of User Stories to Implement the Solution

A good place to start building your work item list is to decompose your features from your vision statement into user stories. Each of the features from the vision statement shown previously may be too large to implement fully in one iteration. They are also at too high a level for properly describing and prioritizing the functionality. We therefore decided to decompose each feature into a set of user stories. For example, Table 12.4 shows some of the user stories that together fulfill the requirements of the feature *A cashier can transact a purchase of groceries on behalf of the customer in the traditional manner.*

---

3. Mark used his smart phone to take this picture and used one of the many software packages available to clean it up.

Table 12.4 The Start of a Work Item List with User Stories (US) from Feature 1

ID	Work Item
US1	As a cashier I can scan barcodes for grocery items so that the price may be added to the purchase total.
US2	As a cashier I can weigh produce items so that the cost of the produce may be added to the purchase total.
US3	As a cashier I can apply store coupons against purchase in order to reduce the transaction total.
US4	As a cashier I can complete a purchase transaction.
US5	As a cashier I can print a receipt.

We made sure to include Pete, our architecture owner, in this session to ensure that we ask him for possible technical stories such as requiring online backups, fault tolerance, job scheduling, and other technical requirements to add to our work item list. As we identify each technical and user story, we make sure that we capture the acceptance tests that need to be passed to consider the story complete.

Architecture Envisioning

Figure 12.7 shows a simple context diagram[4] that Pete sketched on the whiteboard to help understand what type of information moves between the point of sale terminals, the back office system in the store, and the head office.

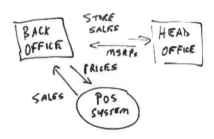

Figure 12.7 Context diagram

In addition to the context diagram, Pete led the team through creating a deployment diagram of showing the hardware configuration for the store and how it connects to the head office. The team felt that this was a useful diagram to help understand conceptually how the new system

---

4. The use case diagram of Figure 12.6 could also be considered a context diagram.

will look and communicate with the head office. Pete spent 45 minutes using a drawing tool to create the diagram that you see in Figure 12.8. The team understands that the actual hardware configuration could change as we learn more about the solution, but this serves to get alignment on the understanding of how it might work conceptually.

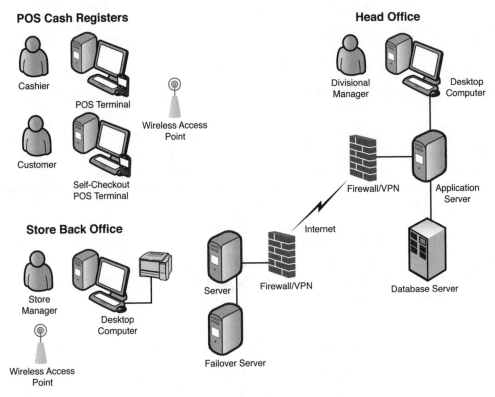

Figure 12.8   Deployment diagram for the AgileGrocers POS system

Pete takes a picture of the hand-drawn context diagram and pastes it into our evolving vision statement together with the deployment diagram file.

Release Planning

As discussed in Chapter 6, "The Inception Phase," during Inception we need to identify the initial release plan, which is a breakdown of the phases and iterations with start and end dates for the expected duration of the project. DAD teams deliver potentially consumable solutions at the end of each iteration. The high-level release schedule for the project is depicted in Figure 12.9. The team decides to run 12 two-week iterations of Construction. The Transition phase is longer than a typical project. It will take some time to roll out the new system across all the stores in Canada, so an eight-week effort is planned for the rollout.

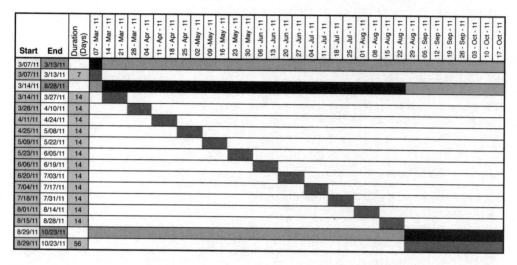

Figure 12.9 Release as a Gantt chart for our new AgileGrocers POS system

Estimating

The estimating for our AgileGrocers system for all the work items in the list came up with a number of 314 relative points (using the planning poker estimating technique described in Chapter 10, "Initial Release Planning"). Table 12.5 shows the same user stories from Table 12.4, but they now have estimates against each story.

Table 12.5 Relative Estimates for Items on the Work Item List

ID	Work Item	Relative Estimate (points)
US1	As a cashier I can scan barcodes for grocery items so that the price may be added to the purchase total.	13
US2	As a cashier I can weigh produce items so that the cost of the produce may be added to the purchase total.	8
US3	As a cashier I can apply store coupons against purchase in order to reduce transaction total.	5
US4	As a cashier I can complete a purchase transaction.	30
US5	As a cashier I can print a receipt.	5

Identifying Initial Risks

A partial example of the risk list that we created for this project is shown in Table 12.6. Notice that it is ranked by magnitude, with the biggest risks at the top.

Table 12.6   Example of a Ranked Risk List for the AgileGrocers POS System

Risk	Probability (%)	Impact (1-10)	Magnitude
The continuous connection to head office (required for inventory management) cannot be made sufficiently fault tolerant.	70%	10	7
We may not be able to send sufficient payroll details to SAP.	80%	4	3.2
We may not be able to get 3 second response time on credit transactions.	60%	4	2.4
The users are not sure what kind of operational reports they need.	50%	2	1.0

As you can see from these examples, it is not necessary to create a lot of documentation in the Inception phase. However, this minimal information is indeed required to make sure that the interests of all stakeholders are aligned before we go off and deliver a solution that does not meet their expectations.

Other Inception Phase Activities

There is more to Inception than producing documents and models. For our AgileGrocers project, we did a number of activities to prepare the environment for the Construction phase, including

- Set up a common work area where the team can work together.
- IBM Rational Team Concert was installed for the developers to manage the agile plans, work items, source code, and builds.
- Mark and Scott conducted IBM's three-day Disciplined Agile Delivery (DAD) workshop for the team to bring them up to speed with agile practices.
- The development team participated in the envisioning sessions so that they could develop an understanding of the solution and the various alternatives that were considered.

Alternative Approach to Running Your Inception Phase

For our case study, we used a set of work products and modeling techniques that we preferred for the situation. However, you may have your own preferences for how you put together your work products. Since we strive to produce no more than 20 pages of documentation in an agile Inception phase we chose to put our work into one document that we call a vision statement. If this does not work for you, you may choose to put them in several documents such as a Project Plan, Business Case, or Software Requirement Specification (SRS). The problem with having multiple documents is that you may unintentionally end up creating many more pages of documentation in aggregate than is necessary. It is important to understand that DAD is a framework, to which you adapt the techniques that you find most effective. The key is to satisfy the goal of the Inception phase, providing just enough written documentation to achieve stakeholder concurrence on the vision and gaining agreement to start building the appropriate solution. Table 12.7 shows alternative approaches that you may have taken in our situation.

Table 12.7   Alternatives to the Approach That We Took for Our Inception Phase

Where Our Goal Was To:	The Technique/Work Product We Used Was:	You May Have Chosen Instead:
Practice: Shared Vision		
Brainstorm the current business problem and root causes.	Mind map.	Fishbone diagrams.
Brainstorm potential needs and features that could address the root causes of the business problem.	Brainstorming session to elicit needs and features as sticky notes on a whiteboard.	Interviews of key stakeholders. (However, this is not particularly agile!)
List the key benefits and functionality for the proposed solution.	A list of features/stories in the vision statement.	Go straight from the brainstormed features to a list of coarse-grained user stories/epics.
List key stakeholders, project constraints, acceptance criteria, and key risks.	Identified these as tables in the vision statement.	Listed in sections in the above Project Plan.
Practice: Requirements Envisioning		
High level overview of system processes.	Use case diagram to show goals and actors.	Business process diagram, UML activity diagram.

(continued)

Table 12.7   Alternatives to the Approach That We Took for Our Inception Phase (continued)

Where Our Goal Was To:	The Technique/Work Product We Used Was:	You May Have Chosen Instead:
Practice: Architecture Envisioning		
High level overview of "to be" architecture.	Context and deployment diagram.	UML class, component diagrams. Informal sketches could have been used as well.
Practice: Release Planning		
Create a prioritized work item list of things that need to be done to implement the solution.	Features decomposed into a list of user stories inserted into the work item list.	Insert your user stories created in the previous step into the work item list. Disaggregate larger stories (epics) into smaller user stories.
Specified target release date(s), number of iterations, lengths, and dates.	A high-level Gantt chart to show the timeline, iterations, and milestones.	A simple phase plan schedule in a table as a section of the vision statement. A Kanban board.
Create high-level estimates for the work items.	Planning poker estimating session using relative points.	Estimating with actual hours.

Concluding the Inception Phase

Mark, Louise, and Pete meet with Dean, the project sponsor, and Terry, the enterprise architect, to have a one hour lightweight milestone review for the phase. Louise walks Dean through the document.

Louise: Dean, we have spent a few days fleshing out the problems of continuing to use our current store systems and how it is contributing to declining sales in our stores. We have outlined a suggested solution for replacing the store systems in the vision statement that we have here.

Dean: Remind me again what's in this "vision statement"?

Louise: The vision statement summarizes the current business problem, the suggested solution, the key features that will be delivered, the project timeline, key stakeholders, constraints, and risks. It is like a brochure that explains what you will get for your investment.

Dean leafs through the document.

Dean: Wow, what is this, hand-drawn diagrams?! Mark, for an expensive consultant this is very unprofessional! <frowns>

Mark: As an expensive consultant, I could have billed you an extra 4 hours to make these diagrams look pretty, but I believe that they are readable as they are. On agile projects, we try to eliminate unnecessary work to save you money. I would suggest that it would actually be *unprofessional* of me to charge you for frivolous work of gold-plating documents, wouldn't you agree?

Dean: I suppose you are right. Continue....

Louise: As you can see from the schedule section, we plan to deliver increments of your solution for your review every two weeks.

Dean: Okay. Now I understand that based on your findings, you don't think that it is realistic from a time and cost perspective to give this new application to all of our 250 stores?

Mark: Yes, that is correct. The budget doesn't allow us to upgrade all of the stores in the first release. Additionally, rolling out the solution to all stores across Canada will take many months. It will take time to configure and ship the hardware to all of the stores, and we have a limited number of trainers to help the staff convert to the new system. So we are planning to install the new system in 54 stores over a six-week period in Q3.

Dean: That makes sense to me. We will have more budget next year to roll out the system to the remainder of the stores. We don't want to be changing systems in our busy holiday season.

At the end of the session, Mark asks for and receives approval from Dean to continue into the next phase of the project (Construction) to start implementing the solution.

Dean: Well, congratulations! I would never have believed that you could put together such a concise picture to frame the project and its business case.

Mark: Thanks. Finally, as you requested we've summarized how our time was spent throughout the project (see Table 12.8 for the listing), and I think you'll agree that we stayed focused on the high value activities and didn't get down into the "specification weeds." We achieved this by structuring our time in a timeboxed manner and by capturing just the essentials at a high level. This is how we're going to proceed through the rest of the project.

Table 12.8   Summary of Tasks Completed and Work Products Produced in the Inception Phase

Tasks Completed
Brainstormed business problem root causes with a mind map (1 hour)
Summarized root causes into a problem statement (in the vision) (1 hour)
Brainstormed needs and features of solution using stickies (1 hour)
Listed these needs and features (in the vision) (1 hour)
Requirements and architecture envisioning (photos of diagrams pasted into the vision) (3 hours)
Carved our project timeline out into a set of iterations and determined deployment schedule (described as a section in our vision statement); also set up this release plan in RTC (3 hours)
Created a Work Item List of functional and technical user stories, together with acceptance tests derived from our list of features (in RTC) (12 hours)
Completed other sections of the vision statement related to stakeholders, project constraints, and risks (2 hours)

(continued)

Table 12.8   Summary of Tasks Completed and Work Products Produced in the Inception Phase (continued)

Tasks Completed
Reviews with various stakeholders (8 hours)
Prepared the development environment and work area for the team (8 hours)
Set up team members and roles in RTC (1 hour)

Work Products Produced
An eight page vision statement used for the final phase review, approval to proceed, and continuing guidance to the team
Work item list of prioritized user stories with relative estimates created in IBM Rational Team Concert (RTC)
Release plan with phases, iterations, and dates set up in RTC

Concluding Thoughts

So there you have it. A successful ending for this project's Inception phase. Granted, on some projects things do not always work out so smoothly. Sometimes upon completing Inception there is not a clear indication that the project makes good financial sense. In this case the project may be cancelled, or another iteration started to investigate alternatives, such as a changed business process or buying a package. Although some organizations see cancelled projects as a sign of failure, the truth is that cancelling hopeless projects should be considered a success if they are cancelled *before* a substantial investment is made in them.

We stress strongly that this case study shows only one possible way of getting to the same result. DAD is not a prescriptive methodology. Rather, it is a *goal-driven framework* from which you can draw ideas to achieve these goals. In this case, we want to achieve stakeholder concurrence that it makes sense to invest in a proposed solution to a given business problem.

CHAPTER 13

The Construction Phase

"Besides the noble art of getting things done, there is the noble art of leaving things undone."
—*Lyn Yutang*

Agile development has always entailed creating a solution in a series of increments. Each increment is completed in a fixed, timeboxed period of time, called an iteration or sprint. Disciplined agile teams work closely with their stakeholders throughout each iteration, focusing on performing the highest value work as defined by their stakeholders. The primary goal of the Construction phase is to produce a consumable solution that provides business value to your organization and meets or exceeds the minimum required functionality to justify the cost of deploying it. In each Construction iteration we evolve the current version of the solution toward that goal.

This chapter shows a goal-driven approach to completing the Construction phase of your DAD project. We then discuss detailed execution of your Construction iterations in Chapters 14 through 16. Chapter 17 continues our case study from Chapter 12, describing a typical Construction phase. Figure 13.1 shows a mind map of the structure of this chapter. We describe each of the topics in the map in clockwise order, beginning at the top right.

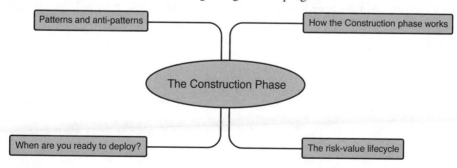

Figure 13.1   Outline of this chapter

THE BIG IDEAS IN THIS CHAPTER

- Early in the Construction phase the team proves the architecture with working code.

- Team members work together to learn from each other, to improve the way they work together, and to improve the overall solution they're providing to their stakeholders.

- The team will regression test their solution to the best of their ability and will potentially adopt test-driven approaches to specifying their work at both the requirements and design levels.

- Agile testing practices dramatically improve quality and maintainability of your solutions.

- The team will collaborate with enterprise professionals—such as enterprise architects, operations staff, and enterprise administrators—to ensure their solution reflects the overall strategy of your organization.

- Construction iterations produce consumable increments of the solution that are suitable for deployment when the stakeholders are ready.

- At the end of each iteration the team demonstrates their work to key stakeholders both to provide concrete visible status and to obtain feedback on their work.

How the Construction Phase Works

As described later in this chapter, DAD suggests that in the early iterations we reduce delivery risk by proving the architecture with working slices of the solution that validate the key components of the architecture. In subsequent iterations we produce additional increments of the solution that are of sufficient quality to be potentially consumable if deployed to the customer. Once we actually have sufficient functionality to deploy the solution to the customers, we conclude the Construction phase by ensuring that the solution is ready for deployment.

The Construction phase has a number of specific goals, all of which are indicated in Figure 13.2.

Goals for the Inception Phase	Goals for Construction Phase Iterations	Goals for the Transition Phase
- Form initial team - Identify the vision for the project - Bring stakeholders to agreement around the vision - Align with enterprise direction - Identify initial technical strategy, initial requirements, and initial release plan - Set up the work environment - Secure funding - Identify risks	- Produce a potentially consumable solution - Address changing stakeholder needs - Move closer to deployable release - Maintain or improve upon existing levels of quality - Prove architecture early	- Ensure the solution is production ready - Ensure the stakeholders are prepared to receive the solution - Deploy the solution into production
Ongoing Goals		
- Fulfill the project mission - Grow team members' skills - Enhance existing infrastructure	- Improve team process and environment - Leverage existing infrastructure - Address risk	

Figure 13.2 DAD lifecycle goals

Let's explore how each of the goals indicated in Figure 13.2 is addressed:

- **Produce a potentially consumable solution.** To say that "code is only what matters" is clearly an exaggeration. However, code is what makes our delivered solution run. We need to get to working software as quickly as possible. One of the key agile principles is "Simplicity—the art of maximizing the amount of work not done—is essential." It is important to keep this in mind when choosing whether to work on an artifact and to what level of detail. Show your users a working solution as quickly as possible and at regular intervals. This begins in the first iteration of Construction and continues for each subsequent iteration. Customers will soon tell you whether you are on the right track. Often they will tell you that you have missed the mark. This is a natural outcome. It is a good thing that you found this out early while you still have the opportunity to adapt your solution toward what they truly need and expect.

- **Address changing stakeholder needs.** A work item list (known as a backlog in Scrum) is a priority ordered stack of work items that need to be completed to deliver your solution to your customer. It is meant to be dynamic and reflective of the current priorities of your customers. As such, anything that hasn't been built yet, and remains in the stack of work items, can be changed at any time. This is a huge advantage over traditional methods that require customers to specify their requirements in exhaustive detail at the beginning of the project, and punishes them through change control procedures when they inevitably discover that their priorities have changed, or new requirements become visible as they start to see their solution materialize. Encourage your product owner to adjust the backlog at any time as scope and priorities change. This is a healthy approach to building solutions and ensures that features delivered to customers are actually those that are most valuable to them. As described in Chapter 14, "Initiating a Construction Iteration," it is useful, however, to set expectations with your customers as to what is achievable by the end of the last planned iteration. Your work item list should show groups of work items that are achievable in each of the remaining iterations so that your customers understand that anything below a certain point in the list is currently out of scope. This encourages them to self-manage their scope accordingly.

- **Move closer to a deployable release.** Ideally, at the end of each Construction iteration we have a solution that is potentially consumable by our customers. By consumable, we mean that it is not only "shippable" but is actually usable by the customer. However, for many projects it is often not feasible to deploy the solution at the end of each iteration. Your organization should strive to deploy your solutions to customers as frequently as possible. Only when they are actually using features of the solution can they realize a return on their investment. Many companies are getting good at deploying often, some even deploy many times *per day*, which gives them a huge competitive advantage.

- **Maintain or improve upon existing levels of quality.** A key differentiator of agile over traditional methods is that we have a working, consumable solution early in the project lifecycle. It is only consumable if it has a high level of quality. Building quality into the process from the start of the project and using techniques such as test-driven development (TDD) makes this possible. As described later, systems tend to become more difficult to maintain as they grow unless technical debt, which we describe in Chapter 15, "A Typical Day of Construction," is continually addressed.

- **Prove architecture early.** Flawed architectures are a common cause of project failures. A large application is difficult to rearchitect without considerable rework. It is therefore critical to determine early in the project that the architecture can indeed support the requirements once it has been fully built. DAD suggests that requirements that touch key points of the architecture should be implemented as high priority items to prove the architecture. More on this later in the chapter.

In addition to these phase-specific goals we also need to continue focusing on the ongoing goals:

- **Fulfill the project mission.** We spent some time in the Inception phase coming to a consensus with the stakeholders on the project vision. It is important to evaluate progress toward achieving this vision on a continuous basis. It's also important that the mission is clearly articulated to new team members, and an easy way to do that is to have a common project vision.

- **Grow team member skills.** As described in Chapter 4, "Roles, Rights, and Responsibilities," tools don't build software, people do. Invest in your team. Hands-on agile coaching can greatly speed your adoption and increase your chance of success. Infusing experienced agile professionals who take on key roles such as team lead can be helpful. Pairing of team members with different skill levels can also help increase the effectiveness of your team.

- **Enhance existing infrastructure.** Look for opportunities to establish and socialize patterns and assets that can be reused.

- **Improve team process and environment.** Effective agile teams are constantly looking for ways to improve their effectiveness. Teams should be empowered to change any aspect of their process or environment.

- **Leverage existing infrastructure.** Look outside your team for assets that can be reused for your project. This could include standards, patterns, mechanisms, code, or services, for example.

- **Address risks.** Consistent with DAD's risk-value lifecycle, the project should actively indentify risks and take steps to address them early in the lifecycle.

Figure 13.3 shows the 3C rhythm of the Construction phase, depicting the high-level flow of work throughout the phase. A critical point to understand is that the activities of traditional development disciplines, such as architecture and testing, occur iteratively and incrementally throughout the Construction phase. These traditional disciplines are not phases in their own right, and DAD should not be tailored in such a way as to make them phases.[1] These disciplines are so important to agile teams that we strive to do them every single day. What may vary is the amount of work that we do in each discipline as we proceed through the Construction phase. This is another reason that it is important to have team members with cross-functional skills so that they can do the work that is emphasized at a particular point in the phase. To see this, let's explore how each discipline is addressed during the DAD Construction phase by describing the practices shown in Figure 13.4 within the context of the discipline to which they apply:

- **Architecture.** The most critical architecture work is done in the early Construction iterations. While we have already done some architecture envisioning in the Inception phase, in Construction we need to prove that the architecture can indeed support both the functional and nonfunctional requirements by implementing stories that have good architectural coverage. We describe this later in the chapter as the risk-value lifecycle.

---

1. A common failure pattern of Rational Unified Process (RUP) adoptions was to tailor the RUP phases of Inception, Elaboration, Construction, and Transition into Requirements, Architecture, Programming, and Testing phases (albeit keeping the original names). Sadly many organizations didn't recognize that this mistake was why they didn't achieve the benefits that they should have, and that many agilists who denigrate RUP often do so because their only RUP experiences are with these sorts of RUP adoptions.

Other practices within the realm of architecture include proof-of-technology "spikes" or set-based design whereby a story is implemented with two separate architectural approaches in case one doesn't work or is inferior. The architecture owner may also recommend refactoring be added to an iteration's work where necessary to minimize technical debt. Just-in-time (JIT) model storming occurs frequently to solve architecture and design problems.

- **Analysis.** Using an agile approach, we resist the traditional approach of writing extensive requirements specifications up front. Instead, the product owner (often with the assistance of business analysts and domain experts) applies the prioritized requirements practice to maintain an ordered work item list that continues to evolve over the life of the project as the requirements and their priorities change. An alternative to writing requirements specifications is to write your requirements as executable tests. This is described further later.

- **Design.** On agile projects there is seldom much value in creating detailed design documents as they tend to become stale quickly. However, it is common to do some JIT model storming perhaps on a whiteboard between team members to review designs before committing them to code. Good, proven designs from these models may, however, be documented in a lightweight manner in an architecture notebook or in a tool such as a wiki, as were your architecture models created during Inception. Patterns, design mechanisms, and development standards are an accelerator on agile projects, particularly for large teams or teams with a mix of senior and novice developers. For application code the detailed design information is captured in the form of executable tests by teams that have adopted a test-driven development (TDD) approach. For database schemas you may choose to capture the design in a physical data model, particularly if you're using a tool with support for both schema generation and reverse engineering of changes to the schema.

- **Programming.** Many agile practices, notably from the Extreme Programming (XP) method, relate to programming. Catching defects early is a critical part of the efficiencies derived from agile techniques. Developer regression testing allows the developer to run automated tests against all code including their own every time even a small change is made so that defects are caught before they are injected into the integration stream. Programmers periodically refactor their code to improve its design without affecting what it does, so that it is easier to maintain in the future and performs better. A more advanced version of developer regression testing is TDD. It requires discipline and skill to write unit tests prior to writing the code itself, but results in better designed code and ensures good test coverage since new code (including defect fixes) shouldn't exist without a test first.

- **Testing.** The nature of testing has changed dramatically with the adoption of agile methods. The days of large testing cycles at the end of the project are largely behind us except for those stuck using the traditional approach. Automated regression testing now replaces much of the manual effort of testing. Testers are freed from the drudgery of repeatedly executing manual test cases and can focus more on exploratory testing to detect things that automated tests are not good at. In addition to developer TDD, acceptance test-driven development (ATDD) is also a practice that has changed the way testing is now done. Business analysts need to start thinking about how to test a story as part of eliciting the requirements of a story. Defining the tests up front allows the developers to understand what "done" means for the story—that is, when the specified tests pass. These business-readable tests can also be automated as a regression suite using acceptance testing frameworks. Independent testing by people outside the team is a good supplemental practice to the team's testing practices to ensure that the testing process has not been compromised by the team's natural bias to focus on happy-path testing. In Chapter 15 we discuss and compare these different testing approaches in more detail.

- **Technical writing.** Technical writing activities, particularly around deliverable documentation such as operations manuals, user documentation, and support manuals, typically occur throughout the project. Ideally a person or persons with technical writing skills will be team members, following practices such as continuous documentation or document late.

- **User experience (UX).** To the end user the user interface (UI) is the system. People with UX skills should be actively involved with the project throughout the entire lifecycle to ensure that what the team produces is consumable by your stakeholders. This includes working closely with end users to ensure that the user interface is usable, with operations people to ensure that the scripts/routines provided to them are usable by them, and with all stakeholders to ensure that the deliverable documentation is understandable and easy to work with.

- **Project management.** Team leads, people who might have been project managers in a previous life, should create an environment for the team that allows them to excel. He or she should foster transparency and accountability by visualizing work with techniques such as taskboards, velocity, and burndown charts, and through facilitation of team interactions such as the daily coordination meeting. The need for planning does not go away with DAD, so the team lead facilitates an iteration planning session at the beginning of each iteration. Look-ahead planning also occurs to ensure that the work item list is well formed and prioritized before each iteration begins. Your agile processes should be designed to capture automated metrics as a byproduct of the work that is being done. Thankfully team leads do not need to spend a lot of time gathering and reporting information about the progress and quality of the system since tooling that supports agile metrics captures this in real-time and presents it in a variety of ways using dashboards (see Chapter 20, "Governing Disciplined Agile Teams"). Collocated and near-located DAD teams can also achieve this benefit through swarming around a shared taskboard.

Continuous process improvement is an integral part of effective agile teams. While it can happen at any time during the project, normally at the end of each iteration the team lead facilitates a retrospective to review the team's success and discuss opportunities for the team to improve. Other aspects of project management that occur during the Construction iterations include the team lead responsibilities of addressing issues in a timely manner that surface during the daily coordination meetings, scheduling demonstrations and other milestone reviews with stakeholders, and other administration that is usually required on even the most trivial projects.

- **Quality assurance.** Continuous integration utilizes the practice of regression testing and integrates the team's unit tested work into an integration area frequently to ensure that developers' changes do not break the system as a whole. Continuous deployment takes the integration-tested application and automates the deployment and its validation to any environment. Continuously performing developer regression, system integration, and deployment testing increases the confidence in the system quality dramatically compared to the traditional late-lifecycle integration approach. Technical debt is the tendency of systems to become increasingly difficult to support and maintain as they grow in size. Quality assurance understands the need to incorporate regular refactoring as a necessary investment and part of any system's evolution to keep technical debt levels manageable. An important part of quality assurance is that there are good configuration management practices in place. All work products should be versioned and managed in your configuration management tool so that any version of your system, with all its supporting collateral such as deployment scripts and tests, can be restored and rebuilt at any time in the future. As described previously, independent testing is a good mechanism for ensuring quality of the solution as well.

- **Common to all.** Many agile practices apply to all team members regardless of discipline. All team members participate in the daily coordination meeting to plan their day's work, report progress, and surface issues. JIT model storming is done by all team members to solve issues as they arrive. These models could be to flesh out requirements or designs. Continuous documentation should be done in a minimalist way for information that is not already captured in code and tests. Non-solo development is an extension of XP's pair programming practice. DAD extends the idea to include all team members, suggesting that working in pairs, regardless of specialty, often makes sense, increasing both productivity and quality. The need for a sustainable pace suggests that if the team is expected to execute iterations successfully over long periods of time, it is unacceptable to expect the team to work more than reasonable hours. Quality deteriorates for team members that are tired or stressed for long periods of time.

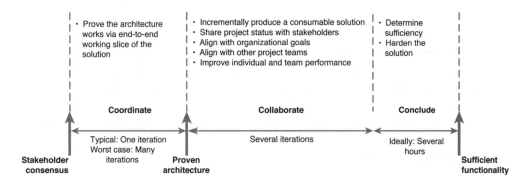

Figure 13.3 Construction phase overview

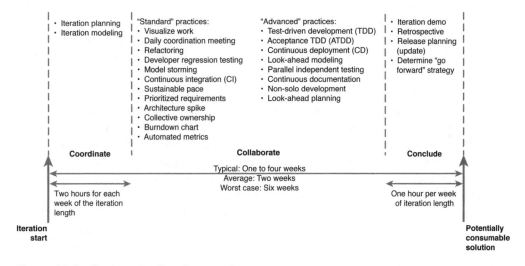

Figure 13.4 Construction iteration overview

The Typical Rhythm of Construction Iterations

Figure 13.4 shows the typical rhythm of a single Construction iteration. Prior to an iteration starting, the team will have worked with the product owner to groom the work item list so that the priorities and scope of the upcoming iteration are current and accurate.

During the iteration the team collaborates and interacts throughout the day face-to-face if possible to maximize their effectiveness in building the solution. Figure 13.4 also lists a number of common agile practices that your team may apply during Construction iterations—remember, you will tailor your approach to address the situation that you face. These practices are described in their context in the next few chapters.

The team concludes the iteration by focusing on stabilizing the release to ensure that there is a potentially consumable increment of the solution. Other end-of-iteration activities include retrospectives, milestone reviews, and demonstrating the solution to stakeholders.

Figure 13.4 forms the basis for our discussion for the next three chapters as we describe how to initiate the iteration, collaborate to complete the work, and then conclude the iteration.

The Risk-Value Lifecycle

Agile methods such as Scrum use a value-based prioritization method, known as a value lifecycle in the spirit of "the customer is always right." That is, the product owner ranks the backlog (work item list) according to the highest value features. It does indeed make sense that we prefer to build the functionality that provides the greatest return on investment (ROI) to the customer first. This is consistent with the mainstream agile preference to deliver value into the hands of the customer on a frequent basis, ideally at the end of each iteration. However, as you learned in Chapter 10, "Initial Release Planning," it often isn't realistic to deploy into production at the end of each iteration.

For large enterprise DAD projects, it is typical to spread the implementation of functionality across a number of iterations before actually deploying into production. With this extended time window, we are free to reprioritize features to include risk as a consideration in addition to value. We know from history that deferring implementation of features related to high risk is a big mistake. There is a saying that you need to attack risk before it attacks you. In the early stages of a project, we encourage teams to have a *maniacal* focus on reducing risk and uncertainty. We do this by implementing features of the software related to the difficult stuff. Mark refers to this as building the "tricky bits" (high risk) versus the "juicy bits" (high value). In Chapter 2, "Introduction to Agile and Lean," we introduced the DAD lifecycle, which is shown again here in Figure 13.5. Note in the diagram that early in the Construction phase we have the "Proven Architecture" milestone. Many of the technical risks of the project are related to architecture, and by implementing the hard stuff early we prove that the architecture can support the nonfunctional requirements such as performance and usability. Of course we may also find that the original architecture vision doesn't work and therefore we'll need to evolve it accordingly. This is an example of adjusting early (what some people call failing fast).

Delivering high-value features as early as possible is still important, and more often than not high risk work items also prove to be of high value.[2] Often agile teams ignore or forget project risks. So when you rank your work item list, it is important to consider ranking by both risk and value. As described in Chapter 10, you create a ranked risk list during the Inception phase.

---

2. When a high risk item proves to be of low business value, you should stop and consider whether that item is really required at all.

Actively use your risk list to help determine your implementation priorities and whenever possible link risks to work items that help to mitigate the risk. Figuring out how to deal with technical risks early in your project by actually building working code to prove that they are no longer risks will save you grief later in the project.

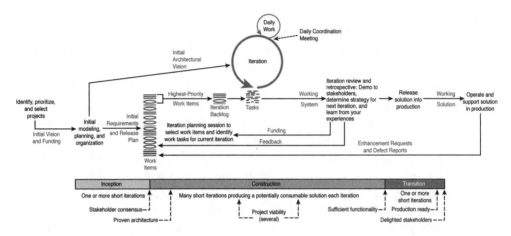

Figure 13.5   The Disciplined Agile Delivery lifecycle (basic)

When Are You Ready to Deploy?

After a set of Construction iterations have been completed, and the product owner believes that together it is ready to be deployed to the customer—a minimally marketable release (MMR)—it is probably appropriate to have a milestone review. The purpose of the review is to achieve consensus among key stakeholders that the solution is ready for deployment, and that the stakeholders are actually prepared to receive it—that is, documentation is complete, training has been done, user environments have been set up. If there is agreement that we are ready to deploy the solution to the customer, the Construction phase ends and we proceed into the Transition phase, described in Chapter 18, "The Transition Phase."

The characteristics of this review are similar to any implementation, agile or not. Considerations would include assessment that the functionality complete meets the criteria of an MMR, and that the quality (defects outstanding) is adequate. If the stakeholders agree, we move into the next phase of DAD, which is the Transition phase. For projects that do periodic or regular deployments, there can be multiple Transition iterations. These patterns are described in Chapter 18.

Construction Patterns

Several common strategies applied during the Construction phase seem to work well in practice, and several seem to work rather poorly in practice. The success of this phase is determined by your ability to understand and adopt the successful patterns appropriately and avoid the anti-patterns when you can. Let's begin with some patterns for success:

- **The team can be reliably depended on to demonstrate increments of software at the end of each iteration.** As described earlier in this chapter, if we cannot display a high-quality increment of working solution at the end of each iteration, we have not had a successful iteration. Well-functioning agile teams understand this and ensure that everything that they do is a value-added work toward this goal. They are quick to raise issues or roadblocks to the team lead, resist perfectionist work, and resist scope creep.

- **Team members finish their tasks ahead of schedule and ask to help others with their tasks.** On traditional projects that use silo approaches, team members are encouraged to do their job, and do it well, rather than ensuring that the team delivers its iteration goals. A sign that things are going well on your Disciplined Agile project is that team members finish their tasks and actively seek to "sign up" for additional tasks on the taskboard. On traditional projects, where people are encouraged to stick to their tasks, this is not normally seen. Detailed work breakdown structures are often buried in an MS project plan, and it is not easily visible what other tasks someone could help out with. Taskboards make this visible, and team members can easily see what work needs to be done and volunteer to work on anything. Any agile team lead has seen this self-organization in action, and it is a beautiful thing to witness. You see team members move their items to the Complete column and pick off other stickies in the "not started" column to start working on them.

- **Iteration dates never move.** If the team cannot deliver demonstrable software at the end of each iteration, this is a sign that they are not committed to agile development (or that they are still learning). If the iteration was planned in a self-organizing fashion, not delivering to their own commitments is problematic. It could be that the team is not cohesive and some individuals are not carrying their weight. It could also mean that team members are not being truthful with their daily reporting of status. Or the team could still be gaining experience in estimating. Perhaps scope is changing during the iteration (which is not acceptable). If the team is falling behind during an iteration, they should feel comfortable admitting this to each other and choose to pull out scope if necessary to ensure that the work items remaining in scope for this iteration are properly tested and shippable.

- **Any stakeholder can walk into the common work area and request to see a demonstration of the working software as it currently sits, at any time.** Agile teams build their software many times a day and run their automated tests continuously. They often deploy successful builds to a demo environment so that stakeholders can work with it whenever they want.

Construction Anti-Patterns

There are several common *anti-patterns* that we've seen teams exhibit during this phase:

- **A work item list that is too big to easily manage and comprehend.** The work item list should be filtered to contain only items related to the current release so that it is easily understood. Defer breaking down features into stories for future releases until your next release planning sessions.

- **Inattention to risk mitigation.** It is important to constantly be conscious of the project's highest outstanding risks and proactively take steps to mitigate them as quickly as possible. In many cases, this means implementing work items that can determine whether the risk is a real concern. Post your risks on a whiteboard or flipchart in the work area so that they are not out of mind, and better yet link them to work items that mitigate the risks.

- **Assuming that the architecture will work without proving it with code.** Elaborate designs in tools or on paper are not sufficient for proving that the architecture can support the requirements. These "paper-based" architectures are no substitute for working code as proof that the architecture is solid.

- **Assuming that an iterative approach alone ensures that you will build the right solution in an *effective* manner.** Carving work into a series of iterations is no guarantee that you are being agile. We have seen some projects do requirements specifications in the first iteration, design specifications in the second, and so on which is nothing more than a traditional waterfall approach in disguise. We have also seen many projects doing the easy "high value" functionality first, leaving the hard things until the late iterations and then discovering that their architecture cannot handle the complexity.

- **One or more of your team members are working on other projects in addition to yours.** As stressed in lean thinking theory, task-switching between projects takes time and is a huge source of waste that should be eliminated by ensuring that all team members are dedicated to the project. Unfortunately having people assigned to multiple projects is a reality in far too many organizations, often due to overspecialization of staff members.

- **A work item isn't done.** None of its points count toward the amount of functionality delivered. Finish it next iteration. Ask why this happened, and try to improve your process.

- **Last iteration we planned for X points but delivered Y.** Next iteration your velocity is Y, regardless of any wishful thinking or schedule pressures. A more moderate approach is to consider the average of the last few iterations or the general trend. Decreasing achieved velocity trends are a troubling sign. It could be that the team is feeling over-worked or that there are some morale issues.

- **During the iteration we missed some tasks when iteration planning.** Update the task list when you realize you missed the tasks. More importantly, ask why this happened so that you can improve your planning efforts in future iterations. Put a big asterisk on the task sticky to indicate that it was an unplanned task. Mark prefers to use a special color sticky note so that it is obvious that we missed a task, and to help remind us not to forget it next time. Seeing these colored stickies on the board is a good reminder to discuss it in the retrospective. Teams that are using electronic tools to manage tasks often have the ability to simply set an attribute or add a tag to indicate that the task was originally missed.

- **During the iteration we realized we missed a requirement that another depends on.** Identify the new requirement, prioritize it, estimate it, and put it on the stack. Stub out the missing functionality, or swap out the blocked requirement for something else. Learn from this and improve your requirements exploration efforts.

- **During iteration planning sessions, the product owner is trying to decide whether new items should be added to the work item list, or be reprioritized.** As described earlier in the chapter product owners should be continually "grooming" the backlog. This can be done at any time, but can be formalized with iteration preplanning meetings. If this is done properly, the product owner should have the work item list updated and current before the iteration planning session starts. Manipulating the work item list in the planning session wastes the team members' time and gives the impression that the product owner is not clear on the immediate objectives and priorities. It also makes it difficult to conclude the planning session in a couple of hours.

- **Defect counts are increasing in each iteration.** Avoid the "snowplow" effect of defects piling up. The longer they remain outstanding, the more expensive they are to fix. Needing a "stabilization iteration" to fix defects before releasing is a sign that too much time was focused on making progress, in lieu of maintaining acceptable quality. Leaving defect fixing to later in the lifecycle is also an indication that your solution may not be truly shippable every iteration after all.

Concluding Thoughts

The Construction phase iterations as described by DAD are not materially different from how other methods such as Extreme Programming (XP) and Scrum describe them. DAD, however, pulls the majority of these practices together into a cohesive set that provides guidance across all disciplines. We supplement Scrum/XP with additional practices related to agile modeling, addressing risk early, and working within an agile governance framework. In coming chapters you see how the Construction phase works in detail.

CHAPTER 14

Initiating a Construction Iteration

Sometimes the work we want to do is not the same as the work that needs doing or the work we're getting paid for.

This chapter describes how to smoothly initiate a Construction iteration. How you begin each iteration is critical for your successful execution of Disciplined Agile Delivery (DAD) projects. You also learn that these initiation activities can potentially be streamlined by some look-ahead work in the previous iteration, albeit at risk of doing a bit of needless work if your direction subsequently changes. The two key activities are iteration planning and iteration modeling.

This chapter uses terminology that assumes that your team is following a tailoring of the Disciplined Agile Delivery (DAD) process framework, which includes organizing your work into iterations. Advanced DAD teams following a leaner approach replace iterations with a continuous stream of work. Instead of an iteration planning meeting held at the beginning of each iteration, these teams perform planning meetings whenever it makes the most sense for them. Similarly, iteration modeling evolves into just-in-time (JIT) model storming.

Figure 14.1 shows a mind map of the structure of this chapter. We describe each of the topics in the map in clockwise order, beginning at the top right.

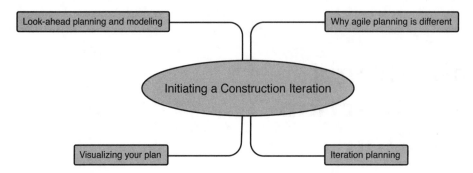

Figure 14.1   Outline of this chapter

THE BIG IDEAS IN THIS CHAPTER

- Teams invest a short period of time at the beginning of each Construction iteration to learn about the product owner's highest priority items, and then plan and commit to deliver this work by the end of the iteration.

- Successful agile teams incorporate modeling as a critical part of understanding the requirements and designs of the iteration's work.

- Effective DAD teams enter a Construction iteration having done some preplanning to ensure their work item list is well formed, as well as possibly researching technical options for implementing the high priority items.

Why Agile Planning Is Different

During the Inception phase, your team should have developed an initial release schedule that shows the planned iterations, when they occur, and when you believe you will release into production. This schedule captures important high-level information required to guide the project but not the tactical details required to organize your day-to-day work. The goal of iteration planning is to think through the work that needs to occur during the coming iteration. This planning is done as a team.

It is important to recognize that an iteration is not a mini-waterfall where activities such as requirements, design, coding, and testing are executed sequentially. Rather, team members conduct work for these disciplines and more in *parallel* throughout the iteration. For instance, at any given time some team members may be implementing requirements while others are modeling upcoming work and others still writing test scripts. Working iteratively is made easier if the team members are cross-functional generalizing specialists who can work on a range of tasks as needed, thereby reducing bottlenecks and increasing overall team efficiency.

Another important observation is that agile teams work collaboratively. Several people may work together to implement a single functional requirement, perhaps even following non-solo development practices such as pair programming and modeling with others. DAD team members work closely together as needed, sometimes for a few minutes before they go back to working individually and sometimes for several weeks or even months at a time. Who is working with whom changes dynamically throughout the iteration as needed.

Iterative and collaborative ways of working have a significant effect on detailed planning. Investment in a detailed Gantt chart or PERT diagram that depicts dependencies and timings between activities is futile because the work on agile teams is so fluid. A simple list of tasks with indications of the person(s) who intend to work on that task proves to be a better strategy to capture a detailed plan. Furthermore, because of the dynamic nature of the work you need to coordinate regularly throughout the iteration. In Chapter 15, "A Typical Day of Construction," we discuss the practice of holding a daily coordination meeting, which helps to reduce the need for sophisticated plan documentation.

Iteration Planning

The morning of the first day of the iteration may be the most critical. You may choose to start your iteration on a Monday, but interestingly some teams prefer to start their iterations midweek. This might be because team members for distributed teams need to come in from out of town. Also, in our experience some team members sometimes choose to start their Mondays later than usual and may drift into the office late, missing part of the planning session. The team needs to be focused to plan the work for the next few weeks, ideally doing so in a couple of hours. Mark likes to schedule a lunch the morning of the iteration planning workshop. If the workshop runs late, the planning can be completed during lunch since you have everyone there anyway. The first time the team goes through this exercise it can be a bit awkward, so don't be surprised if it takes a full day or more, but subsequent planning workshops can become amazingly efficient. Experienced agile teams often organize into small groups and do the planning themselves with little intervention by the team lead.

This chapter discusses how self-organizing teams estimate and plan their work. In Chapter 4, "Roles, Rights, and Responsibilities," we argued that the role of a team lead differs substantially from a traditional project manager and is a bit more robust than a ScrumMaster. Agile approaches such as DAD recognize that the team members themselves are best suited to plan their work since they are the ones committed to delivery of the work items and are most familiar with what technical tasks are required to implement them. The team lead facilitates and leads the planning session but should *not* list and assign tasks to team members. This is sometimes difficult for experienced project managers acting as team leads to do. When coaching teams we often see leads say "I need you to do this…" In a light-hearted way we remind them that this is not allowed.

The goal of your planning workshop should be to identify a realistic plan to address one or more work items for your stakeholders that is formed and then committed to by the team. Figure 14.2 overviews the iterative workflow of a planning workshop. DAD teams that have adopted a lean approach to managing work items perform planning on a just-in-time (JIT) basis for an individual work item instead of a collection of work items. When this is the case the first step of Figure 14.2 isn't needed (lean DAD teams pull work into their process only when they have capacity to do so).

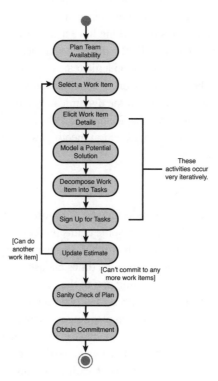

Figure 14.2   Iteration planning workshop workflow

LESSONS FROM THE TRENCHES—START ITERATIONS MIDWEEK

Andy Pittaway, an executive project manager in IBM Global Services in the UK, has found that it is better to start and stop iterations midweek. This is because on many of our projects people are not fully available on Mondays or Fridays due to other obligations or the need to travel. As a result he's found that these days are not great for the starting and closing activities, which require the whole team. In addition he has found that midweek teams have easier access to the enterprise support people they need if they run into some difficulty and need to ask for additional help.

Let's review each activity of the iteration planning meeting.

Plan Team Availability

For the team to be able to commit to delivering a set of stories for a particular iteration, we need to understand everyone's availability. Ideally, you should seek dedicated commitment from each team member on your project. When team members work on more than one project at a time their productivity goes down dramatically. Worse yet, the team may not feel that these people are truly committed to the iteration outcome.

Despite what some managers believe, team members never have eight hours per day to do productive work. We need to determine how many "ideal hours" per day each team member can actually dedicate to tasks that they are responsible for. Time that each person spends in meetings, or helping other team members complete their tasks is not included in their estimate of daily ideal hours. A typical number might be five or six hours per day for someone actively dedicated to the team. For situations where you are pairing people to work on tasks this number might be even lower.

Create a simple spreadsheet that tallies the hours for each team member for each day of the iteration. Refer to the case study in Chapter 17, "Case Study: Construction Phase," for an example of a resource planning spreadsheet and how to estimate ideal hours. Team members should have their calendars available during this planning session. Ask each team member how many ideal hours they expect to be available each day. Put zero for the days that they are on vacation or leave. Adding up all the ideal hours that each team member can dedicate to tasks for each day of the iteration gives a total number of ideal hours available to the team. This total is important, and we refer to it later in this chapter when we plan the details of the iteration.

The next six activities are performed for each work item that we plan to deliver in the iteration, as depicted previously in Figure 14.2.

Select a Work Item

The next agenda item in the planning session is to select the highest priority item from the work item list to complete within this iteration. Prior to this meeting your product owner will have ordered the work item list according to a combination of various drivers, compared in Table 14.1, such as the following:

- **Business value.** Agile is about delivering high value to customers on a frequent basis. Once the highest risks of your project have been mitigated, value typically becomes the primary determinant of your work item priorities.

- **Risk.** As described in Chapter 13, "The Construction Phase," DAD recommends a risk-value approach to prioritizing your work. You should implement technically risky work items in the early construction iterations to reduce project uncertainty, the goal of meeting the proven architecture milestone. Technically risky work items, such as integrating with existing legacy systems or accessing legacy data sources, often support high value requirements to your stakeholders so these work items are usually toward the top of a value-driven work item list anyway.

- **Due date.** Sometimes work items are due on or before a given date. This occurs due to legislation requiring specific functionality in your solution or a contractual obligation such as a promised feature to an important customer in the case of a commercial product.

- **Operational emergency.** Many DAD teams are working on the new release of a solution already in production or the marketplace. When this is the case it is possible that an operational emergency, such as the solution being down or experiencing a significant defect, can motivate the team to drop whatever they are currently working on to do the work to address the emergency. Addressing operational emergencies is an important aspect of your overall DevOps strategy.

- **Dependencies.** Sometimes it may be necessary to implement lower value work items before high value due to requiring certain functionality in place to make something else work. Note that there are strategies to reduce the impact of these dependencies such as building a "mock" to simulate the functionality that eventually will be required. However, sometimes it is just simpler to reprioritize a work item or two and just build the real thing.

We recommend that business value be the primary driver of your prioritization strategy, but that it be tempered by the recognition that you should also adopt a risk reduction strategy to increase the chance of project success. Many DAD teams also need to prioritize some work items by due date and operational necessity, an important aspect of your overall DevOps strategy. We're leery of prioritization by dependency except in rare cases where doing so clearly reduces costs associated with mocking out that functionality.

Elicit Work Item Details

The goal of this activity is for the team to learn more about the detailed requirements pertaining to the work item—to perform JIT requirements exploration. At this point many DAD teams have no written details about a work item beyond a simple sentence or two on an index card or in your planning tool. These work items could be user stories, defect reports, feature statements, technical stories, or other various items that need to be completed to implement the solution. The team obviously needs to understand some basics around what each work item is all about before they can decide how it will be implemented. So the team must talk with someone who understands those details. For functional requirements such as user stories or use cases this would be a stakeholder, the product owner, or a domain expert. For nonfunctional requirements, such as a technical story, a technically oriented stakeholder such as an operations person or enterprise architect may be your best source of information, as would your architecture owner. The team asks questions to clarify details related to the work item. Regardless of who is providing the details the product owner should make the business benefit of each work item clear to the team. Providing this context minimizes the risk of delivering the work in a manner inconsistent with the product owner's vision.

Table 14.1 Comparing Work Item Prioritization Strategies

Prioritization Driver	Advantages	Disadvantages	Considerations
Business value	Provides greatest return on investment (ROI) for your stakeholders. Reduces functional and political risk by producing most important business value at all times.	Requires stakeholders to agree to prioritization. May lead to inefficiencies and a lower level of reuse (but may be worth it if business value is high).	Should be your primary driver but cannot be the only driver in most enterprise situations. Long term ROI will be impacted if technical debt accrues due to a desire to deliver business value quickly in the short term.
Risk	Increases chance of project success by reducing technical and business risks.	May initially decrease ROI provided by team due to focus on lower business value items.	High-risk items are often high-value items, so impact on ROI is typically negligible.
Due date	Enables the team to fulfill legal obligations.	Potential to impact ROI when a large number of such items are done at the same time.	Avoiding fines or bad publicity due to noncompliance of legal obligations, or losing customers due to lack of required functionality, should be seen as high business value anyway.
Operational emergency	Work critical to the success of your existing solution is performed by the people best suited to do it.	Team is distracted from the job of working on the next release.	If operational emergencies occur frequently it is a sign that you need to invest in better quality in your upcoming release and that you should consider creating a subteam specifically for doing that sort of work.

(continued)

Table 14.1   Comparing Work Item Prioritization Strategies (continued)

Prioritization Driver	Advantages	Disadvantages	Considerations
Dependency	Enables the team to reduce reliance on mocks or stubbed out functionality, thereby decreasing work they need to do.	Can be used as an excuse to push low priority work to the top of the work queue, thereby reducing ROI.	When functionality is mocked out your solution is effectively not potentially shippable until that functionality is in place.
			Try to develop requirements that are loosely coupled to one another, but recognize that dependencies between requirements are an unfortunate reality.
			On large DAD teams the dependencies between the work being performed by different subteams will motivate more prioritization by dependency than is normally experienced by smaller teams.

The team also needs to have a discussion with the product owner regarding when the work item will be considered "done." For now a good way to define this is to identify acceptance tests for the work item—for example, "The successful withdrawal of cash will result in cash being removed from the customer account, the customer's card returned, and the cash dispensed." Another might be "Verify that the ATM will not allow a customer to withdraw more than $600 in the last 24 hours." For expediency it is not necessary to capture all these tests during the short planning workshop, but you need to have enough to ensure that you understand the scope of the work item. The complete collection of tests needs to be implemented before the end of the iteration for the work item to be considered sufficiently done for it to be potentially consumable. The work item isn't truly done, however, until it is part of an operational solution in the hands of your stakeholders—in other words, DAD teams define done as up and running in production (or the marketplace).

You need to consider the behavior that should occur when the desired functionality works appropriately, often referred to as the happy path. You must also think about what could go wrong, often referred to as alternate courses of action. Finally, for functional requirements you need to consider nonfunctional issues, such as security, usability, performance, availability, and many more and capture relevant acceptance tests for those issues. Handling nonfunctional requirements was discussed in detail in Chapter 8, "Identifying the Initial Scope."

This part of the planning meeting will go much smoother if part or all of the team has been involved in any look-ahead iteration preplanning meetings since they will already have a basic understanding of the work items to be delivered and may also have some agile modeling already done on proposed designs of these work items.

LESSONS FROM THE TRENCHES—GREAT TEAMS EMPATHIZE WITH THEIR STAKEHOLDERS

We have often seen teams that mechanically create code according to specifications without truly understanding the real business value of what they are doing. Just as traditional analysts and testers should learn more about development, developers should learn more about analysis and user experience design (UX) to name only two disciplines. This includes learning elicitation skills to explore the problem and how to create a consumable solution to that problem. We have periodically seen a product owner become frustrated at the apparent lack of empathy of team members for the business problems and a lackluster approach to understanding the true nature of the business. In our experience product owners who are full-time employees of a company can be particularly sensitive to an apparent lack of caring when the rest of the team is comprised of external consultants. In all likelihood they have had to explain the details of their business repeatedly over the years to a number of different people, which of course could be frustrating.

Model a Potential Solution

Modeling of the solution occurs at any time throughout the iteration. However, for many teams the majority of "detailed" modeling occurs at the beginning of the iteration as part of their planning efforts. Any modeling that is done should be just enough to understand how to implement the work item. This practice is called iteration modeling, and it will be performed iteratively to explore detailed requirements and to identify a potential solution to those requirements.

Chapters 8 and 9 overviewed a collection of modeling techniques, such as flow charts and UML sequence diagrams to name two, and described how to apply them in an agile fashion. DAD teams do just enough modeling during Inception to obtain stakeholder consensus regarding the project scope. Although this is done early in the project it is typically not a big requirements up front (BRUF) exercise where detailed requirements specifications are written (although in a small minority of situations that can in fact happen). For the purposes of this planning workshop your team references requirements definitions as needed. For small collocated DAD teams the key requirements models are likely captured on whiteboards or paper on the walls of your team room for all to see (a practice called information radiators, big visible charts, or wall of wonder). DAD teams working at scale, particularly those that are geographically distributed, should consider using a software-based modeling tool to capture key model information. If the requirements model is captured electronically the team may choose to project it on the wall for reference.

Team members will stand up around a whiteboard and model alternatives using techniques such as class diagramming, sequence diagramming, flow charts, screen sketches, or other types of models. These modeling techniques were discussed in some detail in Chapter 9, "Identifying an Initial Technical Strategy," as part of identifying a technical strategy. The goal is to go into enough detail so that the developers have a common vision for how the solution would be designed/implemented. They then break down the work item into tasks. You want to keep iteration modeling such as this to a minimum; otherwise, the planning workshop will quickly become an all day exercise.

Lessons from the Trenches—Iteration Modeling Saves the Day

Tony Grout, an executive consultant with IBM Rational in the UK, recently worked as part of the team on a freight forwarding system for a client. They developed the solution with close input by stakeholders, but they still couldn't relate to the solution until they'd pretty much built it to release quality in the iteration. They heard more than once "I'll know when I see it." This was killing them in terms of cost, time, and team morale. By the time they stopped and rethought the process they were 30% over budget.

They stepped back and decided at the start of the monthly iterations to spend the first few days doing iteration modeling by prototyping using low fidelity paper and then click through screen mockups. Then they would finally commit to full-blown code. This didn't completely remove the misundertandings, but they managed to deliver the project without adding any additional cost and time beyond the 30% already incurred.

If more details are needed later in the iteration when you are implementing the work item you can always do some JIT model storming as needed (described in Chapter 15). JIT modeling is more effective than up-front modeling because the details tend to depreciate over time—the longer in advance that requirements are described the less likely it is that they represent actual stakeholder needs at implementation time.

Decompose Work Item into Tasks

Once a work item is understood by the team the goal is to decompose it into the tasks that are required to implement it. For a user story you might identify analysis activities such as "describe business rules," "mock up screens," or "write story tests." You're likely to also identify development tasks such as "write tests and code for the Loan class," "write stored procedure to save a loan," and "refactor the Account component." When the work item describes a functional requirement, you may choose to include specific tasks to ensure that you address applicable non-functional requirements. Examples include "encrypt Account information across network" and "performance test loan update to database."

With collocated or near-located teams these tasks are typically handwritten on index cards or sticky notes and then posted on your taskboard. When the team is using a manual taskboard the index cards end up on a corkboard, and sticky notes are put on a whiteboard. If you're using an electronic tool such as IBM Rational Team Concert (RTC) or a spreadsheet someone will want to transpose the tasks into the tool after the planning meeting. This is usually done by the team lead.

REMEMBER TO CONSIDER DEPENDENCIES

What about dependencies between work items? In theory, well-written functional requirements will stand alone and do not have dependencies. However, there are always exceptions. In these cases, combine work items that are dependent on each other or simply ensure that the work item that is a dependency is built first. If the dependency is on functionality or data that is being delivered by another project team you should not commit to delivering your work item until the other one is delivered. If this is not possible you may need to stub out or mock up the dependency to the other work item until it is delivered (although sometimes this isn't possible if you don't understand the behavior of what you're trying to stub out, a common problem when working with legacy systems). Try to avoid stubs/mocks if possible. Stubbing out interfaces to other components that you need increases risk since it prevents you from truly being able to deliver and test end-to-end functionality. This approach violates the principle of delivering shippable software at the end of each iteration. Finally, if work items have circular dependencies on each other it's an indication they should be implemented in the same iteration.

Far-located teams where some or all team members cannot physically attend a planning meeting may choose to use a tool such as RTC to plan your iteration. This is likely to be done using a combination of either an audio- or videoconference call with the planning tool displayed via a webcast so that everyone can see real-time updates. Some teams cannot find a common time to have a conference call because they are globally distributed. For example, a team with members in Europe, North America, and Asia will have no working hours in common for all team members. Such teams need to focus on using the planning tool and then hold several planning calls to coordinate across the team.

Sign Up for Tasks

A key principle of self-organization is that team members identify, estimate, and sign up (or "volunteer") to do the tasks. But when do team members actually do this? We have seen different approaches. Some teams feel comfortable signing up for the tasks during the iteration planning workshop. They write their initials on the tasks as they volunteer to do them. This can be helpful for the team to collectively understand who is going to be responsible for different bits of the work items.

However, determining who owns tasks in the iteration planning meeting is a type of "upfront" planning, albeit very short-term, that we try to avoid if possible. A more agile approach is to sign up in a just-in-time (JIT) basis when a team member has finished a task and is ready to start another one—in other words, team members pull tasks into their own work in progress (WIP) as their capacity allows. In this case, they would move their current task to "complete" status, and look at the board for another task to sign up for. This works best in a truly collocated environment where the team member says, as he is in front of the taskboard, to his other team members (who are working there in the same room) "I just finished this, how about I start on that?"

In a situation where you are not collocated, picking new tasks in isolation might not be optimal. Another team member might have wanted to do that task, or the rest of the team might have pointed out that it makes sense for another team member to work on it. If you have tooling such as RTC that has integrated work item management and chat built in, you could have this discussion online with the team so this problem would be minimized.

AGILE TEAMS ARE "SELF-LEVELING"

Thankfully, on agile projects, we do not need project managers to assign resources to tasks and worry about "leveling" the plan to ensure that we have the right mix of resource skills on a project. Agile teams are "self-leveling" since they share the workload and pitch in where required, regardless of role.

Update Estimate

For each task the team members estimate the time required to complete it and capture the number on the task card. Each task should be approximately one to five hours long. Tasks longer than eight hours should be avoided if possible and instead be organized into smaller tasks.

As part of release planning completed in the Inception phase iteration we created an estimate of "relative points" for each work item. The scope and intent of the work items that we are going to deliver in this iteration may have changed materially since that estimate was done. Additionally, we have a better understanding of these items now that they have been described in greater detail. As a result, as we understand the requirements better and model the solution we may realize that the point estimate is under- or overestimated relative to the other items. Furthermore, the original estimate may have been based on the ordering of work items. For example, work items A and B share overlapping functionality, so the first one that you implement will include that functionality. If you change the order in which you do A and B, the point values should potentially change to reflect this. Accordingly, it may make sense to change the estimate for some work items as we plan the work to implement them. After this planning workshop, based on an improved understanding of the solution, someone, typically the team lead (possibly in discussion with the other team members), should go back to the work item list to update relative estimate for future planned work items that are similar. This is often called "grooming" or cleaning the backlog.

Can the Team Do More Work This Iteration?

Now that the team has planned the work for delivering a work item, they consider whether they can do more work. If so, they go back and select another item off the work item stack and follow the same process that we have described. How do you know how much work to plan? This depends on the team's "velocity," which is the number of relative points of work that the team can deliver in an iteration. If you are planning the work for an iteration, select enough work items for which their relative point estimate adds up to the team's current velocity. With the exception of your first iteration, the velocity reflects your team's ability to deliver functionality in the previous iteration. So, if your team only completed 18 points of work the previous iteration, it's a good assumption that you'll only be able to accomplish the same amount of work this iteration. Or you may choose to average the delivered points from several previous iterations to determine your velocity. If you are in the first iteration, however, you have no record of how productive the team is, so you have no established velocity and therefore need to make a good guess.

Furthermore, at this point in time we recommend that your teams commit to deliver only work items whose efforts together add up to about 80% of the ideal hours available. This is based on our experience that unplanned tasks inevitably surface during the iteration and that the team tends to be overly optimistic when estimating the time required to complete their tasks.

Sanity Check

We recommend doing a sanity check of the planned work on the taskboard to ensure that the team isn't overcommitted, with a further reality check that individuals aren't overcommitted either. For large teams that are organized into a collection of subteams this process is further complicated by needing to do a sanity check for the individual subteams, too. The basic strategy is to add up the individual estimates and compare the total to the total available hours for the team. If the effort of all the tasks is greater than the total hours available, they cannot commit to delivering the scoped iteration work items. In this case you have several alternatives:

- **Postpone some work.** In this case remove the lowest priority work item from the list of items to be implemented and add it back to your work item list/pool as future work to perform.

- **Drop work.** Are there one or more work items that you pulled from your work item list/pool that your stakeholders don't need any more? Granted, this likely isn't the case at this point in the game, but it can be a good question to ask. Your product owner should actively prune work items that aren't required throughout the entire project as the requirements evolve.

- **Work differently.** Can we take a less formal, more agile way to deliver the other work items? Can we eliminate a work product, document, or meeting for this iteration? Can we work more optimally as a team? For instance, if we normally pair up to write test cases, perhaps we can work as individuals in this iteration, and one of the testers can write some code. Granted in the long term this decision could jeopardize quality and thereby increase technical debt. Sometimes we choose to make prudent trade-offs to get the work done quicker.

- **Get help.** Can some work be performed by another project team? Can someone be brought onto the project? The challenge with this strategy is that according to Brook's law you risk slowing down the team in the short term by bringing on new people.

- **Drop people from the team.** It's a harsh observation, but sometimes you invite someone onto a team who just doesn't fit in well. Maybe it's someone who doesn't have the necessary skills and doesn't seem to be picking them up even in a learning environment common on DAD teams. Maybe it's a senior person who isn't good at working with others junior to him. Maybe it's someone who isn't good at working in a dynamic, agile environment. The point is that you may be able to speed up the team by losing someone who is slowing you down. Of course, you usually can only make this sort of assessment after working with someone for a few iterations.

An important input into your sanity check will be the metrics that have been captured to date by your team. Your team will either have a manual dashboard showing important information such as your ranged burndown chart, which shows progress to date as well as a ranged estimate as to when you may deliver. Some DAD teams have an automated project dashboard; visit www.jazz.net for live examples from several IBM product development teams, showing metrics being generated through usage of various development tools. Some teams of course have both. These dashboards provide insight into your past performance and current status that you can and should use to help you determine the viability of an iteration plan. See Chapter 20, "Governing Disciplined Agile Teams," for a detailed discussion of agile metrics.

Obtain Commitment

Let's review what we have done:

- We have selected a set of work items to tackle in this iteration. The customer for each work item (a stakeholder, product owner, architecture owner, or domain expert) has given us a refresher of what it is all about, and the team has had an opportunity to ask questions to clarify details.

- We have received personal commitments from each team member on the ideal hours that they can commit to the iteration to complete the tasks that they volunteer to do.

- The architecture owner has discussed these requirements with the team and may have spent some time on the whiteboard doing some agile modeling of a potential design solution.

- The team has decomposed each work item into small tasks that are required to implement it. They have collectively provided a time estimate for each task.

- The team, with the assistance of the product and architecture owners, has clarified, added, or refined the story acceptance tests that define what "done" means for each work item.

- In aggregate we have determined that there are enough hours available to the team members to complete the tasks that they themselves have identified and provided estimates for.

Now is the climactic moment of the planning session for the team lead. The team lead asks "Based on *your* understanding of these work items, *your* tasks and estimates, do we (i.e., *you*) agree to deliver these work items at the end of this iteration?" Since the team produced the plan, with their own tasks and estimates, they *should* agree to commit to *their* plan. If they do not, it may be that they feel that their estimates are not accurate due to their lack of understanding of the work items. It could also mean that there are issues—such as mistrust within the team, an organizational culture where people don't commit, or an organizational culture that punishes failure— that need to be resolved.

If there isn't commitment the team lead needs to be frank and ask why so that any issues are surfaced. If the issue is lack of understanding of the work items, spend some time elaborating details with the product owner. Sometimes the product owner may not be able to answer detailed questions about a work item and may need to bring in a stakeholder or domain expert to provide clarity. Have the team discuss other work items while you leave the planning session (or call someone) so that the team can get the answers they need. Of course, this may not be practical at times, but you need to act with urgency in these situations so that the planning can finish and the real work begin.

Well-functioning agile teams understand that they should not leave this short iteration planning session until they have a doable plan to which they have made a commitment of delivery of the work items to the product owner.

Visualizing Your Plan

In the "old" days, we used project planning tools to create detailed work breakdown structures and Gantt charts that never reflected the reality of what actually occurred. To a large degree the effort spent creating and maintaining them was a complete waste of time—the real value is in planning, not in documenting the plan. Agile methods understand this and instead rely on "live" plans visible to the team at all times. The low-tech yet effective way of tracking iteration work is done via a taskboard.

Collocated and near-located teams set aside wall space for a physical taskboard. Physical taskboards are either whiteboards with sticky notes to capture tasks or corkboards and index cards for tasks. As you see in Figure 14.3 the taskboard is organized into columns and rows. The columns indicate the current state of the task, with columns along the lines of Not Started, In Progress, Blocked, Waiting for Validation, and Complete being common. The rows, which are optional, typically indicate who is currently doing the work. This could be individual team members for small teams or subteams for larger teams. Your team needs to identify an approach that makes the most sense for your situation.

Figure 14.3   Physical taskboard example

Figure 14.4 illustrates an example of a virtual taskboard in RTC from a sample jazz.net project (it uses the term "sprint" instead of iteration, but that doesn't matter). This board is a table that has a row for each work item and columns for your tasks that you have just identified to complete the work item. The description of the work item appears in the first column. Initially all tasks go into their respective rows in the Not Started column, *except* for the tasks that each team member expects to start immediately. The names of the other columns can be adjusted depending on how you want to manage the transition of the tasks from "not started" to a "done" or "resolved" status.

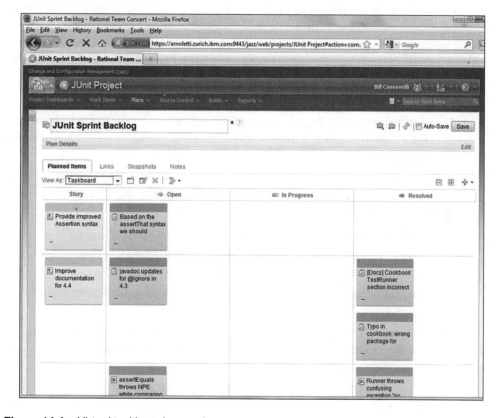

Figure 14.4   Virtual taskboard example

Note that if you are using a Kanban/lean approach to work item management you will use a Kanban board instead of a taskboard. In fact, your strategy approach to managing work is quite different. The Kanban approach uses signal cards to manage work flow—in the case of software delivery projects this may be something as simple as sticky notes on a whiteboard or electronic "cards" in work item management software.

As your team starts working on items from the taskboard, it becomes a living project plan showing the current status of all tasks being worked on. In the next chapter we describe other visual charts that help the team stay on track with completion of the work items that they have committed to.

Look-Ahead Planning and Modeling

DAD explicitly recognizes the need to do preplanning at times prior to iteration in which the related work items are implemented. Look-ahead planning and modeling sessions can be a mechanism for preparing for the iteration planning workshop that occurs on the first day of the iteration. These meetings can occur in the week prior, or even earlier, to an iteration starting. The product owner meets with some or all of the team, and optionally with stakeholders who are subject matter experts (SMEs), or any with other specialists who understand the highest priority work items in the list.

This meeting serves as an opportunity to do the following:

- Discuss details regarding the requirements for each work item to be delivered in the next iteration. Needs for further clarification of requirements details may surface in which case answers can be obtained prior to the iteration planning workshop.

- Model the details via an activity diagram, a screen sketch, or whatever modeling technique is appropriate. But do not let this turn into an up-front detailed requirements specification unless there is a clear need to do so.

- Discuss new work items that have been recently identified.

- Explore large requirements, such as epics or use cases that need to be broken down into smaller requirements to be deliverable within a single iteration.

- Consider dependencies between requirements, resulting in reordering of items in the work item list.

- Consider potential designs to support the work item(s) so you can do accurate task identification and estimating in the iteration planning workshop. Design alternatives may surface, and these discussions can then take place before iteration planning.

- Think through potential blockers that surface during these meetings such as the need for a database designer or tooling specialist or an activity that needs to be completed prior to the iteration starting. Look-ahead planning in advance of the iteration provides some lead time to avoid these blockers.

Consistent with lean thinking you should leave look-ahead planning and modeling exercises until the last possible moment so that you are working with your most up to date understanding of the situation. Scott's January 2012 Agile Mini Survey found that 68% of respondents indicated that they were explicitly doing look-ahead planning, and an additional 19% were doing something similar. More importantly, 28% of respondents indicated that look-ahead planning was very important to their success, and 48% indicated it was important. In short, look-ahead planning appears to be a valuable practice that may not be getting the attention it deserves. Note that there is a context switching implication to this practice—you're focused on the current iteration, then you task switch to think about coming work, and then you switch back to working on the current iteration—so be circumspect in your application of it.

LESSONS FROM THE TRENCHES—MANAGING THE WORK ITEM LIST

We have both seen many projects where the product owners are so busy helping the teams in the throes of an iteration that they neglect keeping the work item list current. As a result they often scramble in the few days before the upcoming iteration to get organized around which work items are highest priority and what the items really mean. They may realize at the last minute that they need the subject matter experts (SMEs) to attend the planning session to explain the story details. A good product owner understands that a key part of their role is to be regularly grooming the work item list so that it always reflects their evolving understanding of the project's priorities and scope. It is natural that new stories will surface and should be added to the list, while some stories may turn out to be unneeded. Priorities can change due to business needs changing, dependencies that surface, or as a better understanding of the desired solution gels. Granted, taking a lean approach with a small pool of work items instead of a large work item list removes the need for such grooming activities.

Concluding Thoughts

The goals of iteration planning workshops, or planning workshops in general, are clear. The team learns the details of the highest priority work items and spends a short period of time planning the effort required to address those work items. Since the team itself identifies the work to be done they should be willing to commit to delivering the work items based on their established velocity from previous iterations. This is an important aspect of self-organization.

You also learned how modeling is an important part of coordinating the work to be done during an iteration. After hearing what your stakeholders require for a given work item you may spend a few minutes discussing it within the team and modeling how you will implement the work item. These models are often simple sketches drawn on a whiteboard.

Spending some time prior to each iteration preplanning, researching requirement details, and technical alternatives will ensure that your Construction iteration planning workshops are efficient and effective. To learn more about how the iteration planning might look on one of your projects, refer to the case study in Chapter 17.

Additional Resources

For more detailed discussions about several of the topics covered in this chapter:

- **Agile planning.** Mike Cohn's *Agile Estimation and Planning* (Addison-Wesley, 2006) is an excellent source of information on release and iteration planning. His approach to planning implicitly includes modeling activities.

- **Agile modeling.** The Agile Modeling (AM) methodology is described in detail at www.agilemodeling.com as are numerous types of models you may choose to create throughout a DAD project. This chapter described three of AM's best practices: iteration modeling, look-ahead modeling, and JIT model storming.

- **Requirements dependency.** The book *A Practical Guide to Distributed Scrum* (IBM Press, 2010) by Elizabeth Woodward, Steffan Surdek, and Matthew Ganis discusses requirements dependencies and how to deal with them on an agile project team.

- **Project management.** Planning, coordination, and leadership were major topics in this chapter—topics that generally fall under the category of project management. Jurgen Appelo's *Management 3.0: Leading Agile Developers, Developing Agile Leaders* (Addison-Wesley, 2011) is a great resource as is Walker Royce's classic *Software Project Management: A Unified Framework* (Addison-Wesley, 1998).

- **Surveys.** Various agile planning techniques, iteration planning, and look-ahead planning were explored in the January 2012 Agile Mini Survey. The results are posted at www.ambysoft.com/surveys/.

CHAPTER 15

A Typical Day of Construction

Agile Principle #9: Simplicity—the art of maximizing the amount of work not done—is essential.

The heart of Disciplined Agile Delivery (DAD) is the Construction phase, and in turn the heart of the phase is an individual construction day. The team collaborates every day to deliver the work items they've committed to. DAD brings together a set of common agile practices that enables you to implement your work items in an agile manner. This chapter provides an overview of agile practices for development, modeling, documentation, build, and governance. We describe the advantages of each approach, as well as our guidance for applying these practices effectively.

Figure 15.1 shows a typical timeline for a Construction iteration, as well as potential agile practices that may be applied during the iteration. Figure 15.1 is meant to be an exemplar—the practices that team members follow will depend on the needs of the situation, the work that needs to be done that day, and the team's skillset. This chapter describes how the team works together on a typical day to complete the work items that they committed to during the iteration planning as described in the previous chapter. We also describe many of the practices indicated in Figure 15.1.

Figure 15.2 shows the rhythm of a typical day of construction. The day begins with a daily coordination meeting where team members organize how they are going to proceed with their work that day. The majority of the day is spent collaborating together to evolve the solution, and ideally the day ends with a stable build that is potentially consumable by others.

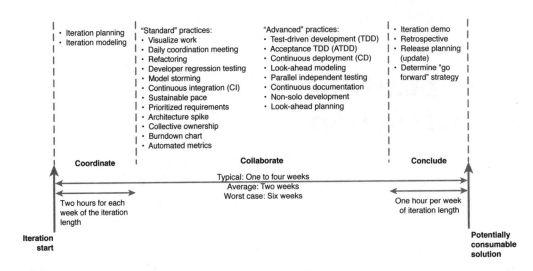

Figure 15.1   Construction iteration overview

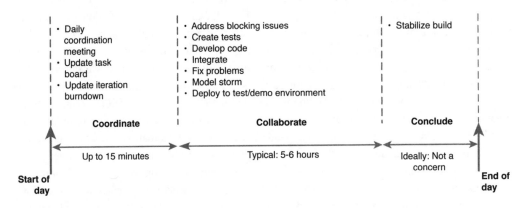

Figure 15.2   A typical day of construction

Figure 15.3 shows a mind map of the structure of this chapter. We describe each of the topics in the map in clockwise order, beginning at the top right.

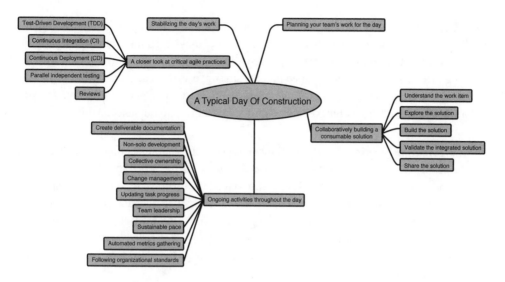

Figure 15.3   Outline of this chapter

THE BIG IDEAS IN THIS CHAPTER

- Team members work together to deliver the work items that they have committed to.

- The team meets daily to plan and coordinate their work for the day in a just-in-time fashion.

- Team members potentially perform analysis, design, testing, programming, and even delivery activities every single day.

- The team should plan to stabilize their work toward the end of the day so a clean build can be created and tested before the team goes home.

Planning Your Team's Work for the Day

In Chapter 14, "Initiating a Construction Iteration," we discussed how the team members themselves plan their own work for the iteration as part of the self-organizing teams practice. Execution of their plan is also done in this manner. The team meets daily to have a short meeting during which they coordinate their work and update any of their "management assets," such as their taskboard or iteration burndown chart. There are several approaches that you can take to plan and report the status of your iteration's work, which are compared in Table 15.1:

- **Daily coordination meeting (Scrum).** The goal of this meeting is for the team members to share their current status, identify any issues they're dealing with, and to plan the day's work. In Scrum, these meetings are called a Scrum, or alternatively a daily planning meeting or daily stand-up meeting. Scrum suggests that each team member answer three questions: What did you do yesterday? What are your plans for today? Do you have any impediments/blockers/issues? The meeting should take no more than 15 minutes.

- **Coordination meeting (Kanban).** Kanban-style coordination meetings are held around the team's taskboard with the discussion focusing on the work itself rather than the activities of each team member. It is useful to read the board right to left or downstream to upstream to emphasize the pull approach to work. The question put to the team is whether there are any blockers or things slowing down the work that reduces throughput. Although these meetings are typically held daily, with a lean/advanced approach this meeting can be held on an as-needed basis (perhaps twice a day, or every second or third day depending on the situation).

- **Weekly status.** This more traditional meeting is held in a room typically away from the work area and may last an hour or more. Team members report status on what they have done in the previous week and are assigned tasks for the following week. They also have the opportunity to surface issues at this meeting. The team lead typically provides an overall update on the project to the team and distributes meeting minutes after the meeting.

- **No scheduled meeting.** In this situation the team elects to bypass regularly scheduled meetings. In these cases the team lead may solicit status on an ad-hoc basis from individuals by visiting them in their work area.

We suggest that you start with Scrum-style daily coordination meetings and once you've stabilized with that strategy, which may take several months, consider moving toward a leaner Kanban approach. Let's discuss how to effectively run Scrum-style meetings in more detail as they're likely to be your starting point.

For collocated teams daily coordination meetings are held in the team's work area and last no more than 15 minutes. In Chapter 14 we discussed how to create a taskboard as part of the iteration planning workshops. Now, as part of the coordination meeting, the team members should gather around their taskboard for this meeting. Figure 15.4 shows Mark facilitating a coordination meeting around a team's taskboard. The taskboard could be either a manual taskboard or a virtual board on a large monitor or projection screen. Pick a time at the beginning of the day when all team members are expected to be in the office, such as 9:00. This meeting is mandatory, and you must ensure that your team members who are new to agile understand this. It's interesting to note that most of the team members shown in Figure 15.4 are in fact standing around the board and are paying attention to the conversation. On the left-hand side are two key stakeholders of the project listening in to get the current status.

Table 15.1 Comparing Planning and Status Reporting Strategies

Strategy	Potential Advantages	Potential Disadvantages	Considerations
Daily coordination meeting (Scrum)	Just-in-time (JIT) discussion of status, planning of day's work, issue escalation, and dependency management. Works well for teams of up to ten people.	Requires team members to be present in the work area at a standard time at the beginning of each day. Can be time consuming if not facilitated well. Team members new to agile will struggle with why it's important to coordinate on a daily basis.	Good choice for teams new to agile as it will help to gel the team.
Coordination meeting (Kanban)	Shorter meetings focusing on throughput issues rather than individual updates. Scales well, with ten minute meetings involving 40 to 50 people commonly reported.	May fail to surface collaboration issues, dependencies, expectations between team members.	Works well with gelled teams who are working together effectively.
Weekly status meeting	Appropriate for team members who prefer to be told what to do.	Difficult to plan a week of work accurately in advance. Time consuming and expensive.	This approach is inconsistent with the agile philosophies of frequent collaboration and self-organization.
No scheduled meeting	Reduces planning overhead. Good for team members with differing work hours.	Lack of structured communication is a risk.	

Figure 15.4   A daily coordination meeting

Team members should stand and face the board so that they can refer to specific items on the board when they are providing status and planning their day's work. If your team has the benefit of agile tooling such as IBM Rational Team Concert, then project the dashboard in the room so that everyone can see the status of the work items as they discuss them. We have even seen some teams have a large widescreen monitor in their work area to project the dashboard at all times.

These meetings are conducted standing up for a reason. Sit-down meetings have a tendency to go much longer than 15 minutes. They often become long status meetings and can last hours, resulting in a huge waste of productive time. What we want is a quick planning meeting so that we can return to doing productive work. The other reason for standing up is that people often feel uncomfortable doing so for long periods of time, encouraging shorter meetings. It also reminds the team of the sense of urgency to get through the meeting so that we can all get back to work.

Why do we ask the three questions?

- The first question tests the team's focus. Question anything done that was not work planned for the iteration.

- The second question allows you to revise the project strategy daily by reorienting the team according to dependency changes revealed by the response to the previous question.

- The third question surfaces issues that may result in new tasks in the work items list. Issues are posted in the work area and are reviewed in the next daily meeting to ensure that action has been taken to eliminate them. It is a key responsibility of the team lead to ensure that these issues are dealt with and escalated if necessary in a timely fashion.

This process continues around the room, allowing each team member to give a summary of his or her status and plan for the day. These meetings are typically facilitated by the team lead, although any team member may do so. The facilitator is there to provide order making sure the meeting is being addressed with respect and order. The meeting facilitator does *not* make decisions for the team or assume a position of power.

It is important to recognize that daily coordination meetings are not:

- Opportunities to assign blame for slipping schedules—the team should work together outside the meeting to get back on track.

- Problem-solving or issue-resolution meetings—team members work together outside the coordination meeting to deal with any issues that are identified.

- Detailed status reporting meetings—if status reporting is needed, automate it as best you can.

- A forum for non-team members to voice their opinions—they are invited to listen and observe.

Remember that in the planning workshop in Chapter 14 we asked each team member for the "ideal hours" to which they can commit to working on the tasks that they volunteer for. For instance, Katherine might estimate that she has six hours/per day to dedicate to her tasks. Therefore, one could expect that she should be able to reduce the number of hours for her tasks that she is working on each day by approximately that amount. Later in this chapter we describe how team members update this board with their progress during the day. Daily coordination meetings ensure transparency and accountability with regard to work being done by each team member. Daily coordination meetings are far more effective than traditional sit-down meetings. We have all seen meetings with large groups where only a few people are actually contributing to the discussions. The people not participating are like tourists who show up, listen in, and sit back, with nothing to contribute. Standing up at daily meetings and sharing prevents tourism. The taskboard plan is "live" and its status is clearly visible to all team members and any other stakeholders who attend the meeting. Having each team member describe his daily work and progress against his objectives keeps all team members accountable to the team and product owner.

LESSONS FROM THE TRENCHES—DAILY MEETINGS ARE NOT AN OPTIONAL AGILE PRACTICE

Mark recently worked on a project where a VP initially discouraged the 15-minute coordination meetings, saying that they were a waste of time and not required. He instead suggested going around and collecting status from individual team members so that they could focus on doing work alone in their cubicles. Clearly this was not consistent with close and regular team collaboration. Fortunately he started attending the stand-ups and soon saw the value of frequent coordination. He quickly became a committed attendee of these meetings and one of the best supporters of our agile approach.

These coordination meetings are limited to 15 minutes, but they often last 5 minutes or less. The key is to have the quick round-the-table (or rather, round-the-taskboard) discussion to keep everyone informed, determine daily strategy, and reduce feedback loops. Here are some tips for ensuring they provide value:

- **Coordinate the day, don't just share status.** The purpose is *not* to report status to the team lead as in traditional status meetings. Rather, coordination meetings are about team members' communication with *each other* about what they are doing today, where they need to collaborate with other team members, or what blockers they see coming from other team members. For instance one developer might need another developer to finish his work before starting on another task the next day.

- **Each update is short and meaningful.** When team members answer their daily questions, they should ensure that what they say is valuable to the team. For instance, saying "I will be in meetings for most of the day" says nothing of value to the team. Rather he could say "I have a half-hour meeting with the DBA today to discuss indexing for optimizing our account searches and a 1-hour meeting this afternoon to review the Account design with Scott (the architecture owner)." The team lead should ensure that all team members articulate their activities clearly. With some prodding like "Which meetings are you attending?" or "Which test cases are you creating?" the team quickly learns to be clear about what they are doing. Here is an example of an effective update by a team member:

  John points to a task on the board and says, "Yesterday I finished coding the order screen and have moved this to the Ready to Test column as you can see. (Pointing to another task) I have started writing tests for the payment authorization story. I spent 2 hours on it yesterday and I have 1 hour left. I should be able to finish that today. I will then start working on the design for the daily sales report. I will move that task from the Not Started to the In Progress column (moves task card). Pete, I am going to need 20 minutes of your time to review the design this afternoon."

- **Take issues offline.** Issues are identified during coordination meetings but resolved outside of them; otherwise, it is difficult to keep the meeting short and valuable to attendees. People can stay behind after the stand-up to discuss the issue without wasting other team members' time. It is an important responsibility of the team lead to ensure that the meeting is effective and efficient. We have found that team members new to agile tend to want to provide details about every task they are working on rather than simply describing the status of the work, blockers, dependencies, and time remaining on each task. Team leads should coach team members to get better at providing updates.

- **Team members should not be distracted by questions from observers.** While the meeting is primarily for the team, anyone outside the team is free and indeed encouraged to attend them. Anyone outside the team will typically stand outside the circle of team members and will not talk unless asked to. For instance a manager might show up for the meeting and hear something that a team member is doing that he may disagree with, but the manager should *not* speak up and distract the team from their stand-up. He may voice his issues to the particular team member *after* the meeting. While it should be made clear to any observers of the stand-up that they should be quiet during the meeting, this is a guideline, not a rule. There are times when someone observing might want to clarify a detail (such as correcting an incorrectly stated meeting time). Also, the team may reach out to observers to get clarification on the status of an issue, for example, "Has the order for the new server been placed? When can we expect it to arrive?"

- **Facilitation is critical.** Effective facilitation of coordination meetings is a sign of a good team lead. Coach the team to keep their updates short and to the point, and coach people to discuss issues outside the meeting. Congratulate your team on significant milestones. Encourage the team to stay focused if the iteration burndown indicates that the team is falling behind or if other metrics indicate that quality is slipping. Also, once the team is comfortable with coordination meetings start rotating team members into the role of facilitator, perhaps letting a different team member facilitate each day. This helps to expand their skills and increases their understanding of the need to effectively participate during other meetings when they're not facilitating.

- **Reference your project dashboard(s).** A project dashboard may be manual, such as an iteration burndown and a ranged release burndown chart hand-drawn on a whiteboard or electronically displayed on a computer screen. Either way, these dashboards often provide important insight into your current project status that you should consider when planning your day.

Before concluding the daily coordination meeting, the team assesses their progress against their iteration goals by updating their iteration burn-down chart. By design iterations are short in duration. A two-week iteration is just ten business days. We cannot afford to wait for a weekly status meeting to assess whether we are behind schedule. An iteration burndown chart is a simple low-tech way of tracking progress on a daily basis on the basis of "burned down" hours. As you see, Figure 15.5 plots on the Y axis the number of total remaining hours of work for all work items against the day of the iteration on the X axis. Initially we draw a trend line from the top left of the chart indicating the total number of hours of tasks to complete down to zero in the bottom right. Every day during the coordination meeting we plot a new value indicating the remaining hours to be completed for all the remaining tasks. If we finish on schedule, by the last day of the iteration the number of hours remaining should have burned down to zero. Refer to Chapter 17, "Case Study: Construction Phase," for an example of a how to use a burndown chart on your project.

LESSONS FROM THE TRENCHES—DEAL WITH BLOCKERS RIGHT AWAY

Andy Pittaway is an executive project manager in IBM Global Services in the UK who has worked with organizations for years to adopt disciplined approaches to agile, often at scale. One of the behaviors that he encourages in daily coordination meetings is to have a principle that if someone raises a blocker or decelerator, then someone else at the meeting will volunteer to help them with that. If no one comes forward quickly the team lead takes it on. This really helps get the team focused on team commitment and building strong bonds. The presence (or lack) of this kind of behavior is a good measure as to the mindset of an agile team.

At the beginning of the iteration, you should know what your expectation is for burning down hours per day. For instance, if the total hours for all work item tasks is 300 and you have a 15-day iteration, you expect to knock off 20 hours/day from your tasks. So for instance, in the previous example, if yesterday the team reduced the hours on the all remaining tasks by a total of 20 hours, you had a good day. Congratulate your team on their efforts. Your taskboard should reflect the reduced number of hours remaining. Resist the temptation to create your burndown charts in a spreadsheet. If they are stored out on the network somewhere, no one will see them. Some tools can automatically update your burndown and display it on your own dashboard. Values plotted above the burndown trend line indicate the project is behind schedule, below the line you are ahead of schedule. This amazing yet simple technique keeps the team focused on progress versus objectives. The burndown chart should obviously be posted in the work area alongside other visual tools such as the taskboard and agile models. Figure 15.5 shows an example of an iteration burndown chart after 11 days of a 15-day iteration (three weeks).

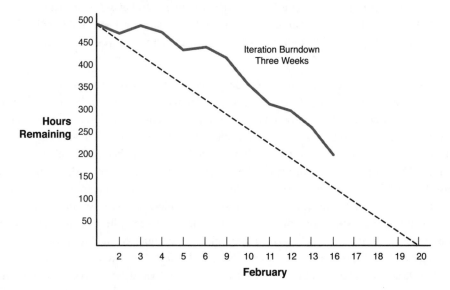

Figure 15.5 Iteration burndown chart

Once the burndown has been updated, issues posted, status reported, and daily work planned, thank everyone and wish them a good day. This is an indication that the stand-up has ended. Often you will subsequently see team members and observers get together to have discussions on items or to plan the day. You will hear people discuss topics like "when can we get together today for 15 minutes to discuss the proposed database changes?" This is agile communication, and it is a beautiful thing to see. On collocated teams you don't need to resort to emails, instead it's just self-organized, proactive, face-to-face collaboration as it should be. Refer to the case study in Chapter 17 to see an example of how a typical daily planning meeting would go, and how teams can effectively "work the board" when planning their work on the taskboard.

Collaboratively Building a Consumable Solution

Now that we have planned our day's work, how does the rest of the day unfold? We have already described in this chapter the agile philosophy of using many practices to ensure a quality solution is delivered. These practices include considering how to test and building test automation before each increment of code is written. Beyond that, the cycle of implementing work items is what you might expect on any iterative project that builds software in small increments. For each work item or user story, you should typically follow this pattern:

- Understand the work item.
- Explore the solution.
- Build the solution.
- Validate the integrated solution.
- Share the solution.

Repeat these steps for each work item that can be delivered in the iteration. Figure 15.6 shows potential activities related to delivering a planned work item that we suggest are applicable for an *ideal* project. These activities are performed as part of delivering *each* work item. In the figure, we have purposely not drawn lines between the activities as many of them occur in parallel and the order may vary. Also many of them are automated processes triggered by completion of another activity.

Notice in the diagram that activities related to the initial steps can help to prevent problems downstream in the development and integration of each work item. Indeed we know from experience that the effort to find and fix problems can be dramatically reduced by using these prevention practices. While we believe that the practices shown in Figure 15.6 increase your chances of success on your agile projects, you may choose alternative strategies to delivering your work using the steps listed previously. In this chapter we review these alternatives and provide considerations for choosing the optimal approach.

DAD recognizes that the "ideal" approach to implementing agile practices on your projects may not be practical due to organizational constraints, scaling factors, and other reasons. So in this chapter we cover these steps for delivering your work items and provide alternative approaches to applying practices for each.

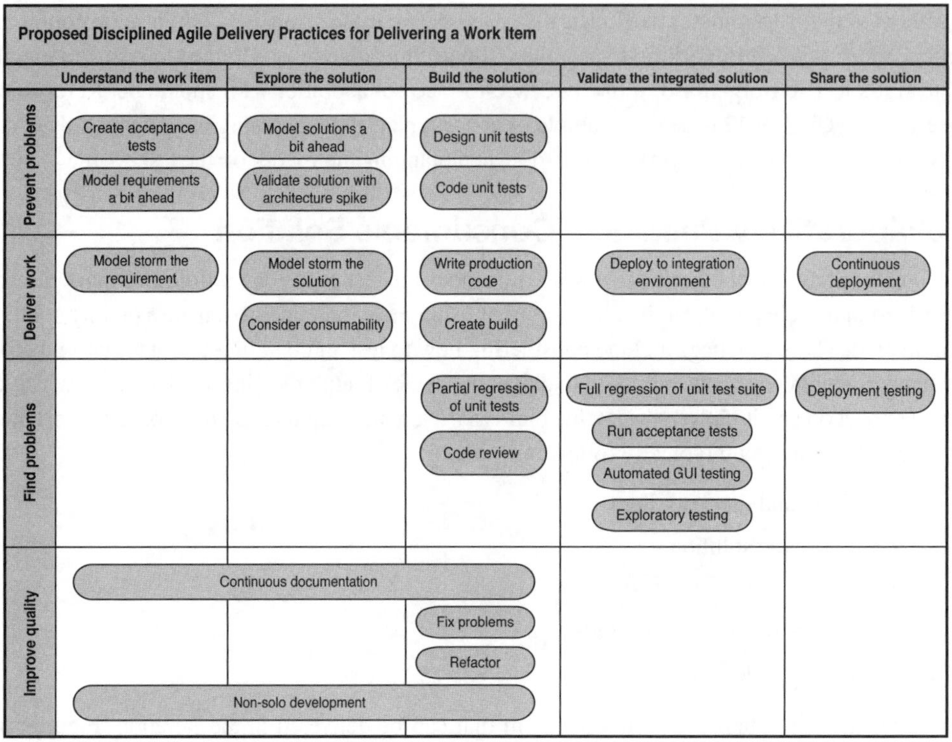

Proposed Disciplined Agile Delivery Practices for Delivering a Work Item				
Understand the work item	**Explore the solution**	**Build the solution**	**Validate the integrated solution**	**Share the solution**
Create acceptance tests / Model requirements a bit ahead	Model solutions a bit ahead / Validate solution with architecture spike	Design unit tests / Code unit tests		
Model storm the requirement	Model storm the solution / Consider consumability	Write production code / Create build	Deploy to integration environment	Continuous deployment
		Partial regression of unit tests / Code review	Full regression of unit test suite / Run acceptance tests / Automated GUI testing / Exploratory testing	Deployment testing
Continuous documentation / Non-solo development		Fix problems / Refactor		

(Row labels, top to bottom: Prevent problems, Deliver work, Find problems, Improve quality)

Figure 15.6   Potential Disciplined Agile Delivery practices for delivering each work item

Understand the Work Item

When we choose an item from the work item list, it may be a user story. So why don't we call this section understand the "requirement"? Well, the work item might actually be a defect or something else to deliver as part of the solution. So we use the generic term work item. Requirement type work items are typically expressed as user stories. Stories are not intended to *be* requirements themselves, but rather to *represent* requirements. They are placeholders for further elaboration or discussion when it is determined that they should be delivered in a particular iteration. As such, the team members need more information about the work item before it can be implemented. How much requirements detail should we specify? There are several approaches that you can take to elaborating your requirements during construction. The different approaches are summarized in Table 15.2:

- **Create acceptance tests.** Acceptance tests (also called story tests, customer tests, or customer acceptance tests) describe black-box requirements, identified by your project stakeholders, that your system must conform to. In traditional software development acceptance tests are typically thought of as testing artifacts, which they are, but when you step back and think about it acceptance tests really are first class requirements artifacts because they describe the criteria by which stakeholders determine whether the system meets their needs. In short, they're executable specifications. Business rules, features, technical (nonfunctional) requirements, and even detailed usage requirements can easily be captured as acceptance tests. Mike Cohn likes to call acceptance tests "conditions of satisfaction." Ron Jeffries measures project progress via the tested feature metric, and the only way you can capture this metric is by having an acceptance regression test suite.

Acceptance tests help us answer the question "How do I know when I am done?" These tests are used to test the workflows or business rules of the application. Examples of these types of tools include Fitnesse, Twist, JBehave, Concordion, and Cucumber. The beauty of this type of testing is that the product owner and other customer stakeholders can document their acceptance tests in a user-friendly format such as a table in a spreadsheet or business-readable text. These test cases can be fed as a set of regression tests into the system, and the results reported back in a colored format to show visually the results of the tests. This is the concept of writing "tests as requirements." The practice of writing a single acceptance test before writing the production code to fulfill that test is called acceptance test-driven development (ATDD) or behavior-driven development (BDD).

When setting up a new type of test, some simple programming for a "driver" or "fixture" is required to feed the test case values into the system. Once the fixture is available, however, it is simple for someone to add any number of test cases. One key advantage of acceptance tests is that they can often be maintained, enhanced, and run easily by nontechnical testers. They often run faster than tests that run against the user interface, such as record-playback tools. Another advantage is that agile teams can write their requirements as executable test scripts. Rather than updating a requirements document when requirements change, you instead update the test scripts. Acceptance testing tools can use these scripts to generate requirements documents ensuring that they are up to date and match what is being actually built at all times.

- **Detailed static requirement specification.** This is the traditional technique of writing a detailed specification[1] of requirements in advance of any design or coding of the solution. This strategy was described in detail in Chapter 8, "Identifying the Initial Scope," in terms of writing a detailed requirements specification for the entire project. It is also possible to do so for the scope of a single iteration, either in advance of the iteration "starting" or at the beginning of the iteration.

---

1. We like to call these detailed requirements of questionable accuracy "detailed speculations."

- **High-level static requirement specification.** With this approach you do just enough requirements specifications to start implementing the solution. For example, for a user story or outlined use case you may choose to explore it with one or more screen sketches, a sketch of the business process or logic it describes, or a point-form list of text. There is an understanding that the specification will evolve during the project as understanding of the requirements improves.

- **Look-ahead modeling of requirements.** As described in Chapter 14, the product owner should investigate details of work items prior to the iteration planning workshop as part of grooming the work item list. This can uncover details such as business rules requiring clarification from other domain experts. Doing some modeling and other elicitation of requirements a bit ahead of implementing them is a practice not officially endorsed by agilists, but according to our research is something that most successful agile teams do.

- **Model storm the requirement.** Model storming is an effective way to elicit the requirements details just-in-time (JIT) during an iteration. Our experience is that the vast majority of modeling sessions involve a few people, usually just two or three, who discuss an issue while sketching on paper or a whiteboard. These "model storming sessions" are typically impromptu events—one project team member will ask another to model with him—typically lasting for 5 to 10 minutes (it's rare to model storm for more than 30 minutes). The people get together, gather around a shared modeling tool (e.g., the whiteboard), explore the issue until they are satisfied that they understand it, and then continue on (often coding).

- **No requirements specification.** Some teams may choose to not capture requirements in any form but instead simply start coding what their stakeholders have asked them to build.

We suggest model storming the requirement and then writing acceptance tests to automate the regression testing of the solution. Your models of the requirements are a type of transitory documentation that is typically useful only until the requirement is implemented. Leaving the diagrams on the whiteboards and modifying if necessary may be all the documentation you need.

Explore the Solution

An important reason why you want to invest some time in designing what you build before you actually build it, even if that design effort is only a few minutes at a time, is to avoid unnecessarily increasing the technical debt within your organization. Technical debt is the accumulation of defects, quality issues (such as difficult to read code or low data quality), poor architecture, and poor design in existing solutions. Although much of the focus of technical debt is on code-related problems, the reality is that technical debt occurs at all architectural levels, including but not limited to the user interface, domain logic, communication, and data storage levels.

Table 15.2 Comparing Strategies for Exploring Requirements

Strategy	Timing	Potential Advantages	Potential Disadvantages	Considerations
Create acceptance tests	Ideally just before coding the individual work item. Could also occur in parallel to implementing the work item or even after the work item is implemented.	Allows stakeholders to create automated tests in business readable format. Unlike record and playback tools they potentially do not need a developer to maintain. Forces the stakeholders or product owner to clearly define how to validate that the solution meets their expectations. With an ATTD/BDD approach the tests do double duty as requirements.	Large libraries of tests may need to be maintained and updated as the solution evolves.	Requires training of stakeholders or their representatives to write requirements as tests. Otherwise, this task falls to the team members.
Detailed static requirement specification documented up front	Documented in advance of the iteration. May even occur during Inception, before any construction begins.	Useful in contractual situations to create a requirements baseline for the solution.	Difficult to keep up to date as requirements continually change. Duplication of requirements and test cases makes maintenance difficult.	It is difficult to create accurate requirements documents before starting to build the solution. This is often a symptom of teams working in mini-waterfalls, not in a truly iterative manner.

(continued)

Table 15.2　Comparing Strategies for Exploring Requirements (continued)

Strategy	Timing	Potential Advantages	Potential Disadvantages	Considerations
High-level static requirement specification	During the iteration JIT before design and coding.	Useful in regulatory compliance situations where you must have documented requirements. Provides sufficient information to begin development of one or more work items. Details are evolved during the iteration in parallel to the requirement being implemented.	Some team members may be uncomfortable with lack of detail if they are used to coding from a detailed specification.	Keep the specifications as lightweight as possible. Use in combination with acceptance tests, with the static specification providing context for the details captured by the tests.
Look-ahead modeling of requirements	Performed for work items to be delivered in upcoming iterations. Ideally model at most one or two iterations, with a maximum of four weeks, ahead of time.	Reduces the risk of being caught off guard by domain complexities. Can improve effectiveness of upcoming iteration planning. Can help evolve the architecture in the right direction.	Distracts team members from delivering work committed to for the current iteration. If the requirement becomes a lower priority and is not implemented the modeling work becomes a waste of time.	The further ahead you model the greater the risk that the requirements will change and your modeling work will be for naught.
Model storm the requirement	Done during the iteration just before design and coding.	Gathering details when you need them streamlines the development process.	Requires easy access to the product owner or stakeholders.	People like pictures and they are useful as supplementing text. Visual pictures (such as UML diagrams) of what the requirement is and its context in a workflow reduces miscommunications with stakeholders.

Strategy	Timing	Potential Advantages	Potential Disadvantages	Considerations
No requirements specification	Never.	Very fast approach.	Not suitable for complex business domains or life critical systems where miscommunications can have large consequences.	Difficult to test a solution based on dated conversations about the requirements.

The easiest way to deal with technical debt is to not incur it in the first place. Figure 15.7 presents Martin Fowler's technical debt quadrant, with the reckless quadrants extended to explicitly address non-code issues. One of Fowler's points is that there are sometimes prudent reasons to take on technical debt, such as to potentially reduce your time to market or as a learning opportunity. However, what we should strive to avoid are reckless mistakes, such as deliberately not investing any time in architecture or design, or inadvertent mistakes resulting from having an insufficient range of delivery knowledge on your team.

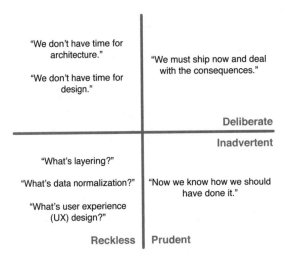

Figure 15.7   The technical debt quadrant

There are several approaches that you can take to understanding and designing the optimal solution as summarized in Table 15.3:

- **Look-ahead modeling.** For complex work items such as epics (large user stories) it may be worthwhile considering a larger design problem than the current work item warrants to avoid problems in the future. Also, one might spend some time evaluating how to generalize a design pattern or mechanism so that it could be applicable for other work items. This is also a good opportunity to think about whether there is any functionality or data within your organization's existing infrastructure that your team can leverage.

- **Model storm the solution.** Just as you can model storm requirements on a JIT basis you can do the same to explore the design. You identify an issue that you need to resolve, you quickly grab a few teammates who can help you, the group explores the issue, and then everyone continues on as before. It is useful to spend some time with your team members and the architecture owner model storming design alternatives for a particular requirement. As described in Chapter 14, you may have already done some of this modeling as part of your iteration planning session.

- **Architecture spike/prototype.** An architecture spike is a technique used to explore a technology that is new to you. The idea is that if you are thinking about using an unfamiliar technology, perhaps you're thinking about using a framework or collection of web services that are new to your team, you write just enough code to familiarize yourself with it. This may take several hours or several days, and the code is likely to be discarded afterward—because your goal is to learn about the technology you don't need to write production quality code. Alternatively you could choose to do some architecture prototyping writing some code that touches all significant parts of the architecture. The code goes vertically through all tiers, such as the user interface to the database, or to an external system. This can be a worthwhile investment of time to ensure our architecture works before we write too much code based on our architectural designs, which may be flawed. As such, this practice is a technique to support DAD's risk-value lifecycle approach.

- **Consumability design.** If you want to satisfy or better yet delight your end users you will need to invest time in consumability design, also called user experience (UX) design or simply design. Because the user interface (UI) is the system to your end users, you need to ensure that your solution is consumable, that it is understandable and easy to work with. To do this you need someone on your team with UX skills to think about how to create an optimal user experience by considering things such as avoiding unnecessary complexity or unneeded features, simplifying the UI design, and where appropriate applying user interface guidelines.

- **Information design.** The vast majority of systems process information in some way. If data is to be a true asset within your organization, DAD teams need to adopt practices that help support this goal. Such information design practices include identifying the best source(s) of existing data, and when no such sources exist, designing a normalized source for that data and writing tests to validate that the data source works as desired.

- **Other "ility" design.** When you're exploring the solution for a functional requirement you'll want to consider nonfunctional requirements (NFRs) that pertain to it. This includes consumability (called out as a special case), security, availability, reliability, and many others described in Chapter 8.

- **Detailed design specification up front.** Creating detailed and fixed design specifications up front as input to coding is a practice that was popular using traditional approaches but is now seen as not being an effective strategy. With the complexity of modern architectures the final code seldom matches a design produced up front.

- **Model-driven development (MDD).**[2] Sophisticated tools such as IBM Rational Software Architect (RSA) allow automated synchronization between visual models and code. These diagrams typically use the Unified Modeling Language (UML) as the standard notation. RSA transforms these diagrams into the implementation language of the target platform java. Changes then made to the code are reflected back up into the model. This technique of keeping the code and models synchronized is called round-trip engineering. Using model-driven development, you can have designs that are always consistent with the code. It can, however, lead to more time than one would expect on an agile project being invested in the modeling effort rather than writing code.

- **Test-driven development (TDD).** With test-first development (TFD) you write a single test before writing the production code to fulfill that test. With existing code you may need to refactor the small portion that you are currently working on at this time to ensure that it meets acceptable standards. TDD is TFD plus refactoring. TDD is described in detail later in the chapter.

- **None.** For one- or two-man teams, a strategy of coding without a design is sometimes used for simplistic solutions.

As indicated in Figure 15.2 we recommend model storming the solution to the work item in a just-in-time fashion in the iteration that the work item is implemented. Scott's surveys indicate that about two-thirds of teams invest some time in look-ahead planning or modeling. Architecture spikes are also often useful for exploring architectural choices before committing a lot of effort pursuing a flawed approach. We also recommend adopting TDD to improve your design and maintainability of your code.

In his work on the Toyota manufacturing process Shigeo Shingo suggests that we engineer our processes to prevent defects rather than focusing on processes to find defects. This is a critical part of lean thinking that bears repeating: *Use processes that prevent defects rather than relying on those that try to find them.* If it is impossible to prevent all defects, make sure that you detect them as quickly as possible by properly testing after every small change. Focusing on quality first results in a method of building software that is radically different from the plan and requirements document-driven traditional approach. As a result the order that we do things may seem backward at first if you are not familiar with test-driven development practices.

---

2. MDD is an industry term for round-trip engineering of code or working software using sophisticated software-based modeling tools, sometimes referred to as CASE tools. When this is performed in an agile manner it is one of several approaches to Agile Model Driven Development (AMDD). The two other AMDD categories are inclusive modeling (solely using simple modeling tools such as whiteboards and paper) and using case tools to generate code but not reverse generate.

Table 15.3 Comparing Strategies for Understanding the Solution

Strategy	Timing	Potential Advantages	Potential Disadvantages	Considerations
Look-ahead modeling of the solution	Done for work items to be delivered in upcoming iterations. Ideally model at most one or two iterations, with a maximum of four weeks, ahead of time.	Allows teams to consider how designs need to evolve to meet upcoming requirements.	If business priorities change, work invested in look-ahead modeling may be wasted if the related work item becomes low priority.	Look-ahead modeling is a useful technique for team members to investigate design alternatives before committing to an approach during iteration planning.
Model storm solution	Done during the iteration just before coding.	You think through the details when you need them and are motivated to do so. Streamline the programming effect by thinking through issues that test-first approaches aren't suitable for.	May miss the big picture, hence need for envisioning.	Keep the sessions short. Look for existing enterprise assets to leverage rather than reinventing new designs.
Architecture spike/prototype	In the early days of an iteration, usually in early construction iterations.	Spikes can quickly prove the ability of the architecture to support the requirements before building the solution.	Takes time and may result in throwaway code.	Used to validate one or more technical approaches (set-based design) before adopting one design over the others.
Consumability design	Typically performed early in the project with consumability a constant consideration throughout construction. During iteration modeling and potentially modeling storming as required.	Increases stakeholder satisfaction with the solution. Consumable solutions are easier to support and potentially to operate, thereby improving your overall DevOps efforts.	Requires the team to understand the importance of UX and to invest in it. Many developers think they have much better UX skills than they actually do. They run the risk of producing difficult-to-consume solutions that they are reticent to change.	For user-interface intensive solutions consider bringing a UX expert onto the team early in the lifecycle to help get your team going in the right direction and to mentor people in UX skills.

(continued)

Table 15.3 Comparing Strategies for Understanding the Solution (continued)

Strategy	Timing	Potential Advantages	Potential Disadvantages	Considerations
Information design	During iteration modeling and potentially model storming as required.	Improves the quality of the information produced by the system. Supports your organization's efforts to address data quality projects.	Requires adoption of agile database techniques such as database refactoring and database testing, which your existing data professionals may not be familiar with.	Working with existing data sources and producing new, high-quality data sources are an important aspect of enterprise awareness.
Other "ility" design	During iteration modeling and potentially model storming as required.	Helps to ensure that your solution addressed the full range of stakeholder needs, not just functional requirements.	Functional requirements that appear to be easy to address on the surface may prove not to be once all of the "ilities" are considered, which can be frustrating for stakeholders who are new to the realities of IT solution delivery.	The team must be constantly vigilant to ensure that they do in fact address all relevant "ilities." Parallel independent testing can help ensure that "ilities" are in fact being addressed.
Detailed design specification	Often documented in advance of an iteration before any construction occurs. Sometimes documented after the development work is performed to capture what was actually built.	When performed before the iteration starts it can shorten iteration planning. Useful in regulatory situations that require design specifications.	When performed as a hand-off between senior and junior team members the junior team members may become unmotivated because they don't get to do the "fun design stuff." Detailed design specifications and the actual code can easily get out of sync.	This can often be a symptom of a lack of collaboration between team members. When team members are collaborating closely they don't need detailed specifications to drive their work. This can also be a symptom of overspecialization of some team members, in this case in modeling.

Strategy	Timing	Potential Advantages	Potential Disadvantages	Considerations
Model-driven development (MDD)	Done during the iteration just before coding (or code generation), and continues in parallel with other development activities.	Analysis and design models allow for portability by transforming code to multiple platforms. Visual models that are synchronized with code result in good documentation.	Can be time consuming to perform detailed modeling. Requires team members to have sophisticated modeling skills.	MDD is fairly common in embedded software development and systems engineering environments but not very common in IT environments (the focus of this book).
Test-driven development (TDD)	Performed throughout the iteration.	TDD leads to higher quality code. Refactoring code as a matter of course throughout the Construction phase keeps technical debt manageable.	Requires skill and discipline on the part of team members. Existing legacy code and data sources may not have existing regression test suites, requiring investment in them.	This can be a difficult, albeit incredibly valuable, practice to adopt.
None	Never.	You get to coding right away.	No modeling of the solution prior to coding often results in rewrites for poorly thought out designs or because of miscommunications between team members.	This strategy is applicable only for very simple situations.

Build the Solution

Writing code[3] for solution in DAD is not materially different from coding with any other method. However, what agile has contributed to the coding discipline is a variety of practices that increase the maintainability and supportability of the code base over time. Several approaches to writing code worth considering are summarized in Table 15.4:

- **Test-driven development (TDD).** In addition to applying TDD to explore the detailed design of your solution it is also an approach to writing your code in a disciplined manner. It ensures that you write just enough code to pass the unit tests and no more.

- **Test after development.** With this approach the developer first writes a bit of production code and then writes the tests that validate that the code works. The developer iteratively gets that bit of code working before continuing on. Unit tests (a.k.a. developer or component tests) are fundamental to disciplined agile development. Well-designed software is made up of classes, modules, or components behind the user interface that expose operations (or services) to implement the required functionality. Unit tests are code that is written to test that an operation such as this works as expected by calling the operation and validating that we get expected results. Writing a library of unit tests as you go ensures that you have an automated regression suite that can be run at any time to ensure that a recent change has not broken something elsewhere. You should strive to have at least 80% unit test coverage of your code.

- **Code now, fix later.** For those who do not have time to do things right, but somehow find time to do things over, this is another approach. Due to time pressures, developers sometimes knowingly take shortcuts to get the solution working without considering the consequences of having to maintain and extend their software in the future.

At a minimum we suggest that you take a test after approach to development and better yet a test-driven approach. As with exploring your solution, technical debt is an important consideration when building your solution. Our philosophy is that as you're building your first strategy you should do no harm and do what you can to not increase technical debt. Better yet, as you run into technical debt try to invest some time to pay it down through refactoring for simple issues. For serious problems that require significant effort to fix, say more than an hour or two, the appropriate response would be to identify one or more work items that are then prioritized appropriately and put on your team's work item list (or into the work item pool for lean DAD teams).

---

3. When we refer to writing code we include the work required to access or persist any relevant data.

Table 15.4 Comparing Strategies for Building Your Solution by Writing Production Code

Strategy	Potential Advantages	Potential Disadvantages	Considerations
Test-driven development (TDD)	Results in better code since it needs to conform to the design of the unit tests. Gives greater confidence in the ability to change the system knowing that defects injected with new code will be caught. Refactoring code as you go reduces the cost of maintenance and makes it easier to evolve the solution in the future.	Takes discipline to ensure tests are actually written before the code. Takes time; tests may have their own defects or be poorly designed.	Test-driven development is an advanced practice. While some feel TDD is mandatory for effective agile development, others question its value. Refactoring is a necessary discipline to ensure longevity of the application through managing technical debt.
Test after development	It is easier to write tests after the code itself has been written.	Teams often find reasons to not write unit tests, such as time pressures or forgetting.	Developer regression unit testing is a good step toward doing TDD.
Code now, fix later	Quick approach to writing code that appears to work.	Leads to poor quality designs, which in turn are more difficult and expensive to evolve later.	Valid approach for prototyping code that will be discarded afterwards. Valid for production code only if your stakeholders knowingly accept the consequences, perhaps because time to market is a greater consideration for them than quality.

Validate the Integrated Solution

There are many agile testing approaches that you can take to integrate each developer's work and validate that it works as an integrated solution. These approaches, compared in Table 15.5, include

- **Acceptance test-driven development (ATDD).** We described the practice of ATDD earlier in the chapter as a requirements specification technique, but as the name implies it is also a validation technique. Simply include your acceptance tests in your regression test suite to ensure that your solution continues to conform to the requirements of your stakeholders.

- **Continuous integration.** Agile teams continually integrate and test their changes to ensure that their solution works. Upon completing any change to code, developers first build the solution and then run tests and analysis of the software in their isolated developer sandbox before delivering it to the integration environment. Defects are therefore caught and fixed before introducing them into the shared code base. Once delivered to the integration environment, the system is again built and a larger regression of unit tests are run against the solution. Running the build, tests, and code/schema analysis can be done automatically using tools such as IBM Rational Team Concert's (RTC) build manager or Jenkins (formerly Hudson). This essential agile practice ensures that there is working and tested software at all times.

- **User interface (UI) testing.** The goal of UI testing is to ensure that the UI meets the needs of its stakeholders. UI tests, sometimes called customer facing tests, can be automated by record-playback tools, such as IBM Rational Functional Tester, that work by recording the actions of a manual test and translating the actions into a script. The system-generated script usually needs some custom crafting to introduce variability (such as random data values) and log expected versus actual results at certain places in the test.

- **Parallel independent testing.** On a regular basis the development team makes their working build available to an independent test team, or perhaps they automatically deploy it via their continuous deployment tools, so that they can test it. The goal of this testing effort is to identify any defects that have fallen through the cracks. The independent testing effort focuses on production-level system integration testing, investigative testing, and formal usability testing that the development team is often not very good at. More on this practice later in the chapter.

- **End-of-lifecycle testing.** An important part of the release effort for many agile teams is end-of-lifecycle testing where an independent test team validates that the system is ready to go into production. If parallel independent testing has been adopted, this testing effort can be short as the issues have already been substantially covered.

- **Code/schema analysis.** Static code analysis tools check for defects in the code, often looking for types of problems, such as security defects, which are commonly introduced by developers, or code style issues. Static code analysis enhances project visibility by quickly providing an assessment of the quality of your code. Dynamic code analysis is a bit more complicated in that it examines the executing code for problems. Schema analysis checks a data source schema (a data source could be a relational database, a hierarchical database, an XML file, to name a few) to ensure it is well formed and conforms to your organizational naming conventions. Code/schema analysis is often included as part of your continuous integration strategy, although usually as part of a nightly or weekly build.

- **Reviews/inspections.** Reviews, including walkthroughs and inspections, are a validation technique in which one or more artifacts are examined critically by a group of qualified people. One goal is to determine whether the artifact fulfills the demands of its target audience and is of sufficient quality to be easy to develop, maintain, and enhance. Potential problems/defects are reported to the creator of the artifact so that they may potentially be addressed. Another goal of reviews is to transfer skills and knowledge within the team. By discussing what is good and not-so-good, and more importantly why and how to approach the same sort of thing next time, people can quickly learn from one another.

- **Nonfunctional testing.** Systemwide requirements, also known as nonfunctional requirements, address quality attributes such as usability, reliability, availability, performance, and supportability to name a few. Parallel independent test teams often test for systemwide requirements because this sort of testing can be difficult or expensive to perform. For example, for performance testing, you may need a productionlike environment where large quantities of data can be used to stress the system during testing.

- **Manual testing from detailed test case specifications.** For traditional siloed teams it is common to have analysts write requirements specifications and then pass them off to testers who then proceed to create detailed test cases against these specifications. Often the testers joined the project late and were not there to hear the customer describe their requirements and conditions of satisfaction. As a result it is not uncommon for testers to evaluate the quality of the solution based on criteria that is inconsistent with the customer's expectations.

- **None.** An appropriate strategy for those who feel that success is optional.

A good regression suite of automated regression, unit, and acceptance tests allows your product owner, domain experts, and other testers to do more interesting testing to possibly find things that automated testing tools are not good at detecting, such as user experience issues.

Table 15.5 Comparing Strategies for Validating the Integrated Solution

Strategy	Timing	Potential Advantages	Potential Disadvantages	Considerations
Acceptance test-driven development (ATDD)	An acceptance test is written just before enough production code to fulfill that test.	Business-readable regression tests can be written by stakeholders. The code is continually validated against the requirements.	The product owner or stakeholders will likely need coaching on how to write well formed tests.	Technical expertise is required to hook up the tests to the underlying system (or to the appropriate developer tests). This requires maintenance of the test framework.
Continuous integration	Potentially every time code is checked into your configuration management tool. Long-running builds may be scheduled during nonwork hours.	Automated build and running of regression tests ensures working software at all times. Changes that break other parts of the solution are detected immediately.	Can take some time for the team to initially set up the environment for running continuous integration.	Complex solutions will likely need several types of test suites, to be run at different times and frequencies, as part of their overall CI solution.
User interface (UI) testing	UI tests are typically executed each time a new build is deployed to the integration environment.	Automated tests are useful for "smoke testing" to ensure the basic aspects of the system work properly after a new release is deployed.	Automated UI testing typically requires developers to maintain test scripts. UI tests prove to be brittle if the UI changes frequently. Manual UI testing is time consuming and people are not good at executing manual tests consistently. UI tests can be slow to run because they are limited by the refresh speed of the screens.	Some organizations adopt UI testing as the only type of automated testing even though it is often the most expensive type of automated testing.

Strategy	Timing	Potential Advantages	Potential Disadvantages	Considerations
Parallel independent testing	Occurs in parallel with development. A new testing cycle typically starts when a build is delivered to the testing team.	Speeds delivery of value to customers by reducing end-of-lifecycle testing. Independent testers avoid tester bias of the business and development teams.	Requires the development team to deploy their working builds to the independent testing team on a regular basis. Requires a mechanism for the test team to easily report defects back to the development team.	The development team should still do the majority of testing. The independent testing effort should be risk-based, focusing on the issues that the development team isn't able to address effectively.
End-of-lifecycle testing	During the Transition phase.	May be required to satisfy the operations team that the solution you intend to deploy has been fully testing.	Tends to be very expensive and time consuming if this is your primary source of testing. Can result in project schedule slippage if defects discovered are more than expected.	Ideally this should just be the rerunning of the regression test suite(s) created by the development team and by the independent test team (if any).
Code/schema analysis	Should be done as part of your continuous integration strategy.	Easy way to ensure conformance to organizational quality standards. Dynamic code analysis can detect defects that can only be captured at runtime.		This analysis is particularly important for scaling situations where code may be written in isolation. This is particularly true on large teams, geographically distributed teams, and organizationally distributed teams (e.g., where outsourcing is involved). Analysis can help to partially fulfill the burden of proof in some regulatory situations.

(continued)

Table 15.5   Comparing Strategies for Validating the Integrated Solution (continued)

Strategy	Timing	Potential Advantages	Potential Disadvantages	Considerations
Reviews	Any time.	Can identify bad practices before too much technical debt accumulates. Opportunity for team members to learn better techniques from one another. Opportunity to come to agreement around quality issues.	Reviews take time. Reviewers can resent the time taken away from their own work.	Keep reviews as lightweight and informal as possible.
Nonfunctional testing	Occurs in parallel with development.	If started early in the project it can find architectural and design problems while they're still inexpensive to address.	Some nonfunctional requirements are difficult to test, such as availability and security.	A good strategy is to deploy your releases to a separate environment and test them there.
Manual testing from detailed test case specifications	Whenever a new build is delivered into your testing environment. Potentially as part of parallel independent testing.	Some defects can only be detected through manual testing.	Labor intensive. The test specifications become stale if the requirements change often.	Keep manual testing to a minimum. When a defect is found write automated regression tests whenever possible.
None	Never.		When no testing is done at all any defects are first detected by end users in a production environment. On average this is the most expensive approach to testing.	If your solution isn't worth testing it isn't worth building in the first place.

A Lean Approach to Defect Management

Traditional defect management strategies, which focus on running testing cycles, logging defects, triage meetings, fix, and retest, are a costly and time consuming process. The communication that occurs across the boundaries of the testers and developers and lengthy queues of defects creates huge inefficiencies. We prefer to use a lean strategy of fixing defects *immediately on the spot* as they are found. For any defect that is found the developer creates a unit test first to catch the defect, and then fixes it so that the defect is caught immediately should it ever resurface. No logging of a defect in a defect tracking system (DTS) is required with this strategy. This approach naturally requires a close collaboration between team members. Periodically defects arise that may be determined to be low priority and not worthy of fixing at that time. Or perhaps what was perceived as a defect is really an enhancement. For these types of situations we add them to the work item list to be prioritized like any other work.

Share the Solution

Waterfall approaches to building applications deliver a solution into the stakeholder's hands for initial validation and testing near the end of the project, often months or even years since requirements were identified. This is obviously a risky strategy that delays delivery of value and opportunities for feedback until far too late in the lifecycle. Iterative and agile methods improved this practice by insisting on working software at the end of each short iteration. DAD takes this even further by striving to have consumable solutions available for demonstration on a regular, in some cases daily, basis. We have already described how automated build and testing via continuous integration results in working software at all times. The next step is to automatically deploy this solution into an environment for the product owner and other stakeholders to test. The degree to which organizations can coordinate regular deployments of complex software across many projects on a frequent basis is a competitive advantage. It ultimately means that you can deliver high quality, high value increments of your solutions in an agile fashion.

Ongoing Activities Throughout the Day

Let's describe some of the things that may occur at any time during the day:

- Creating deliverable documentation
- Non-solo development
- Collective ownership
- Configuration management
- Change management
- Updating task progress

- Team leadership
- Sustainable pace
- Automated metrics gathering
- Following organizational standards

Creating Deliverable Documentation

Deliverable documentation is the documentation that you need to provide to your stakeholders as part of your overall solution. This documentation of course varies between projects, but deliverable documentation typically includes user manuals, training materials, operations manuals, support manuals, and system overviews. It typically does not include requirements specifications or design specifications, except in regulatory situations where such documentation is required or in contract negotiations where it's required as part of the contract. Otherwise, such documentation is known as "transitory" documentation in that it is has short-term value required to help specify and deliver the system but is not required to support it.

Because many people are overly focused on programming within the agile community, documentation has been a controversial subject for many years, and some people still seem to be confused about how it fits into agile delivery. This has been particularly frustrating for Scott considering the early work that he did in agile modeling and documentation practices. Over the years Scott has explored how agile teams approach documentation via several surveys. The Dr. Dobb's Journal (DDJ) 2008 Modeling and Documentation survey found that agile teams were just as likely as traditional teams to write deliverable documentation. The DDJ September 2009 State of the IT Union found that the quality of the deliverable documentation being produced by agile teams is at the same level as that of traditional teams.

We suggest producing "just barely good enough" documentation that does the following:

- Focuses on stable, not speculative concepts
- Is executable if possible, static only if you have to
- Maximizes stakeholder ROI
- Is concise
- Fulfills a purpose of value to your stakeholders
- Describes information that is less likely to change
- Describes "good things to know" that you couldn't infer from the code
- Has a specific customer and facilitates the work efforts of that customer
- Is sufficiently accurate, consistent, and detailed

How much documentation is enough? Our experience suggests that the amount of documentation required is negotiable. We have been known to ask provocative questions such as "Mr. Customer, this is an interesting document that you would like me to produce. However, it would require me to divert resources that are currently building functionality for you. Which requirements would you like to remove from scope so that you can have that document?"

The strategies for writing deliverable documentation, compared in Table 15.6, are as follows:

- **Continuous documentation—same iteration.** Update deliverable documentation to reflect any changes made in the iteration where the changes occur.

- **Continuous documentation—following iteration.** Update deliverable documentation to reflect changes in the iteration immediately following the iteration where they occurred.

- **Document late.** Write deliverable documentation just before the solution is to be deployed into production.

- **None.** Produce no external documentation at all but instead rely completely on the code.

Our suggestion is to adopt the practice of continuous documentation. To be effective at this practice you want to wait for the information to stabilize during the iteration, which implies that documentation will be left toward the end of the iteration. When you document information that isn't yet stable you run the risk of having to rework your documentation. If your iterations are short, you will likely need to take the approach of documenting in the following iteration, or at least letting some documentation slip a few days into the following iteration.

Note that with this practice many teams include criteria around updating deliverable documentation in their definition of done for the iteration. In other words, documentation becomes part of the acceptance criteria for determining whether a work item (such as a user story or defect report) has been fully implemented.

An important decision about deliverable documentation is the tool to capture it with. This should be determined by the needs of your stakeholders who will be using the documentation. For example, support people will likely prefer online documentation so a wiki may be your best bet. Wiki-based documentation may only be a start for operations people because many organizations also maintain deployment configuration information for their overall environment in models or a database. The team responsible for maintaining and evolving it over time, which may be your team, will similarly want online documentation overviewing the solution. This documentation may be supplemented with models in more complex situations. Training materials are often captured using word processors, presentation software, and in many cases audiovisual recording software. The fundamental point is that you need to work closely with the stakeholders of the documentation to ensure you produce what they need in the format they need it in.

Table 15.6   Comparing Documentation Strategies

Strategy	Timing	Potential Advantages	Potential Disadvantages	Considerations
Continuous documentation— same iteration	Ongoing throughout the project, but primarily in Construction iterations.	It is easier to write documentation when it is fresh in your mind. The effort to write documentation is spread throughout the project. Transition phase is potentially reduced.	Evolving requirements may motivate changes to previously written documentation, slowing you down (the XP community would say you're traveling heavy).	This approach is hard to make work in short iterations, say two weeks or less, because the information to be documented may not stabilize in time for it to be documented that iteration.
Continuous documentation— following iteration	Ongoing throughout the project, but primarily in Construction iterations.	See above.	Evolving requirements may motivate changes to previously written documentation.	This approach works well for short iterations. Your solution is in effect not consumable until the documentation is up to date.
Document late	Completed during the Transition phase, although notes may be taken throughout the lifecycle.	Minimize the overall effort to write the documentation because the information to be captured will have stabilized.	You run the risk of not being able to complete the documentation due to project schedule and budget pressures. You may have forgotten important information from earlier in the project. Increases the manual work during the Transition phase.	This approach effectively prevents you from fully adopting the practice of continuous delivery due to the additional work during Transition.
None	Never,	No overhead due to documentation.	It is very difficult to operate, support, and maintain a solution without deliverable documentation.	This strategy is appropriate for research and development projects where the solution isn't going to be deployed.

LESSONS FROM THE TRENCHES—SOME AGILISTS ARE ANTIDOCUMENTATION

Both Scott and Mark have run into agile programmers over the years who did their utmost to avoid writing deliverable documentation. Their reasoning usually went like this: "Documents cost money. Code costs money. Given our choice, we would prefer code that makes the system run and provides functionality over documents that might be read by no one." While this is an interesting philosophy, it needs to be tempered by the reality that some deliverable documentation will be required by your stakeholders. The implication is that you need to work closely with your stakeholders to understand what their real needs are, so that when you do write documentation it will be read because it provides real value to someone.

Non-Solo Development

Extreme Programming (XP) has a practice called "pair programming," which suggests that two developers should work together sharing one keyboard as they code. This is a type of "extreme" design/code review, that is, real-time as one person watches the other code. The key benefit is better quality by detecting defects before they are coded. Other benefits include better documented code and designs that are better thought through. While initially there were many skeptics that having two people write the same code is a luxury that companies cannot afford, studies are emerging that show that pair programming is actually *more* productive than individual coding when you look at its full impact.

In DAD we certainly agree that pair programming is beneficial, but we extend the idea to all team members, not just coders. It is common for analysts to work together, modeling at whiteboards, or for testers to pair up with business experts to help validate the solution. In fact Agile Modeling includes the practice "model with others" to specifically capture this strategy. Two heads are indeed better than one. We refer to this general strategy as non-solo development.

Collective Ownership

Many people think of collective ownership as the concept of allowing any team member to modify and enhance any other team member's code. However, it extends beyond code to any work that the team creates as well, such as documents, tests, environments, and tools such as taskboards. The team also collectively owns the team's process itself. For instance, the team should take ownership of the decision-making process related to issue resolution, standards, work responsibilities, and knowledge sharing. Collective ownership can be thought of as the "secret sauce" that makes self-organization practical and successful. The team collectively does whatever is needed to create and maintain the "whole" system, rather than creating individual owners with isolated "silos" of responsibility.

Configuration Management

Any development team knows that it is a best practice to store their code in a common repository to enable revisioning, locking, and sharing, of their source code streams. However configuration management is more than simple check-in and check-out of files. This discipline includes management of developer "sandboxes," integration streams, baselines, and potentially cataloging of reusable assets as well.

It is important to note that configuration items that need managing extend far beyond code to include all work products that your team produces such as requirements, tests, data, and plans. You should have the ability to take snapshots (baselines) of your entire project at a given point in time and be able to restore the status of all assets accordingly.

Change Management

There are three strategies for dealing with change on a project. These are compared in Table 15.7 and include the following:

- **Change prevention.** Many organizations still believe that the best way to guarantee on-time and on-budget delivery is to define a detailed specification at the beginning of the project. To protect themselves from this business decision IT delivery teams do their best to ensure that the requirements do not change, and if they do then the stakeholders must pay for that change. They do this by putting what often proves to be a slow and onerous change control process in place. Because it is painful to change requirements stakeholders often don't. There are two reasons, often co-related, why IT organizations choose to work like this: cultural and business process constraints. The cultural problems often stem from organizations not having moved away from traditional thinking that tells them that changing requirements are a bad thing. Fact is that a changed requirement late in the lifecycle is a competitive advantage as long as you can act on it. A common business constraint is for senior management to insist on fixed price and/or fixed schedule for the IT project, often in a futile attempt to minimize business risk. Unfortunately they don't realize that this increases rather than decreases the overall risk to the project.

  The impact of change prevention is twofold. First, it promotes significant waste. Because stakeholders have learned that change will be prevented once the requirements specification is accepted, they are motivated to make up potential requirements during the requirements gathering phase in the hopes that they correctly guess what they're going to need. Compounding this is the fact that requirements change over time, either due to changes in the business environment or because of a changed understanding of the domain. The second impact is that when requirement changes are prevented your organization doesn't get the solution that it actually needs. Instead it merely gets what it specified at the beginning of the project when the least information was available to stakeholders to make decisions. Not only is money being wasted on implementing features that aren't required, it's not being spent on features that are required but unfortunately were missed during the up-front requirements specification effort.

Without question, the concept of change prevention procedures is contrary to the spirit of agile development. There is nothing agile about restricting changes that stakeholders require.

- **Flexible work item management.** Flexible work item management allows stakeholders, often via the product owner, to adjust their requirements, priorities, and scope of the release at any time during the project. When a delivery team works in priority order and produces a potentially consumable solution on a regular basis, they are able to fulfil the true needs of their stakeholders while maximizing ROI.

- **Uncontrolled change.** This approach allows change in response to changing stakeholder needs with no record or management of the change. Some teams do this in the spirit of "the customer is always right."

Our suggestion is that you take a flexible work item management approach, either with a work item list or work item pool as described in Chapter 8.

Updating Task Progress

At any time during the day, but at minimum before the daily stand-up, team members update the taskboard to reflect the progress on their tasks. For instance, a team member, upon finishing a task, might cross out the remaining hours on the task sticky and write "0" on it, and then move the sticky from the In Progress column to the Ready for Review or Complete column.

Mark likes to have an additional column between these two called Done Today. When team members finish a task, they can put it into this column indicating their accomplishment. This is positive for morale. The next day, the tasks in that column are moved to the "Complete" column. The team members then update the hours remaining (at the right side of the board) for the Work Item row, as well as the total number of hours of tasks remaining in the iteration (bottom right).

Team Leadership

Regardless of all this cool agile stuff, without a competent team lead your project is likely to fail. Team leads may not actually do the work (although in many cases they do indeed volunteer for work item tasks themselves, including possibly coding). If they are acting only in the capacity of team lead they rely on the commitment of their team members. Team leads need to exhibit the following characteristics:

- Motivational skills.
- Visible humility in that they realize that the team members deserve the credit. Mark makes it a point to let all stakeholders know that as a team lead he deserves no credit for the success of the teams.
- Clearly visible confidence in the agile approach.
- Proactively addressing risks with a sense of urgency to keep the team productive.
- Clearly expressing expectations that the team members deliver their own commitments.

Table 15.7   Comparing Approaches to Change Management

Strategy	Potential Advantages	Potential Disadvantages	Considerations
Change prevention (a.k.a. change control)	Potentially enables the development team to come in on time and on budget.	You build the solution to specification, but this is often not what they actually need. Not consistent with an agile approach of encouraging flexibility and just-in-time adaptation to any new understanding of the customer's need. Many teams are still late and over budget. Can prove to be a relatively expensive overhead, upwards of 5% of project costs on some teams.	May be suitable for some contracting situations where the customer insists on a defined scope, budget, and schedule.
Flexible work item management	Delivery of a system that meets the true needs of the customer. Reduced bureaucracy cost to manage the change control process.	Constant grooming of the work item list by the product owner can prove to be expensive, taking 20% to 25% of their time on some teams. You cannot predict at the beginning of the project exactly what will be delivered.	This approach requires a degree of trust between the team and their stakeholders that the team will deliver the maximum scope achievable for their investment.
Uncontrolled change	Reduced bureaucracy.	Likely to result in scope creep and schedule delays.	

One of the underemphasized aspects of a good team lead is the ability to resolve team issues. Closely located, highly collaborative teams often exhibit family-like behaviors. Mark has seen petty arguments, egos that get in the way, a focus on organizational hierarchies and roles within the team, and other team dysfunctions on almost every project.

People skills that are found in good project managers are equally required on agile projects. Ineffective managers often avoid conflict or constructive feedback or they may be unwilling to escalate issues. These attributes will also cause your agile projects to fail.

Allowing your teams to self-organize and manage themselves requires a lot of trust. But, if your team is not capable and highly motivated they will still run into trouble. A good team lead recognizes when the teams are taking advantage of the freedom to manage their own activities and takes action to replace team members if necessary. Fortunately self-organizing teams tend to self-police themselves through peer pressure. They typically take their iteration commitments seriously, and poorly performing team members often become visible quickly. One of the positive byproducts of the daily stand-ups is the individual daily accountability because individual contributions, or lack thereof, are visible to the entire team.

On a healthy team, experienced team members spend time coaching more junior members and help them accomplish their tasks if necessary in the interest of the entire team meeting its iteration commitments to the product owner.

Team leads encourage team members to become cross-functional generalizing specialists. For instance, a developer might sign up to do a testing task, or update the database schema. This is consistent with the agile practice of collective ownership of all project work products. Cross-fertilization learning between team members results in systems that are of higher quality and easier to maintain. It also minimizes the resourcing risk of losing key knowledge through attrition.

Sustainable Pace

Due to the focus on short-term results delivered every few weeks team members can become increasingly stressed over a number of iterations. When people become burned out the quality of their work and productivity decreases dramatically. Sustainable pace is the pace at which the team can perform effectively over an extended period of time. Brief spurts of overtime can typically be tolerated by the team but cannot be maintained over time.

Automated Metrics Gathering

In DAD we show low-tech methods of capturing metrics such as taskboards and burndown charts. The advantage of these techniques is that they are simple to maintain. For more advanced metrics, such as defect rates, status of builds, and work item management, some tooling is worthwhile. We want to avoid developers having to maintain and tabulate metrics since it detracts from their primary task of creating the solution. Modern tooling enables in-depth reporting of many metrics related to progress and quality via dashboards that are updated unobtrusively as a byproduct of team members working on the solution. More on this in Chapter 20, "Governing Disciplined Agile Teams."

Following Organizational Standards

We would be remiss in our lengthy discussion of practices to deliver quality solutions if we did not mention standards. In our experience, agile teams often neglect development standards that exist in their organizations. Using existing standards actually speeds up delivery by reducing rework, defects, and support costs of the solution. The team should select from available standards but be empowered to adopt their own standard if suitable for their specific situation. Standards should be identified and refined in early iterations. Be proactive in communicating these standards to your teams to avoid nasty surprises later. DAD teams are naturally expected to follow their own coding standards and conventions tailored from appropriate guidance defined at the larger organizational level.

Having said this, the true goal is to produce a high-quality solution for your stakeholders, not to produce a solution that fulfills a collection of standards. Follow standards and guidelines that lead to this.

A Closer Look at Critical Agile Practices

Earlier in this chapter we gave short shrift to a few important agile practices that deserve more detailed treatment. These practices are the following:

- Test-driven development (TDD)
- Continuous integration (CI)
- Continuous deployment (CD)
- Parallel independent testing
- Reviews

Test-Driven Development (TDD)

The key aspect of TDD is the practice of test-first development (TFD) as shown in Figure 15.8. The first step is to quickly add a test, basically just enough code to fail. Next you run your tests, often the complete test suite although for sake of speed you may decide to run only a subset, to ensure that the new test does in fact fail. You then update your functional code to make it pass the new tests. The fourth step is to run your tests again. If they fail you need to update your functional code and retest. Once the tests pass the next step is to start over.

Some people may think that writing code to test code before any actual code is written is backwards. However, if we do not write the tests first, then often the tests are never written. There is always the need to write code for more functionality, and developers sometimes "forget" to write the tests. Having a standard in place to write the tests first ensures that they are never forgotten. It is important to have good test "coverage" of your code—that is, there should be automated tests that cover all the code that has been written. TFD is an advanced practice that all teams should move toward but may take some time to achieve.

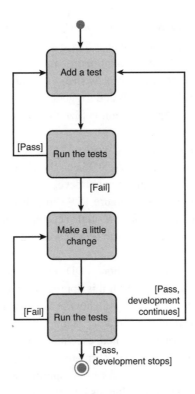

Figure 15.8   The steps of test-first development (TFD)

TDD is TFD plus refactoring. Refactoring is a disciplined way to restructure your code to improve its quality. The basic idea is that you make small changes to your code to improve your design, making it easier to understand and to modify. Refactoring enables you to evolve your code slowly over time, to take an iterative and incremental approach to programming. A critical aspect of a refactoring is that it retains the behavioral semantics of your code, at least from a black box point of view. For example there is a simple refactoring called Rename Method, perhaps from getPersons() to getPeople(). Although this change looks easy on the surface you need to do more than just make this single change; you must also change every single invocation of this operation throughout all of your application code to invoke the new name. Once you've made these changes, you can say you've truly refactored your code because it still works again as before. It is important to understand that you do not add functionality when you are refactoring. When you refactor you improve existing code, when you add functionality you are adding new code. Yes, you may need to refactor your existing code before you can add new functionality. Yes, you may discover later on that you need to refactor the new code that you just added. The point to be made is that refactoring and adding new functionality are two different but complementary tasks.

Refactoring applies not only to code, but to your database schema and user interface (UI) as well. A database refactoring is a simple change to a database schema that improves its design while retaining both its behavioral and informational semantics. For the sake of this discussion a database schema includes both structural aspects such as table and view definitions as well as functional aspects such as stored procedures and triggers. A UI refactoring is a simple change to your UI such as Align Fields and Apply Common Size that improves the quality of the look and feel of your solution.

Earlier in the chapter we described two types of TDD, acceptance test-driven development (ATDD) and developer TDD. The focus of ATDD is on the JIT specification of detailed requirements and validation thereof, whereas the focus of developer TDD is on the JIT specification of the detailed design and validation thereof. Figure 15.9 shows how ATDD and developer TDD fit together. The basic idea is that the creation of a single acceptance test in turn requires you to iterate several times through the write a test, write production code, and get it working cycle at the developer TDD level.

We have three concluding thoughts about TDD. First, many teams start by adopting the practice of developer regression testing. With this approach the tests are often written after the production code, a practice that still requires skill but not as much discipline. Second, from a testing point of view TDD is a form of confirmatory testing, the equivalent of testing against the specification. Because the tests form the detailed, executable specification, by definition this must be confirmatory testing. The challenge with confirmatory testing is that it doesn't catch the issues that you weren't told about, hence the need for other approaches to testing. More on this later. Third, an enabling practice for TDD is continuous integration (CI).

Continuous Integration (CI)

CI is the practice of regularly integrating and testing your solution to incorporate changes made to its definition. Such changes include updating the source code, changing a database schema, or updating a configuration file. Ideally, when one or more changes are checked into your configuration management system the solution should be rebuilt (recompiled), retested, and any code or schema analysis performed on it. Failing that, you should strive to do so at least once if not several times a day. As you see in Figure 15.10 there are several steps to CI:

1. **Ensure build readiness.** If a build is currently running, this new build should be queued up. If the build is currently broken and there have been no changes to the solution definition since that build attempt. you should not attempt a new build until changes have been checked in.

2. **Obtain current source.** The CI tool should obtain the latest source code, configuration files, and schema definition (if the database is going to be rebuilt) from your configuration management system.

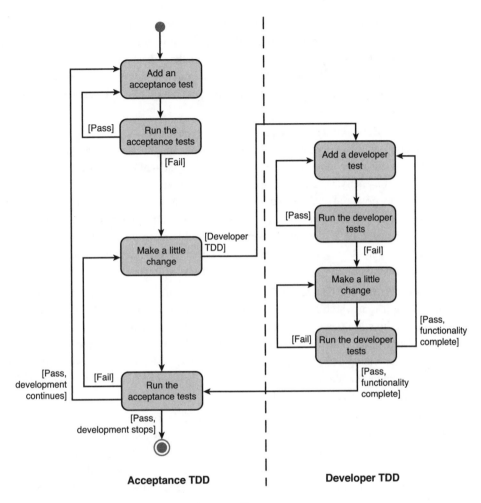

Figure 15.9 Acceptance and developer TDD together

3. **Build solution.** This includes both compiling your code and potentially rebuilding your test database(s). This sounds straightforward, but for large systems composed of subsystems you need a strategy for how you're going to build both the subsystems as well as the overall system (you might only do a complete system build once a night, or once a week for example, and only build subsystems on a regular basis).

4. **Run regression test suite(s).** Which test suite(s) you run will be determined by the scope of the build and the size of the system. For small systems you'll likely have a single test suite of all tests, but in more complex situations you will have several test

suites for performance reasons. For example, in the project integration sandbox you may have a test suite that runs in less than 30 minutes that is run several times a day, one that runs in a few hours that is run once a day, and one that takes many hours so it is run once a week. In your preproduction test environment you may have a load/stress test suite that is long running, a security test suite that should be run at least once each build, a UI test suite, and several others.

5. **Perform code/schema analysis.** If the regression tests pass you will optionally perform static code analysis, dynamic code analysis, and maybe even data schema analysis. Although this is an optional step we highly suggest that you do this. The results of code/schema analysis are typically warnings about potential quality problems as opposed to potential defects that are noticeable by stakeholders. For example, your analysis may reveal that you're not following certain coding conventions in some places, that you have cyclomatic complexity problems in your code, or your database schema may not be adequately normalized. These are problems that you should be concerned about, but they're not serious enough to stop you from releasing into production.

6. **Report results.** The CI system should record the results of the run, such as when it ran, how long it ran, which baseline was built, how long it took to build, which test suites were run, how long each test suite took, how many tests were run, which ones (if any) failed, and so on. This information must be available to the team immediately so that they can act on it. Furthermore it should be captured so that trend analysis could be done on it to enable the team to manage itself effectively and potentially to support your IT governance effort (see Chapter 20).

The next section describes continuous deployment (CD). Figure 15.11 illustrates the practice of deploying automatically between different sandboxes/environments. For example, when the build is successful on a developer's workstation they may automatically deploy their changes to the project integration environment, which would invoke the CI system there. A successful integration in that environment could trigger an automatic deployment into another environment and so on. Figure 15.10 doesn't show this happening.

In your personal sandbox your integration job could run at specific times, perhaps once an hour, or better, every time you check in a new version of a component (such as source code or schema definition) that is part of the build. This whole process of continuously integrating a developer's code with the rest of a team's code in and then running automated test regressions in an integration environment is a critical part of agile done right. Continuous integration ensures that we have high quality working software *at all times*.

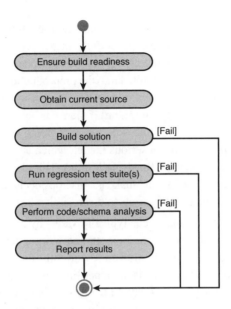

Figure 15.10 The process of continuous integration

Continuous Deployment (CD)

The agile practice of continuous deployment (CD) extends continuous integration (CI) to automatically deploy your work into the next environment when your work integrates successfully. Figure 15.11 overviews this strategy, depicting several important aspects of CD:

- **Environments.** It shows how your team will have several environments, also called sandboxes, in which they're potentially working: development sandboxes where individuals develop the solution; the project integration sandbox where the work of individual team members is combined into a working solution; a demo sandbox where people, including stakeholders, can see and even use a working version of the solution; a preproduction testing environment (this is where your independent test team works if you have one); and your production environment where the solution is used. Your physical strategy may vary from the logical strategy shown previously in Figure 15.11. For example, smaller teams may not have a separate demo environment but instead may simply use the project owner's laptop. Very large teams may have several preproduction testing environments, each of which supports different types of testing.

- **Deployment between environments.** Deployment between development sandboxes and the project integration environment should automatically occur whenever a developer has a successful integration. This deployment often automatically runs an integration build in the project integration environment. Deployment between the project integration environment and the demo and preproduction environments may occur whenever the solution integrates successfully in the project integration environment. When it comes to the preproduction environment, in many cases the build will be put into a staging area first and then pulled into the preproduction environment by the testers when they're ready to take it. A common strategy is for it to be scheduled to occur on a periodic basis (nightly, weekly, and so on) if there has been a successful project integration build since the last time the solution was deployed into these environments. Deployment into production is a serious matter, which is why the DAD process framework includes the Production Ready milestone. This decision is typically not automated, instead one or more people make a conscious decision that the solution is ready to be deployed and then run the scripts to do so.

- **Level of testing.** Your testing focus typically varies by environment. In your development sandboxes you'll typically be running and writing developer tests and hopefully acceptance tests for the work items you're currently implementing. These test suites need to run quickly—10 minutes is an upper limit although shorter is better—because these tests are run many times a day. In the project integration sandbox you may have tests that are focused on testing the solution from end-to-end. These tests often take longer to run and therefore are run less frequently, perhaps every evening. You will also have some tests that run quickly, perhaps in 30 minutes or less, which may run several times a day. Testing in your preproduction environment can be complex—see the discussion about independent parallel testing later in this chapter—and can be very long-running. For example, one of the teams in IBM that works on a middleware product has a test suite that purposefully runs for three months straight to simulate long-term load.

- **Average cost of fixing defects.** The average costs of fixing defects rises exponentially the longer it takes to find the defect. The implication is that you want to test as often and early as you possibly can in the delivery lifecycle. Continuous deployment helps to address this problem by streamlining the effort required to get your solution to the next testing level as quickly as you possibly can.

Here are some attributes of a good CD solution:

- Strive for automated or push-button deployment where no manual steps are required.

- Scripts and configuration values should be versioned in your configuration management system with your code so that you can redeploy any previous version of your system if you need to.

- Use one deployment script that is usable for all environments.

- Log the results of the deployment tasks so that you have an audit trail of any errors.

- Run automated tests after the deployment to smoke test the system and to validate that the target environment has been configured correctly and is running as expected. This is often referred to as deployment testing or installation testing.

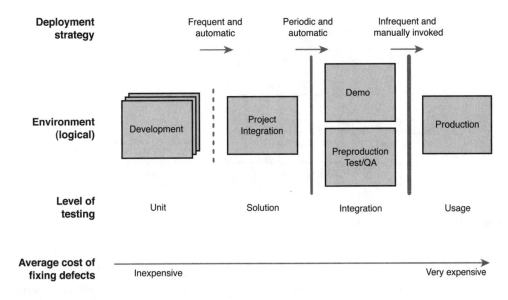

Figure 15.11   Deploying between various environments

Parallel Independent Testing

There are limits to the whole team approach to development where agile teams test to the best of their ability. In many situations, described later in this section, you need to consider instituting a parallel independent test team that performs some of the more difficult forms of testing. As you can see in Figure 15.12, on a regular basis the delivery team makes their working build and an indication of what has changed since the last drop available to the independent test team. Ideally this occurs automatically as per the continuous deployment (CD) practice. The independent test team then tests the drop as they see fit and reports any defects back to the delivery team. These defect reports are put into the work item stack/pool and addressed by the team appropriately. Although Figure 15.12 and Figure 15.13 later in this section indicate that your team has adopted iterations, this practice is also applicable if you're following a more advanced/lean strategy based on a continual flow of work instead.

The goal of this testing effort is not to redo the confirmatory testing that is already being done by the developers but instead to identify potential defects that have fallen through the cracks. The implication is that this independent test team does not need a detailed requirements specification. They may however need architecture diagrams, a scope overview, and release notes (a list of changes) since the last time the development team sent them a build. The independent testing effort focuses on preproduction integration testing, exploratory/investigative testing, and anything else that they suspect the delivery team isn't testing effectively.

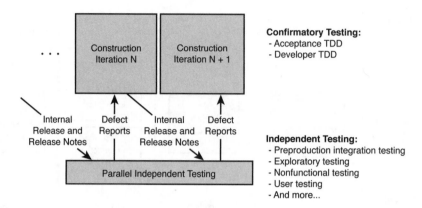

Figure 15.12   Parallel independent testing

There are several reasons why you should consider parallel independent testing:

- **Investigative testing.** Confirmatory testing approaches, such as TDD, validate that you've implemented the requirements as they've been described to you. But what happens when requirements are missing?

- **Potential inconsistencies between project teams.** Independent testing could potentially uncover inconsistencies in business rules as tested by separate project teams. For example, your stakeholders could tell you that platinum customers receive a 10% discount, whereas the stakeholders of another project team have told them the discount is 8%. Who's right? Your stakeholders or their stakeholders? Maybe both are right, but the full context of the actual business rule hasn't been communicated to either team explaining when each discount is applicable. An independent test team responsible for supporting both of these project teams may catch this inconsistency.

- **Lack of resources.** Many development teams may not have the resources required to perform effective preproduction integration testing. This form of testing often requires expensive test environments that go beyond what an individual project team will have. Economically it makes sense to centralize and share these resources.

- **Lack of skills.** Sometimes your team isn't truly a "whole team" with all the skills and knowledge that they require. For example, they may not have expertise in security testing to properly perform vulnerability testing, penetration testing, and similar issues. Similarly it can be hard to staff all teams with people who have experience with open source software (OSS) licensing validation, consumability testing, and database testing. Because some forms of testing require specialized expertise it can be most effective to staff the independent test team with this expertise and have them address these sorts of issues.

- **Large or distributed teams.** Large or distributed teams are often subdivided into smaller teams, and when this happens system integration testing of the overall system can become complex enough that a separate team should consider taking it on. Whole team testing works well for agile in small teams, but for more complex systems and agile at scale you need to go beyond it.

- **Complex domains.** When you have a complex domain, perhaps you're working on life critical software or financial transaction processing, whole team testing approaches can prove insufficient. Having a parallel independent testing effort can reduce these risks.

- **Complex technical environments.** When you're working with multiple technologies, legacy systems, or legacy data sources the testing of your system can become difficult.

- **Regulatory compliance.** Some regulations require you to have an independent testing effort. The most efficient way to do so is to have it work in parallel to the development team.

- **Preproduction integration testing.** The solution that you're building must work well with the other solutions currently in production when your solution is released. This is an aspect of enterprise awareness. To do this properly you must test against versions of other solutions currently under development, implying that you need access to updated versions on a regular basis. This is fairly straightforward in small organizations, but if your organization has dozens, if not hundreds, of IT projects underway, it becomes overwhelming for individual development teams to gain such access. A more efficient approach is to have an independent test team be responsible for such enterprise-level system integration testing.

As you see in Figure 15.13 the independent testing efforts stretch into the Transition phase of the delivery lifecycle. This is because the independent test team still needs to test the complete system once the final Construction iteration is complete and give the team time to fix any found defects as appropriate. Ideally this testing effort is just rerunning the appropriate regression test suites to show that everything works as expected.

There are several reasons why you still need to do end-of-lifecycle testing:

- **It's professional to do so.** You'll minimally want to do one last run of all your regression tests to be in a position to officially declare that your system is fully tested. This would occur once iteration N, the last construction iteration, finishes.

- **You may be legally obligated to do so.** This is either because of the contract that you have with the business customer or due to regulatory compliance.

- **Your stakeholders require it.** Your stakeholders, particularly your operations department, will likely require some sort of testing effort before releasing your solution into production to feel comfortable with the quality of your work. Ensuring that your solution is production ready is an important milestone that supports effective governance and DevOps strategies.

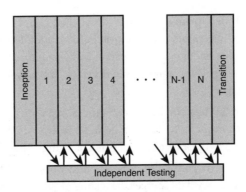

Figure 15.13   Independent testing throughout the DAD lifecycle

Some agilists claim that you don't need parallel independent testing. In simple situations this is clearly true, but not every situation is straightforward. Luckily it's incredibly easy to determine whether your independent testing effort is providing value: Simply compare the likely impact of the defects/change stories being reported with the cost of doing the independent testing.

Conversely some organizations believe firmly that all testing should be done by a group external to the development team. The rationale for this is that the development team will be biased and tend to test basics such as "happy path" scenarios rather than abnormal scenarios that might be encountered in real life. The independence and objectivity of an external group also makes the auditors happy. In DAD we understand that some degree of independent testing is a good part of proper diligence and is a supporting practice that we endorse. Note, however, that it occurs in *parallel* with the development of the solution; that is, we do not want to defer the testing to the end of the lifecycle as is done in traditional methods.

Reviews

First and foremost, we consider the holding of reviews and inspections to be a process smell indicating that you made a mistake earlier in the lifecycle that could likely be rectified by another, more effective strategy (non-solo development, for example) that has a much shorter feedback cycle. However, in several situations it makes sense to hold reviews:

- **Regulatory requirements.** When your project is subject to regulations, such as the Food and Drug Administration (FDA)'s 21 CFR Part 11, you may by law be required to hold some reviews. Our advice is to read the relevant regulations carefully, determine whether you actually are subject to them, and if so identify how much additional work you actually need to do to conform to the regulations. If you let the bureaucrats interpret the regulations you will likely end up with an overly bureaucratic process.

- **To obtain stakeholder feedback.** Stakeholder demos are an example of a review, and they're a valuable mainstream agile technique. Demos provide stakeholders with a consistent opportunity to provide feedback about work in progress. Chapter 16, "Concluding a Construction Iteration," discusses stakeholder demos in greater detail.

- **To keep stakeholders informed.** Stakeholder demos are an important opportunity to communicate the level of progress your team has made to date by showing them your potentially consumable solution.

- **To ensure your strategy is viable.** In Chapter 20 we argue that you should have the occasional lightweight milestone review to determine whether the project team is on track.

- **A work product wasn't created collaboratively.** We are eager to review artifacts where only one or two people have actively worked on them *and* that can't be proven with working code (e.g., user manuals, operations documents, and so on). These situations do occur; perhaps only one person on your team has technical writing skills so they've taken over the majority of your documentation efforts. However, if this is actually the case, you should really consider adopting non-solo development techniques to spread around these skills a little more widely.

Stabilizing the Day's Work

Toward the end of the day team members' attention turns to stabilizing their code so that it can be tested and checked into source control. This is of course code that has been tested and does not break the build. Any code checked committed must be tested to ensure that the build is not broken.

LESSONS FROM THE TRENCHES—USING AGILE TECHNIQUES ON TRADITIONAL PROJECTS

We are periodically invited into traditional waterfall projects to help apply agile techniques where possible. On one such project Mark and his team's challenge was to clean up a large backlog of defects before going into production. This is a typical problem for large waterfall projects with exhaustive testing at the end of the lifecycle rather than the modern approach of continuous regression testing throughout the project. For this project, we had 10 business days to clean up the remaining defects prior to the user acceptance testing before going live. The team members committed their final defect fixes for the day late each afternoon, whereupon a build was created and deployed into the system's integration environment. Integration testing took place offshore overnight and into the morning by an independent testing team. The team (including the independent testers) reviewed the new defect outstanding count each morning and discussed the plan for the day for who would be fixing the remaining high priority defects. The reduction in defect count was plotted on a defect burndown chart to ensure that the team was on pace to retire the key defects within the 10 days.

Concluding Thoughts

This chapter described how work occurs on a typical construction day and discussed many potential techniques that your team may apply. You saw how these activities help your team to fulfill several of the goals of the Construction phase:

- **Produce a potentially consumable solution.** By following the daily pattern of planning your work, creating automated tests, writing code, and integrating it with the rest of the solution you can have a working and tested solution at all times.

- **Address changing stakeholder needs.** Working closely with stakeholders and adopting a flexible change management strategy are key to your success. Showing stakeholders your work in progress to get feedback from them and performing just-in-time (JIT) model storming to elicit domain information from them are effective strategies for working closely.

- **Move closer to a deployable release.** Practices such as continuous integration (CI) and continuous deployment (CD) enable you to reduce the cycle time between writing code and having a running solution that could potentially be deployed into production.

- **Maintain or improve upon existing levels of quality.** Investing in writing automated tests first ensures that defects injected into your application are caught and fixed almost immediately, saving a huge amount of testing and integration pain later on. Periodically refactoring your code base as you go avoids technical debt, which impedes your ability to extend and support your solution in the future.

- **Grow team member skills.** Adopting non-solo development practices such as pair programming and modeling with others is an easy way to share skills among the team. The team lead should actively strive to give team members opportunities to pick up new skills, including giving up some of their own responsibilities to other team members.

- **Leverage existing infrastructure.** DAD team members actively seek to reuse existing functionality and data whenever they can, reducing costs to their stakeholders and speeding up delivery of new functionality as a result.

Additional Resources

For more detailed discussions about several of the topics covered in this chapter:

- **Surveys.** In this chapter we shared statistics about agile documentation practices from two surveys, the results of which are posted at ambysoft.com/surveys/. This included data from the Dr. Dobb's Journal (DDJ) 2008 Modeling and Documentation survey and the September 2009 DDJ State of the IT Union survey.

- **Sustainable pace.** Extreme Programming's practice of sustainable pace is described at extremeprogramming.org/rules/overtime.html.

- **Daily coordination meetings.** Mike Cohn has a great article about daily coordination/Scrum meetings at mountaingoatsoftware.com/scrum/daily-scrum/.

- **Agile modeling and documentation practices.** This chapter described several practices from Agile Modeling that you are likely to perform throughout construction. This includes JIT model storming at agilemodeling.com/essays/modelStorming.htm and the Continuous Documentation practice at agilemodeling.com/essays/documentContinuously.htm. General agile documentation advice is presented at agilemodeling.com/essays/agileDocumentation.htm.

- **Agile testing.** This chapter described a collection of agile testing and quality techniques. Lisa Crispin and Janet Gregory's book *Agile Testing: A Practical Guide for Testers and Agile Teams* (Addison-Wesley, 2009) is the best single resource to get you started on this topic. Scott has a survey article summarizing agile testing and quality techniques, and how they work together, at ambysoft.com/essays/agileTesting.html. Scott also has a detailed article about TDD, ATDD, and developer regression testing at agiledata.org/essays/tdd.html and one about database regression testing at agiledata.org/essays/databaseTesting.html.

- **Code analysis.** Steve Gutz describes static code analysis at ibm.com/developerworks/rational/library/08/0429_gutz1. William Jackson compares static and dynamic code analysis at gcn.com/articles/2009/02/09/static-vs-dynamic-code-analysis.aspx.

- **Architecture spike.** Scott has written about architecture spikes at agilemodeling.com/essays/agileArchitecture.htm.

- **Status reporting.** We discussed several ways that agile teams share their current status both internally and externally. This reporting enables the team to manage their activities better and senior management to govern them better. A critical technique is to maintain an iteration burndown chart, described by Mike Cohn in his book *Agile Estimating and Planning* (Addison-Wesley, 2006). We also suggest that you adopt tools that automate metric gathering so that they can be displayed in a project dashboard. Examples of live dashboards for several IBM product teams can be found at www.jazz.net.

- **Refactoring.** Refactoring is a fundamental agile quality technique. Martin Fowler's seminal book *Refactoring: Improving the Design of Existing Code* (Addison-Wesley, 1999) is a must-read for all agile developers. Scott and Pramod Sadalage describe how to refactor databases in *Database Refactoring* (Addison-Wesley, 2006), and Rusty Harold describes UI refactoring in *Refactoring HTML: Improving the Design of Existing Web Applications* (Addison-Wesley, 2009).

- **Continuous integration and deployment.** Jez Humble and David Farley provide real-world advice about achieving your goal of push-button deployment in *Continuous Delivery: Reliable Software Releases Through Build, Test, and Deployment Automation* (Addison-Wesley, 2010).

- **Technical debt.** In *Managing Software Debt* (Addison-Wesley, 2010) Chris Sterling describes a host of strategies for avoiding and reducing technical debt. Martin Fowler describes the technical debt quadrant at martinfowler.com/bliki/TechnicalDebtQuadrant. html.

- **Exponential cost of fixing defects.** Barry Boehm has been writing about the exponential cost of fixing defects starting in *Software Engineering Economics* (Prentice Hall, 1981).

- **Writing code.** We would be remiss if we didn't share a few suggestions about how to write better code. The easy answer is pretty much any book written by Robert C. Martin, although if we had to choose it would be *Clean Code: A Handbook of Agile Software Craftsmanship* (Addison-Wesley, 2008). Jon Bentley's *Programming Pearls* (Addison-Wesley, 1999) is a great resource for anyone wanting to learn how to write better code as is *The Practice of Programming* (Addison-Wesley, 1999) by Brian W. Kernigham and Rob Pike.

CHAPTER 16

Concluding a Construction Iteration

Improving software development practices counts for nothing unless it improves software development results.

As you learned in Chapter 15, "A Typical Day of Construction," a properly executed Construction iteration yields a tested working solution every day. If the iteration was successful the team should be able to demonstrate functionality representing the work items that they committed to deliver at the beginning of the iteration. The end of the iteration is also a good time to assess progress against the release plan, evaluate the team's performance, and identify any opportunities for improvement. The end of each iteration is an opportunity to discuss with your stakeholders how, or whether, to proceed—will you continue on the same path, pivot to a new direction, or even cancel the project?

Figure 16.1 overviews the rhythm of a Construction iteration. Toward the end of the iteration focus turns to addressing key defects and hardening of the code base so that we have a potentially shippable increment of the solution. This has been called *iteration hardening* and this chapter assumes that has occurred. In this chapter we discuss the activities required to bring a Construction iteration to a successful conclusion.

Figure 16.2 shows a mind map of the structure of this chapter. We describe each of the topics in the map in clockwise order, beginning at the top right.

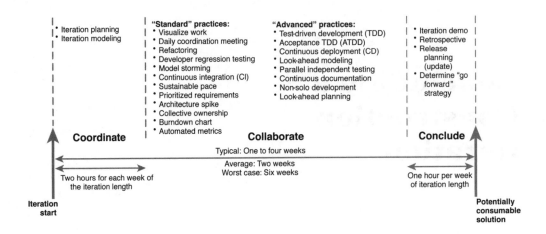

Figure 16.1   Construction iteration overview

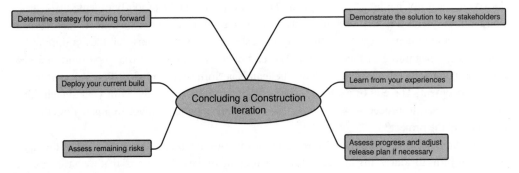

Figure 16.2   Outline of this chapter

THE BIG IDEAS IN THIS CHAPTER

- Completion of documents is not a reliable indication of progress. The only meaningful indication of progress is through the demonstration of a potentially consumable solution.

- Toward the end of a Construction iteration the team's focus turns from building new functionality to stabilizing what has been built and making it potentially consumable by the customers should they wish it to be deployed.

- At the end of an iteration the team typically demonstrates their work to key stakeholders both to provide concrete visible status and to obtain feedback.

- The team should take time to reflect on their success or challenges of the iteration and consider actions to improve how they work together.
- The end of each iteration is an opportunity to gauge the team's pace (velocity) and adjust expectations of what is achievable for the release.

Demonstrate the Solution to Key Stakeholders

If there is one criterion to assess your agile capability it is to be able to demonstrate increments of a consumable solution at the end of each iteration. This demonstration should minimally address changes to the solution (including the software, deliverable documentation, and so on) since the last demonstration. All other techniques described in this book support this common goal. Table 16.1 shows various strategies for showcasing your solution to your stakeholders. These strategies include the following:

- **Iteration demonstration.** A demonstration is conducted once at the end of each iteration to showcase the team's accomplishments. It demonstrates progress to invited stakeholders and provides the team with the opportunity to receive feedback from them.

- **On-demand demonstrations.** A demonstration can take place at any time at the request of any stakeholder. This requires disciplined continuous integration practices in place to ensure that a working solution is available. Better yet, you should consider having a continuous deployment strategy (see Chapter 15) that automatically deploys your working builds into a demo environment at appropriate times.

- **All hands demonstrations.** On a regular basis a demonstration of what you have produced is made to a much larger group than just the key stakeholders directly involved with your project. This is sometimes referred to as a showcase.

- **None.** Some teams choose not to demonstrate their solution to their stakeholders.

If your DAD projects are executed properly, you should be able to book demonstrations in *advance* for the end of each Construction iteration until the solution is released. These demonstrations are also known as *showcases*. Book your key stakeholders, such as the vice president of the pertinent division(s), for these demonstrations. There should typically be no excuse for not being able to deliver demonstrations on these dates. Pre-booking regular demonstrations well in advance can have a remarkable effect on the behavior of your team. They often soon realize that everything that they do is about being able to create a stable, executable solution at regular intervals. If the iteration does not produce a demonstrable increment of your solution, it is not considered a successful Construction iteration. In this situation no individual is to blame; it is instead seen as the fault of the entire team. You succeed or fail together.

Table 16.1　Comparing Demonstration Strategies

Strategy	Timing	Potential Advantages	Potential Disadvantages	Considerations
Iteration demonstration	Typically on the last day of an iteration.	Can be regularly scheduled, making it easier for stakeholders to attend. An opportunity for the team to pause and celebrate their achievement. A constant stakeholder feedback drumbeat is maintained throughout the project. Stakeholders know that they are only one iteration length away at any point in time from the next demonstration, helping overall transparency.	Some stakeholders may have scheduling conflicts and be unable to attend the demonstration.	Keep this demo less than one hour. Large teams need to choose which subsets of the new functionality they intend to demo in a given iteration as they may have developed more than can be easily demoed in an hour.
On-demand demonstrations	Whenever a demonstration is requested by a stakeholder.	Demonstrations can occur at the stakeholders' convenience rather than that of the team.	Can be disruptive to the team although can be manageable if the product owner coordinates these demonstrations.	A good strategy as you move toward a lean approach with more frequent deployments. If you also have iteration demos you can sometimes ask the requester to attend the next demo instead of giving them a personal one.

Strategy	Timing	Potential Advantages	Potential Disadvantages	Considerations
All-hands demonstrations	Typically at major milestones and just before release (sometimes called a pre-release demo).	Keeps everyone involved. Mitigates risk of potentially missing something material at smaller demonstrations. Good way to confirm whether the product owner truly represents the wider stakeholder community. Builds credibility that the team is making progress.	Can be expensive if there are many people and the meeting is long. Can be confused for a requirements elicitation session, making scope management difficult.	A good strategy for effective communication to stakeholders. Allows various stakeholder groups to consider the impact on their business. Typically occurs in addition to iteration demonstrations and may even be considered as a type of milestone review.
None	Never.	Frees up time spent doing the demonstrations.	Possibility for miscommunication regarding what is being built versus what the stakeholders expect.	May be appropriate for small projects where the product owner is the customer and sees the solution evolve every day. This strategy should be rarely considered as it decreases stakeholder visibility into what the team is doing.

We suggest rotating the demo responsibilities among team members. For instance a developer could do a demo, but the next demo could be done by a tester. In many organizations the team lead or product owner does the demos, but is this right? The people who actually did the work to create the software should show it to the users. This gives your team members some visibility and a share of the credit that they deserve. It also helps them to build valuable communication skills. So, consider rotating demo responsibilities between everyone on the team, including the product owner and team lead.

Learn from Your Experiences

One potential activity when concluding an iteration is to reflect on how well your team worked together and whether there are ways in which you could be better. There are several strategies for doing so, which are compared in Table 16.2. These strategies are as follows:

- **Retrospectives.** This is a facilitated reflection meeting with the team. They typically last 30 to 60 minutes although longer retrospectives do occur. In retrospectives we typically ask four questions: What went well? What could we improve on? What should we do differently next time? and What still puzzles us? Variations to these questions are also allowed. For example, some teams choose to identify enjoyable things about their work, frustrating things, and suggestions for things they should consider trying.

- **Structured survey.** The team uses a standard set of questions regarding agile practices and capabilities against which they rate themselves. The result is a scorecard showing the agile capability of the team. Areas where the team rates itself poorly are indications of where they want to consider improving.

- **Measured improvement.** Once process improvements have been identified, consider tracking your progress in implementing them. This tracking should occur for several iterations until the practice is firmly established on your team. The easiest approach is to poll team members at the beginning of a new reflection meeting about how previously identified process improvements are going. These answers can be on a scale of one to ten and then using a spreadsheet to capture, average, and track over time.

- **Project post mortem.** This is one or more facilitated reflection meetings with the team, which occurs near the end of the project or immediately following it. These meetings are often half a day to a full day in length for large projects and often follow a strategy similar to retrospectives.

- **Ad hoc process improvement.** Ad hoc process improvements can be identified and acted upon at any time.

- **None.** Some teams choose not to invest in improving their process.

Table 16.2 Comparing Process Improvement Strategies

Strategy	Timing	Potential Advantages	Potential Disadvantages	Considerations
Retrospective	Typically on the first or last day of the iteration, although can occur at any time.	Structured format allows everyone to provide input. Supports a just-in-time (JIT) process improvement strategy. Potential improvements are identified when people are most motivated to act on them, at the point where they're experiencing problems.	Waiting to identify ideas to solve problems at the end of an iteration may be too late. Can result in a list of potential improvements that you never actually act on.	Requires an environment where team members feel that they can express their opinions in an environment of trust. Consider focusing on identifying one or two pain points that your team can act on immediately. Very effective when used in combination with measured improvement.
Structured survey	Initially to form baseline. Then update regularly, commonly once an iteration.	A standard set of questions allows comparisons across teams.	Questions may not be suitable across all teams and thus require customization. Novice teams may not have the necessary skills to understand the questions adequately. The questions may not cover the entire range of issues faced by your team. Tends to focus on activities, such as following a specific process, instead of outcomes, such as improving quality.	Can be a good way to ease into reflection meetings and measured improvement.

(continued)

Table 16.2   Comparing Process Improvement Strategies (continued)

Strategy	Timing	Potential Advantages	Potential Disadvantages	Considerations
Measured improvement	As part of a retrospective or other type of reflection meeting.	Increases the chance that the team will focus on the improvement long enough to internalize it.	Small overhead to poll the team to track their adoption of various strategies.	IBM found with internal teams that the teams that held retrospectives and then tracked their improvement efforts did better than teams only doing retrospectives.
Project post mortem	At the end of the project.	Provides an opportunity for catharsis on teams on a troubled project. Provides an opportunity to explicitly recognize what a team did well.	Potential improvements are identified when the team can no longer benefit from them. Despite good intentions, many organizations fail to act on the process improvements that are identified.	Project post mortems on their own seldom do much to motivate actual process improvement.
Ad hoc process improvement	At any time.	Shortens the time between perceiving a problem and acting to solve it.	Some problems go away on their own without taking explicit action, so if you act too quickly you risk wasting time.	Ad-hoc retrospectives at the time that a problem is perceived can be very effective in practice.
None	Never.	Avoids the overhead involved with process improvement.	Teams miss opportunities to improve their productivity.	This goes against principle #12 behind the Agile Manifesto. We don't recommend this.

Both of us are firm believers in holding retrospectives and supplementing them with measured improvement. This is a combination of the agile principle of investing time to regularly reflect and then tune your approach appropriately with the age-old observation that what gets measured gets improved. Let's explore how to be effective with these two techniques.

There is nothing that says that process improvements need to be formally discussed and acted upon only at the end of the iteration. Improvements can be identified and then made at any time. For teams new to agile we recommend that you set aside an hour for your team at some point each iteration to discuss your experiences. Mark sometimes prefers to run retrospectives as the first item on the agenda of the iteration planning session. Celebrate your achievements but also discuss how to improve in the coming iteration. Motivated self-organizing teams will feel comfortable recommending improvements to your processes. It baffles us that many organizations spend significant efforts in post mortems *after the project* to document post-implementation reviews. For your next projects you will be dealing with different teams, business domains, technologies, and other things that are situationally dependent. Will these "lessons learned" truly be applicable? Perhaps, but will people be motivated to act and be given the resources to do so? Likely not. It is much better to improve *within* the project between iterations than to do a post-implementation review after the project to explain at length why the project failed. Seek to improve *within* your projects rather than *between* them.

What if the team has ideas for improvements during the iteration? Do they have to wait for the retrospective to discuss and implement the ideas? Of course not, but changing the process mid-iteration may be disruptive. You could potentially choose to discuss the idea at an upcoming stand-up meeting and then decide whether to make a change. If you decide to wait until the end of the iteration to brainstorm ideas or agree on improvements, make sure that you capture the suggestion on the whiteboard so that it is not forgotten.

You should definitely keep a list of action items for team process improvements and, for significant changes, add them as highly ranked items to your work item list. This ensures that they are actually followed up on. You could also organize potential improvements into categories of *internal* or *external* to the team. For improvements external to the team, the team lead should be responsible for trying to effect the changes. It can require significant discipline to concentrate on things that you can actually control. Retrospectives should be kept constructive in the interest of maintaining optimism within the team. Remember that the positives of accomplishing the goals of your iteration should far outweigh the nuisances that impeded your progress.

It is important that the team understands that the retrospective meeting is not a gripe session or an opportunity to assign blame for shortcomings. Norm Kerth, an expert in project retrospectives, describes a "prime directive" for effective retrospectives: "Regardless of what we discover, we understand and truly believe that everyone did the best job they could, given what they knew at the time, their skills and abilities, the resources available, and the situation at hand." This prime directive is all about establishing safety, without which most retrospectives fail. In general it should always be safe for team members to voice their opinions and to share ideas. This is a hallmark of a healthy team.

At the beginning of each retrospective review the previous iterations' retrospectives to see whether you acted on your own recommendations. If you didn't then you need to question what the value would be of running another reflection meeting, the results of which you're also likely to ignore. If you acted on some or all of the recommendations from previous retrospectives it is useful to take a few minutes to discuss how well they are working out. This is what the measured improvement practice focuses on, measuring and tracking your process improvement efforts. This can and should be kept simple. We've seen teams do this successfully by playing "measurement poker" where they use their planning poker cards (shown in Figure 16.3) to vote on how well they've adopted each process improvement. These votes are captured and averaged in a spreadsheet with a simple trend chart to show changes over time.

Figure 16.3   Planning poker cards

One challenge with retrospectives is that most improvements end up being local to the team but don't do much to help the overall organization. It's great that the team is improving their process, but with a bit of enterprise awareness they may be able to do even better. For example, if my team identifies a new strategy that worked well for us, we could easily share it with the rest of the organization through internal social media, during an internal developer conference[1] or some

---

1. Many large organizations run their own internal conferences. Many speakers are internal to the company, although it is common to bring in outside experts. Both Scott and Mark have spoken at such conferences and are happy to come speak about DAD at your company.

other information sharing venue. Furthermore, many teams focus on how they work together internally, clearly a good idea, but often do not consider how they interact with other teams as they feel it is outside of their control. Hogwash! Having discussions with other teams about how you could work together more effectively can be incredibly valuable to the teams involved as well as to other teams you don't even know about. Improving the way that you work with the data administration team may motivate them to apply those improvements to the way that they work with dozens of other teams that they support. When it comes to process improvement, sometimes it's good to think globally while you act locally.

Retrospectives are not just about improving project execution. Granted, that is an important benefit. Retrospectives are also about exploring and evolving organizational culture. They're about discovery, professional fitness, and, as Steven Covey counsels, sharpening the blade by improving your own skills.

LESSONS FROM THE TRENCHES—FOCUSING YOUR RETROSPECTIVES

Andy Pittaway is an executive project manager in IBM Global Services in the UK, having led and coached agile teams for years. He says, "In our retrospectives we are focusing on finding mainly two types of improvements: a) those that the team can fix themselves very quickly with the equivalent of a squirt of oil on the process (we call these WD-40 actions) and b) more strategic actions which get fed into larger scale enterprise process initiatives or transformation projects.

"I have found that retrospectives are so important that I tend to insist on them. If time is short then the team may reduce the time spent, but we try hard to always do it.

"I believe that great teams challenge themselves to definitely find something at the end of iteration to improve for the next iteration, i.e., improvement changes which are applied every single iteration."

Assess Progress and Adjust Release Plan if Necessary

At the end of an iteration your team should honestly assess how much consumable functionality was produced. In other words, what did you actually get done? This is important information for reporting purposes—at the beginning of the iteration you promised X points worth of progress, so your stakeholders expect you to have accomplished that. Furthermore, as you learned in Chapter 14, "Initiating a Construction Iteration," the number of points of work you accomplished this iteration is called your velocity. The velocity of this iteration is typically used to estimate how much work you're likely to accomplish next iteration.

Getting to "done" is one of the real challenges in building a consumable solution. Classically in agile we do not grant partial points for work items that are not fully complete. Granting partial credit for work items may delay us from finishing a piece of functionality and can result in endless churn as a particular work item seems to carry over from iteration to iteration. It is therefore important to make sure that "doneness" is defined well at the beginning of the iteration when committing to deliver a set of work items. Ideally these criteria are defined by the acceptance tests created for the individual work items. A common definition of done is that all of the acceptance test cases run for a given work item.

A more advanced, and more difficult to conform to, definition of done comes from the lean community. In this definition of done a work item is done only when it has been delivered into the hands of the end users and they like it. The general thinking is that a solution really shouldn't be considered consumable until it's been successfully "consumed" by its intended audience. As you evolve your agile adoption toward lean approach, you may adjust your definition of done accordingly.

Once you've calculated your velocity for the iteration you should update your release burndown chart to update your estimated completion date. With a ranged burndown chart you can extrapolate a more narrow range of estimated remaining iterations to completion based on an increasing understanding of your true velocity. An example of a ranged burndown chart is shown in Figure 16.4 and is described in detail in Chapter 10, "Initial Release Planning."

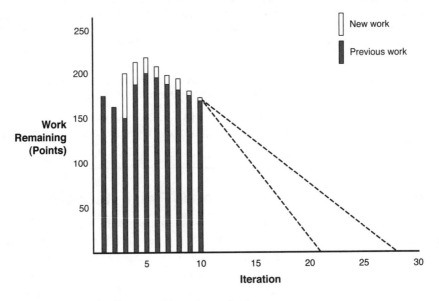

Figure 16.4 An example of a ranged burndown chart

Assess Remaining Risks

At the beginning of the project during the Inception phase you should have identified the key project risks, a list that needs to be maintained throughout the project. You should strive to mitigate risks at the most appropriate time for doing so, which for many risks is early in the life-cycle. During a Construction iteration you may have mitigated one or more risks through addressing a work item. If so, now is the time to update the risk list.

The end of an iteration is a good time to reflect on the remaining risks and potentially identify additional risks that may be surfacing. One result is that the priorities of the remaining work in your work item list may need to be revised to reflect these new risks.

Deploy Your Current Build

At the end of a successful iteration you should consider deploying your final working build for the iteration into one or more environments. For the sake of simplicity we call this your iteration build. As described in Chapter 15 there are several environments that you will consider deploying your working builds into. Note that you may have chosen to deploy into some of these environments during the iteration too. These environments are as follows:

- **Demonstration.** Most teams deploy their iteration build to their demonstration environment in time for the iteration demo.

- **Pre-production testing.** Some DAD teams, particularly those in regulatory or complex situations, have a parallel independent test team supporting them. A common practice is to make your iteration build available to this team.

- **Production.** You may decide to deploy into production at this point. This decision may be made as the result of a specific milestone review, because the release date for your solution has come up (some DAD teams work under hard deadlines), or because it's common practice to release regularly into production. The appropriate milestone— milestones are described in greater detail in Chapter 20, "Governing Disciplined Agile Teams"—would be the "Sufficient Functionality" milestone. In lean parlance this is often referred to as the Minimally Marketable Release (MRR) decision point, which we find to be quite a mouthful. The purpose of the milestone is to determine whether the additional value provided by this release exceeds the costs of deployment *and* that the new functionality in the release is sufficiently consumable by the end users. There are several approaches, described in the next section, for coming to this decision.

We suggest that you deploy into your demonstration and preproduction testing environments at the end of each iteration. We also suggest that you release into production as often as your situation warrants.

Determine Strategy for Moving Forward

At the end of an iteration an important issue is to identify how your team will proceed next iteration. You typically make this decision based on a successful demo and better yet clear feedback from actual usage of the solution in production. There are several sources of information to consider when making this decision:

- **Input from your iteration demo.** One of the primary reasons to run the demo is to get feedback from your stakeholders. Sometimes this feedback is specific to an aspect of your solution, and sometimes it is applicable to the success of your team. In the case of the latter you likely want to act on it sooner rather than later.

- **The team.** Your team itself should have a good sense as to how well the project is going. This is particularly true if they have been interacting closely with stakeholders or their representatives (such as the product owner).

- **Usage statistics.** Chapter 8, "Identifying the Initial Scope," discussed how some operations groups require you to track statistics for your solution—the features people are using, what screens or reports they're running, what help screens they are viewing, and so on—so that you have a better understanding of actual usage. If you're doing this, and if you're deploying your solution on a regular basis, these usage statistics can be a good indicator of what end users find valuable, what they find difficult to use, and what they appear to be uninterested in.

In the book *The Lean Startup*, Eric Ries describes several common options that you should consider when determining how to proceed. These strategies, compared in Table 16.3, are the following:

- **Persevere with the current strategy.** In many cases this is the decision that you make. Hopefully your team is working together effectively and you are getting clear feedback that your solution is providing value to your stakeholders and better yet is delighting them. Note that this strategy may or may not include deploying your current build into production.

- **Run a split test.** You often reach a point where it isn't clear how to proceed, particularly when you have one or more stakeholder goals/requirements that can be fulfilled in several ways. For example, one of the AgileGrocers user stories is "As a store manager I want to increase future sales via targeted coupons." In the look-ahead modeling sessions the store managers agreed that the solution should print one or more coupons on customer receipts. But they couldn't agree on the strategy for identifying what coupon(s) to provide. One strategy was to give a coupon for something they just purchased so they continue buying that from you. If the customer bought Brand X hot dogs then give them a coupon for that. A second strategy was to give a coupon for a similar but higher margin replacement product and thereby motivate them to "upgrade" their food purchases, in this case give them a coupon for Brand Y hot dogs. A third strategy was to give them a coupon for a complementary product. So if they bought hot dogs but no mustard, then give them a coupon for mustard because they're likely to need it at some point in the future. You could argue about these three options forever and get nowhere. With a split test approach you would implement all three strategies, deploy them at different cash registers, and then track the rate of coupon submission to determine which of the three strategies leads to the best outcome. The implication is that what appeared to be a fairly simple requirement on the surface evolved into a serious strategy decision that could potentially consume one or more iterations worth of work. The split test strategy is effectively set-based design at a feature level instead of a product level.

- **Pivot in a new direction.** Sometimes things don't go well. You work closely with your product owner and stakeholders, the demos are successful, everyone tells you that they love what they're seeing, and then you deploy into production and your end users don't use the solution. If you continue with the current strategy you run the risk of continuing to build something people don't want. Another strategy is to pivot, to start going in a new direction, in the hope that this new direction results in a solution that is more attractive to potential end users. At this point in time the next step is likely to get key stakeholders together to discuss the problem, to gain their agreement to pivot, and then to discuss likely options. This will probably be a difficult and contentious discussion but a valuable one to have sooner rather than later.

- **Cancel the project.** An important consideration is whether the project is still viable. Although DAD explicitly includes a potential milestone called Continued Viability this is an issue that you may choose to consider at the end of each iteration (Scrum suggests this). There are several reasons that you may want to cancel a project. First, the business environment may have changed. For example in the Autumn of 2008 Scott was brought into a U.S. financial organization to assess the work of an agile team that was about to finish the release of a system that would support its subprime mortgage business. A few weeks earlier this market had crashed. Although the team had done great work there was no sense in proceeding because the solution simply wasn't needed by the business any more. Second, even after several pivots it may become clear that the team is struggling to produce a solution in which people are interested. Third, the team simply may not have the ability, either due to a lack of skills or resources, to produce a viable solution within the constraints that they face. Healthy organizations consider cancelling a troubled project to be a success, although Scott found in one survey that only 40% of organizations think this way.

Table 16.3   Comparing Go-Forward Strategies

Strategy	Advantages	Disadvantages	Considerations
Persevere	Stakeholders are most likely to feel that the project is on track.	Many teams choose to persevere even where there is clear evidence not to because this is often the easiest short-term decision to make.	Stakeholders who are actively involved with the project become politically motivated to keep the project going even when it's clearly in trouble. You may need to get input from outside the immediate team. In Chapter 20 we discuss the need for an explicit milestone review to determine the viability of your project.
Split test	Concrete strategy to identify the best of several approaches.	Requires extra work to monitor the effectiveness of each implemented strategy. Some stakeholders may view this as wasteful because you're implementing and deploying several competing features with the intention of potentially removing some of them later.	Two or more alternatives may tie for best, potentially requiring you to choose one after all. Requires the team to be able to easily deploy the solution, monitor the results, and act on them swiftly.
Pivot	Helps a team that is starting to get into trouble get back on track.	Stakeholders who weren't part of the decision may think that the team doesn't know what it's doing. Your estimated costs and schedule may diverge sharply at this point from what you've been previously reporting.	It requires significant discipline to regularly consider whether you need to give up on the current strategy that you're following and pivot to a new one. Clearly communicate the decision behind why you decided to pivot to your stakeholders. Better yet, include them in the process of identifying the new strategy to pivot to.

Strategy	Advantages	Disadvantages	Considerations
Cancel the project	Cancelling a troubled project stems losses early.	Many organizations still consider cancelling a troubled project to be a failure. This motivates teams to continue working on a project far longer than they really should, thereby increasing the overall loss.	It requires significant discipline to regularly and fairly consider whether to cancel a project. When you cancel the project there is likely to be some shut down work to do. For example you may need to write a justification report to present to your organization's governance board. You may need to package up the assets created so that they may be recovered at some point in the future if the project is revived. You should likely hold one last retrospective (yes, a project post mortem) to identify and share any lessons learned. You may even need to fire some or all of the people on the team, something that is particularly true in the case of any consultants or contractors who were on the team.

There are several ways that you can go about making these decisions, compared in Table 16.4. These strategies are

- **Team meeting.** Most times you hold a team meeting to discuss this issue. This meeting typically follows your demo to your stakeholders.

- **Lightweight milestone review.** You may choose to schedule a specific milestone review meeting that includes key stakeholders. Chapter 20 describes how to keep these meetings lightweight. This review meeting doesn't necessarily need to be held at the end of an iteration although often is because you already have your key stakeholders there for the demo. This review may address either the Sufficient Functionality or Continued Viability milestones.

- **Formal milestone review.** Your team may decide to run a formal milestone meeting where the results are officially recorded and a defined protocol to run the review may be followed. Formal reviews are common in regulatory environments.

Our advice is to make these decisions a regular part of iteration closing activities via a short team meeting specifically for that purpose. However, to temper the risk of groupthink within your team or worse yet the tendency to avoid hard decisions such as pivoting or even cancelling you should consider holding milestone reviews occasionally. We prefer keeping such reviews as lightweight and informal as your situation allows.

Concluding Thoughts

Completing a successful iteration is an important milestone and is worth celebrating. On either the last day of your iteration or the first day of the subsequent iteration, congratulate your team publicly in the daily stand-up on their iteration achievements. If they found ways to overcome unpleasant surprises during the iteration (as commonly occur!) and nevertheless delivered on their commitments, the team lead might lead everyone in the room in a round of applause to show your appreciation. Any observers in attendance should participate to show gratitude for the hard work in the previous weeks. You may also consider ordering in lunch as a small token of your appreciation.

Finishing an iteration is an opportunity to recognize and demonstrate your team's good work to your stakeholders. The achievement is also an opportunity to pause, catch your breath, and reflect on how the team might have done things better. Finally, the conclusion of an iteration should include consideration of how to proceed. You may decide to deploy to production, pivot to a new direction, continue in the same direction, or in some cases cancel the project.

Table 16.4   Comparing the Decision Approaches

Strategy	Advantages	Disadvantages	Considerations
Team meeting	Easy to schedule. Inexpensive to run as long as you keep it focused and short.	You may not get the insights that people from outside the team may bring to the discussion.	Requires an environment where people can safely discuss potentially touchy subjects.
Lightweight milestone review	Forces the team and stakeholders to address a specific issue.	Requires additional time from key stakeholders.	Consider having someone from outside the team facilitate the session.
Formal milestone review	Forces the team and stakeholders to address a specific issue. Supports regulatory compliance concerns.	Potential for overhead as compared with lightweight reviews.	Consider having a professional facilitator run the review.

Additional Resources

For more detailed discussions about several of the topics covered in this chapter:

- **Retrospectives.** Norm Kerth is the father of retrospectives and was a key founding member of the patterns movement in the early 1990s. His Web site about retrospectives is at www.retrospectives.com and is a great source of information.

- **Structured surveys.** Per Kroll and William Krebs described this technique at http://www.ibm.com/developerworks/rational/library/edge/08/may08/kroll_krebs/ in their description of the IBM Rational Self-Check product.

- **Lean techniques.** This chapter overviewed several lean techniques, in particular pivoting and split tests, that are described by Eric Ries in his book *The Lean Startup* (Random House, 2011).

- **Surveys.** In the section on strategies for moving forward, the project cancellation statistic is from the Dr. Dobb's Journal 2007 Project Success Rates survey, the results of which are posted at www.ambysoft.com/surveys/.

CHAPTER 17

Case Study: Construction Phase

The project is 90% done. I hope the second half goes as well. —Unknown

Chapter 12, "Case Study: Inception Phase," introduced the AgileGrocers Point of Sale (PoS) Case Study. The focus of this chapter is the continuation of the project into the Construction phase for the PoS system. Our goal is to show what to expect in *typical* construction iterations. Your organization's experience and the techniques and agile practices that you choose to apply will definitely differ, depending on many things such as your culture, need for governance, capabilities, and experience.

Continuing Our Scenario with the AgileGrocers POS Case Study

We have just completed our one-week Inception phase. The following Monday, the team meets at 9:00 a.m. for two hours to plan the first two-week iteration of the Construction phase.

Figure 17.1 shows the team as it looks when we start the Construction phase. Ashok, Ann, Brian, Katherine, and Gunther have joined the team as team members. Their specialty is programming, but each of them also has other general strengths in areas of testing and analysis. Using the DAD framework, we realize that in an enterprise IT environment, we usually need to collaborate with people outside our immediate team to get the work done. We need to draw on the expertise and skills of people acting in these secondary roles, but we are not sure who yet.

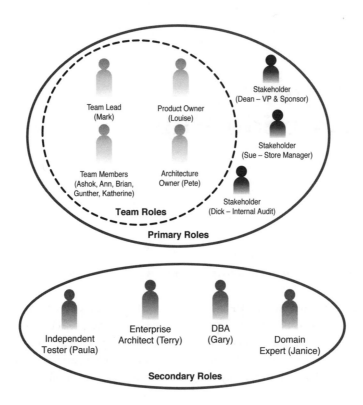

Figure 17.1   The AgileGrocers project team

As described in Chapter 1, "Disciplined Agile Delivery in a Nutshell," each phase and iteration has a 3C rhythm of coordinate, collaborate, and conclude. For our case study, the initial coordination activities for the phase focus on proving that the architecture works.

Planning the First Construction Iteration

As facilitator of the planning session, Mark started with some basic resource planning for the team to verify their time commitments to the project for the new iteration. For the team to be able to commit to delivering a set of features for a particular iteration, we need an understanding of the availability of each team member. Ideally, every team member should be solely committed to one project. When team members work on more than one project at a time, their productivity goes down dramatically, and the rest of the team doesn't feel that these people are truly committed to the iteration outcome.

For each of the team members we need to determine how many "ideal hours" per day they can dedicate to tasks that they are responsible for. This is similar to the Kanban technique of using constraints to limit the work to which the team can commit. Time that each person spends in meetings or helping other team members complete their tasks is not included in their estimate of daily ideal hours. A typical number might be five or six hours per day.

Mark displays the simple spreadsheet of Table 17.1 via a projector. He uses this to tally the hours for each team member for each day of the iteration. Prior to the meeting Mark asked the team members to have their personal calendars available for the purposes of the planning session. The resource planning part of the meeting unfolds as follows:

Mark: Let's start with Pete, our architecture owner. Pete, I hope that you are dedicated solely to this project.

Pete: Yes, I am, but I have an off-site strategic planning session next Tuesday and Wednesday. I also have approximately one hour per day that I need to handle administration, meetings, and emails. I will also be helping some other team members with their tasks for probably about two hours per day. That leaves about five hours per day to work on my own work items.

Mark: Okay, I'll mark you down for five hours per day then. Any vacation or other leaves of absence in the next three weeks?

Mark: Ashok, how many ideal hours can you dedicate to your tasks?

Ashok: I have no leaves of absence planned, and I think that I can do six productive hours per day against the tasks I volunteer for.

Brian: You can make mine the same, please.

Mark: Okay, Gunther?

Gunther: Well, I would normally also say six hours per day, but this iteration I will be pairing with Katherine to do non-solo development of a few stories together. She is new to Java and our environment so working together will be an opportunity to bring her up to speed. So in effect, I am only working half time on tasks dedicated to me.

Mark: That is a good practice as it helps to spread skills and knowledge throughout the team. When we decompose our work items into tasks in a few minutes, only one person can take ownership of each task, so you and Katherine will need to take some tasks each and split your time between your own and the other's.

Katherine: Okay, then I too will sign-up for three hours per day to complete tasks that I own.

Mark: Sounds good.

Mark: Louise, I assume that you will be busy this iteration managing the work item list, clarifying requirements and priorities with other stakeholders, and other tasks. So you won't be doing any tasks directly related to implementing the work items?

Louise: Actually, I should have some free cycles to help create acceptance tests. Probably about three hours per day.

Mark: Excellent! While classically in mainstream agile, the product owner is not a direct contributor, practically speaking, if you want to roll up your sleeves and help with tasks, there is nothing wrong with that.

Louise: Okay. And I promise not to tell other team members what to do or how to do their tasks <grin>.

Mark: That's right. We need you to tell us *what needs* to be done, and in *what priority*, *not how* to do it. We trust the team members to know the best way to meet your needs in the most efficient way. Well, I can see from our resource sheet that our team contributors have a total of 250 hours in the iteration to do productive work related to work items, and that based on ten working days in the iteration, we should be able to knock off about 25 hours per day of work. Let's proceed to reviewing the work item list and pick our work for the iteration.

Table 17.1   Ideal Planning Sheet Hours

	Pete	Ashok	Brian	Gunther	Katherine	Louise		
Mar 14	5	6	6	3	3	3	Total Hours in the Iteration	**250**
Mar 15	5	6	6	3	3	3	Days in the Iteration	10
Mar 16	5	6	6	3	3	3	Ideal Hours/ Day to Burndown	25
Mar 17	5	6	6	3	3	3		
Mar 18	5	6	6	3	3	3		
Mar 21	5	6	6	3	3	3		
Mar 22	0	6	6	3	3	3	Pete - On leave	
Mar 23	0	6	6	3	3	3	Pete - On leave	
Mar 24	5	6	6	3	3	3		
Mar 25	5	6	6	3	3	3		
Totals	**40**	**60**	**60**	**30**	**30**	**30**		

EFFORT VERSUS DURATION

Note that hours in our planning sheet are *not* hours of effort. If Ashok is working on a difficult bit of code that is expected to take two hours and asks Gunther to pair program the code fragment, the task is "owned" by Ashok and counts for two hours, not four. It is a duration number, not effort. This is an example of why Pete cannot commit to six ideal hours per day. He is working on other things not related to his specific tasks that he has volunteered for.

Planning the Iteration's Work

At this point, after having determined the team's capacity to do productive work via "ideal hours," Mark turns over the meeting to the product owner, Louise. Louise brings up the work item list (called a backlog in Scrum) that she created in IBM Rational Team Concert (RTC) and displays it to the team on the projector.

Louise: This list shows what needs to be done, in priority order. For each item in the list, there is a relative point estimate. We know from our estimating that there is a total of 314 points to be delivered over the next 12 iterations. That is approximately 26 or so points per iteration. However, we know from experience that additional work items will be discovered, or that our initial estimating was overly optimistic. So Mark has suggested that the actual amount of work is probably about 10% to 20% more. So let's round up the work to 360 points, indicating that we need to complete about 30 points for each of the 12 iterations to finish on schedule. This allows for some contingency.

Louise continues: From our estimating session we thought that the "Complete purchase transaction" story was 30 points all by itself, and I know that it is not realistic to complete this in the first iteration of our project! A story of this size is commonly known as an "epic." I have broken this epic down into five separate smaller user stories, and moved all but one of them lower in the work item list to be built in future iterations. In the first iteration, I would be happy to see the framework of a basic PoS transaction working.

Mark: Our risk list that we have posted on the wall shows that we are concerned that we may not be able to achieve 3-second response time when validating a payment transaction. Perhaps we should add a work item to the list to validate that our architecture can support this requirement?

Louise: I don't see this as big value for me. I will need it at some point, but it is not as important to me as some reports for example.

Mark: I understand that system performance may not seem as high value for you, but for us techies this can be difficult. We need time now to figure this out, as the solution may be easy, but could also be extremely expensive and time consuming. We just don't know. This work item is one of the highest risks on the project so we want to deal with it now. Hopefully fast response time is easy to accomplish, but if not, at least we discover this now and have time to figure out a solution. Does that make sense?

Louise: I guess so. You know, I went to a Scrum course, and they told me that I am the boss. I get to decide priorities of anything that they put in the backlog (and you now call a work item list). So are you saying that I need to talk to Pete the architect about risky bits that he needs to add as priorities to my backlog? Oops. Work item list?

Pete (architecture owner): Precisely. Louise, you and I need to work closely on this project. I need to help you prioritize work items in the early iterations. I need to inject some "tricky bits" as high priority items in your list so that we can figure out how to do this stuff. We need to balance these bits with your high value stories, which I like to call "juicy bits." DAD calls this balancing the risk-value lifecycle practice. Once our team has figured out how to deal with the technically challenging parts of this project, we can focus on delivering the highest value stories to you in each iteration. A key differentiator of DAD versus some other agile methods is that we recognize that it is a mistake to deliver high value work items without resolving essential technical challenges early in our project. And we figure these technical things out not by doing elaborate designs, but rather building code related to actual implementable stories to prove that we have mitigated these risks.

Louise: Like a proof of technology prototype?

Pete: Our preference is to validate our architecture by doing this work against actual stories so that we have something we can keep at the end. However, sometimes we do indeed do these prototypes, known as "spikes" to explore candidate design solutions. This can be a valuable learning opportunity for the team.

Louise: That makes sense. Now I understand why you asked me to move some of my items such as printing the receipt, lower down the list into other iterations so that he could work on some high risk items in the first iteration. By the way, I added my own work item into the list. It is item #6 "Run a workshop and identify the needs for operational reports."

Mark: I have no problem with you inserting the reports workshop into your work item list as a high priority, first iteration work item. From the risk list, we can see that the users are not really sure what kind of reports they need. This is a different type of risk, related to delivering a solution that meets the needs of our stakeholders. It is important that we get a better understanding of what they want before we get too far into this project. It may mean that we have to insert additional stories into our work item list based on what you discover in your work item list, which is why we added some contingency into our estimates.

Brian: Wait a minute! That sounds to me like you are letting Louise change scope on us! Shouldn't we lock down the requirements list right now?

Mark: Um . . . no. Agile methods have long since realized that it is pretty much impossible to have an accurate requirements document at the beginning of the project. So a better approach is to build some contingency into the budget and schedule, expecting a degree of change to naturally occur, and continually evolve the requirements through "grooming" your work item list as the product owner's understanding of the true requirements evolves over the life of the project.

Louise continues: Okay, so with our revised work item list I have highlighted the first four work items that add up to 30 points for implementation in this iteration. My hope is that you can complete the work items up until this point. Of course I understand that this is your first iteration, so the amount of work you can complete is a bit unknown at this point. Mark, do you think that this is a good estimate?

Mark: My role is not a project manager, but speaking on behalf of the team, they are probably a bit unsure of what they can accomplish until they go through an iteration or two. How about we go to the next step and have the team do some planning among themselves by identifying the tasks that they need to do to complete these work items and how long they are going to take?

Louise: Shouldn't you be listing tasks and assigning them to the team members?

Mark: Actually, no. On an agile project I recognize that the team can best make these decisions among themselves. I trust them, and they trust each other to do this properly. They truly know better than I what it takes to complete these work items, and how long it will take. I don't "manage" them. My job is to facilitate this process and remove any impediments that interfere with them delivering work items to you. If I have any spare cycles, however, I plan to help in any way I can. I might help model some requirements, build some tests, or perhaps write or review some code if possible. I will do anything I can to help the team meet their commitments to you.

Ashok: Mark, it is good that you have built a buffer in for unplanned work items, but you have assumed that we can deliver 30 points of work items in each iteration. What if we discover after a couple of iterations that we can only deliver 20 points per iteration?

Mark: That is an excellent question. This is where traditional project management comes in. DAD, or any agile method is not a silver bullet, but what it does do is expose the truth of what we can accomplish early in the project. If we find that we can only deliver 20 points, then we have some basic and traditional choices to make; we can promise to deliver fewer work items (reduce scope), add additional iterations (increase schedule and budget), add resources (people), or compromise on quality (take shortcuts). But . . . we don't know what is possible until we get through a few iterations. So let's not jump to any conclusions until we have some real metrics from which to make these decisions.

LESSONS FROM THE TRENCHES—PLANNING FOR RELEASE CONTINGENCY

When setting expectations with your stakeholders about how much work you can deliver from the work item list (WIL), it pays to be conservative. Given your expected velocity in terms of number of relative points of work that you can deliver, multiplied by the number of Construction iterations *should* give you an idea of where in the backlog you run out of schedule. However, our experience is that the WIL will change dramatically from the original version created early in your project. Stuff always gets added to the list. Sources of "point creep" usually include defects deferred to future iterations, unexpected refactoring or do-overs, inaccurate relative point estimates for items, and new or changed stories. We typically either add extra iterations to deliver the additional work items, or set the expectation that original scope will probably need to be cut by 25% if the schedule is to be adhered to. Of course, when items are added to the list, items below the priority of these new items are pushed down in the stack. The product owner understands that this usually requires removing items at the bottom of the list for this release altogether to make room for new items. We encourage our product owners to manage the scope of the release just like a project that uses a traditional approach.

What do we do with defects? Should they be added to the work item list? Our approach is to fix defects in the iteration that they are found, and treat them as tasks in the iteration. However, there are times where for various reasons, defects need to be carried over to subsequent iterations. In these cases, we add the defect to the WIL. Most agilists consider a defect a type of change, similar to a requirement, that must be prioritized by the product owner like any other story. Therefore we reserve some contingency points available to deal with defects added to the WIL.

Mark adds: Okay, team, Louise has presented the first four work items as her highest priorities (depicted in Table 17.2). Now we—that is, *you*—need to determine how we deliver them and how much effort it will take. Hopefully we have enough time in this iteration to deliver them. We will do some estimating to find out. But before we do, Louise, can we please go through each of the work items for this iteration and explain how they should work and what you are expecting? I believe that you wanted Janice, the domain expert from the business, to join us for this part of the planning session so that she can answer any tricky questions about the functionality. I just texted her while you were talking, and she says she is on her way.

Table 17.2   Highest Priority Work Items Showing First Four Work Items to Be Delivered in the First Iteration

ID	Work Item	Relative Estimate (points)
27	As a cashier I can complete a purchase transaction. (1 item, no persistence, draft UI, no scanning or PLU look-up).	12
6	Run a workshop and document list and summary of operational reports.	5
8	Ensure data feed to SAP on payroll details works properly.	5
9	As a customer, I can pay with debit or credit card with 3 second response time.	8
1	As a cashier I can scan bar codes for grocery items so that the price may be added to the purchase total.	13
2	As a cashier I can weigh produce items so that the cost of the produce may be added to the purchase total.	8
6	Run a workshop and document needs for operational reports.	13
7	Ensure store systems operate when connection to head office is disrupted.	8
5	As a cashier I can print a receipt.	5
3	As a cashier I can apply store coupons against purchase in order to reduce transaction total.	5
10	As a store manager, I can update stock prices from the back office in real-time.	13
11	System shall automatically failover to a backup server in the event of failure of the main system.	10

Janice arrives with Sue, the store manager representative.

Louise: Welcome, Janice!

Janice: Hi, Louise. I have brought Sue along. She has 20 years experience working in our stores and has been asked to represent the store managers when we define the requirements for the new system. As you know, Sue is also going to move into this work area to be closer to the team to be available to provide details on the requirements as well as give feedback as the system is developed. I can't be here full-time, but I am always available on chat if you need me to pop by.

Louise: That's wonderful. It is great to have the domain expertise readily available to our team members. Welcome, Sue.

Louise then describes each of the work items for the iteration. Janice adds clarification on certain details in response to questions from the team. Fortunately, Louise has been preparing for this planning session by making sure that her work item list is well prioritized and formed (sometimes called "grooming" the backlog in Scrum).

Louise also came to the meeting with a list of acceptance criteria for each of her priority work items. She will consider the work items complete when they meet these criteria. By thinking about testing *before* implementing the work items, it is easier for the team to understand what they need to do to make the project owner happy. Table 17.3 shows an example of these acceptance tests for the "As a cashier I can scan bar codes" user story:

Table 17.3 Example Acceptance Test Criteria

Test ID	Acceptance Criteria
1	Scanning an item causes the system to beep and display the price on the terminal.
2	If a quantity has been entered before scanning the item, the quantity should be displayed, with the unit price, and total for that item.
3	The total for the quantity x the price of the scanned item should be added to the transaction total and a running total be displayed on the terminal.
4	If the scanned UPC code does not find the item on file then the system should display an error message and prompt the cashier to enter the code number.
5	UPC code scan errors and the numbers that are then entered should appear on the PoS closing report at the end of the day so that they can be fixed.

During the discussions about each work item, Janice draws screen mockups on the whiteboards as thought starters for the user interface. For each item the team spends a few minutes discussing among themselves how it would work. They agree that they can use the existing data model as a start, with some redesign required. Mark listens as Ashok asks Pete "are we allowed to change this database schema? Isn't that Gary, the DBA's, responsibility?" At this point Mark interjects:

Mark: Yes, that is part of AgileGrocers' overall governance strategy for this project; the data administration group will be responsible for database changes that eventually end up in production. Contrary to what you may have heard out there in the agile world, sometimes our teams need to collaborate with people *outside* the team. If you create a task in your plan to review your suggested database changes, I will make sure that Gary is available to do the review immediately so that there is no roadblock for you.

At times during the team's discussions of how they are going to implement a work item, the team gathers around the whiteboard to model storm the solution. They sketch a simple class diagram, showing the key entities and their relationships, so that the entire team is naming their classes consistently. These examples of doing screen mockups and designs on a whiteboard are examples of Agile Modeling in practice.

Once the team agrees to an approach for the first work item, which is about scanning items, Pete asks Mark, "Okay, we think we know how we'll structure a PoS transaction and how we will capture scanned items. What now?"

Work Item Breakdown and Estimation

Mark: We'll I'm not your project manager, I am just here to help. We need to take this work item and disaggregate it into a set of tasks. So I would like you to write the names of each task that you will do for this work item on a separate sticky note, with a number of hours that you think it will take for that task. Decide among yourselves who should do each task and put that person's initials on the task. Each team member should make sure that they don't sign up for more hours of tasks than they have committed hours for in the previous part of this planning session. For instance, Ashok has 60 hours available that he can commit to his own tasks, so the total hours for the tasks that he plans to do should not exceed that or he is over committing.

The team then works together to do the task identification and estimating for the scanning work item that Louise has just reviewed. Louise does not participate in this planning, but is there to answer or clarify any questions that the team has about the work items.

While the team is doing their estimating, as they complete their sticky notes with tasks and estimates, they pass them to Mark, who enters them as tasks in the planning section of RTC. The review of each work item, modeling, task identification, and estimating continues for each of the planned four work items.

Completing the Estimating Session and Sanity Check

After the estimating completes, Mark quickly adds up all the hours for the tasks that the team has identified to complete. The hours add up to 210, which is a lot less than the 250 that the team said they had available to do tasks in the iteration. The choice now is whether to add another work item into the iteration. Based on Mark's experience he suggests that we don't add another work item in this iteration, as often the estimates may be overly optimistic, or more likely, unplanned tasks surface during the iteration. Also, the scope of the work item may turn out to be larger than thought in this estimating session. After this sanity check that the work is achievable in the iteration, according to the *team's* plan, not Mark's, Mark asks the team whether they "commit" to delivering these four work items based on what they know. The team agrees to this commitment.

The iteration planning finishes around noon. Mark had ordered pizza for the team in case the planning session ran late. The team uses the lunch to have discussions on how they are going to jump into their work in the afternoon.

Over lunch Ashok says to Mark: You have said that project, iterations, and even days have a 3C rhythm of "Coordinate, Collaborate, and Conclude." Is what we did this morning the "Coordinate" for the iteration?

Mark: Precisely. This afternoon, the team will begin collaborating to achieve the iteration's goals.

Ashok: Awesome.

After lunch the team jumps into their work. For each of the tasks that each team member starts to work on, they change the status of the tasks to from "not started" to "in progress" and assign themselves as owner.

LESSONS FROM THE TRENCHES—PLANNING FOR ITERATION CONTINGENCY

Mark has seen that iterations *always* have unplanned tasks. Handling them can be tricky as adding new tasks with hours to the taskboard makes it difficult to track progress against the plan on the burndown chart. There are many variations to handling this situation, but this is Mark's approach. Realizing that change happens, he ensures that the team undercommits in terms of tasks planned compared to available ideal hours in the iteration. For instance, in this iteration, the team's planned hours totaled 210 against 250 hours available for the iteration. So Mark often creates an extra sticky note (or a task in RTC) for contingency hours. In our case Mark created a contingency task of 40 hours (250-210). The number may seem high, but the team is new to this agile approach, and new teams tend to forget tasks that they need to do or be too aggressive with their estimates. In future iterations, as the team gets better at planning their iterations, he will let them create tasks that consume most of their ideal hours available, and reduce the contingency task accordingly. The contingency task hours are treated like any other task being added into the total planned hours that goes into creating the burndown chart. Now when an unplanned task surfaces, for instance, "refactor the Account class—ten hours," it is added to the board, and the hours on the contingency task are reduced by the same amount. This approach keeps the burndown progress looking healthy and helps avoid team members' resistance to being honest and surfacing an unexpected task in fear of making the burndown look bad. Having new tasks visible on the board helps to make sure that similar tasks are not forgotten in future planning sessions. In fact, for manual taskboards, Mark uses a different color sticky note for newly added tasks so that they are extra visible to the team and hopefully not forgotten in the next planning session.

The Morning of Day 2: 9:00 a.m.—The Daily Coordination Meeting

The next morning, in the work room where the collocated team works, they all stand up at 9:00, and gather around the taskboard, which is being projected from RTC. Mark has sent an email to the stakeholders inviting them to come and watch the meeting but has asked them not to interrupt the meeting to ask questions. Several stakeholders, including Dean (the sponsor), Janice (the domain/business expert), and Terry (the enterprise architect) show up and stand behind the team who is gathered around the projected taskboard.

Dean: Why is everyone standing?

Mark: We hold the meeting standing up to stress that it is a short meeting with a degree of urgency to complete and get back to productive work. The classic weekly status meeting sitting around the table with coffee and donuts has gone the way of the dinosaur in our new agile world.

The team wants to have a quick 15-minute planning meeting to plan their day's activities, and questions from people outside the team would make it difficult to finish the meeting in 15 minutes. This daily coordination meeting (alternatively called daily stand-up, or daily Scrum) constitutes the *coordination* component of the 3C rhythm for the day.

As Mark starts the daily coordination meeting for each day after the first day of the iteration, he first reviews the progress of the team in the previous day.

LESSONS FROM THE TRENCHES—BIG VISIBLE CHARTS

For the purposes of this book's case study, we have shown hand-drawn burndown charts. Tools like RTC provide automatic burndown (or burnup) charting as part of its customized dashboards. However, even when using tools like RTC, Mark finds that updating a manual burndown chart is so simple (once per day) that he usually has a hand-drawn burndown chart on a whiteboard in the team room so that it is always visible to the team. If you don't feel like hand drawing your burndowns, an alternative to consider is to display key metrics on a specific monitor, effectively a virtual "wallboard," all day long. This virtual wallboard shows key metrics such as your iteration burndown, defect trends, build status, and so on.

Tracking Iteration Progress with Iteration Burndown Charts

Starting on the second day of the iteration, part of Mark's responsibility at the daily coordination meeting is to review the team's progress against their plan. A common visual chart to show this progress against plan is the iteration burndown chart. Mark has hand-drawn the iteration's burndown and posted it in the work area as shown in Figure 17.2.

Before going around the room in the normal, "3 question" format of the daily stand-up meeting, Mark reviews the team's results overall from the day before:

Mark: Good morning, team. I have updated the iteration burndown as you can see. We got off to a slow start yesterday, but that is mostly due to spending the morning in the planning session. We expect to knock off 25 hours during the day, but we only knocked off 13. The green line that I have drawn for our progress is above the straight blue line, which indicates our expected burndown trend if we are on schedule. As you can see, we are trending above the expected burndown line, but we have technically only done one-half day of work, so I am sure that we can make it up. This is normal for the first day of the iteration; hopefully we can complete more hours today.

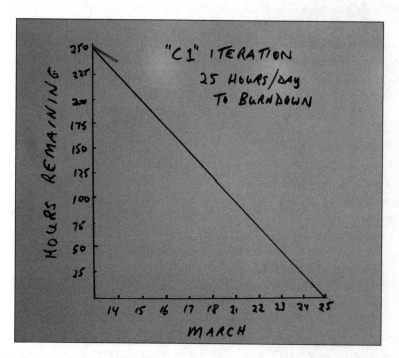

Figure 17.2 Iteration burndown chart

Coordinating the Day's Work

Now, after having reviewed the team's overall progress for the previous day, Mark continues by asking each member to answer three questions: What did they do yesterday, what do they plan to do today, and do they have any issues or blockers that are stopping them from making progress on their work items?

Mark also asks team members to do a little "look-ahead planning" (a practice we highly suggest) and consider dependencies on their upcoming work items. For instance, Ann may need some changes made to a database table before she can start working on a new user story two days from now. In this case it would only be fair to ask Gary the DBA (external to the team) to approve the database change so that Ann can make the change in the team's sandbox database. In this particular case, Ann should mention this dependency in the daily meeting in advance so that Mark can contact Gary and get the change approved in time so that she can stay focused on their current tasks, but be ready to start the next story.

Ashok: Okay, I'll start. As we all know, yesterday morning was used up with the iteration planning session. So I didn't actually work my expected six hours per day yesterday due to

Mark's planning overhead <chuckle from team>. I think, Mark, that next iteration, you should reduce our ideal hours available on the first day of the iteration because of this.

Mark: Duly noted. I will record it in our retrospective log so that we learn this lesson and action it.

Ashok points out the task "model PoS transaction collaboration": I started working on this task yesterday afternoon. I have moved it from "not started" into the "in progress" column as you can see. It should not take more than another hour. As you can see, I am doing it on the white-board on that other wall <points to the other wall where there is a draft of a UML communication diagram>. I originally estimated the task as three hours. Even though I worked on it for two hours, there are still two hours remaining. I changed the time remaining for the task in RTC to two hours. Is that correct?

Mark: Yes, it is. The time remaining should be actual time, not the original time minus time spent. What we are really concerned with is how much is remaining, not expended.

Ashok: Okay. When I am done with that task, I will create any new classes, their operations, attributes, and signatures. I called that task "code classes," which should take me the rest of the day. I have no impediments blocking my progress. However, Pete, can I ask you to spare 15 minutes this afternoon to review my model before I commit it to code?

Pete: Sure. Thanks for the heads up.

Ann continues the meeting with her update. She mentions to Louise that she has a few questions about the current user story that she is implementing.

Louise: Sure, what are your questions?

Mark: Pardon me for interrupting, but this meeting is not the place for detailed requirements or design discussions. Let's get through our planning, and then you two can work together on your questions.

Louise nods.

An important part of a team lead's responsibilities is to ensure that the daily meeting runs efficiently so that meeting time is minimized and team members can get back to working on their tasks.

When it is Pete's turn to give his update, he mentions that RTC has just released a patch that the team could use, but he is unsure what the procedure is to download it and get it installed for the team. He asks if he should spend some time surfing the Net to figure out where to get the update.

Mark: No, Pete, I don't think that is a good use of your valuable time. I will talk to Terry and find out what the policy and procedure is for getting the update installed. I'll write this as an issue on our Issue List on the whiteboard. Hopefully when we have our daily meeting tomorrow, I can strike this issue off as dealt with.

This is an example of a team lead's responsibility to remove any impediments (or blockers) on behalf of the team. Unlike traditional project managers who often find procedures such as status and time reporting steal productive time from the team, an agile team lead *reduces* bureaucracy and time wasting tasks for the team wherever they can. Team leads also prod the team to do this as well. This is one reason why teams will take a team lead over a traditional project manager any day.

The team finishes giving their updates to each other and goes back to work. Janice has been watching the meeting with interest and has some questions, but she knows not to interrupt the team's meeting. Now that it is over, she approaches Louise and asks her questions.

Janice: Thank you for answering my questions, Louise. Do you mind if I also sit in on your discussions with Ann?

Louise: If you can spare the time that would be great.

Mark: Wonderful. This is an example of just-in-time ad hoc meetings that spawn between the team and interested stakeholders after the stand-up meeting. This is the power of daily communication between the team and stakeholders without the need for time wasting emails. I have seen many potential miscommunications avoided when these type of things are caught by interested observers at our daily coordination meetings.

LESSONS FROM THE TRENCHES—TEAMS REPORT TO EACH OTHER

Mark finds that when he coaches new teams, and they give their update, they tend to face him as they answer their three questions. Mark repeatedly reminds the team that it is *their* meeting, not his. They are not reporting to him. They are reporting to each other. They have made commitments to each other and to the product owner, not the team lead. So Mark asks them to point out what they are doing on the taskboard and talk to each other. It is a powerful team dynamic once they realize that they own the success of the iteration and start working together as a team. The team lead helps to streamline their processes. Once the team becomes comfortable with the basic idea, other team members can take on facilitation responsibilities and pick up new skills.

Collaborating Throughout the First Day

Once the team has finished coordinating their day's work, they spend the rest of the day collaborating to complete their work items. During early afternoon, the team gives Louise an interim build to do some acceptance testing. She discovers that scanning an item is displaying 0.00 for the price, yet she knows that the item's price is in the system.

Louise: Mark, I discovered this problem with the scanned price. Should I enter it into the company's defect tracking system? We can then start prioritizing these bugs and assigning them to different team members. I hear that is called "defect triage" and that sounds like a cool job for me.

Mark: Well, Ann wrote the code for that this morning, and she is sitting two desks away from you. Why don't you just tell her what you found.

Louise: I suppose that is a more agile approach. I'll go talk to her. . . . Ann, I found this defect. Can you fix it in the next few days?

Ann: Why don't I fix it right now, and you can retest in 15 minutes.

Louise: Wow, that is quick turnaround. Quicker than the time it would take me to log the defect!

Ann: Before I fix the defect, though, I am going to code a unit test to detect this defect. As part of our continuous integration practice, we will automatically run this test on a regular basis. Should the problem ever recur due to some other change, we will catch it before it gets to you. This gives us confidence to make changes to our code base without having to do extensive manual regression testing.

Concluding the First Day

As part of *concluding* the day, the team focuses on stabilizing the application. Any new code written during the day was tested by the team member who wrote it. They did this by integrating their new code with a snapshot of the system that they have in their own developer sandbox. When the developer is satisfied that his changes not only work as expected but don't break the rest of the system, he delivers his changes to the shared code base (or "trunk") known as the integration stream. This delivery fires a build of the system and automatically runs all the developer unit tests to ensure that the changes have not broken other parts of the system.

A key responsibility of every developer is to ensure that new unit tests are written to support any new code, and that these tests are added to the suite that is run in the integration stream every time a new piece of code is checked in/delivered. Ideally, the team adopts the test-driven development (TDD) practice whereby the tests are written *before* the actual code is written. This ensures that the tests are not forgotten, or neglected due to time pressures. The practice of building and integration testing continually for each new code delivery is called continuous integration and is a key agile practice that all teams should incorporate. Having working, consumable software on a regular basis (ideally daily) would be impossible without this practice.

Toward the end of the day, critical defects are fixed. The team decides to defer some minor defects so that they can concentrate on getting the remaining stories implemented, with hopefully some time to fix the minor defects toward the end of the iteration. In these cases, they log the defects in RTC as work items so that they don't lose track of them, and so that they can be prioritized like any other work item.

Day 2

Mark spends some time with Paula, a test lead assigned to this project.

Paula: Hello, Mark. I have been told that I and one of my fellow testers have been assigned to this project to do independent testing. Why are we meeting so early in the project? Shouldn't I be joining the team when the application is built and ready to test?

Mark: Actually, on an agile project we have features to test as early as one week into the project. If there are problems, we save a lot of time and effort catching them early. It will reduce our user acceptance testing required significantly at the end of the project, and we expect far fewer problems to be found. In fact, we expect the testing at the end of the lifecycle to be more of a formality.

Paula: Why don't I just join the team as a tester?

Mark: Well, we do indeed have a significant focus on testing within the team. However, there can be a tendency for team members to be biased to testing "happy paths" of testing and not consider more esoteric scenarios. Having someone outside the team adds a degree of confidence that the testing process is not compromised.

Paula: Where can I find the requirements documents?

Mark: We don't produce much in the way of requirements documents on an agile project, as we find that they are costly to produce and usually don't reflect the true needs of the solution. The effort to write a requirements document, as well as the cost and resulting delays to keep these documents up to date, can discourage change to any requirements. This is not an efficient way to work. Therefore, we rely more on discussions with our domain experts in lieu of written requirements documents.

Mark continues: We would prefer to spend time writing acceptance tests based on what our stakeholders tell us as we implement the actual functionality, and ideally just before we do so. These tests are like requirements and are used to validate that the system meets the stakeholders' expectations. Louise has some experience writing these tests and she can provide you with some samples. Louise is busy, so I can walk you through the technique, and then you can spend some time thinking about other tests that she has not covered.

Day 3

On the third day, Gunther realizes that he needs to do a task that is not on the taskboard and asks Mark what to do.

Gunther: I need to spend two hours reviewing the existing database schema and the related data dictionary documentation, but I forgot to identify this task in our planning workshop. Should I add a sticky to the taskboard for this?

Mark: Sure. It is typical to discover new tasks that need to be done. That is why we planned to do 210 hours of work when the team actually has about 250 ideal hours available. We have about 40 hours of contingency built into the plan to do this unplanned work. Let's categorize this as an "unplanned task" in RTC, so that when we do our retrospective at the end of the iteration we can observe the degree of work that we did not plan for and perhaps learn and plan better for the next iteration.

The Next Several Days

Work continues over the next several days following the daily pattern that we have described.

During the daily coordination meetings, as part of reviewing the team's progress, Mark reviews any outstanding issues that have been prominently displayed using sticky notes on a whiteboard. Having them displayed this way ensures that they are not forgotten and are dealt with in a timely fashion. Clearing these issues is a critical part of a team lead's role.

As new capabilities become available, Janice and Louise spend part of every day running manual "smoke tests" to ensure that from a functionality point of view, the system works as expected.

Midway through the iteration, Janice informs Louise that they completely forgot a few stories. Ann is panicking, and Mark steps in to help out.

Janice: We absolutely *have* to have these stories in the first release of the system.

Mark: Well, in that case, let's add them to the work item list in the priority that you and Louise agree upon. It will obviously mean that the other items will go down in priority, and some may not make it into the final release. But let's defer that discussion until we have a better idea of how we are progressing.

Janice: Since these are high priority items, can we get the team to stop working on some of their current items and work on these instead?

Mark: No, that would not be wise. It is a good practice to not add new work items to the current iteration since the team already has committed to a given set of items. We don't change scope during the iteration. If, for instance, it is a material addition to an existing story that we are working on, we add an additional story to the work item list, and they can start working on it in the next iteration.

Louise: Mark, I also have some bad news. In discussing some of the future planned stories in more depth with Ann, we have discovered that some of them are far more complicated than we thought and in fact quite different from the way we originally understood them. So the relative estimates for them are too low. What should we do?

Mark: Well, the good news is that we now have a better understanding of the requirements. It is a good thing that we didn't spend a bunch of time in a traditional manner to document the wrong requirements. I recommend that you adjust the relative point estimates for these stories in your work item list. Again, it means that some more work in the list may not get implemented, but we will see.

Louise: Janice, I have to admit that I am getting a bit frustrated that you aren't answering my emails promptly when I have questions about the requirements. It means that I can't give timely answers to the team sometimes. And I take a long time typing up those emails.

Janice: I am usually at my desk, but sometimes I take my laptop to another desk or to work in a quiet corner of the cafeteria.

Louise: Well, that explains why you don't answer my phone calls.

Janice: And often I make a point of not reading my email so I can get my other work done.

Louise: Ahhhhhh!!!

Mark: Hang on. Can I suggest something different? Janice, I believe that you have IBM Sametime® on your desk for instant messaging/chat (IM)? Louise, why don't you just ping Janice when you have a question? Or better yet use RTC as it's integrated with Sametime and then the chat can be automatically logged against the corresponding work item. That is probably quicker than typing up a long email.

Louise: I guess we could try that. But then I wouldn't have an audit trail of the decision in case Janice changes her mind.

Mark: Actually, modern chat tools allow you to save and file your conversations so that shouldn't be a concern. And to be honest, making a decision to be more trusting reduces the need for elaborate time-consuming audit trails.

For the remainder of the iteration, the team collaborates to complete their work items.

Day 7

Dick, the internal auditor, pays a visit to Mark.

Dick: I understand that you are doing an agile project. I want you to understand that my job is to make sure that you follow our processes. I insist that the application be verified by doing some testing by an independent party.

Mark: I actually agree with you, Dick. We have asked Paula to independently test our application so that the verification process is not biased by our own team members.

Dick: Excellent. Additionally, I will want to have a weekly meeting with you to review progress, risks, issues, and adherence to schedule. I'll set up a weekly meeting in my office.

Mark: Well, Dick, we have no secrets on this project; all of our work is transparent. We talk about all of these things in our daily coordination meeting, and our metrics are both posted on our walls, as well as viewable via a dashboard in RTC. Please feel free to attend our meetings to observe how our project is progressing. If you are unsure about anything that you hear, stay behind after the 15-minute meeting, and I would be happy to clarify any details.

Day 8: The Team Has Fallen Behind Their Plan

As can be seen from Figure 17.3, the team has fallen behind and has an open discussion during their daily coordination meeting on Day 8 about their progress.

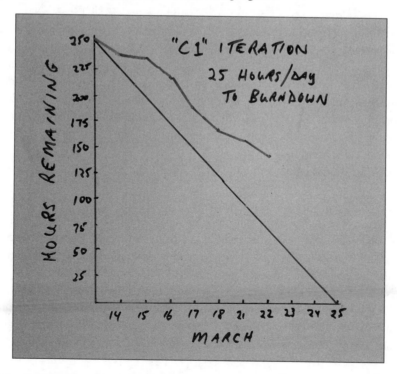

Figure 17.3   Iteration burndown chart toward the end of the iteration

What's the Purpose of the Iteration Burndown Chart?

Iterations are by design, short in duration. A two-week iteration is just ten business days. We cannot afford to determine whether we are behind schedule on merely a weekly basis. An Iteration burndown chart is a simple way of tracking progress on a daily basis by plotting "burned down" hours. We plot the number of total remaining hours of work for all work items on the Y axis against the day of the iteration on the X axis. Every day we plot a new value based on the total task hours remaining in the iteration and draw a line from the previous day's plotted value. (If you are using a tool like RTC it automatically plots the new day's value.) The straight line on the chart depicts the expected burndown trend if the team is on track to complete all their task hours by the end of the iteration. On the last day of the iteration, the number of hours should have burned down to zero. Values plotted above the burndown line indicate the project is behind schedule; below the line and you are ahead of schedule. This amazing yet simple technique keeps the team focused on progress versus objectives.

At the beginning of the iteration, you should know what your expectation is for burning down hours/per day. For instance, in our case, for this iteration we have written tasks that add up to 250 hours (including contingency). Since we have a ten-day iteration (considering the statutory holiday), we can expect to knock off 25 hours/day from our tasks.

Mark: Team, this is no surprise, as we have seen from our burndown that we are increasingly falling behind on this iteration. With only three days remaining in our iteration it is obvious that we are not going to get all four of our work items completed. It does seem achievable that we can complete everything except programming the interface to the SAP system for sending payroll details. Let's concentrate on getting the other three stories into a stable and tested build in preparation for our iteration review on Friday with Dean and some other interested stakeholders.

Dean is in attendance at the stand-up meeting, and while he knows that he isn't supposed to interrupt, he can't help himself:

Dean: Wow, we are falling behind already. I guess this agile approach isn't working too well!

Mark: Well, Dean, we are indeed disappointed that it appears right now that we won't meet our commitment to Louise; however, to be fair, this is our first iteration, and the team is just learning how to work together in the most effective and productive manner. We have learned some lessons to streamline our work. We will discuss them more at our retrospective on Friday so that we make sure that we adopt these process improvements for our future iterations.

Louise adds: And I have to admit that I wasn't as organized as I had thought during this iteration. Turns out that I didn't understand exactly what Ann (our store manager representative and domain expert) really wanted in these stories, and the team had to wait for me to get answers. They also had to redo some work because I had given them the wrong information.

Mark: I'll add that frankly, we bit off more than we could chew in terms of number of points worth of work items that we can realistically deliver in an iteration. We call that velocity. I am hopeful that as the team adapts to become more productive from iteration to iteration, their velocity increases so that they can take on more work. For the next few iterations, however, we will assume that we have a lower velocity and will accept fewer points of work items to commit to delivering.

Dean: Remind me again why this is better than the traditional approach?

Mark: In agile, we accept the reality that teams don't know at what pace they can deliver work until they start working together and get comfortable with the domain, technology, and people aspects of the project. Likewise, Louise will admit that she doesn't really know exactly what the end solution will look like until she starts to see and use increments of the solution.

Concluding the First Iteration

In the last few days of the iteration, the team is focused on "hardening" their work—that is, focusing on fixing the quality of their work rather than building new functionality so that it is at a minimum suitable for a demonstration, but preferably a potentially shippable, consumable solution should the stakeholders wish to deploy it as it is.

Iteration Review

On the last day of the iteration, the team books a one-hour iteration review meeting (called a Sprint review in Scrum) in the work area with interested stakeholders to demonstrate the team's accomplishments for the iteration. A PoS system is available in the work area to do the demonstration. The team is in attendance for this short meeting. (It is their work area after all!) It is good to have the team present to take credit for their work, receive feedback about how they are progressing, and ensure that they are meeting the stakeholders' expectations. Mark asks Ashok to lead the demonstration of the solution's new features.

This meeting is more than just a demo—it is an opportunity to get feedback from the stakeholders on their perception of the project and the recent iteration in terms of meeting their expectations. The demo is a good way to show objective progress, but the review is also an opportunity to discuss other topics related to the project.

Mark facilitates the meeting.

Mark: First of all, let's review our progress against our plan. I would like to congratulate the team on its accomplishments for this iteration. We were able to complete three of the four planned work items in the iteration. The team in fact worked some overtime to get this much work accomplished. However, we don't want to continue this pattern of overtime as it is inconsistent with the sustainable pace agile practice. The team will burn out if we keep this up. Rather, we will adjust our expectations for the number of "points" of work items that we can deliver (velocity) down from 30 to 25 points since that is what we delivered in this iteration. I am optimistic that, as we learn to work more effectively, we can increase our expected velocity, but we will wait until we have evidence that this is possible before we commit to do so.

Louise: But if we reduce our expected velocity, doesn't this mean that if we extrapolate this out for the remaining 11 iterations, that we will not be able to complete all of our planned release work items?

Dean: Looks like we're off to a rough start!

Mark: That could possibly be true. But having a lot of experience with agile projects, I added some contingency into our plan so that we do have an extra iteration in the schedule to be able to handle flexibility in our productivity and project scope. If we maintain a pace of 25 points over the 12 Construction iterations, that means that we will deliver 300 of the 314 identified points, which is 95% of the expected functionality. I am still optimistic that we will be able to improve our velocity. In most projects, it takes some time for the team to learn to communicate and work most effectively. In the next meeting the team will discuss ways of working better together. We expect to reap the benefits of these improvements for the remainder of the project.

However, I do anticipate more points of stories and other work items to be added to our list. So we may have to make some difficult trade-offs regarding scope if we are to deploy on our planned dates. I will keep track of additional points of scope and plot it on a ranged burndown chart so that we can show a realistic team velocity of what our team can deliver during an iteration.

Dean: I have a waterfall project going on as well. They are three months into the project, and the project manager tells me that they are on schedule. We are one month into this project, and you are already behind!

Mark: Respectfully, how do you know that you are on schedule for the other project? Do you think that the remainder of the schedule is accurate considering the team of developers has not even been hired, and you probably don't know how productive they will be? When will you see some of your solution working?

Dean: The Microsoft® Project plan schedule says that we will have a working system in six months.

Mark: Well, we are about to show you a working, tested piece of your solution now, and we are four weeks into the project. We will continue to show you increments of the solution every two weeks, and if you need to deploy something to your users, we can do that at any time. With your waterfall project, early deployment is not an option.

Dean: Well, let's see what you have done <frown>.

Louise: Ashok will now demonstrate what we have accomplished during this iteration. Ashok?

Ashok demonstrates scanning of items, including weighing of produce items. He also demonstrates that while they were able to verify payment for debit and credit transactions they take roughly 6 seconds, not the 3 that were expected.

Louise: Yes, this was disappointing. However, I now realize that my requirement expectations might be a bit unrealistic. So I am changing the acceptance criteria to 6-second response time.

Mark: I understand that, while the PoS transaction works, the team had to take some shortcuts and also had no time to create a proper set of unit tests.

Pete: Yes, to be honest the code is a bit sloppy and would be hard to maintain and extend as it is. We simply did not have enough time to do it properly if we planned to be able to demo the functionality.

Mark: That is not uncommon, especially in the early iterations. While the agile community might blast me for this, I am going to suggest that we give you credit for the 10 points for completing this work item, but we need to add a new work item to refactor this functionality so that the code is of good quality. Failure to do so would build some "technical debt" that we would have to pay back in the future when we would be forced to rewrite the code when it becomes too brittle and unmaintainable. The refactor work item needs to be high priority; otherwise, it might never be done.

Louise: What's the big deal? If it ain't broke, why fix it?

Mark: Well, if we don't fix it, poorly written code will lead to an unmaintainable system. Allowing bad code and designs to accumulate in the code base is known as accruing "technical debt." Like interest debt, it compounds over time. It's pay me now or pay me later. If later, it will cost much more to fix. In fact it can often require a substantial redesign and rewrite of the code base.

Louise: Okay, it doesn't provide me immediate benefit, but I can see that investing some time in refactoring now will benefit me in the longer term.

Dean: Well, despite not getting as much work done as we had hoped, it is comforting to see some of the solution working at such an early stage in the project.

Mark: Agreed. So to summarize, we completed 25 points of functionality in this iteration, and we plan to deliver at least the same, but hopefully more in the next iteration of the Construction phase (C2). With 11 iterations remaining, it would indicate that we could complete another 275 points. The usual pattern is that the team's productivity increases as the project proceeds so hopefully we can deliver most of the expected functionality. I do expect some additional work items to surface and be added to the WIL, but my hope is that it can be balanced with some increase to the team's velocity as the team gels.

This ends the iteration review, and those in attendance from outside the team are dismissed.

Iteration Retrospective

Since the iteration review meeting ended 15 minutes early, the team saves some time by moving straight into the retrospective.

Mark continues to facilitate this meeting. He brings up a spreadsheet where he tracks retrospectives, and he has already logged an item that was surfaced earlier in the iteration by Ashok during a daily stand-up:

The team should not plan to complete a full day of ideal hours the first day of the iteration, since almost one-half of the day is used for the iteration planning workshop.

Mark: It is a good thing that we captured this in this spreadsheet so that it was not forgotten! Mark asks each team member to consider these things:

- What things went well in the iteration that if we don't discuss we might forget?
- What did we learn?
- What things could we improve on?
- Are there things that still puzzle us?

Going around the room, each team member takes turns giving feedback on how things went:

Katherine: First of all, I would like to say that I am really enjoying the agile approach to building our solution. It is gratifying to be able to see working software so early in the project. It is also good that we don't have to sift through piles of documentation. Having Louise and Ann available to answer our questions immediately really helps and saves time on emails. Regarding what could be improved, to be honest, sometimes the team is a bit rowdy. It is nice that the team is enjoying themselves and getting along well, but sometimes it is difficult to concentrate.

Mark: Thanks for being honest about that Katherine. This is common when we have a number of people working in the same area. I am sure that the team will be more sensitive to this in the future. I'll make a note of it in our retrospective log, so that we can review this at our next retrospective and see whether the situation has improved. Brian, your thoughts on the iteration?

Brian: I am happy with the way things are going. I had a thought about the need for a user manual for the PoS. When should we start writing it?

Mark: Well, an Agile Modeling practice is "continuous documentation." You bring up a good point, so let's start documenting the manual as we go. Louise, can we add a work item to the work item list for this?

Louise: Sure, I can do that right now. But it will happen every iteration; should it be a work item?

Mark: Good point. It probably makes more sense to create a task to update the user manual as part of each new story. Let's do that. I will mention this in the retrospective log so that we don't forget it in our iteration planning.

The retrospective continues in this manner so that each team member has an opportunity to provide his or her perspective on the effectiveness of the team's process and make suggestions for improvements.

When the retrospective wraps up, Mark invites the team to leave an hour early on this Friday to celebrate the team's achievements over a drink. On Monday morning, they will meet to plan the next iteration in the same manner as they did for this one.

LESSONS FROM THE TRENCHES—DIGITAL VERSUS MANUAL TASKBOARDS

In this case study we used RTC as an example tool for planning the release, managing the work item list, and the task board. Do you need to have your agile planning managed in a tool? Like anything, it depends. Mark prefers to use manual taskboards for small, collocated teams. A manual taskboard prominently displayed in the work room with a variety of colored sticky notes gives immediate and live status to everyone in the room on what is going on. Having to find the dashboard in a tool isn't quite the same. Having said that, for larger teams, or organizations where those outside the team are interested in the team's dashboard (such as a PMO), a virtual dashboard is necessary. Another example is in situations where some team members are geographically dispersed and cannot personally attend the daily coordination meeting. In this case, using a manual taskboard becomes awkward. In situations like this, Mark has resorted to taking pictures of the taskboard and sending them to off-site team members, and the team members in return send him daily updates on their tasks by email with which he then updates the board. Clumsy! Clearly, a tool would have saved time in this situation.

Subsequent Construction Iterations

Space limits us from describing what happens in each of the subsequent 11 iterations, but the following section discusses some of the more interesting issues that surfaced in subsequent iterations of the Construction phase.

The Second Construction Iteration

As the second iteration of Construction starts, Mark produces a release ranged burndown chart to track progress of developing the release on an iteration by iteration basis. He posts this chart (see Figure 17.4) on the wall. The total estimated points to develop the solution (from the planning poker estimating session) were 314. If everything were to go according to plan, the points remaining would burn down to zero by the end of the 12 iterations. However, in the first iteration only 25 points of functionality were delivered compared to an expected 30. The hope is that the team picks up its velocity over the next few iterations as they learn to work better together and to streamline/optimize their processes. Eight points of work items were added into the work item list as unplanned scope, which is indicated on top of the iteration bar in the chart. The 25 points delivered, less the additional 8 added to the work item list, brought the total remaining work down to 297, which was plotted on the bar chart.

At one of the coordination meetings, Dick asks a question about this new chart:

Dick: Mark, what do the dashed lines mean?

Mark: Well, we have already fallen a bit behind, and some new scope was added to the list of work items. If the trend continues, it is difficult to say for sure that we can indeed deliver everything you need in 12 weeks. If we were draconian about it, we could rigorously reduce scope to hit the 12 iteration schedule, but in that case you may not have sufficient functionality to actually go live. A more practical approach is to consider the possibility that we *may* have to extend the schedule. The dashed lines represent a "ranged estimate." It says that with only this one data point for the iteration just completed, we have a predicted range of 10 to 18 iterations needed to complete the application. This is a variation of an estimation model referred to as the "cone of uncertainty." It suggests that our estimating fidelity is poor early in the project, but will become more accurate with a lower range of estimates as we get more information about our progress.

Dick: But you told me that you added some contingency to the schedule, allowing us to add extra points of functionality to our work item list.

Mark: Yes, I did, and I hope that it is enough to allow for unplanned work that is added. However, based on one iteration, there is still too much that we don't know about what your true requirements are, about our delivery velocity, and other unknowns that are a part of every project. So we feel that showing you this range of schedule estimates is prudent. As I said, as uncertainty is reduced as we move through our iterations, the planned schedule variance will reduce dramatically. This is common on IT projects, with a wide estimation range at the start of the project reflecting the uncertainty of the stakeholders' understanding of their needs. As the stakeholders' understanding of their requirements improves, and the most effective way to do that is to iteratively show them a working solution, the estimate range will narrow.

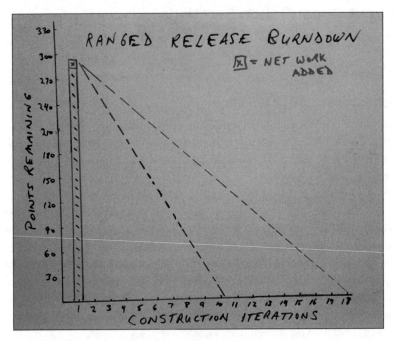

Figure 17.4 Release burndown chart showing progress for the release against plan

The Third Construction Iteration

During the third iteration of Construction, Dean, the VP, pulls Louise aside and says that they must add another new feature to the system. Competitors are adding automatic ordering of stock from vendors when inventory for an item falls below a certain level. Orders are sent to suppliers without the need to create a manual order. Dean asks Louise to insert the work item as a high level priority. Louise figures that on a relative basis, this new feature would add at least 100 points to the estimate. Louise discusses the new feature with Mark.

Louise: I am the product owner, and you said that I own the priorities and scope of the project, so I am adding this to the work item list.

Mark: Yes, you can make that call. However, can I remind you that this is why we created a Vision document in the Inception phase? Does this new functionality solve the problem of reducing the lineups in stores, or reducing the maintenance costs for the system?

Louise: Well, I guess it doesn't relate to those problems.

Mark: Then can I suggest that we discuss this with Dean and remind him that he asked us to solve those business problems with this release. Perhaps we can address his inventory management problems in the next release.

Louise: Okay, I will review the Vision with him and ask him to put this off for now.

Mark: I think that would be best. Let's do our best to meet our existing commitment rather than introducing such a fundamental change in scope.

The Fourth Construction Iteration

An additional chart that Mark posts in the work area shows the team's velocity in terms of number of points of functionality that they are delivering in each iteration. The bar chart in Figure 17.5 shows the trend of the productivity of the team. It shows that while the trend is not straight up, the team is succeeding in increasing their productivity as the project progresses through the iterations. This is typical as teams learn to work more effectively.

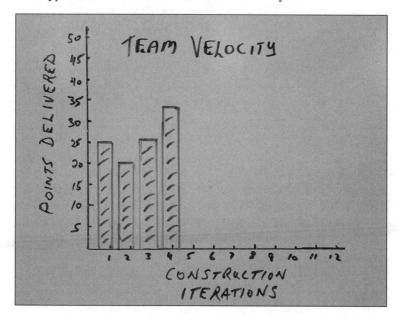

Figure 17.5   Velocity by Construction iteration

The Fifth Construction Iteration

During this iteration, Janice has a discussion with Mark.

Janice: Mark, I had lunch with Sandy, the data center manager working in our operations group. She has heard about our project and says that she really needs to learn about the expectations we have for her to run the system in production. Sandy says that she wants to work with our DAD teams to help facilitate a more frequent and automated deployment to our customers.

Mark: Sandy is definitely a stakeholder. We need to add her to our list of stakeholders in the Vision statement. I'll set up a meeting with Louise, Sandy, and myself to bring her up to speed with our plans. We need to start doing some look-ahead planning for the Transition phase, when we deploy the solution to the stores and in the data center. We may need to order some production servers and perform other related deployment activities.

It is also great to hear that she wants to work with us to streamline our deployment. In DAD, we call the practice of frequent deployment "continuous deployment." We will be deploying our application in a controlled fashion in the Transition phase. However, because we have already automated the deployment into our systems integration environment we deliver deployment artifacts into that environment frequently. It is relatively straightforward to extend these scripts for deployment into the Staging and high-availability clustered Production environments.

Mark continues: Another stakeholder we should engage with is the Customer Support group. When we have problems in the stores, they will call our help desk and they need to know who the contacts are to address any issues.

The Sixth Construction Iteration

During this iteration, the team brings up a new issue to Mark.

Ashok: Mark, we are getting really frustrated with Gary, our DBA. It takes forever to get a database change "approved." He insists that database design must be done up front before any code is written, and must be properly thought through to consider future usage of the data.

Mark: Have you suggested that if there is a problem, the database can be changed to support the new requirements that arise, and then refactored if necessary to support a longer term solution?

Ashok: I have indeed, but he says that is ridiculous. He says that refactoring is for code, not databases.

Mark: I would respectfully disagree. I will talk to him about this. Did he give you an example of why databases need to be designed up front?

Ashok: Yes, he did. He said that if we pick a column name without thinking about it properly, and then he needs to change it, it will break our system all over the place and we will be faced with a lot of code changes.

Mark: Well, it needn't be that way. If he needed to change the column name, he could use a refactoring pattern whereby the new column is created with the new name. A simple script could populate the new column's data with the old column's values. Then a trigger could be used to populate the new column every time our system updates the old column. When we have time, we could refactor our code to use the new column, and then the old column could be removed. This is just one example of a pattern for refactoring databases.

For more information on these agile database patterns, there is a phenomenal book called *Agile Database Techniques* by Scott Ambler. I will buy him a copy.

The Ninth Construction Iteration

When the Construction phase started, Mark created a work item for contingency in the amount of 46 points (360 expected points less 314 estimated initially). As the iterations proceeded, sure enough, additional work items were identified as required scope. As the stakeholder priorities changed, some items were actually *removed* from the work item list since they were no longer priorities. The estimates for net added items were taken from the contingency work item, totaling the 46 points of contingency available. Some of the contingency points were used for new work items; other points were consumed when it was realized that some user stories were larger than thought during the initial estimating session. Also, some technical refactoring ("do-overs") was required, using up some points. Once the contingency points were used up, Louise had agreed that any additional work items would need to be deferred to future releases. This proved to be an effective scope management technique.

However, this scope management technique didn't save the team from the fact that they were delivering fewer points of functionality per iteration than they had expected. In fact, after nine iterations, they were delivering an average of 25 points compared to their initial expectation of 30 points. During the iteration review for the ninth iteration, Mark leads the discussion of what to do in their situation, referring to the ranged release burndown of Figure 17.6 for the purposes of this discussion.

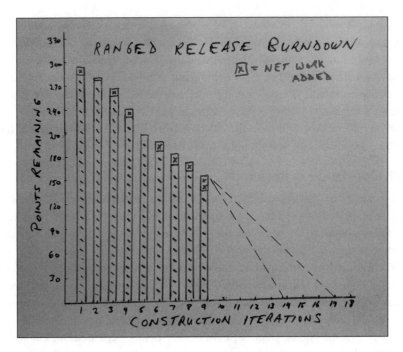

Figure 17.6   Ranged release burndown after nine Construction iterations

Mark: Drawing trend lines from the bar chart out to the X axis, we can see clearly from our ranged release burndown chart that it is unlikely that we can finish all of the functionality by the end of the twelfth construction iteration. We can, however, see that the range of schedule variance is much smaller than our view after the first iteration of the project (refer to Figure 17.4). This is because our stakeholders now have a much better understanding of what they want based on what they've seen the team produce. We now believe that if we keep up this net velocity we will finish construction sometime between week 14 and week 17.

Dean: Not good. What are our alternatives?

Mark: Well, there is no magic here. The good news is that we expect to deliver the functionality that is most valuable to you. Since Louise has agreed to defer some functionality, we still plan to complete the Construction phase in 12 iterations, which was the original schedule. The remaining user stories that we will not complete are lower in priority than what we have already delivered. They pertain to setting up sales promotions in advance to automatically adjust a basket of items' prices for the sales period. Louise, would you agree that this functionality is not critical to our first release of the solution?

Louise: Well, I am not pleased, but I understand that we couldn't really understand what was possible to deliver in advance. I know that the team has worked very hard, and that we have cut out a lot of the normal bureaucracy that we've seen on our past traditional projects. We have definitely more functionality than in the past, and what we are getting is exactly what we need. There have been no surprises on *this* project! And that's a good thing; I don't like surprises. So I suppose we can live without the remaining functionality. It is good that we can go live with the system on the timeline that we expected, and having spent exactly what we had budgeted.

Iteration #12—The Last Iteration of the Construction Phase

The team cleans up the remaining functionality as per the adjusted agreed upon scope and prepares to move into the Transition phase to deploy the solution to the stores.

Construction Milestone Review

On Friday of the last iteration, Mark and Louise (the product owner) meet with Dean (the VP), Terry (the enterprise architect), Dick (the internal auidtor), and Sue (the store manager representative) to go through a comprehensive demonstration of the solution. They want to assess the product's readiness to proceed into the Transition phase to deploy the solution into the stores.

Louise: Well, Dean, I am happy to say that although we were not able to complete all the functionality that we had in mind at the beginning of the project, we at least have sufficient functionality to deploy what we have completed, on time, and on budget!

Dean: Well, two out of three ain't bad <smiles>. And, Louise, since you were there the whole time the system was built, there are no surprises at this point about what we are getting. Terry, are we confident that the system will scale properly when we eventually deploy to all of our 250 stores?

Terry: Yes, we ran testing under simulated load early in the project to ensure that our architecture as designed can support this load. We found a few issues, but fortunately it was early enough to make the required changes before we had invested too much coding around a flawed architecture.

Dean: Dick, from an internal audit perspective, do you have any concerns?

Dick: No, I have been involved regularly during the process, attending many of your daily coordination meetings, as well as attending each of the 12 iteration reviews and voicing any concerns I had at the time. However, before we approve the system to go into production, we want to spend one week of final independent verification testing across all the functionality. This will be done by Paula and three additional testers from outside the development team so that we can do a complete regression. This will begin in week two of Transition, that is, the week after next.

Terry: Yes, our operations folks set up a separate environment for this.

Dean: Louise, how is the quality over all? What is the status of the testing and known defects?

Louise: Well, in our initial Vision that we created in the Inception phase, we determined that all high priority defects, that is, priority one and two, must be fixed before we can go "live." We have no high priority defects remaining. However, we have 45 lower priority defects, and one simple enhancement that we need to carry over into our Transition phase.

Dean: Mark, how will we deal with these?

Mark: In week two of our eight-week Transition phase, we will be piloting the system in two stores. Next week the team will fix the lower priority defects, as well as implement this small story that was introduced into the work item list at the last minute. The defect fixes, as well as the new story, will be merged into the code base at the end of the week, so that it will be ready for the independent testing and the pilot in week two. The final build will be done at the end of week two for deployment to the production systems starting in week three of Transition.

Dean: Sounds good. So what else happens in Transition; is there a plan?

Louise: I have a work item list for the activities related to Transition. We will be reviewing them with the Transition team on Monday morning.

Dean: Excellent. I would like to continue our weekly reviews to be kept abreast of the progress and issues during Transition.

Other Construction Phase Activities

In the Construction phase, we needed to do some "look-ahead" planning for the Transition phase when we will roll out the system to the stores. We added and completed some work items to the work item list. These activities included

- Procurement of production hardware and software licenses for the 60 stores.
- Defining user ids for the store managers for access to the back office system and connectivity to the head office systems.
- Work with operations and independent testing to ensure high-availability requirements will be met.
- Populating the database tables with data such as grocery items and their prices.
- Sue selected 10 people to become trainers for the rollout of the new system to the stores.
- Store manuals were produced in both electronic and hard copy format.
- The Communications department was engaged to create a rollout campaign to generate excitement among store employees.
- Creation of a high-level rollout plan detailing which stores will be installed in what order.
- Travel arrangements for the trainers were made.
- Determine on-call schedule.
- Establish incident reporting process with call center.

Concluding the Construction Phase Iterations

In the last Construction iterations, more thought starts to be given to deployment. Some look-ahead planning occurs to prepare for the Transition phase. This includes activities such as ordering the new Production servers for the back office for each of the stores.

Concluding Thoughts

In our case study, the team was relatively successful in its first iteration of Construction, producing an increment of the working solution in the first week. However, in our experience, this is not typical of teams trying agile for the first time. In reality, it is difficult producing consumable software after just one week. It normally takes some time and a few iterations for the team to learn how to effectively work together. Examples of reasons for teams failing to deliver software in the first week include misunderstood requirements, unwillingness to adopt lightweight approach to creating work products, poor team cohesion, lack of commitment to iteration goals, overly optimistic productivity expectations, environments not ready (such as developer environments, build machines, database availability), and misunderstandings about what constitutes "done" for implemented stories. There are many more reasons why you may not get the results you expect in your early iterations. We find that teams that successfully produce consumable increments of their solution in early iterations have usually worked together on previous agile projects. They typically understand agile practices, how to most effectively work with each other with minimum bureaucracy in a self-organizing manner with little direction, and are dedicated to helping each other meet their teams' commitments to their stakeholders. So if you are new to agile development, approach it with reasonable expectations, expecting to improve your performance as you progress through your iterations. We of course believe that your success can be accelerated with some coaching by experienced agile mentors in your early iterations.

CHAPTER 18

The Transition Phase

It isn't sufficient to build a solution. You must also be able to ship it successfully.

Mainstream agile methods describe the goal of creating "shippable software," meaning that the software is both of value and of sufficient quality to deploy at the end of every iteration. In DAD we prefer to use the phrase "consumable solution" indicating that shippable does not necessarily mean usable software, and that in many cases more needs to be delivered to the customer than just software as the overall solution.

A simple stand-alone application such as a Web site can be easily deployed regularly as part of the end of an iteration. As we already discussed in Chapter 10, "Initial Release Planning," some organizations deploy their software many times a day. However, for nontrivial enterprise deployments, the Transition phase is usually a significant effort. Typically the software is completed and stabilized in the prior Construction iterations. The Transition "phase" might entail fixing some remaining defects and final acceptance testing, but the majority of the effort is usually in the actual deployment preparation, training, and often transitioning of the solution to the operations group for running in production. In the November 2010 Agile State of the Art survey Scott found that the average agile team spent six weeks in their Transition efforts, with some respondents indicating spending one day or less and some indicating 12 weeks or more.

This chapter describes what to expect in these enterprise deployments. In our experience the Transition phase can require careful planning and coordination across many stakeholder groups. This is particularly true for large-scale, high-availability systems that need to integrate with other mission critical systems. Figure 18.1 shows a mind map of the structure of this chapter. We describe each of the topics in the map in clockwise order, beginning at the top right.

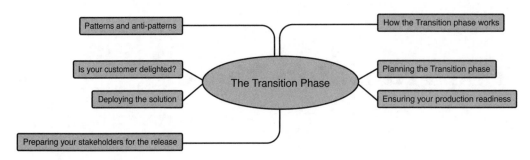

Figure 18.1   Outline of this chapter

THE BIG IDEAS IN THIS CHAPTER

- For enterprise DAD projects, transitioning the solution into production is an important effort worthy of being described as a Transition phase.

- A properly executed Construction phase greatly reduces the risks of deploying the solution to the stakeholders compared to traditional projects.

- The Transition phase typically involves collaboration with many external stakeholders who should have been prepared for this release in the Construction phase.

- The Transition phase typically extends for at least a few days past the date of deployment to help support and transition the release to the stakeholders.

- A DAD project properly executed results in delighted stakeholders.

How the Transition Phase Works

The Transition phase is a special type of iteration devoted to deploying the solution into the hands of the customer. For phased rollouts, the Transition phase could consist of multiple iterations. The length of each iteration should be as short as possible and seldom longer than a Construction iteration. Figure 18.2 highlights the Transition phase specific goals and the ongoing goals that apply to all phases.

Figure 18.3 depicts a high-level timeline for a typical configuration of agile practices that address the goals of the Transition phase, but you need to tailor and perform these activities to the extent they make sense for your situation. An interesting observation, one supported by the survey results mentioned earlier, is that the lower bounds on the times add up to less than an hour to get to the point of being production ready. This time is clearly the ideal, the majority of which is the time it takes to run your regression test suite(s) one last time to verify that your build actually works. Granted, sometimes regression test suites take days or even weeks to run for complex solutions, so at scale Transition efforts take longer. The point is that in situations where teams are following a leaner approach where continuous deployment techniques are fully adopted that the "Transition phase" can be very short—in these cases the phase has effectively evolved into an activity.

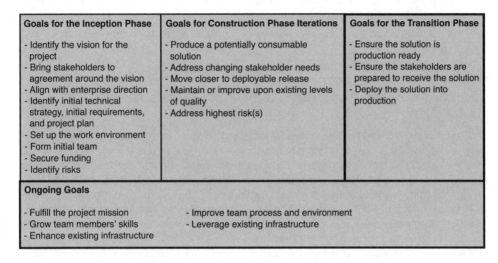

Goals for the Inception Phase	Goals for Construction Phase Iterations	Goals for the Transition Phase
- Identify the vision for the project - Bring stakeholders to agreement around the vision - Align with enterprise direction - Identify initial technical strategy, initial requirements, and project plan - Set up the work environment - Form initial team - Secure funding - Identify risks	- Produce a potentially consumable solution - Address changing stakeholder needs - Move closer to deployable release - Maintain or improve upon existing levels of quality - Address highest risk(s)	- Ensure the solution is production ready - Ensure the stakeholders are prepared to receive the solution - Deploy the solution into production

Ongoing Goals

- Fulfill the project mission
- Grow team members' skills
- Enhance existing infrastructure
- Improve team process and environment
- Leverage existing infrastructure

Figure 18.2 DAD lifecycle goals

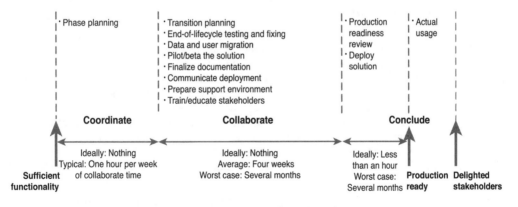

Figure 18.3 Overview of a typical approach to the Transition phase

Planning the Transition Phase

Previous chapters described a responsibility of the product owner to maintain the work item list and its priorities. As the project nears the Transition phase, the work item list needs to be supplemented with work related to putting the solution into the hands of the customer and ensuring that it is adequately consumable. The team lead helps the product owner collaborate with stakeholders external to the team to elicit these work items to ensure that the work is identified. Doing this look-ahead planning in the late iterations of Construction provides input to the planning workshop at the beginning of the Transition iteration. Activities that should be planned as work items include the following: planning the implementation/cutover, installation of deployment artifacts, data conversion, communications to stakeholders, marketing activities, training, and finalizing documentation.

LESSONS FROM THE TRENCHES—UNDERSTAND DEPLOYMENT TRADE-OFFS

It is easy to buy into the simple answer of releasing continuously as always being the "correct" interpretation of lean thinking when it comes to transition. It is equally as easy to fall into the trap of establishing a policy of batched and infrequent releases to production under the auspices of enterprise risk management. This dichotomy was one of the real-world challenges faced by Mark Kennaley, president and principal consultant of Fourth Medium Consulting and author of SDLC 3.0, on a recent engagement for the world's largest mutual fund company. Applying a DAD approach in this context meant questioning the value of mitigating change-event risks by reducing their frequency while simultaneously being sensitive to the realities of the broader business enterprise. Compliance departments often incorrectly design controls that require the batched delivery of value to stakeholders to drastically reduce the frequency of releases. However current management science supports state-of-the-practice lean and agile practices, which recommend increasing release frequency and reducing transfer-batch sizes.

Sound advice in this instance meant striking a reasoned balance to ensure that business agility was maintained in a fast-paced enterprise while being cognizant of the realities of regulatory compliance. Exceptions handed out by auditors in this business can lead to massive outflows of capital amounting to billions of dollars at this scale. At the same time failure to deliver value can introduce equally damaging risks to the business. A critical strategy is to peel the onion to get at the true intent of the compliance tests. Disciplined agility for these endeavors means leveraging risk-driven, multifrequency, and near-continuous releases accompanied with the required practice of parallel independent testing recreatable automatic builds, and cross-stakeholder notification and approval workflow.

You should have an iteration planning workshop for each iteration in your Transition phase executed in the same manner as your Construction iterations as described in Chapter 14, "Initiating a Construction Iteration." The practices of reviewing the high priority work items from the work item list and working with your team to plan the work are consistent with the approach you applied in previous iterations. A key difference is that unlike the Construction iterations where most of the work was done by the team members, in the Transition iterations it is common for most of the work to require collaboration with stakeholders *external* to the team. These external stakeholders such as security experts or other DevOps specialists are often service providers to many teams so they can have conflicting priorities. As such if they are not warned in advance that you will require their time it is likely that they may be unavailable at critical times resulting in delays to your release. In this regard look-ahead planning is critical to minimize these road-blocks. In the next section we describe some of the work items that you would expect to have prioritized and decomposed into tasks during your workshop.

Ensuring Your Production Readiness

Let's explore each of the goals depicted previously in Figure 18.2:

- **Transition planning.** For sophisticated deployments into mission-critical production environments your Transition phase typically includes the requirement to create a detailed implementation plan. Sometime these deployments need to be completed in a small implementation window, usually overnight outside normal business hours. Many organizations plan their deployments for midweek so that in the event things do not go smoothly business and IT personnel are available the next day to troubleshoot any issues. Since these deployments are so time-critical it is not unusual to see deployment steps documented in detail with expected start and end times, dependencies, and responsibilities. These plans are often captured using simple tools such as word processors or spreadsheets. Rollback instructions are usually part of the plan as well. These plans can be complex, especially if data conversion and migration between technology platforms are involved.

- **End of lifecycle testing and fixing.** In the days leading up to solution cutover, when the existing release in production is replaced by the new release, the team may spend some time fixing final defects. The solution is "hardened" by focusing on defect fixing instead of adding new functionality. Your stakeholders may choose to accept the existence of some known low-priority defects in the current release. Outstanding defects remain on the work item list for prioritization with other work for the next release. If your organization follows a strict user acceptance testing (UAT) cycle-based approach, injecting defect fixes at the last minute may be strictly controlled especially during a testing cycle. Hopefully it will be unusual to find new defects in the Transition phase. An important metric for judging the effectiveness of your quality practices is to track the number of defects, by severity, found during the Transition phase as well as those found once the solution is running in production. As an aside, Scott has found this metric to be an important motivator to adopt agile methods over traditional ones.

- **Deployment testing.** For many traditional projects the actual deployment of the solution into production is fraught with risk and peril. Fortunately, teams using a continuous delivery approach will have been deploying into a production-like environment frequently, so this risk will have been greatly reduced.

- **Data migration preparation.** If your solution includes migrating from an existing system to a new platform you need to prepare to migrate the data from the old system to the new. Classically this involves creation of programs to extract the data from the old systems, transform them into a format suitable for the new platform, and then loading them into the new system. Creating and testing of these migration programs is an important part of this phase that may have been started in your Construction iterations. Note that if you adopted the practice of database refactoring these migration scripts will already be in place for the portion of your database schemas that you evolved. You also want to consider how to migrate your security model with its existing users and their authorizations to the new model.

- **Pilot/beta of the solution.** Betas or pilots are often deployed whereby the solution is given to a subset of your user base to obtain feedback based on actual usage in production. It is a strategy that mitigates many risks related to the following:

  - Surfacing new defects in the production environment for situations that could not be tested adequately in nonproduction environments.

  - Customer support requirements and processes. This risk is mitigated through a pilot with a smaller group of users.

  - Tuning production environment aspects such as servers, databases, networks, and security without the risk of affecting the entire user base at one time.

  - If there is a big problem with the deployment it is simpler to roll back.

- **Finalize documentation.** If your team has been practicing continuous documentation the majority of your documentation will be in place prior to transition. Supporting documentation may need to be finalized including user manuals, operations manuals, installation guides, disaster recovery documentation, system overview documents, and so on.

LESSONS FROM THE TRENCHES—CONSIDER DRESS REHEARSALS FOR CRITICAL DEPLOYMENTS

Julian Holmes, cofounder of UPMentors with Mark, has deep experience in agile coaching. He has found that in many regulated or mission-critical environments release rehearsals may need to be conducted and possibly recorded in a production-like environment by the personnel responsible for the actual deployment. These rehearsals may also include failover and disaster recovery testing. The goal of these rehearsals is to increase the chance of successful deployment.

Preparing Your Stakeholders for the Release

Deploying a system to your users before they are ready is not advisable. Communication needs to start far in advance of releasing the solution. In fact, regular communication to key stakeholders starts from the beginning of the project. As the project progresses, the frequency and detail of planning related to transitioning the solution to your customers should increase. Let's now discuss key components of communication and training that you should consider to prepare your stakeholders for the solution:

- **Communicate deployment to stakeholders.** Your stakeholders should be well prepared for any release of your solution. For some solutions there is a need to formalize communications to both internal users and external customers. The style and content of communications for these stakeholders could be quite different. You should consider the unique communication needs of these stakeholders:

  - **Operations.** They need to support the application by running jobs, performing backups and recoveries, and other hardware and software troubleshooting. In large environments it is often necessary to produce documentation to describe the deployment activities to move the solution into production and then provide this documentation to a service provider to perform the actual deployment.

  - **Marketing.** If the solution is a product some lead time may be required to distribute appropriate information to existing or potential customers.

  - **Other internal employees.** For some solutions the changes in business processes or job descriptions affect internal employees. They need to be aware and prepared for these changes.

  - **Regulatory bodies.** In some circumstances changes to solutions need to be communicated to regulatory bodies in advance of deployment.

  - **Project sponsors.** Sponsors of your project obviously need to be kept informed of your release plans.

  - **Change management bodies.** DAD recognizes that deployments in large enterprises are seldom possible without coordination with other projects that share services and data. Many organizations have committees, sometimes called change management boards, that meet regularly to review any new changes going into production to assess impact to other systems already in production. At this stage in the project, you will have been attending these meetings well in advance of going into production so there should be no surprise impacts to other projects.

  - **Governing body.** Your project's governing body, which may be your Project Management Office (PMO), should be made aware of the upcoming solution deployment. However, they should already be aware of your schedule as part of being continually involved with regard to your progress throughout the lifecycle. They will have been involved with the decision to proceed into the Transition phase as part of the milestone review for sufficient functionality at the end of the Construction phase. Agile governance is described in Chapter 20, "Governing Disciplined Agile Teams."

- **Train/educate stakeholders.** As part of preparing your stakeholders to accept the solution you should train and educate end users, support staff, operations staff, and more. This training may occur at any point in time, not just during the Transition phase, although it is best delivered on a just-in-time (JIT) basis. Solicit feedback on the consumability of the solution through pilot team training. The earlier you deliver the training, the better.

- **Prepare support environment stakeholders.** Production environments are usually supported by independent bodies that are keeping many systems up and running. There will also be a support system in place such as a help desk to support your customers. To ensure that a good service level is provided you typically need to help prepare these stakeholders for supporting your system:

  - **Help desk.** These people may be the first line of support to your customers. The process for capturing these incidents and allocating them to the appropriate support staff needs to be determined. On-call schedules need to be updated. We have found that many teams are often surprised to hear that they are expected to be on call when the system goes into production, so setting expectations early is good in this regard.

  - **Disaster recovery.** Most enterprises have procedures in place to recover from a sudden loss of the system. These procedures are usually tested periodically to verify that the systems can be recovered and brought back online in a timely fashion. Your documentation to install the system from scratch needs to be up to date and the procedures should be tested to ensure that the documentation is accurate and usable by operations personnel who may not be familiar with the details of your architecture.

You will likely have a checkpoint in this phase designated as the final "go-live" decision. This is called the Production Ready milestone in the DAD process framework. There is often an "entry criteria" document that specifies the conditions of acceptance by the stakeholders to make this decision as objective as possible. The list of conditions might include an acceptable number of defects of a certain severity outstanding, acceptable results of performance testing, adequate support documentation in place and procedures defined, deployment artifacts are ready, and approval from the business sponsor and possibly other key stakeholders to deploy the solution. More on milestone reviews in Chapter 20.

Deploying the Solution

At some point during your Transition phase you will choose to deploy your solution to your stakeholders. In fact, you may schedule multiple deployments in Transition if a phased deployment makes sense, such as in the case of delivery across geographies. In large organizations the capability to deploy solutions into production is carefully controlled. It is typical to require independent operations personnel to do the actual deployments. In these situations team members do not have access to production servers to deploy artifacts, run database scripts, and other deployment related activities.

Most solutions go through these steps to deploy their system into production. They often follow the implementation plan that lays out the detailed steps to perform these activities. For time-critical implementations, the plan may have steps broken down into start and end times, durations, dependencies, and responsibilities. The overall high-level activities might include the following:

- **Running of any batch jobs against the existing system.** It is typical to want to "close the books" on the transactions for the legacy system before migrating the data to the new system.

- **Backup of existing system.** In the event of an unsuccessful deployment there needs to be a backup.

- **Migrating source data to new formats or even to new technologies.** In our experience, migrating data from existing legacy systems to new technologies is seldom trivial. Earlier in the project data quality problems often surface and should have been fixed before this point, likely using database refactoring techniques. Data issues can result in failures of the data to be accepted by the new system due to violation of business or data integrity rules. If the system needs to be migrated during nonbusiness hours, there is a small window to extract, transform, and load (ETL) the data into the new system. Adequate testing of these activities well in advance of the Transition phase is obviously essential as it is a significant source of risk. Being able to roll back data changes is crucial if the deployment is not successful.

- **Deployment of solution artifacts to target environment.** The artifacts for running the new solution will have been built in advance of the "go-live" decision. They now need to be deployed to the target platform, and necessary configurations, such as server configuration, need to be performed.

- **Execute deployment testing.** Testing of the new system in production needs to take place to ensure that the solution is working as expected. This is often referred to as "smoke testing." Some organizations resist testing with real transactions in a production environment since it typically results in having to back out the business transactions afterward. However, it is better to go through this inconvenience than to have a customer discover a material problem and be faced with some business downtime and the embarrassment of having to roll back to the old system. Smoke testing such as this is often a requirement identified by your operations and support staff, and may be considered part of your overall DevOps strategy.

- **Back up the new solution.** The new system should be backed up and is typically stored off-site for disaster recovery purposes.

- **Make the new solution available to customers.** Often this can be as simple as redirecting a URL to the new solution to make the system "live."

- **Enable your support system.** Your support system, including your help desk, should now be ready to support the system should your stakeholders require it.

- **Communicate successful deployment.** Planned internal and external communications should be sent out at this point. Note that is it advisable to have communications prepared in the event that the deployment is unsuccessful that are ready to send if necessary.

Are Your Stakeholders Delighted?

After deploying your solution to your customers you will want to complete your Transition phase. Some people believe that a project is complete after we have "gone live," but from the point of view of your stakeholders this is rarely the case. Indeed, we know that a lot needs to happen before we turn over the keys for the new solution to the stakeholders and wish them luck. Sometimes "hot-fixes" need to be deployed to fix defects found by customers. It would be a mistake to disband the team the day after deployment in case this happens. In fact many activities typically need to be completed before the team can focus on starting a new Inception or Construction phase for the next release of the solution.

The lean community is fond of describing a goal of "delighting" the customer. It is not enough to have satisfied customers. DAD takes this one step further to suggest that we should strive to delight all stakeholders, not just end users. Wouldn't it be nice to delight the help desk, the shareholders, IT management, and the governing body?

At this milestone, called Stakeholder Delight, you should achieve the following:

- **Business stakeholder acceptance.** The business stakeholders are delighted with and accept the system.

- **Operations acceptance.** The people responsible for operating the system once it is in production are delighted with the relevant procedures, supporting documentation, and the running system itself.

- **Support acceptance.** The people responsible for supporting the system once it is in production are delighted with the solution, particularly the support documentation and relevant support procedures.

- **Cost and estimate acceptance.** The current expenditures are accepted, and reasonable estimates have been made for future costs.

Transition Phase Patterns

Several common strategies applied during the Transition phase seem to work well in practice, and several seem to work rather poorly in practice. The success of this phase is determined by your ability to understand and adopt the successful patterns appropriately and avoid the anti-patterns when you can. Let's begin with some patterns for success:

- **Short and sufficient.** If the quality of the solution has been adequately validated during the Construction phase your transition effort can be short. Look-ahead planning in areas such as creating the implementation plan, communication, and training can expedite transition. In some extreme cases the transition phase can consist of running your full regression test suite one more time and if successful someone running the deployment scripts. This can be on the order of minutes or hours. Of course for the Transition phase to be truly considered successful you must wait for confirmation of stakeholder delight.

- **Multiple iterations.** For some situations it may make sense to deploy your solution over several iterations during the Transition phase. Examples could include the need to deploy the solution to a geographically dispersed set of users or where the number of users is large and a scaled rollout makes sense. The case study in the next chapter shows an example of where this might make sense.

- **Proven deployment/installation.** If you have a solid continuous deployment practice in place as described in Chapter 15, "A Typical Day of Construction," your deployment to a production environment will go much more smoothly. It is often difficult to test your production deployments unless you have a production-like environment. Experience shows that if you do not test your deployment in such an environment there is a high degree of risk that the deployment will be troublesome.

- **Choose your release patterns.** In Chapter 10 we described various strategies for planning your releases and their cadences. Together, a set of planned releases constitutes a solution plan. The three phases of DAD have different goals depending on the stage of the project lifecycle. We want to make it clear that you have complete flexibility to introduce Inception iterations into your solution plan at logical points where there is a need to revisit or update the vision for the solution. Often this coincides with a funding gate. Similarly, since you want to deploy your system into the hands of your customer as frequently as possible you inject Transition iterations into the solution plan as often as makes sense. As you move more to an advanced DAD or lean approach your need for Transition iterations may actually disappear. The key point here is that you customize your mix of the three types of iterations in your solution plan based on your situation. Figure 18.4 shows examples of various patterns. The first pattern in this diagram is the Classic DAD Pattern, which appears in the DAD lifecycle diagram introduced in Chapter 1, "Disciplined Agile Delivery in a Nutshell." The second example in this figure shows a long project of many Construction iterations with one big deployment at the end. This is not an approach that we recommend as it has many of the risks of delivery that we see with traditional approaches. The third example shows one Inception phase with multiple releases. This example also illustrates that a Transition phase could happen at any interval that makes sense for the stakeholders, resulting in varying lengths of Construction. The last example shows a lean approach whereby we deploy as frequently as possible as part of the Construction phase. In this example we do not have timeboxed iterations, but rather deliver the solution to customers in a continuous stream as work items are implemented.

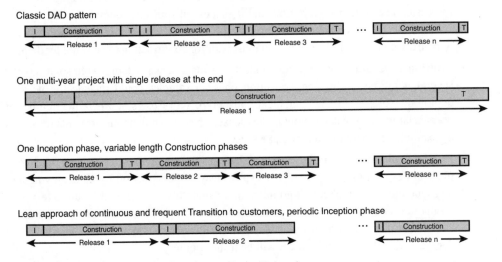

Figure 18.4   Examples of solution plans with multiple releases

---

LESSONS FROM THE TRENCHES—TRANSITION IS NOT JUST ANOTHER CONSTRUCTION ITERATION

We have both experienced some complex Transition phases on large projects. On one such project Mark had to adapt the classic agile approach to handle some of this complexity. On this particular project the solution included both introducing a new software application as well as changed business processes to support the new application. This is an example of why we talk about delivering "solutions" rather than "software" in DAD. The stakeholders for this solution included external customers that used the application in branches across Canada as well as internal employees who used the application for other aspects of the workflow. New business processes were designed to use the new software, and because it was a unionized environment, requiring new job descriptions introduced a number of issues not typical of most projects.

So we supplemented our agile team in the late Construction iterations with team members dedicated to internal and external communication work items, as well as some specific items to work with the union. These team member specialists provided updates at our daily coordination meetings. Their work was also planned on the taskboard with everyone else's, with special colors of sticky notes for their tasks. This was a successful approach. They immediately grasped the value of the agile approach to planning. Communicating their work and plans to the team, as well as the meeting observers (chickens in Scrum parlance) proved extremely valuable and surfaced issues that were dealt with in a timely fashion.

Transition Phase Anti-Patterns

There are several common *anti-patterns* that we've seen agile teams exhibit during this phase:

- **Not having a productionlike environment for integration, acceptance, and deployment testing.** Replicating a production environment for testing purposes can be costly, but there are some alternatives for simulating production. If deployment and configuration scripts need to be changed materially between the testing and production environments there is a risk of it not being done properly when it matters.

- **Not having an agreed upon set of entry criteria for going "live."** We have both seen situations where the decision to go into production was delayed because the project had not understood the entry criteria to obtain approval for going into production such as having a documented and tested disaster recovery plan. It is important to negotiate and document these criteria early in the project, preferably in Inception to properly prepare for the Production Ready milestone.

- **Requests for new functionality.** As the date for going live approaches users often realize that they have forgotten a feature or want to make last-minute cosmetic changes. Set expectations in advance with your users that these changes cannot be made in Transition and that anything new will need to be assigned to the next release once you're in Transition.

- **Releasing the system to unprepared users.** Unfortunately users are often caught by surprise when the system is actually deployed to them. For some this stems from disbelief that the system will actually be delivered based on a history of missed deadlines in the past using traditional approaches. Regular demonstrations of the solution help your stakeholders to understand that the system is indeed coming and to prepare accordingly.

- **Lengthy integration and user acceptance testing (UAT) cycle in Transition.** Traditional approaches often have a long testing phase at the end of the project prior to going into production. This can add months to your schedule and is certainly not consistent

with frequent deployments to customers. As described in Chapter 15, running preproduction integration testing and UAT in parallel with your development during your Construction iterations minimizes the length of end-of-lifecycle testing.

- **Transferring responsibility for maintaining the system to a maintenance group.**
  Disciplined agile development teams follow through. In our view transitioning a solution to a support or maintenance team so that the delivery team can work on the next
  release or another project is not a good idea. This is a disincentive to create well
  designed solutions that are easy to maintain.

- **Moving all of your developers to another project at the end of Construction.** Keeping teams together enables you to retain high productivity levels. It takes times for teams
  to gel, for team members to learn how they can work together effectively. An all-too-
  common mistake in traditional IT shops is to disband solution delivery teams at the end
  of a project, making the individuals available to become members of new project teams.
  The problem with this is that these new teams need to now suffer through the process of
  gelling again. A better approach is to keep effective teams together, or more realistically
  to keep a core portion of the team together to move on together either to the next release
  of the solution they just produced or to begin working on addressing a new opportunity.

- **Not investing in stakeholder training.** All but the simplest of systems require training.

- **Believing that installation is going to be easy.** Installation problems witnessed by the
  user can dramatically reduce their perception of the quality of your solution even though
  the installation process may have nothing to do with the solution itself.

Concluding Thoughts

The activities in your Transition phase are unique to the type of solution that you are deploying
and the degree of governance for managing deployments in your organization. You should take
some time at the beginning of the phase to do an iteration planning workshop to plan your work
for the phase. Some work related transition activities such as procuring production environments,
preparing a support team, and training for the new system and potentially changed business
processes need to occur during your last Construction iterations prior to the Transition phase
actually starting.

Recognizing the complexities and interdependencies of deploying mission critical solutions in large enterprises, DAD takes a disciplined approach to managing your solution's deployments. We recognize the need to collaborate continuously with stakeholders external to the team
to prepare and minimize the deployment risks. Adequate attention to testing your deployments
before the Transition phase starts helps to ensure that your deployment goes smoothly.

You will want to adapt your release patterns for your solution to take advantage of more
frequent deployments as you become capable. As discussed in Chapter 20, an agile governance

framework needs to be in place if you are to be successful with frequent deployments. As your DAD capability increases you may consider continuous deployments into production, sometimes referred to as continuous delivery, by adopting the advanced DAD or lean approach. Using this lean approach to solution delivery you may no longer require a specific Transition phase.

Additional Resources

For more detailed discussions about several of the topics covered in this chapter:

- **Release practices.** Scott has described many of these concepts in his book *The Unified Process: Transition and Production Phases* (Elsevier Publishing, 2001). The book *Software Release Methodology* by Michael E. Bays (Prentice Hall, 1999) gives a solid overview of release management practices as does the book *Release It!* by Michael T. Nygard (Pragmatic Bookshelf, 2007).

- **Data migration.** Data migration practices are described in *Practical Data Migration* by John Morris (British Informatics Society, 2006) and *Refactoring Databases* by Scott Ambler and Pramod Sadalage (Addison-Wesley, 2006).

- **Surveys.** We referenced results from the November 2010 Agile State of the Art survey, at ambysoft.com/surveys/agileStateOfArt201011.html.

CHAPTER 19

Case Study: Transition Phase

This chapter describes the Transition phase of the AgileGrocers Point of Sale (PoS) case study. We want to provide an example of what to expect in a *typical* Transition phase, but from our experience there is no typical transition. They all are different. As we have said in the other case study chapters your approach will differ depending on many things, such as your culture, need for governance, capabilities, and experience.

The team has just completed our 12 two-week iterations. All the functionality has been delivered for the PoS system, as well as for the new back office system.

For the Transition phase a small team is responsible for rolling out the system. Ann, Katherine, and Gunther are not part of the Transition team. They do, however, continue work on items remaining in the work item list. These items will be deployed in a subsequent release of the system several months from now. Figure 19.1 shows the team as it looks when we started the Transition phase.

As described in Chapter 1, "Disciplined Agile Delivery in a Nutshell," each phase and iteration has a 3C rhythm of coordinate, collaborate, and conclude. For our case study, the initial coordination activities focus on planning the activities related to the rollout over the eight-week Transition phase.

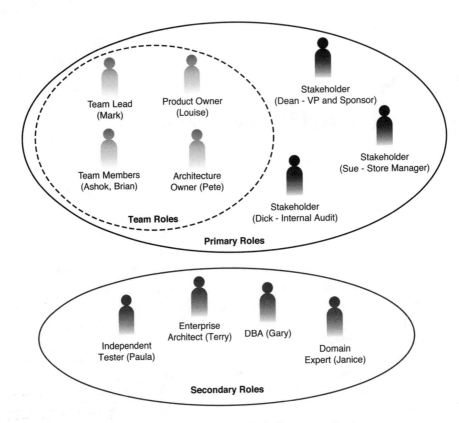

Figure 19.1   Roles for the Transition phase of the AgileGrocers project

Planning the Phase

On Monday, the team meets at 9:00 a.m. for two hours to plan the Transition phase.

Mark: I have displayed on our projector a breakdown of goals by week for our eight-week Transition phase (see Table 19.1). As you can see from this schedule, we will spend the first two weeks fixing remaining defects, preparing our trainers, and doing our final user acceptance testing. We need to ensure that the solution meets the requirements of our acceptance criteria as set out by Dean (the VP) and Dick (the internal auditor) when the vision was defined in the Inception phase at the beginning of the project. Some of the criteria changed during the project as we discovered together what was actually possible to achieve over our tight project timeline. During the remaining six weeks we will deploy the system into ten stores a week.

Table 19.1 Goals for Each Week of the Transition Phase

Week	Goals
1	Fix remaining low priority defects. Establish support process and on-call schedule.
2	Independent final regression testing in User Acceptance Environment. Final build of software and installation scripting complete. Install of software and configuration of equipment for ten stores. Use these ten systems for "train the trainer" workshops. Friday—retrospective and improve process.
3	Ship the equipment for the four stores that will be part of the first installation. Setup of system on Sunday, go-live and support of four stores on Monday. On-site support by trainers Monday–Thursday.
4	Install of software, configuration, and shipping of equipment for ten stores. Setup of system on Sunday, go-live and support of ten stores on Monday. On-site support by trainers Monday–Thursday.
5	Install of software, configuration, and shipping of equipment for ten stores. Setup of system on Sunday, go-live and support of ten stores on Monday. On-site support by trainers Monday–Thursday.
6	Install of software, configuration, and shipping of equipment for ten stores. Setup of system on Sunday, go-live and support of ten stores on Monday. On-site support by trainers Monday–Thursday.
7	Install of software, configuration, and shipping of equipment for ten stores. Setup of system on Sunday, go-live and support of ten stores on Monday. On-site support by trainers Monday–Thursday.
8	Install of software, configuration, and shipping of equipment for ten stores. Setup of system on Sunday, go-live and support of ten stores on Monday. On-site support by trainers Monday–Thursday. Friday—Trainer and team celebration hosted by Dean (VP).

Ashok: Is this planning session for the entire eight-week phase?

Mark: No, we will review our overall plan for the Transition phase today, but do our detailed planning for the next two-week period, similar to what we did for construction iterations. We will decompose our higher level work items into tasks as we usually do. These two weeks coming up are ideal to plan as a regular iteration as the work for the most part is similar to the other iterations. The work items that we need to complete can be planned in the normal self-organizing fashion, whereby the team members can decide among themselves who will do what work. The work, like our previous agile work, can be difficult to estimate yet is time critical, so we are counting on the team to work together to get it done.

Brian: Why are we only planning the first two weeks in detail then?

Mark: In the third week we are "live," and for the rest of the Transition phase we are simply executing the rollout tasks. This can be planned and executed in a traditional project fashion. These weeks need not be planned using the just-in-time agile fashion that we have been using in the Construction iterations. We can indeed do up-front planning for the last six weeks of project work with a degree of certainty. Granted, although we have prepared for this deployment it is still possible that things can happen that could cause delays in our project. If so we will deal with them as they arise just like during any other part of the project.

Ashok: How about finishing fixing any remaining defects? Where is that on the work item list?

Mark: The acceptance criteria, as described in our initial vision, indicates that we must fix all Priority 1 and 2 defects. We are permitted to go live with the system with the lower priority defects still outstanding. It is difficult to plan what new defects will be discovered in the next week, so it is difficult to estimate this work. However, you and Brian will be dedicated in the first two weeks to cleaning up these defects. Pete (the architecture owner) will create the final build and deployment artifacts. He will also update the installation scripts.

Louise: I am concerned about our ability to be able to start doing installs onto the store systems in week 3. On my last project it took a long time to write the installation programs and then when they tried them they seemed to not work properly. A file was left behind, or the wrong version of something was installed.

Mark: Well, fortunately, using our agile approach, we have been practicing installation constantly since the beginning of the project. So there is not much risk in creating the production deployment artifacts.

Louise: How are we scheduling our rollout to the 54 stores?

Mark: Since there may still be unforeseen problems with the installation we are only rolling out to four stores in week 3. Then we will start doing ten store installations per week for each of the next five weeks.

Mark continues: The same can be said about our final user acceptance testing. It is low risk and won't take long since we have been doing continuous integration testing throughout the project. Finally, our documentation effort at this point in the project is minimal since we have been practicing continuous documentation since the first iteration.

Louise: I understand that Sue is training our trainers this week. Why is this not on the work item list?

Mark: While Sue is definitely critical to the success of our Transition, this is a predictable task that will be done outside our team. We need to be aware that it is happening, but we only put items on our work item list that our own team is responsible for.

Louise: I know that a Scrum backlog typically contains only user stories related to functional requirements. Since we have finished building the system I see that the only work items left related to requirements are defect fixes. The rest of the requirements seem to be technical in nature.

Mark: Precisely. This is the flexibility that we have with the DAD work item list. It contains all types of work items.

Pete: Yes, I have lots of things that need to be done to get this system into production. Data migration and security is a real nuisance.

Mark: How so?

Pete: Well, we need to change the schema of the head office corporate database and import some data, such as user ID information, store email addresses, as well as other changes to some production tables. We are not allowed to make the changes ourselves.

Mark: How are they getting implemented then?

Pete: The good news is that we have made the changes in our development and systems integration environments. We have scripts to make the schema changes and import the data. Since we have been recreating the database periodically using these and other scripts, we know that they work. We just have to provide the scripts to the release team, and they will run them for us at the end of next week.

Mark: It is comforting that the risk related to running this script for the first time in production has been mitigated by working out the kinks in our other environments. To make these changes in production, we have to document a Request for Change and provide it to the release team with the scripts, as well as scripts to back out the changes should any problem occur. I took care of this paper work last iteration.

Mark continues: It was a good thing that we did some look-ahead planning where we met with the release team to find out what we needed to do. They require a two-week lead time for these types of changes, and if we hadn't planned ahead we might have not been able to go into production on time.

Once Mark and Louise have reviewed the items on the work item list with the team (see Table 19.2), they decompose the highest priority items that they intend to finish in the first week (in the same manner as described for the Construction iterations in Chapter 17, "Case Study: Construction Phase"). Mark creates items in RTC as usual, and then the team spends the rest of the day working on these items.

Table 19.2 Highest Priority Work Items (a Subset of the Work Item List) for the Transition Phase

Work Item
Finish installation scripts.
Finish user manuals.
Create final build and deployment artifacts.
Provide scripts to release to change tables in production environment.
Provide scripts to release to import user data into production environment.
Provide implementation plan, deployment artifacts, and installation scripts to operations team.

(continued)

Table 19.2   Highest Priority Work Items (a Subset of the Work Item List) for the Transition Phase (continued)

Work Item
Review plan with operations team.
Defect—Date format is incorrect on receipt.
Publish store newsletter announcing availability of new system.
Defect—Incorrect price being received from head office item file.
Establish on-call schedule for support.
Record YouTube video of interview with president announcing rollout of new system.
Configure firewall.
Finalize contract for store off-site backups.
Ship manuals to stores.
Update disaster recovery documentation.
Set up production message queues.
Create additional indexes on databases.
Steering committee meeting to make "go-live" decision.
Execute "go-live" for cutover of back office system into Production.

As in the Construction iterations, the team has a daily coordination meeting to plan their day's work. An iteration burndown is used to track the team's work for the first two weeks.

Collaborating to Deploy the Solution

While the team struggles a bit in the first two weeks to get their planned work completed, the burndown helps keep people motivated, focused, and on track. Due to the repeatable and predictable nature of the rollout to the rest of the stores for the remaining six weeks, the tasks were planned using a traditional work breakdown structure.

There were, however, some unforeseen events during the rollout. In week 3 some employees from each of the four stores that had training sessions did not show up due to personal holidays or other reasons. Apparently they were not aware of the upcoming training. In one store they did not even have enough cashiers show up for the training to open the store on Monday with the new system. As a result the trainers actually had to work as cashiers for the first two days until the cashiers were ready to use the system. This was a learning experience, and the team decided that they needed to set expectations better with the stores regarding their training plans. They immediately sent out a training schedule to all stores and decided that they would follow up with a call the Monday before each installation to confirm attendance of the employees for their training sessions. Also in week 3 several stores planned for conversion in week 4 indicated that they had not had enough notice and that they could not accept the new system. These stores had to be rescheduled for different weeks, the equipment diverted to other stores, and travel arrangements for the trainers rebooked.

On Monday of week 4 Canada observed its Beaver Day[1] statutory holiday. The team members who did the scheduling of the store installations forgot about the holiday and booked travel arrangements for the store trainers anyway. The trainers did not appreciate that they had to not only work on the Sunday of the holiday weekend but also had to stay there during the holiday while waiting for the store to open the next day before they could start their training. There was at least some consolation in their being able to experience the traditional Beaver Day parade and fireworks display in a different town.

AgileGrocers' Delight

On the last Friday of the project Dean, the VP and sponsor of the project, threw a party to celebrate the project's success. The development team, trainers, and those outside the project who contributed to its success were invited.

Dean gave a speech thanking all those in attendance for their efforts.

Dean: I am really proud of what together we have achieved. Based on my experience with other traditional projects, I thought that this new system would be just another late and over budget PoS. But actually this is a great solution, and I am delighted with the result! We came in on budget and on schedule. We didn't get all of the functionality that we eventually will need, but we got the most important things done. As a result we will have happier customers, with shorter lines in the stores. We were not able to complete our new sales promotion scheduling feature for this release, but I understand that the team is starting work on it next week after we run a one-day Inception phase to update our vision for the next release. With our new sales promotion capabilities, we will be able to respond to competitors' pricing much more quickly than in the past. And using our new technology and a more reliable system, we will save a lot on maintenance costs next year.

Despite some logistical problems during the early weeks of the store system rollout, I was amazed at how smoothly the deployment went. I was delighted with the quality of the solution that your team delivered, and that our independent final user acceptance testing turned up so few defects. I guess that using the continuous integration, testing, and deployment really paid off and reduced our deployment risk significantly.

---

1. Beaver Day celebrates the historical fact that much of Canada was explored, and then exploited, to support the growing fur trade with Europe in the 1700s and 1800s. Beaver was the most popular fur traded, used for coats and hats for wealthy Europeans and in some cases corsets for royalty. To this day the Canadian 5-cent piece, the nickel, shows a beaver on the back face, and the beaver is Canada's national animal. Beaver Day is held every year on the day immediately following March 31st.

One thing I really enjoyed was seeing the software evolve and seeing the new capabilities demonstrated every two weeks. It was much better than reading requirements and specification documents, and arguing about whether the features that we asked for met these specifications. Louise tells me that it is a less stressful experience for her, knowing that she could change her mind on requirements and priorities without going through a painful change request process. Being able to juggle priorities as we went along meant that we got the best bang for our buck.

I have decided to fund another release of this project to incorporate the remaining features that did not make it into this release. As well we need to continue the rollout of our existing version to the remaining stores. At some point the new stores need to be upgraded to the new release, and I am sure that will carry some challenges with it. However, I now feel confident that the risk of this can be managed appropriately using a DAD approach. I would like to keep the existing team in place for development of the next release and to support any defects should they arise with the new system. Thank you all again!

LESSONS FROM THE TRENCHES—DETERMINING WHEN YOUR PROJECT ENDS

Mark Kennaley, president and principal consultant of Fourth Medium Consulting and author of SDLC 3.0, weighs in on when a project is really over. "The question of when the project is over and when Production begins I believe can be found by answering the question of when does capital expense (Capex) cease and operations expense (Opex) begin from a financial perspective. In my experience this is a key point of consideration regarding the temporary structure of a project and its governance milestones. If you look at 'early life support' in ITIL, it is part of Opex, post project and part of sustainment. In my experience, if an organization is taking a product lifecycle approach, then the sustainment/maintenance team is seeded with some expertise from the project team to ensure that the biz is not left in a lurch. However, this team is working from a different budget. So this would point to the milestone of 'delighted stakeholder,' which would hopefully be achieved (at the latest) after early life support within operations."

Concluding Thoughts

This case study illustrated some of the things that can occur during the process of transitioning the solution to the customers. This small project was a straightforward deployment. For simple, stand-alone projects, deployment can indeed be simple, but in many cases it is not. Mainstream agile methods tend to trivialize the effort of releasing the system to the customers. But in our experience, on large multimillion dollar projects, going into production can be extremely complex. As described in the previous chapter, managing issues such as high-availability deployments, security concerns, release planning and transition, customer support, and communications to stakeholders can be difficult to plan and execute. In DAD we recognize that these activities are markedly different from those of a typical Construction iteration. For this reason it makes sense to have a separate phase to acknowledge this reality.

Governing Disciplined Agile Teams

Is your governance strategy designed to enable the work or control the workers?

Governance establishes chains of responsibility, authority, and communication in support of the overall enterprise's goals and strategy. It also establishes measurements, policies, standards, and control mechanisms to enable people to carry out their roles and responsibilities effectively. You do this by balancing risk versus return on investment (ROI), setting in place effective processes and practices, defining the direction and goals for the department, and defining the roles that people play within the department.

Let's begin with some bold claims:

- **Bold claim #1:** Agile teams are significantly easier to govern than traditional teams.
- **Bold claim #2:** Traditional approaches to governance are guaranteed to harm agile teams.
- **Bold claim #3:** Disciplined Agile Delivery (DAD) teams must demand good governance by their organization.

For many "agilists" governance is a dirty word that isn't used in polite company. For many information technology (IT) professionals, agile or not, governance has been the primary justification of many obvious dysfunctions throughout their careers. Like it or not, every IT delivery project is governed in some way—it may not be explicit, it may not be effective, but there is governance of some sort going on. Furthermore, considering breach of trust events surrounding companies such as Lehman Brothers, Enron, and Worldcom to name a few there has been a clear movement within the business environment toward better governance. This mindset has seeped into the IT world too. Given the choice between being governed effectively and being governed ineffectively, wouldn't effective governance that reflected the situation you find yourself in be preferable? This chapter shows how to govern DAD teams in an appropriate manner that actually enhances their activities.

Governance and management are two different things. Governance looks at a team from the outside, treating it as a system that needs to have the appropriate structure and processes in place to provide a stream of value. Management, on the other hand, occurs inside the team and ensures that the structure and processes are implemented effectively. The DAD process framework characterizes governance as an element of enterprise awareness from the team's point of view because governance looks at the team from the outside.

Figure 20.1 shows a mind map of the structure of this chapter. We describe each of the topics in the map in clockwise order, beginning at the top right.

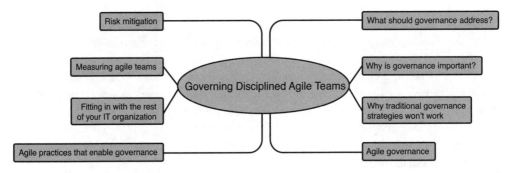

Figure 20.1   Outline of this chapter

THE BIG IDEAS IN THIS CHAPTER

- Effective governance in knowledge-based endeavors is based on motivation and enablement, not command and control.
- Agile project teams must be governed in an agile manner; a traditional strategy only increases project risk.
- Agile teams are significantly easier to govern than traditional teams, but only if the people doing the governance are willing to act appropriately.
- Effective metrics strategies focus on automated gathering supplemented with a few manually gathered measures as needed.

What Should Governance Address?

To understand what governance should address there are two issues to explore. First is the scope of your governance strategy and second are the issues that governance strategies should address. Figure 20.2 depicts various governance scopes and their relationships that your enterprise should consider. At the highest level is corporate governance, which as the name suggests, focuses on your organization in its entirety, including IT and the business division(s) that it supports. Your IT governance strategy in turn should address a range of issues, each one of which has its own governance strategy that reflects the overall IT governance strategy (which in turn reflects your corporate governance strategy). The focus of this chapter is delivery governance, and more specifically the effective governance of DAD project teams. This governance strategy is shaped by the parallel governance strategies surrounding your operations and support efforts, data administration, security, how IT investments are made, and by major technology infrastructure initiatives such as services (sometimes called SOA governance) and your internal cloud.

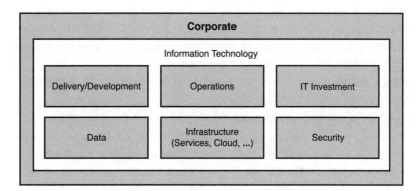

Figure 20.2   Scope of governance strategies

Your governance program may address a range of issues:

- **Team roles and responsibilities.** Your IT organization is likely organized into a collection of teams or groups, such as delivery teams, a data administration group, an operations team, a support team, a project management office (PMO), and many others. Each of these teams has a role to play and a collection of responsibilities to other teams they must fulfill. Sometimes team responsibilities are referred to as service level agreements (SLAs). For example, within your organization you may decide that a DAD team is responsible for producing a consumable solution in an incremental manner that meets the evolving needs of stakeholders in a timely and cost-effective manner. Your data administration team is responsible for supporting development teams, responding to database change requests within 24 hours, and fulfilling 90% of appropriate changes within three days. Before you fall on the ground laughing, this is in fact possible even in complex environments with the adoption of database refactoring techniques. Our advice is to have well-defined roles and responsibilities for teams and to let them self-organize to determine how they will fulfill those roles and responsibilities.

- **Individual roles and responsibilities.** Your governance strategy often defines the roles and responsibilities taken on by people within your organization. People are judged, and hopefully rewarded, based on their ability to fulfill these roles and responsibilities effectively. The challenge is that the roles and responsibilities vary based on the overall role of the team(s) that people are a part of and the process followed by the team. For example, an enterprise architecture team has different roles than a delivery team. A DAD delivery team has a certain set of roles and responsibilities, see Chapter 4, "Roles, Rights, and Responsibilities," which are similar but different from those on a Scrum development team, which in turn differ from a Unified Process (UP) delivery team and different again from a traditional delivery team. Our advice is to keep individual roles and responsibilities as simple and straightforward as possible, to support overlapping responsibilities between roles, and to allow people to determine what they'll do within their teams in a self-organizing manner.

- **Decision rights and decision making processes.** Your IT governance framework should specify a decision rights and accountability framework that encourages desirable behavior in the use of IT. From a delivery point of view the challenge is to create an environment that results in the development organization performing in such a way that business goals are met. This framework must reflect the fact that individual teams have their own unique business goals to meet that should reflect the overall organization's goals (another aspect of enterprise awareness).

- **Governing body.** Your governance strategy should define who performs the actual governance—a group of people often referred to as your governing body, governance board, or simply the governors—and how the group itself will be governed. This group often has rotating membership to ensure that the governance strategy remains fresh and to spread the work among a greater range of people. In some organizations the project management office (PMO) takes on the responsibility of governance, but we find that results in a narrow focus that often shortchanges the needs of stakeholders. Our advice is to have a range of people in your governing body, several of whom should be senior stakeholders. Furthermore some if not all of the governors must be familiar with the realities of how DAD teams work in practice because if you don't understand what you're governing you can't possibly govern it effectively.

- **Exceptions and escalation processes.** No governance program can be all encompassing in that it defines rules and guidance for all situations. Furthermore people and teams don't always work well together, so there is a need for a strategy to handle any problems that do arise. Our advice is for team leads to be constantly on the lookout for any problems between people and to help them resolve the problems as quickly as possible. When the issue is between teams they should strive to first resolve the issue by working with the team lead/manager on the corresponding team(s). When this doesn't work then they should approach the governing body for help. In the case of potential exceptions our advice is similar. For example, perhaps your team believes that they need to adopt a new product that isn't on your organization's technology roadmap. You should first ask yourself if you really need this technology and then if so work with the team responsible for making this decision, in this case your enterprise architecture team, and negotiate a strategy with them. Only if this fails, and if you still believe in your cause, should you escalate to your governing body.

- **Knowledge sharing processes.** An important aspect of enterprise awareness is for teams to understand the need to share their lessons learned with other teams. But how should you do this? Your governing body should provide mechanisms for doing so, perhaps supporting social media tooling such as IBM Lotus® Connections or online documentation tools such as shared wikis. You may also have knowledge sharing strategies, such as internal conferences (both of us are available as external speakers for such events), ongoing education and training sessions, and internal magazines to name a few. Portfolio retrospectives, where key members from several teams attend the retrospective, are also a good option for many organizations.

- **Metrics strategy.** Your governing body should monitor and then guide IT project teams. Ideally the majority of these metrics are automatically generated by the tools used by people to do their regular jobs, thereby reducing or even eliminating the metrics collection burden on people. These measures should be fed into a data warehouse where they can then be displayed as needed by project and portfolio dashboards. In effect our advice is to apply the principles of business intelligence (BI) to your IT environment, a strategy IBM refers to as development intelligence (DI). However, some measures, such as stakeholder satisfaction ratings, may still need to be captured manually and input into your DI system. More on metrics and DI later in this chapter.

- **Risk mitigation.** The guidance and monitoring of risk mitigation activities is an important aspect of governance. The DAD process framework builds in some risk mitigation via its risk-value lifecycle, and as you saw in previous chapters suggests that you create, maintain, and most importantly work down a ranked risk list.

- **Reward structure.** Your organization compensates people for the work that they perform, and for exemplary work may even give people additional "bonus" rewards.

A challenge with agile teams is that because people collaborate closely with one another it can be difficult to identify when an individual has performed in an exemplary manner. Although people are clearly motivated by intrinsic rewards such as knowing that they've solved an important business problem or mastering a new skill, extrinsic rewards such as your pay are clearly critical—stop paying someone and see how long they stick around. Although the complexities of reward systems are beyond the scope of this book, the fundamentals are that you need to reward people fairly both in comparison with their coworkers and with other organizations that could potentially hire away your staff.

- **Status reporting.** Like it or not, your project team will likely be required to provide an indication of their status in some way to the governing body. An automated project dashboard goes a long way toward doing this, but your team may still need to provide a regular summary status report. For example, Scott is currently on a large geographically distributed team that has a sophisticated DI strategy in place, yet they still have a monthly operational review (MOR) call where subteams verbally summarize their current status.

- **Audit processes.** Verifying that teams are actually doing what they say they are doing, particularly when it comes to financial concerns and regulatory compliance, is an important part of governance. Team members may be required to keep track of the time that they spend on a project, not only so that costs can be allocated appropriately to the right "cost bucket" but also for tax reporting purposes—many countries allow organizations to claim some aspects of software development as R&D and thereby receive tax benefits for doing so. Furthermore, not every team is as honest as your team is. Scott once worked in an organization where an outsourced project team was billing for 20 extra people than they actually had on the team, and did so for a long time until caught as the result of a financial audit. Organizations working in regulatory environments, such as pharmaceutical companies, often have a team of internal auditors who perform surprise audits on their own teams to ensure that they are in compliance with appropriate external regulations—far better to fail an internal audit and then fix the problems than to fail an external audit and be punished for the failure. Agile or not, a team ultimately has to meet legal and essential organizational needs, and audits help to ensure this.

- **Policies, standards, and guidelines.** Your governance strategy should indicate which guidance, such as coding conventions and user interface (UI) guidelines, should be followed by your team. This guidance is likely to be supported and evolved by other teams within your organization, and ideally should be easily consumable by your team and applicable to the situation that you face.

- **Artifacts and their lifecycles.** Your governance strategy should identify key artifacts— in the case of DAD teams executable tests, production source code, and supporting models to name a few—and then monitor how these artifacts evolve throughout the delivery effort. This is also true of other artifacts, such as coding guidelines owned by a centralized development community of practice that are developed and evolved based on feedback from delivery teams over many years; enterprise architecture (EA) models initially developed by your enterprise architects and evolved based on their learnings working with development teams to apply their EA strategy; and operational infrastructure models owned and used by your operations team to guide their decisions. The Agile Modeling (AM) methodology promotes a lean perspective that you should know who will consume an artifact and for what purpose. It is particularly important to understand what decision(s) an artifact supports.

Why Is Governance Important?

There are several important goals that your IT delivery governance should address. Effective IT governance should enable and motivate IT delivery teams to do the following:

- Sustain and extend your IT strategies and objectives, which in turn should reflect your corporate strategies and objectives.
- Determine how the company will execute its strategy by selecting and prioritizing the most valuable initiatives to undertake.
- Regularly and consistently create real business value.
- Provide appropriate return on investment (ROI).
- Deliver consumable solutions in a timely and relevant manner.
- Work effectively with their project stakeholders.
- Work effectively with their IT colleagues.
- Adopt processes and organizational structure that encourage successful IT solution delivery.
- Present accurate and timely information to project stakeholders.
- Mitigate the risks associated with the project.
- Empower teams to carry out their work.

Three supporting aspects of the previous list are worth noting. First, effective delivery governance should make it more likely that DAD project teams will be successful. Second, although every item in the list is important your organization has its own unique prioritization that causes it to focus on one or more items over the others. Furthermore, prioritization is likely to vary by project team given the unique situation that they face. No one governance strategy fits all situations. Third, notice how we say "enable" and "motivate" instead of "ensure" or "enforce." This is an important philosophy based on the observation that delivery professionals are intellectual workers, and as such it is more productive to convince them that it's best to work in a certain way (motivate them) and then make it as easy as possible to do so (enable them). For example, if you want developers to follow a certain set of coding conventions you could tell them to do so and let them know that their code will be inspected at some point for conformance to the programming guidelines. This is an example of command and control governance. Yes it works but can prove to be expensive and demoralizing in practice. A better approach is to share a sensible collection of coding conventions with the team, let them know that other teams are also following these conventions, discuss the value of having reasonably consistent code written across teams, and be open to suggestions for improving the conventions over time. This should motivate them to follow the conventions. To enable them to do so, provide them with static code analysis tools that automatically inspect the code and provide feedback to the programmers on the spot, providing an opportunity for them to learn and improve their programming skills (another motivator for many people). As an aside, pair programming is a complementary strategy that promotes continuous code inspection and peer reviews as a learning/coaching opportunity.

Although there are a lot of good reasons why delivery teams should embrace effective governance, it doesn't seem to be happening yet in practice. The Dr. Dobb's Journal December 2010 State of the IT Union survey found that 16% of respondents don't know what governance is and 38% indicated that their organization has no governance. We believe that these two statistics are indications that many organizations either haven't explicitly defined their governance programs or that the programs are poorly communicated to the people being governed. The good news is that 46% of respondents did know about their governance programs. Of them 41% (of the 46%) indicated that their governance strategy generally helped, 46% found it neither helpful nor harmful, and only 13% found the governance program was generally a hindrance. However, the DDJ November 2009 State of the IT Union survey found that only 11% of respondents indicated that their existing governance strategy works well with agile teams, an indication that their organization was likely to apply traditional governance strategies to their agile teams.

Why Traditional Governance Strategies Won't Work

Traditional governance focuses on managing and directing development project teams explicitly, using gateways and triggers that attempt to enforce rules and catch violations. An example of a traditional governance strategy is shown in Figure 20.3, which depicts lifecycle phases as rectangles and quality gates (milestones) as diamonds. This is different from the basic DAD lifecycle shown in Figure 20.4, let alone the lean/advanced version shown in Chapter 1, "Disciplined Agile Delivery in a Nutshell." Granted, if your organization currently has a traditional governance strategy in place it may have fewer milestone points than what is depicted in Figure 20.3. Then again it may have more—Scott once worked with an organization that had more than 40 governance checkpoints in its delivery process. The point is that it is easy to see a dissonance between traditional governance and the DAD delivery lifecycles.

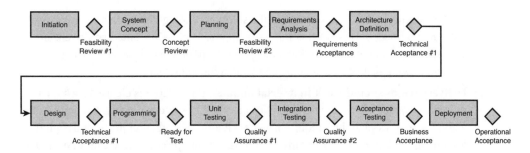

Figure 20.3   A traditional artifact-driven governance strategy

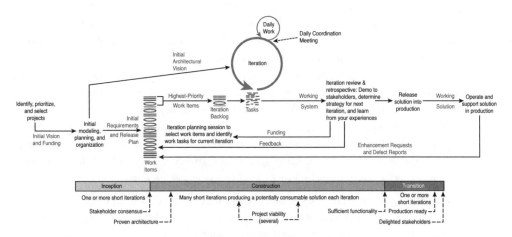

Figure 20.4   The Disciplined Agile Delivery (DAD) lifecycle (basic)

There are several common assumptions behind traditional governance strategies that make them an anathema for agile teams:

- **You can judge team progress from generation of artifacts.** This is observably not true. In Figure 20.3 the Technical Acceptance #1 quality gate focuses on reviewing the team's architecture model. Once the team passes through this quality gate the only thing that I could tell you is that an architecture model has been created and some smart people seem to like it. It's still possible that the architecture doesn't work. In your own experience, how many projects have you seen with an architectural strategy that was reviewed and accepted, only to see that team run into technical problems later in the lifecycle? Contrast this with DAD's Proven Architecture milestone where the team should have a working end-to-end skeleton of the solution running that implements technically risky requirements. This reflects the agile approach of being outcome-driven, in this case showing that the architectural strategy works in practice, instead of being artifact-driven, showing that you've documented your architectural strategy.

- **Delivery teams should work in a serial manner.** Figure 20.3 is clearly based on a traditional V-model lifecycle where activity-based phases occur serially. On agile teams, activities such as planning, requirements elicitation, testing, architecture, design, programming, and so on occur iteratively throughout the project. How can a governance strategy that assumes otherwise possibly be effective for agile teams?

- **You want teams to follow a common, repeatable process.** A common theme throughout this book is that project teams find themselves in unique situations. DAD teams vary based on team size, geographic distribution, and the domain complexity that they are addressing, to name a few scaling factors. Clearly a team of five people works differently and organizes themselves differently than a team of fifty or five hundred. Surely a collocated team works differently than a team that has people working from individual cubicles and than a team that is geographically dispersed across multiple locations. Surely a team that is building a Web site works differently than a team building a financial transaction processing system than does a team building an artificial intelligence-based system. Different teams, different situations. What you should really strive for are repeatable results, such as spending your IT investment wisely and providing solutions that meet stakeholder needs, not on following repeatable processes.

- **Projects should be driven by senior IT management.** This is an interesting philosophy, but it assumes that senior IT management is best suited to do this. Agile approaches are based on the concept that project teams should work in a stakeholder-driven manner. The philosophy is that stakeholders should be allowed to change their requirements, stakeholders should decide how their hard-earned money is being spent, and stakeholders should decide when they've received sufficient functionality for their investment.

A common governance strategy in traditional IT shops is an approach called Earned Value Management (EVM). The gist of EVM is that you track your actual schedule and budget results throughout a project against what you planned at the start of the project. The theory is that this comparison provides valuable information that you can use to steer the project and also judge the percentage of expected value you've earned to that point. So, if you've budgeted one million dollars for the project and have spent $400,000, then you should be about 40% through your expected schedule. You may even choose to assume that you've earned 40% of the value for your investment. This is clearly a false assumption for traditional teams because they don't have a potentially consumable solution until near the end of the lifecycle—cut funding 40% of the way into a traditional project and you've likely got a stack of documents and maybe some unfinished code. Not a lot of stakeholder value in that.

What about EVM for agile? It arguably makes a lot more sense to apply EVM to agile projects because agile teams are producing incremental value throughout the project. But because agile teams work in priority order they're earning more value earlier in the project—an agile team that is 40% of the way through the project budget may have produced 55% of the expected value by that point. Or, it may not have produced sufficient functionality yet to justify releasing it into production, so it too has arguably produced zero value for stakeholders at that point. Regardless, EVM doesn't seem to offer much for agile teams other than catering to governing bodies that require EVM.

What both Mark and Scott find frustrating is that many IT governance bodies within organizations seem to be oblivious to the impedance mismatch between their existing governance strategy and agile processes. They need to recognize that agile teams should be governed in an agile manner.

LESSONS FROM THE TRENCHES—TRADITIONAL FINANCIAL GOVERNANCE REDUCES AGILE BENEFITS

Richard Knaster, IBM Rational's worldwide agile practice manager, works with customers around the world to apply agile approaches. He worked with a large financial institution that allocated funding to projects once per year: "Due to the large budget of most projects, departments are very concerned to get the requirements right for the project. Consequently, it is not uncommon for them to spend a year gathering the high level requirements (e.g., epics and stories) and then squeeze the construction phase to just three months and then spend another six months to a year testing and deploying the software. Even though the construction is done in an agile manner, the surrounding traditional governance processes greatly reduce any gains from using agile practices. The resulting time to market is just as poor as before." An unfortunate example of inappropriate business governance practices motivating a "water-scrum-fall" approach.

Agile Governance

The previous section begs the question of how to govern agile teams? Our experience is that the most effective way to govern agile teams is to focus on collaborative strategies that strive to enable and motivate team members implicitly. For example, the traditional approach to motivating a team to provide good ROI would be to force them to develop and commit to an "accurate" project budget, and then periodically review their spending to ensure they're on track. An agile approach would be to ask the team to provide a ranged estimate of what they believe the cost will be so as to set expectations about future funding requirements. Then the team works in priority order as defined by stakeholders, visibly providing real business value through the incremental delivery of a potentially consumable solution. Costs are tracked via the team's burn rate (the fully burdened cost of the people on the team plus any capital outlays for equipment or facilities), and value is tracked by the stakeholders' continuing satisfaction (hopefully) with what the team is delivering for that cost. In short, a traditional approach often measures financial progress against a budget, whereas an agile approach seeks to maximize stakeholder value for their investment by always working on the most valuable functionality at the time.

We'd like to share the following philosophies about effective agile governance:

- **Trust and respect are the foundation of effective governance.** If you believe that the people governing you don't trust your judgment or respect you as a person what are the chances that you're going to do what they tell you? You may do just enough to make it appear that you're conforming to their strategy, but that will be it. Bottom line is that if the governors don't have a good relationship with the governed, effective governance is incredibly difficult to achieve.

- **Be stakeholder driven.** Your IT governance strategy should support your overall enterprise governance strategy. If your stakeholders' primary objective is to expand the business quickly this will motivate an IT governance strategy, which motivates delivery teams to provide timely and competitive solutions. If the primary business objective is to protect life, as it would be in a company building medical systems, the IT governance strategy would want to motivate delivery teams to build safe, high-quality solutions.

- **Collaboratively define your governance strategy.** An implication of trusting and respecting your staff is that you should actively involve them in defining how they will be governed. This may take a little longer than simply mandating a governance strategy defined by some really smart people sitting in their ivory tower somewhere, but it will have a much greater chance of being accepted and followed by the people being governed.

- **Be transparent.** Your governance team should have nothing to hide. The goals of the governance program, the way that the governing body works, the way that teams will be monitored, how people can seek help from the governing body, and all other aspects of your governance strategy should be clear and unambiguous. A governance program that is opaque will soon be perceived as unfair and soon after that people will begin undermining it.

- **Motivate, don't dictate.** Your governance strategy should focus on motivating people to "do the right thing" instead of dictating what that right thing is. The difference could be as simple as setting a goal, explaining why that goal is important, and letting teams determine how the best way to achieve that goal is. A dictatorial approach would set the goal and define how it will be achieved, for example, through using a new test management tool. The problem with this approach is that improving their testing strategy may not be the most pressing improvement need on every team, and some teams may have an existing test management tool that works well already.

- **Enable, don't enforce.** It is common human behavior to take the easiest path available. To increase the chance that people exhibit the behaviors desired by your organization your governance program should make it as easy as possible for people to have those behaviors. Furthermore, if it's hard to do things that aren't desirable, chances are they'll stick with what you want them to do.

- **Optimize the "IT whole," not the "governance part."** A common problem that governance programs can suffer from is that they effectively get out of control because, ironically, they're not governed well. An example of this is a governance program that requires teams to produce artifacts in a certain manner so that they can be easily reviewed by the governing body. For example—every team must produce an Architecture Overview Document using documentation template 1701-E.doc and submit it before the third Monday of the month so that it may be reviewed in time for the monthly architectural review meeting held on the fourth Thursday of the month. In this case the delivery teams are very likely doing a lot of extra work to conform to the governance process. The governance process may work smoothly when you look only at the activities of the governing body even though the overall IT organization suffers from needless work. Far better for the governing body to be flexible in the way that they monitor the architectural strategies of delivery teams. For example, architecture board members could simply pop into the team room at the request of the team and be walked through the architecture strategy by someone at a whiteboard. For another team it may be more appropriate to do a walk-through of a collection of models captured in a software-based tool. Different teams, different strategies for supporting them.

- **Optimize corporate performance.** Figure 20.2 made it clear that delivery governance is one part of IT governance that in turn is part of your overall corporate governance strategy. Your real goal should be to optimize your overall corporate performance through effective corporate governance.

- **Collaboratively set reasonable guidance.** The conventions, standards, and guidelines that delivery teams are expected to follow should be collaboratively defined by the teams following them. This doesn't imply that you rewrite your Web usability guidelines every time a new Web-based project comes along, but it does imply that when you first set those guidelines that actual Web developers and user experience (UX) people should be involved in their creation (or more realistically adoption and modification of existing guidelines that can be found online). It's also possible that subsequent teams will evolve the guidelines, particularly as new HTML standards are released, but that's evolutionary improvement, not complete rewrites.

- **Collaboratively define rights and responsibilities.** Although Chapter 4 suggests a collection of rights and responsibilities (R&R) that DAD teams should consider adopting, you should still adopt and tailor appropriately the R&R that fit well with your organization. For example, the responsibility to share information with your colleagues may not be appropriate if you're working on a top secret project for your country's military.

- **Be suitable to task.** The needs of the organization and of your team's situation determine how the level and style of governance are tailored. For example, delivery teams building life-critical software need a tighter governance approach than teams building an informational Web site. One governance size doesn't fit all. In general, the most effective governance strategies reflect what teams would naturally do or at least require the least deviation from such.

- **Automate wherever possible.** Technology can make your governance solution empowering and unobtrusive. The more you embed, or automate, your development governance practices through automation and culture, the more likely they are to be followed. For example, adopt development tools that are instrumented to record important events that are possibly of interest to someone. If your build tool records the time and results of a build (success versus failure, X tests run, Y tests passed, and so on), this information can be reported on by your project dashboard. If you include test coverage analysis as part of your build process, perhaps for nightly builds as this sort of analysis can be too time consuming for developer builds, and if the tool records important quality statistics, you can also report on this in your project dashboard. These are both examples of development intelligence. Furthermore, modern development tools can enact process rules programmatically, such as under what circumstances people can check code into your production build. For example, most of the time you may want anyone on the team to be able to check in source code. But when you are close to releasing into production you may want code to be checked in only by the team lead to reduce risk of inappropriate code getting into production.

LESSONS FROM THE TRENCHES—SUCCESSFUL AGILE REQUIRES AGILE GOVERNANCE

Paul Gorans is the Accelerated Solution Delivery (ASD) practice lead within IBM Global Services. Paul has spent the last 14 years delivering agile projects, agile assessments, planning and enabling agile transformations. His advice: "Let there be no doubt; transforming to an agile delivery approach is difficult. Companies or government agencies that have been in existence for decades have built up layers of deep and wide waste, many of them around governance. Business or IT governance constructs and processes that do not support new technology-centric go-to-market models and products must be either replaced or substantially evolved; otherwise, they increase risk on the agile projects."

Agile Practices That Enable Governance

Enough with philosophies, let's discuss some concrete strategies your governance strategy can promote that enable effective governance of DAD teams. These strategies, compared and contrasted in Table 20.1, are the following:

- **Value-driven lifecycle.** DAD teams should produce potentially consumable solutions every iteration, an improvement over Scrum's advice to produce potentially shippable software every iteration. At the end of each iteration what you have built should be "done" up to that point. If your project loses funding, you should be easily able to put what you have into production on short notice.

- **Risk-value-driven lifecycle.** This extends the value-driven lifecycle strategy to explicitly address common risks early in the lifecycle. This provides the extended team with explicit milestones centered on balancing risk mitigation and value creation. These potential milestone reviews are described in Table 20.2.

- **Explicit, lightweight milestone reviews.** Keep milestone reviews as simple and short as possible. For small collocated project teams milestone reviews could be as simple as a few people from the governing body, or their agents, visiting the team room and having the team spend an hour walking them through whatever is to be reviewed. For larger efforts this could be upwards to half a day and be held in a meeting room. Teams in regulatory environments may need to invest a bit more effort, particularly around creation and baselining of artifacts to be reviewed and recording of action items from the review. With adoption of common agile practices such as stakeholder demos and automated metrics, described later, there is less need for project status discussions in milestone reviews.

- **Agile enterprise teams.** Your enterprise teams, such as your enterprise architecture team, your data administration team, your governing body, your project management office (PMO), and others if they exist, must learn how to interact effectively with DAD teams. This isn't difficult in and of itself as they basically need to be willing to work in a collaborative, open, honest, flexible, and learning-oriented manner. The challenge comes when these same enterprise teams also need to work with other agile teams that may not be as enterprise aware, or with traditional teams that are more document/artifact focused than DAD teams. The implication is that enterprise teams must be sufficiently flexible to support several delivery paradigms in parallel. One strategy does not work well for all teams.

Table 20.1   Comparing Agile Governance Strategies

Strategy	Risks Addressed	Considerations
Value-driven lifecycle	Functional—Ensures that you're building something that reflects the needs of your stakeholders. Political—Visibly communicates that your team is on track and making progress. Financial—Increases the chance that you're spending stakeholder funds wisely. Governance—Stakeholders have the opportunity to steer the project, even to the point of cancelling the project if it appears it isn't viable.	Early in the lifecycle you may not have produced enough yet to get sufficient feedback. As a result if you get going in the "wrong" direction at first you may lose several iterations worth of work. Making a "no go" decision after an iteration demonstration is politically difficult.
Risk-value-driven lifecycle	The risks addressed by a value-driven approach (see above). Functional risk—Helps drive to stakeholder consensus early in the project. Technical risk—Motivates teams to prove the architecture with working code. Governance risk—Inclusion of explicit milestones throughout the lifecycle.	Keep milestone reviews as light as possible. The addition of explicit milestone reviews shouldn't been seen as an opportunity to burden teams with unnecessary overhead. The milestones should be clearly communicated to your stakeholders. Every project needs periodic checkpoints to ensure that expectations are being met and that the project is on track. Your organization may have existing milestones that need to be replaced by the ones described in Table 20.2 for DAD teams.
Explicit, lightweight milestone reviews	Governance risk—Stakeholders have an explicit opportunity to assess and then steer the team.	To keep these reviews lightweight you should focus on the goals, not on producing artifacts for reviews. Less ceremony is better, so try to keep the review process as simple as you can.
Agile enterprise teams	Financial risk—You decrease your financial risk when teams leverage existing assets. Technical risk—You decrease technical risk when you leverage existing working assets. Operational risk—DAD teams strive to produce solutions that fit into the existing infrastructure.	You may need to work with your enterprise teams to help them understand how agile teams work and how they can take advantage of agile strategies.

Table 20.2 Potential DAD Milestones

Milestone	Fundamental Question Asked	Risks Addressed	Considerations
Stakeholder consensus	Do stakeholders agree with your strategy?	Business—A common vision decreases the chance that conflicting goals derail your project. Political—Public agreement around the strategy makes it harder for a subgroup of stakeholders to dissent. Functional—Agreement around a shared vision focuses stakeholders.	Developing and then coming to agreement around a vision requires a short-term investment of time during the Inception phase to decrease your long-term risk, thereby increasing short-term project risk. Therefore you want to keep your Inception activities as lightweight as possible.
Proven architecture	Can you actually build this?	Technical—You know that your architectural strategy addresses your key technical requirements. Political—People with competing technical visions for your project cannot reasonably claim your strategy isn't viable.	Proving the architecture with working code requires that the people involved with formulating the architectural vision have the development skills required to do so. Some traditionalists may still believe that reviewing an architecture model is sufficient, an indication that they require additional coaching in agile principles.
Project viability	Does the project still make sense?	Business—Determines that the solution makes strategic sense. Technical—Determines that the technical strategy remains viable. Operational—Determines that there is still operational capability to run the solution. Political—Publicly addresses project feasibility and confirms continuing support for the project.	Effective viability reviews should address overall project feasibility. The business environment may have changed, some aspects of the technical strategy may have shifted (perhaps a vendor of a key component has dropped support for it), the political environment may have shifted due to a reorganization, or the strategy may no longer be operationally feasible due to cuts within your operations department.

(continued)

Table 20.2   Potential DAD Milestones (continued)

Milestone	Fundamental Question Asked	Risks Addressed	Considerations
Sufficient functionality	Does it make sense to release the current solution?	Business—Determines that sufficient incremental value to stakeholders has been achieved. Operational—Determines that the operations group is willing to accept a new release.	This milestone is sometimes referred to as minimally marketable release (MMR). There are several key questions to address at this milestone: Is the value added to the solution since the last deployment greater than the cost of releasing the new version? Is the new functionality sufficiently complete to justify deployment? Is the operations staff able to accept a new release of the solution at this time? It is important that acceptance criteria for transitioning the system into production have been agreed upon far in advance of this milestone.
Production ready	Will the solution work in production?	Operational—Verifies that the solution is of sufficient quality to deploy.	The operations and support staff must be convinced that the solution is of sufficient quality to be released *and* the new release will not cause harm to other solutions currently in operation.
Delighted stakeholders	Are stakeholders happy with the deployed solution?	Business—Verification that stakeholders are satisfied with the value they've received for their investment. Political—Public confirmation of the success of the project.	Business stakeholders are delighted with the solution and have officially accepted it. Operations staff responsible for operating the solution once it is in production are delighted with the relevant procedures and documentation. Support staff responsible for supporting the solution once it is in production are delighted with the relevant procedures and documentation. The governing body for the project has verified that expenditures are acceptable and reasonable estimates have been made for future costs.

LESSONS FROM THE TRENCHES—APPROPRIATE GOVERNANCE ENABLES TRUE SELF-ORGANIZATION

Part of effective agile governance as advocated by DAD is the enablement of true self-organization. This means that good governance recognizes that the team is in the best position to define their way of working and establish their approach based on their culture in consideration of the context of the project. One approach we see as forging a pragmatic direction for facilitating good governance for teams as they organize for a software endeavor is with the expert system being built by Software Development Experts (www.software-development-experts.com). According to CTO Mark Kennaley, product architect for this SaaS-delivered system, "our experience with lean and agile transformation governance at an enterprise scale in industries like Insurance, Financial Services, Defense and Government, led us to develop the Software Development Practice Advisor (SDPA). Good governance is typically difficult to achieve at scale, where diverse organization microcultures and differing problem domains mean teams are likely to self-organize differently. Failure to give the boots on the ground, who have the most up-to-the-minute data on what works and what doesn't, the latitude to decide on the tactics to employ on their project is typically interpreted as command and control governance. This obviously leads to all sorts of change management issues. Having management prescribe the 'flavor of the month' on teams is a great example of the type of governance that teams will get if they don't demand good governance. We have found that teams following a balanced hybrid approach like Disciplined Agile Delivery are far more likely to self-organize successfully. Using DAD as a starting point within the system, management is afforded complete visibility into the self-organization process across the portfolio. We have found that that the net result is successful, true change and good governance 'steerage' of the organization towards modern software development practice."

Throughout the book we describe practices DAD teams may adopt that support their appropriate governance. These practices, compared in Table 20.3, are the following:

- **Coordination meeting.** The team meets for a few minutes, typically at the beginning of each day, to coordinate their activities. The team lead facilitates the meeting and is responsible for keeping it short and focused. This practice is often called a Scrum meeting or daily stand-up meeting.

- **Iteration demonstration.** On a regular basis, typically at the end of each iteration, the team either demonstrates the solution to key stakeholders or better yet lets stakeholders actually use the solution. The goals are to show completed work and to invite feedback regarding it. The team often captures new work items generated from this feedback. This practice is also called stakeholder demonstration or sprint demonstration.

- **All-hands demonstration.** On a regular basis demonstrate what you have produced to the larger group of stakeholders than you would normally work with in iteration demonstrations. Holding all-hands demonstrations at major milestone reviews is a common strategy. This practice is sometimes referred to as a showcase review.

- **Follow enterprise development guidance.** Standards and guidelines for the architecture, coding language, data storage, user interface (UI) design, and client-specific needs are defined and readily available to the team. If the guidance does not exist or is insufficient the team is empowered to select, create, or tailor the standards necessary to ensure consistent quality.

- **Retrospective.** This is a facilitated reflection meeting performed by the team, the goal of which is to identify potential areas of improvement. Retrospectives often last 30 to 60 minutes. In retrospectives we typically ask four questions: What went well? What could we improve on? What should we do differently next time? and What still puzzles us?

- **Work closely with enterprise professionals.** Enterprise professionals—such as enterprise architects, data administrators, and reuse engineers—should be actively involved with a development team, particularly in the beginning. Hands-on involvement is what is required, not just grand visions, detailed models, or the threat of compliance reviews. The goal is to ensure that the team leverages and enhances the existing infrastructure within your organization.

- **Development intelligence.** All project teams, including agile ones, should be monitored by your governing body. The basic idea of development intelligence (DI) is that the tools used by your team should be instrumented to record important events when they occur. For example, whenever a build is run your build tool could record basic information such as the date and time it was initiated, the time it took, the number of tests run, the number of successful tests, and so on. Your work item management tool could record when a work item is defined, when work begins on it, when the work is validated (if appropriate), and when it is marked done. This sort of information can be recorded in a data warehouse and later reported on using business intelligence (BI) tooling via a project or portfolio dashboard. In short, DI is simply BI for information technology professionals.

Fitting in with the Rest of Your IT Organization

Figure 20.2 showed the different scopes for governance. This chapter focuses on delivery governance, agile delivery governance to be exact, which is one aspect of your overall IT governance strategy. IT governance in turn is part of your overall corporate governance strategy. Your delivery governance strategy must reflect the constraints placed on it by these higher forms of governance, which is the topic of this section.

Table 20.3 How Common Agile Practices Support Appropriate Governance

Practice	Chapter(s)	Risks Addressed	Considerations
Coordination meeting	15	Organizational—Team members have a better idea of the current project status and what they need to do.	Coordination meetings are primarily an internal team governance strategy. External team governance is supported when project stakeholders, including members of the governing body, who want to understand the current team status, listen in during coordination meetings.
Iteration demonstration	16	Political—Demonstrations provide visibility to stakeholders and thereby help to manage expectations. Functional—Provides an opportunity for stakeholders to steer the project.	Key stakeholders frequently do not have time to carefully review and discuss the results of every iteration, implying that you may need to work with an evolving subset of stakeholders each iteration.
All-hands demonstrations	16	Functional—Ensures feedback from the complete range of stakeholders and validates your product owner truly represents them. Political—Helps set stakeholder expectations.	This is not a replacement for iteration demos nor is it meant to be a formal review, instead it is just a quick update and sanity check. A significant challenge that product owners face is that they have to represent a wide range of stakeholders, including business stakeholders and IT stakeholders. A product owner from the business side may struggle to represent IT stakeholders, and one from the IT side may struggle to represent the business effectively. An all-hands demonstration is a good opportunity to validate whether your product owner represents all stakeholders fairly.
Follow enterprise development guidance	6	Technical—Ensures that your team is working to the enterprise strategy. Technical—Promotes higher quality through consistent artifacts.	You should adopt existing guidance whenever possible and modify it according to the team and project needs. Teams can be motivated to follow the guidance through adoption of tooling such as code analysis tools that validate your conformance to the guidelines.

(continued)

Table 20.3   How Common Agile Practices Support Appropriate Governance (continued)

Practice	Chapter(s)	Risks Addressed	Considerations
Retrospectives	16	Process—Promotes process improvement within the team. Organizational—Enables opportunities for the team to work together more effectively.	Retrospectives primarily support governance within a team. However, when mechanisms exist within your organization to share potential improvements across teams, retrospectives can support IT-level governance.
Work closely with enterprise professionals	7, 8, 9, 15	Technical—Increases the chance that your team leverages existing infrastructure. Operational—Increases the chance that your team will produce a solution that fits into your existing infrastructure. Functional—Ensures that your solution reflects overall business goals.	An enterprise architect may be in the role of architecture owner for the team. It is not only possible but desirable to take an agile approach to enterprise architecture (EA). Having a viable EA, and just as important, an EA team that can work collaboratively with development teams to help communicate and evolve their vision, can have a significant impact on overall productivity. Delivery teams should consult with EAs regarding availability of reusable assets. Related to this, determine availability of existing services, or negotiate design of new components and interfaces (to be subsequently available for reuse), and determine availability of existing EA patterns/mechanisms (to avoid reinventing the wheel, improved quality, reduced technical risk, and reduced defects through consistency of applied patterns).
Development intelligence	11	Operational—Increases the chance that the team will steer itself effectively. Political—Increases stakeholder visibility into what the team is doing.	With DI your team can detect problems quickly and then act when they are easier to address. If your governing body has easy access to accurate and timely metrics they can make more intelligent decisions to help guide your team.

For delivery governance to be effective it must consider the whole of IT governance; otherwise, you risk suboptimization. Other forms of IT governance that impact your agile delivery governance strategy include the following:

- **Operations governance.** Operations governance focuses on your ability to fulfill service level agreements (SLAs) at both the solution and organizational levels. These SLAs typically address issues such as availability, security, accessibility, and reliability to name a few. When your team is working with operations staff these issues are conveyed by them in the form of nonfunctional requirements (NFRs), which must be taken into account by your architecture strategy (see Chapter 9, "Identifying an Initial Technical Strategy") and verified during construction iterations (discussed in Chapter 15, "A Typical Day of Construction"). An important aspect of DevOps is to ensure that your delivery and operations strategies fit together well, including governance.

- **Security governance.** Your organization's security governance strategy focuses on promoting effective practices around information confidentiality, integrity, availability, authenticity, and access control.

- **Data governance.** The goal of data governance is to ensure the quality, availability, integrity, security, and usability of data within an organization. Because DAD teams typically work with, and often enhance, corporate data sources they must conform to the appropriate policies set by their organization's data administration/management group. These policies are reflected in guidance around data design conventions, procedures for working with delivery teams, and any metadata management (MDM) strategy.

- **Quality assurance (QA) governance.** In the world of agile delivery the role of quality assurance needs to adapt from auditing the quality of the process and product that is delivered at the end of the lifecycle to supporting practices that ensure that quality is built in and validated from the beginning of the project. Independent testing is a key practice suggested by the DAD process framework. In addition QA practices need to be embedded within the team rather than treated as purely an audit function external to the project team. QA professionals can add value to agile teams by helping them engineer the process to prevent defects rather than designing a process to detect defects after the fact.

- **Technology governance.** This is a catch-all category for the governance of major technologies or architectures. Examples include service governance, cloud governance, and network governance. Technology governance strategies often overlap into other forms of IT governance. These governance strategies are often introduced in parallel to, or just behind, introduction of the given technologies.

- **IT investment governance.** This is the governance of the financial aspects of IT, in particular how the IT budget is spent. To effectively govern the IT investment in agile delivery projects your stakeholders must be actively involved with the project team, providing feedback on a regular basis either directly or through a stakeholder proxy such as a product owner. They should regularly consider whether the project continues to be viable and whether the current incremental solution is ready to be released. These activities in effect put them in control of how their money is being invested and how much is being invested. Chapter 6, "The Inception Phase," described several ways that an IT delivery project could be funded, including fixed cost, time and materials (T&M), T&M with performance bonus, and staged gate. At that time we argued for a T&M based approach as being the lowest risk option available to you, with the caveat that it requires effective governance to make it work.

In addition to aligning your agile delivery governance strategy with your IT governance strategy, you must also align it with two key organizational governance issues. First you must align your agile people practices and your human resource (HR) strategy. The people on your team must be rewarded for their efforts, they must have career opportunities available to them, they are provided benefits such as health care and vacations, they have educational opportunities, and many other aspects governed by your overall HR strategy. Although DAD teams are self-governing, and it is nice to believe that they are in complete control over their destiny, the fact remains that when it comes to these issues you're constrained by your organization's HR strategy. The implication is that some aspects of the individuals and interactions within agile teams are governed by your HR department.

LESSONS FROM THE TRENCHES—AGILE AND CMMI CAN SUCCESSFULLY COEXIST

Scott has worked with several organizations that were CMMI compliant that wanted to adopt a more agile strategy. This was particularly true for organizations with metrics programs in place, something that's required for CMMI levels 4 and 5, because the metrics typically showed that their traditional strategies weren't as efficient as they'd hoped. The primary challenge for such transitions was invariably around culture; many CMMI compliant organizations tend to have overly specialized staff and the inevitable supporting bureaucracy to make such approaches work. Key events in these organizations were the recognition that they needed to improve, that traditional strategies of yesteryear weren't going to give them the improvements they desired, and that CMMI and agile strategies could work together given open and flexible attitudes.

The second organizational governance pertains to your approach to regulatory compliance, if any. There are two aspects to this—externally imposed regulations and internally imposed regulations. External regulations include the Sarbanes-Oxley (SOX) Act and the Food and Drug Administration (FDA) Code of Federal Regulations (CFR) Title 21 (FDA CFR 21) regulation in the United States. Internal "regulations" are self-imposed standards or specifications managed by external organizations, such as International Standards Organization (ISO) 90003 and Capability

Maturity Model Integrated (CMMI), which your organization has chosen to adopt. Sometimes these regulations impact the way in which IT delivery projects are managed and governed. For example, because SOX requires that an organization be able to prove how some financial calculations are performed a project team may be required to hold a milestone review to verify that this is true.

Measuring Agile Teams

An important aspect of effective delivery governance is the monitoring of teams so that they may be guided and helped by senior management effectively. This is in fact common—the Ambysoft 2009 Governance Survey found that nearly three quarters of respondents indicated that their project teams collect metrics[1] to enable project monitoring by senior management. Although the majority of IT organizations are doing this, one wonders if they are effective at collecting metrics, if they are collecting the right metrics, and if they are using them to improve the way that they guide delivery teams. The goal of this section is to provide answers to these questions.

Let's start with some advice for how to approach metrics in an agile manner:

- **Talk to people; don't manage to the metrics.** Metrics should be considered potential indicators, not hard fact. For example, a defect trend chart showing a spike in defects may indicate that a team is at risk of increasing their technical debt, or it may indicate that they've improved their testing approach, which in turn enables them to identify and pay down their technical debt. Without talking with the team it is difficult to identify what is actually going on.

- **Measure teams, not individuals.** This old adage still applies in the agile world. When people believe that they are going to be affected by the results of measurement programs they quickly find ways to subvert such programs. Furthermore, measuring employees and sometimes even contractors on an individual basis is illegal in some countries.

- **Collect several metrics.** Any given metric provides only a single view of what is happening. Consider the defect trend chart with a spike in identified defects. Alone it provides an indication that something is going on. But if you also know that code complexity is increasing and that code quality trends are decreasing these metrics together likely reveal increasing technical debt. One metric puts another into context. For example, having 20 severe defects for a million line of code (LOC) system is better than one defect with 10,000 LOC.

---

1. Throughout this section we use the term "metric" to encompass measurements as well. A metric is what is to be measured, such as defect trends, and measures are the actual observed values (in this case the defect reports from which the defect trend is calculated). Although metrics and measures are two separate concepts, in practice the majority of practitioners apply the term metrics for both.

- **Trends trump scalar values.** A point or scalar value such as a defect count of 20 at a certain period of time doesn't tell us much. However, knowing that we had 40 defects two weeks ago, 30 last week, and 20 this week is much more informative.

- **Adopt a goal question metric (GQM) approach.** The fundamental idea behind this approach is that you first identify a goal that you want to achieve, a set of questions pertinent to achieving that goal, and then the metric(s) associated with each question. We apply the GQM technique for several potential governance goals later in this section. Of course, as you fulfill your existing goals new goals will emerge, so GQM proves to be an evolutionary strategy in practice.

- **Empirical observation is important but limited.** Much has been made of empiricism, the act of observing what works and what doesn't and then changing your behavior appropriately, in the agile community. Empiricism has its place in both process improvement and in governance, but unfortunately it doesn't scale well if you need to monitor more than a handful of delivery teams. A more sophisticated development intelligence (DI) strategy is likely called for.

- **Prefer automated metrics.** More and more development tools are now logging data about critical events pertaining to their usage, either into files that can later be reported from or better yet into a data warehouse. For example, a defect management tool can easily generate information about defect identification and closure. A work item management tool can track lifecycle events such as creation, starting work, validation, and closing of a work item. A code analysis tool can record when it was run, how many potential issues it identified, the types of issues, and so on. Because this sort of information is generated automatically as a by-product of the work the metrics are inexpensive to collect, do not require developer intervention (thereby reducing the burden of collecting them), are timely, and are more trustworthy than manually gathered metrics because they're captured consistently.

- **Some metrics must be gathered manually.** Some measures, such as stakeholder satisfaction, need to be collected manually, perhaps via surveys or interviews. The challenge with manually gathered metrics is that they can be expensive to collect, they are collected inconsistently, and they are captured infrequently and therefore may not be as timely as desired. Our advice is to collect metrics manually only when you cannot find a way to capture them automatically. The Ambysoft 2009 Governance Survey found that half of respondents indicated the metrics being gathered to do this were manual, and an additional one in five indicated that the majority of the metrics gathered were automated.

- **Prefer pull versus push reporting.** What we mean by this is provide mechanisms for people who are interested in the metrics to view them on their own, perhaps via an automated project dashboard or via big visible charts in your team work room. This enables people to pull the information when they want it. Alternatively, a push strategy would be for your team to prepare a regular status report providing key metrics that is then sent out to the appropriate people.

- **Beware scientific facades.** A serious challenge with metrics is that they can make an inherently stochastic/probabilistic endeavor such as software development appear deterministic to the uninformed. For example, I'm sure you've heard claims by some people that their projects come in on time, on budget, and to specification X% of the time, where X is an impressive number. Sounds like they know what they're doing, which is exactly what they want you to think. But just because they're coming in on budget doesn't mean they're spending the money effectively or they didn't update the original estimate once they knew what their actual cost was. Coming in on schedule doesn't mean they're delivering when the solution is actually needed, just when it was promised. Producing something built to specification doesn't imply they've produced something stakeholders actually want.

- **Measure the value of your metrics program.** The value of your metrics program should be one of the first things that you measure. The value received from better decision making due to the metric should be greater than the total cost of ownership (TCO) of collecting it. Unfortunately the true cost of many metrics can be difficult to calculate. For example, the immediate cost of performing a function point count at the beginning of a project to improve the precision of an estimate is fairly obvious; it's the cost of the people required to perform the work to do so. But this motivates people to do detailed requirement and design specification early in the project, which in turn can motivate significant wastage throughout your project as discussed in earlier chapters. Our experience is that a metrics program that isn't subject to being measured is likely to be a highly questionable effort.

- **Be prepared to educate people.** You can't count on everyone being familiar with the various agile metrics. For example, senior management new to agile may not understand that it is normal for your ranged burndown chart to show an initial spike in new requirements at the beginning of a project. Stakeholders may be confused at first that ranged burndown charts give ranges and not exact estimates, indicating they need to be walked through the realities of IT estimating (see Chapter 10, "Initial Release Planning"). Practitioners may not understand that recording how they spend their time can provide significant value to your organization in the form of research and development (R&D) tax credits.

- **The value of many metrics diminishes over time.** Some metrics are introduced to a team simply to change their behavior. Once the behavior changes, the metric no longer has any value. For example, in Chapter 16, "Concluding a Construction Iteration," we described the practice of measured improvement where a team purposely tracks the adoption of an improvement suggestion. This motivates the team to focus on the given improvement, but there will come a time when it is clear that the team has either successfully adopted the improvement or clearly given up on it. Either way you should stop collecting that metric.

- **If you collect no metrics at all you're flying blind.** Even the most extreme of agile teams find it valuable to collect a few basic metrics such as defect trends and work item burndown because the metrics provide insight into the current operating efficiency of the team.

- **If you collect too many metrics you may be flying blinded.** A common metrics anti-pattern occurs when an organization collects a large number of metrics in an attempt to be thorough. Just like nonpilots are overwhelmed by the number of gauges and indicators in a modern plane cockpit, many people who are not agile experts get overwhelmed by the multitude of metrics on some project dashboards. This is often the case when an organization has adopted tooling that automates metrics collection and reporting—just because it's easy to collect doesn't mean it adds value. By following a GQM approach you can identify the handful of metrics that provide real value to you now.

For the sake of our discussion there are three potential audiences for agile metrics:

- **Your team.** A DAD team wants timely and accurate metrics so that they can self-organize more effectively. For example, they may refer to an iteration burndown chart during a coordination meeting to understand their current status or a defect trend chart to help them to understand how well they're responding to incoming defects.

- **Your stakeholders.** Project stakeholders are often interested in answering fundamental questions such as when will the next release be shipped, is the solution of sufficient quality, what is the expected cost, and are we satisfied with the solution so far. Ideally these questions are answered through a DI-based strategy where stakeholders have access to an automated dashboard that focuses on stakeholder-specific issues.

- **The governors.** Your governing body will want to monitor project teams so they can make better decisions and hopefully guide project teams effectively.

There are many potential metrics that you could collect. The ones that we suggest you consider are summarized in Table 20.4. This list isn't meant to be exhaustive, but it does include the metrics that we've found useful on various projects. The table indicates whether gathering the metric can be automated, how the metric is commonly displayed (scalar, trend, or list), and its timeliness (whether it is predictive or trailing).

Table 20.4 Potential Metrics for Agile Projects

Metric	Description	Automation Strategy	Display Considerations	Type	Timeliness
Acceleration	The change in velocity, often calculated over several iterations.	Calculated from velocity.	—	Scalar	Trailing
Activity time	The length of time of a specific, important activity. Possible activities include deployment to production, running a regression test suite, iteration planning, or initial requirements envisioning.	Requires tools supporting that activity to log basic events.	As a trend shown as a histogram or line chart. For a given activity categorized between wait time and actual activity time.	Scalar or Trend	Trailing
Age of work items	The amount of time that a work item has existed.	Requires a work item management system.	Typically charted using a histogram or line chart to indicate the number of work items for a given age range. Often categorized by work item type (requirement, defect, and so on)	Trend	Trailing
Blocking work items	A list of work items blocking other work items.	Requires an electronic Kanban-style taskboard.	On a taskboard a blocking work item is shown in a warning color, such as red. As a list of the blocking work items and optionally the items that are being blocked. In diagram form as a directed graph.	List	Trailing

(continued)

Table 20.4 Potential Metrics for Agile Projects (continued)

Metric	Description	Automation Strategy	Display Considerations	Type	Timeliness
Build health	Indicates the status of your build. Can be captured at the level of a subsystem or system.	Requires your build management tool to log basic events.	For the current status this is shown using a status indicator (e.g., green = success, yellow = tests passed but some code analysis warnings, red = compile or tests failed). Some teams integrate a physical indicator, such as a flashing light, to indicate a broken build. For an ongoing trend it is common to show a series of colored bars (e.g., green, yellow, red) each of which indicates the status of a build.	Scalar or Trend	Trailing
Business value delivered	Assesses the value being delivered to business stakeholders.	Typically manual as this requires surveys, interviews, or observation to gather this data.	As a trend this is typically shown as a line graph with a numerical estimate of the business value delivered along the vertical axis and time along the horizontal axis.	Scalar or Trend	Trailing
Change cycle time	The period of time from when a requirement, enhancement request, or defect is identified until it is resolved (either cancelled or deployed into production).	Requires change tracking tools that are integrated all the way through the lifecycle, including tracking changes coming from operations and support.	As a trend this is typically shown as a histogram or line chart. Typically categorized by change type.	Scalar or Trend	Trailing

Metric	Description	Automation Strategy	Display Considerations	Type	Timeliness
Code quality	Assesses one or more quality aspects of source code, such as cyclomatic complexity and adherence to coding conventions.	Automated by code analysis tools. Can be manually gathered via code inspections.	As a trend this is typically shown as a histogram or line chart. May be categorized by subsystem or component. May be categorized by type of quality aspect.	Scalar or Trend	Trailing
Defect density	Indicates the number of known defects for a given amount of code (e.g., per thousand LOC) or by size (e.g., per thousand function points).	Automated via code analysis tools.	As a trend this is typically shown as a histogram or line chart. May be categorized by subsystem or component. May be categorized by severity or type of defect (e.g., security, consumability, performance, and so on).	Scalar or Trend	Trailing
Defect trend	Indicates the number of remaining known defects at the end of an iteration that are still to be addressed.	Automated through test management tools.	This is typically depicted by a histogram or line chart. May be categorized by severity. May be categorized by defect type (e.g., supportability, consumability, data quality, and so on).	Trend	Trailing and Predictive

(continued)

Table 20.4   Potential Metrics for Agile Projects (continued)

Metric	Description	Automation Strategy	Display Considerations	Type	Timeliness
Effort/cost projection	Indicates the amount of time (or money) invested to date and any expected time (or money) to complete.	Requires information about team size, charge rates, sunk costs, and estimated schedule.	As a trend this is typically shown as a line chart or histogram. Cost may be categorized by capital (e.g., investment in hardware or facilities) versus expense (e.g., labor costs) spending. You may choose to compare original estimated cost/effort versus current estimate or actual cost/effort.	Scalar or Trend	Trailing and Predictive
Iteration burndown[2]	Indicates the total estimated time required to implement the remaining work items in a given iteration.	Requires the estimated number of hours of work initially accepted by the team and the number of task hours remaining each day.	You may choose to indicate the "ideal burndown," a straight line from the top of the stack on the first day to zero on the last day of the iteration.	Trend	Predictive and Trailing
Lifecycle traceability	Indicates how well majority artifacts are traced/linked to one another. For example, can you trace a stakeholder goal to a detailed requirement to the supporting design to the implementation code and to the validating tests (and potentially in reverse)?	Requires major artifacts to be captured electronically and linked to one another.	In summary a percentage may be calculated per traceability category (such as requirements-to-test or design-to-code). In detail a collection of listings, one for each traceability category, showing actual elements being traced to one another.	Scalar	Trailing

2. Some teams produce burnup charts that start at zero and add the work implemented each day. Both of us prefer burndown charts because they tend to make it clear earlier that a team is in danger of not delivering everything they committed to—burnup charts tend to be perceived in an overly optimistic manner.

Metric	Description	Automation Strategy	Display Considerations	Type	Timeliness
Net present value (NPV)	The sum of the present values (PVs) of a collection of amounts. See Chapter 10.	Simple financial calculation.	—	Scalar	Predictive or Trailing
Ranged release burndown	Shows the amount of work completed to date by iteration, the amount of work added each iteration, and a range estimate of the amount of time remaining to complete the current work. See Chapter 10 for details.	Requires initial size of work items chosen for the release, size of work items completed each iteration, and size of work items added or removed each iteration.	See Chapter 10.	Trend	Predictive and Trailing
Release burndown	Indicates the total estimated time in terms of number of iterations required to implement the remaining work items for a given release.	Requires the estimated number of points of work initially estimated by the team and the number of points of work items remaining at the end of each iteration.	You may choose to indicate the total points of work items for each completed iteration added to the work item list to show additional scope added to the project over time.	Trend	Predictive and Trailing
Return on investment (ROI)	The total value (as an NPV) divided by total cost (as an NPV) over the lifetime of something.	Simple financial calculation.	—	Scalar	Predictive or Trailing

(continued)

Table 20.4   Potential Metrics for Agile Projects (continued)

Metric	Description	Automation Strategy	Display Considerations	Type	Timeliness
Risk mitigation	Indicates the rate at which risks are mitigated.	Requires information about individual risks and when they are considered mitigated.	Typically shown as burndown chart where the total magnitude of the remaining risks at the end of an iteration are indicated. New risks identified in an iteration may be indicated separately from previously known risks. May categorize by severity of the risk.	Trend	Trailing
Stakeholder satisfaction	Indicates the level of satisfaction of your stakeholders with the solution provided.	Typically manual as this requires surveys, interviews, or observation to gather this data.	May be displayed as a bar chart indicating the number or percentage of people who gave a certain rating (e.g., 7 people were very satisfied, 85 people satisfied, and so on). May be categorized by stakeholder issue (e.g., consumability, value delivered, timeliness of delivery, ease of deployment, and so on). May be categorized by stakeholder type.	Scalar or Trend	Trailing
Team morale	Indicates the morale of the team.	Typically manual as this information is gathered via surveys, interviews, or observation.	As a trend typically shown as a line chart.	Scalar or Trend	Trailing

Metric	Description	Automation Strategy	Display Considerations	Type	Timeliness
Test coverage	Indication of the percentage of the code that is exercised by your regression test suites.	Requires test coverage tools.	As a scalar can be visually shown as a heat map organized by software component. As a trend typically shown as a line chart.	Scalar or Trend	Trailing
Time invested	The amount of time spent on the project.	Typically manual as this requires data entry to categorize work.	As a trend shown as a histogram or line chart indicating the amount of time spent each iteration. May be categorized by activity (e.g., development, training, planning, demos, supporting other teams, and so on).	Scalar or Trend	Trailing
Velocity	The number of points of work completed in an iteration.	Can be automated if the team is using a work item management tool.	As a trend shown as a line chart or histogram indicating the velocity each iteration.	Scalar or Trend	Trailing

The potential goals of a DAD project team are driven by the situation that they face. Scott runs an annual IT Project Success survey for Dr. Dobb's Journal (DDJ), and not surprisingly he consistently finds that people's success criteria vary. Furthermore, what they value also varies, and it often isn't what we're told they should value. For example, the 2011 edition of that survey found that three quarters of respondents prefer to ship something only when it's ready, seven out of eight want to provide a good ROI, and almost everyone wants to meet the actual needs of stakeholders and deliver high-quality systems. What is interesting is that only one in eight believe in the definition of success that we often hear about: delivering relatively on time, relatively on budget, and relatively to specification. Potential goals that you may have for your project team include the following:

- **Deploy in a timely manner.** Many people want to have a solution when it is ready to be deployed. This is not necessarily when it is scheduled to be deployed. For example, people don't want a low-quality solution delivered on time, and many times they prefer a solution delivered earlier than originally asked for.

- **Spend IT investment wisely.** Most people want to spend money effectively, investing in the most promising projects and then not wasting the investment when they do so. Spending the money wisely sometimes has little to do with the actual budget.

- **Provide business value.** The stakeholders of a solution want solutions that provide real business value to them that at least satisfies their needs but better yet delights them.

- **Produce a quality solution.** People want a quality solution provided to them. One challenge is that quality is in the eye of the beholder—an end user's quality concerns may be different from an operations person's concerns. Another challenge is that quality is often constrained by time and finances.

- **Reduce technical debt.** Many organizations want to improve the quality of their systems, data sources, and supporting infrastructure so that it is less burdensome to operate and evolve.

- **Provide a healthy working environment.** Many people want a physically and emotionally healthy environment to work in.

- **Regulatory compliancy.** Many DAD teams need to comply to either internally imposed regulations such as Capability Maturity Model Integrated (CMMI) or externally-imposed regulations such as Sarbanes-Oxley or Food and Drug Administration (FDA) regulations.

Table 20.5 maps the potential goals described previously to the likely audience for those goals and then the question and supporting metrics for those goals. Notice how a given metric may be used to answer more than one question and that it often takes several metrics to answer a single question. Also note that the metrics may provide only partial insight into a question; you should not make decisions based just on the metrics alone.

Table 20.5 Mapping Goals, Audience, and Potential Metrics

Goal	Audience	Questions and Supporting Metric(s)
Deploy in a timely manner	Team, stakeholders, governors	Is the team working at a sufficient pace to complete the work? Metrics: Acceleration, ranged release burndown, velocity, iteration burndown, activity time (deployment), deployment testing Is the team working together effectively? Metrics: Team morale, blocking work items Is the team producing sufficient quality work to enable them to continue working at their current pace? Metrics: Build health, code quality, defect trend Are new or changing requirements putting the release date at risk? Metrics: Age of work items, ranged release burndown
Spend IT investment wisely	Team, business stakeholders, governors	How effective is the investment in IT activities? Metrics: Business value delivered, NPV, ROI What future spending do we require? Metrics: Effort/cost projection Is productivity increasing? Metrics: Acceleration, business value delivered, velocity (trend)
Provide business value	Team, business stakeholders, governors	Are we providing sufficient business value? Metrics: Business value delivered, NPV, ROI, stakeholder satisfaction Are we providing business value in a timely manner? Metrics: Ranged release burndown, stakeholder satisfaction, effort/cost projection, change cycle time
Produce a quality solution	Team, stakeholders, governors	What is the level of quality of our solution? Metrics: Code quality, defect density, stakeholder satisfaction Is the team working in a manner that will continue to result in sufficient quality? Metrics: Build health, defect trend, test coverage Is the solution supportable? Defect trend
Reduce technical debt	Team, IT stakeholders, governors	What is our current level of technical debt? Metrics: Code quality, defect density Are we reducing technical debt over time? Metrics: Build health, defect trend, test coverage

(continued)

Table 20.5   Mapping Goals, Audience, and Potential Metrics (continued)

Goal	Audience	Questions and Supporting Metric(s)
Provide a healthy working environment	Team, governors	Are team members happy working here? Metrics: Team morale, attrition rate Does the team's external environment promote high morale? Metrics: Stakeholder satisfaction Is the team working at a sustainable pace? Metrics: Acceleration, iteration burndown, ranged burndown chart, sick days, overtime hours
Regulatory compliance	Team, governors	Is the team fulfilling regulatory requirements? Metrics: Lifecycle traceability, risk mitigation

---

LESSONS FROM THE TRENCHES—DEVELOPMENT INTELLIGENCE HELPS TO SCALE AGILE

Richard Knaster, IBM Rational's worldwide agile practice manager, has helped several organizations to scale agile. He reports: "Development intelligence strategies such as automated dashboards are excellent tools to steer projects and ensure that agile teams are working effectively. In large organizations where there are many projects the physical space and governance needs make the use of whiteboards to track projects (e.g., taskboards, burndown charts) unfeasible. Management cannot be expected to attend ten or more daily meetings to understand if the projects responsible for their strategy execution are on track. A large insurance company found that by using IBM Rational Team Concert (RTC) dashboards they could easily see how well projects were progressing towards their release goals and if the agile practices that they had adopted were being followed correctly. By looking at the dashboards, they discovered that some teams were not writing stories effectively, nor concluding the iteration by either marking stories as being done or moving incomplete stories to the next iteration or to the product backlog. The dashboards also helped them get a handle on their technical debt. It was easy to view the defect trend for a single team or for the entire enterprise and understand if the teams were addressing quality throughout the projects or just towards the end of the release. The insurance company was also able to see whether the team was tracking impediments, performing retrospectives, and taking a few key actions from the retrospectives."

Risk Mitigation

An important aspect of delivery governance is risk mitigation throughout the lifecycle, something explicitly built into the DAD process framework. Earlier in this chapter we described the risk-value lifecycle and how it helps DAD teams to recognize and address common risks faced by delivery teams. This chapter also overviewed several common agile practices and how they support your governance efforts and help to reduce overall project risk. There are of course project-specific risks that must be dealt with. Chapter 10 described how initial risk identification occurs during the Inception phase. Chapter 16 described how the risk list evolves as known risks are mitigated and new risks identified during the Construction phase.

We have a few important points to make about addressing risks effectively. First you should strive to address risks at the most appropriate time to do so, which is not always when you first identify them. There are trade-offs associated with this strategy. On the positive side some risks go away on their own given enough time, and sometimes you are better able to deal with a risk after taking the time to think about it. On the negative side some risks grow harder to deal with over time so you want to be smart about how long you wait. Second, not all risks need to be mitigated, and some can't be mitigated. You may identify a risk and your mitigation strategy may simply be to hope that it doesn't occur and if it does to accept the consequences. Third, some of the biggest risks to your project are political or people oriented. These sorts of risks you may choose to not document or openly discuss outside the team. Fourth, the best risk mitigation strategy is to have good people with a common set of common-sense values.

Concluding Thoughts

This chapter described what an agile governance strategy entails. Effective governance is based on motivating and then enabling people to exhibit the behaviors that you desire. We really can't say this often enough. You need to collaboratively develop a governance strategy that reflects the realities of agile solution delivery. DAD teams should be judged based on regular delivery of real business value to their stakeholders, and your governing body should work in a lightweight and respectful manner that is focused on guiding teams to success. To do this your governing body needs to monitor the progress of DAD teams through a combination of metrics and collaboration with the teams themselves.

This chapter also discussed how too many IT organizations have gotten into trouble by adopting command-and-control based governance strategies. The serial, documentation-focused governance approaches of yesteryear were questionable for the traditional project teams they were designed to govern, but for today's agile teams these traditional governance strategies prove detrimental to the success of the project.

Effective governance is particularly crucial at scale. When it comes to large or geographically distributed teams you want to maximize the independence of the subteams to give them the freedom to succeed. However, the only way this will work is if you have an appropriate governance program in place to guide the teams to ensure they are working together to a common goal. This is particularly true with outsourcing teams working for service providers. We've found that the greater control that the "home/main team" tries to inflict upon the external teams, such as creation of detailed specifications and accompanying sign-offs, the lower the overall success rate of the outsourcing effort. Having said that, lightweight monitoring is critical to ensuring that subteams remain on track.

The maxims "you ship the organization" and "you get what you measure" are primary motivators for organizations to build an effective governance program. Our experience is that truly disciplined agile teams demand effective governance because they realize that they can leverage the resources of their organizational ecosystem by doing so. Governance doesn't have to be a four-letter word any more.

Additional Resources

For more detailed discussions about several of the topics covered in this chapter:

- **Development governance.** Scott and Per Kroll have written an IBM whitepaper titled "Lean Development Governance" that can be downloaded from ibm.com that overviews a collection of practices critical to governing DAD teams.

- **IT governance.** The book *IT Governance* by Peter Weill and Jeanne W. Ross (Harvard Business School Press, 2004) is a great starting point for understanding the fundamentals of IT governance. In "Operational IT Governance" (http://www.ibm.com/developerworks/rational/library/may07/cantor_sanders/) Murray Cantor and John D. Sanders describe seven principles to guide IT governance efforts.

- **Metrics.** The paper "The Goal Question Metric Approach" (http://www.cs.umd.edu/~mvz/handouts/gqm.pdf) by Victor R. Basili, Gianluigi Caldiera, and H. Dieter Rombach is the seminal work on GQM. The book *How to Measure Anything: Finding the Value of Intangibles in Business* by Douglas W. Hubbard (Wiley Publishing, 2007) will help you to find strategies to measure some of the harder aspects of your IT efforts.

- **Agile strategies for enterprise professionals.** Scott has written extensively about how enterprise professionals can work effectively with agile teams. The articles "Agile Enterprise Architecture" (www.agiledata.org/essays/enterpriseArchitecture.html) and "Agile Enterprise Administration" (http://www.agiledata.org/essays/enterpriseAdministration.html) are good starting points.

- **Surveys.** Results from the 2011 IT Project Success survey and the Ambysoft 2009 Governance survey are available at www.ambysoft.com/surveys/.

- **Earned value management (EVM).** Scott has written about the challenges surrounding EVM in "Questioning the Value of Earned Value Management in IT Projects" at http://drdobbs.com/architecture-and-design/207801786. However, if you find yourself in a situation where you still need to support EVM on your agile project team you should find John Rusk's "Earned Value for Agile Development" (http://www.agilekiwi.com/EarnedValueForAgileProjects.pdf) to be a valuable read.

Got Discipline?

Manage chaos if you must, but disciplined practitioners prefer to avoid chaos in the first place.

While in the process of writing this book we often took the opportunity to discuss what we were doing on discussion forums, on Twitter, at user group meetings, and even at a few conferences. A common question we received was "What makes Disciplined Agile Delivery (DAD) more disciplined than other approaches to agile?" It's a fair question, particularly from someone who hasn't yet read this book. In this chapter we explore this question, explicitly summarizing the critical strategies that exhibit the greater levels of discipline in DAD as compared with what we see in many agile projects today.

Figure 21.1 shows a mind map of the structure of this chapter. We describe each of the topics in the map in clockwise order, beginning at the top right.

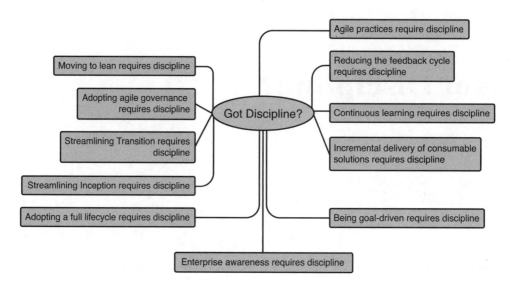

Figure 21.1   Outline of this chapter

Agile Practices Require Discipline

First, let's explore the discipline inherent in many mainstream agile practices. Agile teams have the discipline to do the following:

- Hold short, focused, and to the point daily coordination meetings rather than infrequent and time consuming status meetings. It requires discipline to keep these meetings focused on coordination activities and thereby short and to the point.

- Commit to delivering a set of work items each iteration rather than letting deadlines slip. It requires discipline to consistently fulfill the promises that you make to your stakeholders.

- Remove impediments in a timely fashion rather than procrastinating in pursuing a solution. It requires discipline to tackle tough issues that are easier to ignore in the short term.

- Take the time to write tests before code rather than writing code. It takes discipline to consistently work in a test-first manner instead of leaving testing to sometime in the (distant) future.

- Test to the best of their ability instead of throwing artifacts over the wall to testers or reviewers. It takes discipline to actively take responsibility for the quality of your own work.

- Reflect on the team's experiences and improve their processes proactively rather than relying on process dictated by project managers or external governance bodies. It takes discipline to stop and take time to reflect on how well your team is working and then act to improve it.

- Have a continuously working, integrated, and tested solution rather than waiting to do so when you're "done" at the end of the lifecycle. It takes discipline to stop all work when the build is broken so that it is repaired and the state of working, high-quality solution is restored.

- Work together in a common area rather than in comfortable but isolated workspaces. It takes discipline to work effectively in a team, to do so in a respectful and trusting manner.

- Collaborate constantly with the stakeholders or their representative(s) to ensure that their expectations are met. It takes discipline to accept that it isn't your place to define the requirements or set priorities, particularly when you believe that you know better.

- Create and evolve deliverable documentation continuously throughout the project. It takes discipline to accept that there's more to successful solution delivery than producing potentially shippable software.

- Self-organize and plan the team's work among themselves rather than relying on a traditional project manager to define, estimate, and assign work. It takes discipline to take responsibility for your own work and to respect the collective decisions of your team.

This list is just a start if you want to be successful delivering solutions that will delight your stakeholders. Disciplined Agile Delivery takes discipline to the next level in the ways discussed in the following sections.

Reducing the Feedback Cycle Requires Discipline

Techniques that shorten the time between doing something and getting feedback about it are generally lower risk and result in lower cost to address any changes than techniques with longer feedback cycles. Many of these techniques require agile team members to have new skills and to take a more disciplined approach to their work than they may have in less-than-agile situations. Several ways to shorten the feedback cycle that are common to agile software development have been adopted by the DAD process framework. These techniques, listed in order of immediacy, are as follows:

1. **Non-solo development.** Non-solo development strategies such as pair programming and modeling with others provide feedback within seconds. These techniques are great strategies for reducing the feedback cycle within your team, but they often require initial discipline to adopt because it can be difficult to break your former solo working habits.

2. **Active stakeholder participation.** It can require significant discipline to work closely with your stakeholders, to seek and then respect their opinions, and to allow them to set important aspects of your project direction. Working closely with stakeholders typically has a feedback cycle on the order of seconds when they are collocated with your team to hours or days when you need to wait to interact with them.

3. **Continuous integration.** Building, regression testing, and potentially running your work through code analysis on a continuous basis is a straightforward concept that provides feedback on the order of minutes. Doing it in practice, and more importantly the habit of acting on the feedback provided from the tests and code analysis, requires discipline to adopt at first because you often want to work on the next thing instead of cleaning up the work on what you're currently doing.

4. **Continuous deployment.** By regularly deploying into more complex environments—to your project integration environment from your individual environment, from your project environment to your demo or independent testing environments—you put yourself in a position to receive more meaningful feedback. Continuous deployment requires you to have the discipline to have multiple environments, to work with people external to your team (such as stakeholders and independent testers), and to seek and act on their feedback.

5. **Short iterations.** The length of an iteration defines the feedback cycle between promising your stakeholders you would do a bundle of work, the end result of your iteration planning session, to demonstrating what you actually got done. As described in Chapter 10, "Initial Release Planning," it requires significant discipline to work in short iterations. The average agile team has construction iterations of two weeks, although some teams have shorter iterations, and some advanced teams have evolved beyond iterations to take a lean approach. Then again some agile teams, particularly those at scale, may have slightly longer iterations. The shorter the iteration the greater the discipline required to make it work because you need to adopt many, if not all, of the techniques listed in this section. You also require the discipline to identify, and then address, wasteful activities that add little or no value in your current process.

6. **Short release cycles.** The length of your release cycle defines the feedback cycle from promising stakeholders to deliver a new release of a solution to actual use by end users in production. The feedback from real users is the key information to determine whether you've delivered the right thing for them. All other stakeholder feedback is merely an approximation up until that point. As with short iterations, it requires increasing discipline to move from annual to biannual to quarterly to monthly to weekly or even daily releases into production.

Continuous Learning Requires Discipline

Continuous learning is an important aspect of agile software development in general, not just DAD. However, DAD explicitly addresses the need for three levels of learning: individual, team, and organizational. It also addresses the need for three categories of learning: domain, technical, and process. Continuous learning strategies are summarized in Table 21.1.

LESSONS FROM THE TRENCHES—THE DISCIPLINE OF THE LEARNING ORGANIZATION

According to Mark Kennaley, CTO of Software Development Experts (www.software-development-experts.com), "thanks to the awareness in the industry from folks like Scott and Mark and through DAD and the Agile Scaling Model, enterprises are starting to understand the nature of the discipline required to get to the next level of software development performance. Professional sports teams leverage a system of plays to perform at such a level, and software development teams are very similar. From our work with Japanese clients, we observed that the discipline required for meaningful improvement is only possible when the 'front line' in the project is empowered to adjust course from an established baseline way of working. Rather than just talk about lean thinking principles of kaizen, stop-the-line, value-stream analysis and standard work, we built the Software Development Practice Advisor to concretely enact these principles of discipline. The system instills such discipline by ensuring that past valuable experience in context in the form of hybrid practice-based approaches like DAD is leveraged to achieve benefit. Similarly, by allowing professional teams to rapidly reconfigure their playbook based on their real-time project observations, it's like enabling a half-time strategy adjustment in the big game. Enabling such discipline requires easy access to the data provided by this system aggregated across the organization and the entire industry to indicate practice efficacy. It also requires using such a system to mitigate the effects of cognitive bias towards any one body of knowledge or community to rigorously and pragmatically consider all practice and method experience, one of the goals of DAD. A learning organization performing to its maximum potential continuously inspects and adapts, not only after the IT investment has occurred, but rather during the execution of the investment to yield optimal outcomes."

Table 21.1   Strategies for Taking a Disciplined Approach to Continuous Learning

Strategy	Considerations	Learning Level			Learning Category		
		Individual	Team	Organizational	Domain	Technical	Process
Active stakeholder participation	Working with stakeholders, including those outside the team, regularly allows the team to learn more about the customers' expectations and their domain, as well as the opportunity for external stakeholders to learn about your solution and thus be prepared for its release.	✓	✓		✓	✓	
Coaching and mentoring	Investing in coaching and mentoring from experienced agile leaders is the quickest path to agile capability on your projects.	✓	✓		✓	✓	✓
Individual learning	Individual team members need to have the discipline to learn skills outside their area of specialty. It is often easy to ignore other disciplines in favor of investing education time in becoming even more specialized.	✓			✓	✓	✓
Non-solo development	It takes discipline to recognize that your work might be of higher quality if it receives real-time feedback as it is created. The investment usually results in learning for all people involved.	✓	✓		✓	✓	✓
Proving the architecture with working code	It takes discipline to realize how important it is to learn how to implement the difficult aspects of your solution early in the lifecycle and work on those aspects before the cool stuff.		✓			✓	

Strategy	Considerations	Learning Level			Learning Category		
		Individual	Team	Organizational	Domain	Technical	Process
Retrospectives	A skilled team continues to improve as they become more self-aware of their team's strengths and deficiencies. We have found that teams often become complacent after several iteration retrospectives feeling that they cannot improve any more. We described a measured improvement approach in Chapter 16, "Concluding a Construction Iteration."		✓			✓	✓
Sharing lessons learned with other teams	Teams should share lessons learned with other teams within their organization. See Chapter 20, "Governing Disciplined Agile Teams."			✓	✓	✓	✓
Stakeholder demonstrations	It takes discipline to take the time to regularly demonstrate your solution to stakeholders, and to convince the stakeholders that it is worthwhile when they may not be interested. The feedback is an opportunity to learn whether the solution may not be meeting expectations and the opportunity to adjust accordingly.		✓	✓	✓		

Incremental Delivery of Consumable Solutions Requires Discipline

Being able to deliver potentially shippable software increments at the end of each iteration is a good start that clearly requires discipline. The DAD process framework goes one step further and advises you to explicitly produce a potentially consumable solution every iteration, something that requires even greater discipline. Every construction iteration that your team executes requires the discipline to address:

- **Working software that is "done."** Your software should be tested to the best of your ability. Ideally this includes preproduction integration testing and acceptance testing of the functionality delivered to date. The software should not only fulfill the functional requirements but appropriate nonfunctional requirements (NFRs) as well. Some of this testing may require the help of an independent test team, particularly at scale.

- **Continuous documentation.** Deliverable documentation, such as operations and support, system overview, and end user documentation is part of your overall solution. Evolving this documentation in sync with the software requires greater discipline than simply leaving this documentation to the end of the lifecycle.

- **Consumability.** Your solution should be more than potentially shippable, it should also be consumable. This requires investing some effort in user experience (UX) design throughout the lifecycle, particularly early in the project.

- **Organizational change.** The business processes around using your system, and potentially even the organizational structure of the stakeholders involved with it, may need to evolve. The implication is that your team needs the discipline to recognize and explore these issues throughout the project so that your stakeholders are prepared to receive your solution.

- **Operations and support issues.** Your solution should be consumable by all stakeholders, not just end users. Your operations and support staff should be able to work with the solution efficiently. To understand these needs your team needs the discipline to work closely with operations and support staff throughout the lifecycle, an important aspect of your overall DevOps strategy.

Being Goal-Driven Requires Discipline

The DAD process framework uses a goal-driven approach as illustrated in Figure 21.2. Throughout this book we described each of the DAD phases in turn and suggested strategies for addressing the goals of that phase. For each goal we described the issues pertaining to that goal. For example, in Chapter 10 when we discussed initial project planning we indicated that you need to consider issues such as the amount of initial detail you intend to capture, the amount of ongoing detail throughout the project, the length of iterations, how you will communicate the schedule (if at all), and how you will produce an initial cost estimate (if at all). Each issue can be addressed by several strategies, each of which has trade-offs. Our experience is that this goals-driven, suggestive approach provides just enough guidance for solution delivery teams while being sufficiently flexible so that teams can tailor the process to address the context of the situation in which they find themselves. The challenge is that it requires significant discipline by agile teams to consider the issues around each goal and then choose the strategy most appropriate for them.

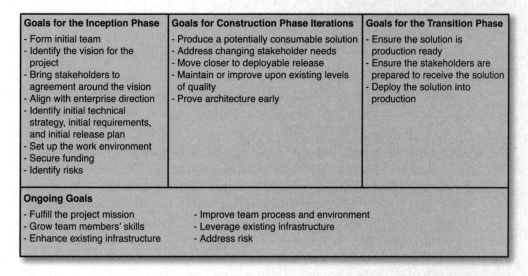

Goals for the Inception Phase	Goals for Construction Phase Iterations	Goals for the Transition Phase
- Form initial team - Identify the vision for the project - Bring stakeholders to agreement around the vision - Align with enterprise direction - Identify initial technical strategy, initial requirements, and initial release plan - Set up the work environment - Secure funding - Identify risks	- Produce a potentially consumable solution - Address changing stakeholder needs - Move closer to deployable release - Maintain or improve upon existing levels of quality - Prove architecture early	- Ensure the solution is production ready - Ensure the stakeholders are prepared to receive the solution - Deploy the solution into production

Ongoing Goals		
- Fulfill the project mission - Grow team members' skills - Enhance existing infrastructure	- Improve team process and environment - Leverage existing infrastructure - Address risk	

Figure 21.2 Goals addressed throughout a DAD project

DAD lays out a set of milestones across the lifecycle that are common across most projects regardless of what agile practices you use. It takes discipline to use a goal-driven approach to reach those milestones. This means that you do not use a cookbook approach to deliver your solutions but rather adapt your techniques to follow the path best suited to you. Prescriptive guidance and rules are common in many agile methods, and people can easily fall into a trap of doing exactly what is dictated by a particular method without challenging how appropriate it is for their own situation.

Enterprise Awareness Requires Discipline

Whether you like it or not, as you adopt agile you will be constrained by the organizational ecosystem, and you need to act accordingly. It takes discipline to work with enterprise folks who may not be completely agile yet and to have the patience to help them. It takes discipline to work with your operations and support staff in a "DevOps" manner throughout the lifecycle, particularly when they may not be motivated to do so. Despite the fact that governing bodies such as project management offices (PMOs), architecture and database authorities, and operations may indeed be a source of impediments to your DAD adoption, these authorities serve important functions in any large enterprise. Therefore a disciplined approach to proactively working with them and being a positive change agent to make collaboration with them more effective is required.

Adopting a Full Lifecycle Requires Discipline

Despite some agilists' reluctance to admit that projects go through phases, the DAD process framework explicitly recognizes that they do. Building serious solutions requires a lot more than just doing the cool construction stuff. It takes discipline to ignore this rhetoric and frame your project within the scope of a full delivery lifecycle. The basic and advanced DAD lifecycles explicitly depict:

- **Predelivery activities.** Portfolio management activities occur long before your project begins, including the initial identification of potential projects, their prioritization, and finding initial funding for the Inception phase.

- **Three-phase delivery lifecycle.** Projects have phases that they go through. All efforts are initiated at some point, all of them go through a construction effort (or a configuration effort in the case of purchased solutions), and hopefully some sort of deployment effort. This is why the DAD lifecycles include explicit Inception, Construction, and Transition phases to respectively address these aspects. From a product point they will go through at least the Construction and Transition phase many times throughout the life of the solution.

- **Post-delivery activities.** The fact that your solution is operated and supported in production, or in the marketplace for commercial products, is included. We do this to reflect the DevOps reality that many DAD teams are in the position of working on a new release of an existing solution, and therefore are likely to be getting defect reports and enhancement requests coming in about previous versions. As a result they require the discipline to treat these things as potential new requirements and act accordingly.

Streamlining Inception Requires Discipline

We devoted a lot of material in this book to describing how to effectively address how to initiate a DAD project. Unfortunately in our experience we have seen many organizations treat this phase as an opportunity to do massive amounts of up-front documentation in the form of project plans, charters, and requirements specifications. Some people have referred to the practice of doing too much temporary documentation up front on an agile project (known as Sprint 0 in Scrum) as water-scrum-fall. We cannot stress enough that this is *not* the intent of the Inception phase. While we provide many alternatives for documenting your vision in Inception, from very heavy to very light, you should take a minimalist approach to this phase and strive to reach the stakeholder consensus milestone as quickly as possible. If you are spending more than a few weeks on this phase, you may be regressing to a water-scrum-fall approach. It takes discipline to be aware of this trap and to streamline your approach as much as possible.

Streamlining Transition Requires Discipline

In Chapter 18, "The Transition Phase," we described different strategies for delivering your solution into production. In most mid- to large-sized organizations the deployment of solutions is carefully controlled, particularly when the solutions share architectures and have project interdependencies. For these reasons release cycles to your stakeholders are less frequent than you would like because of existing complexities within the environment. However, the ability to frequently deploy value to your stakeholders is a competitive advantage; therefore you should reduce the release cycle as much as possible. This requires a great degree of discipline in areas such as the following:

- Preproduction integration and deployment testing
- Regular coordination between project teams and with operations and support staff
- Change management around both technology and requirements
- Adoption of continuous deployment practices to such a degree that frequent deployments are the norm and the Transition "phase" becomes an automated transition activity

Adopting Agile Governance Requires Discipline

It is easier to avoid your traditional governance and tell management that "agile is different" than it is to work with your governors to adapt your governance to properly guide the delivery of your agile teams. As described in Chapter 20 every organization has a necessary degree of governance, and there are ways to make it especially effective on agile initiatives. It takes discipline to work with your governors to help them understand how disciplined agile teams operate and then discipline to accept and conform to the resulting governance process.

Moving to Lean Requires Discipline

Throughout the book when we explored a given goal we provided a range of options to address the issues pertaining to that goal. These options ranged from traditional/heavier approaches that we generally advised against except in specific situations to agile strategies to lean strategies. Generally, the leaner the strategy the greater the discipline it requires. For example, consider the following issues:

- **Change management.** Managing work items as a prioritized stack, the agile strategy popularized by Scrum, clearly requires discipline. However, the lean approach of managing work items as a pool from which you pull work as your team has the capacity requires greater discipline due to the need to honestly assess priority on a just-in-time (JIT) basis across several categories or groupings of work items. Both of these strategies were described in detail in Chapter 8, "Identifying the Initial Scope."

- **Iterations disappear.** A major difference between the agile/basic DAD lifecycle and the lean/advanced DAD lifecycle is that the cadences of activities such as planning, demos, and retrospectives are decoupled with the lean approach. In other words, the Construction phase evolves from an iteration-based strategy to a continuous stream of work. Although it sounds easy to say that you'll plan when you need to, demo when you need to, hold retrospectives when you need to, and so on, in practice it requires great discipline to not push these sort of activities off for a few days or a few weeks in favor of "sexier" development activities.

- **Kanban boards.** When techniques such as Kanban boards are used in an undisciplined manner they can lead to poor productivity if metrics to measure your cycle time for your work items are not rigorously measured.

Concluding Thoughts

Adopting a disciplined approach to agile delivery requires the courage to rethink some of the agile rhetoric and make compromises where necessary for the benefit of the "whole enterprise." In our experience most agile projects make certain compromises that are not classically "agile" to get the job done. Rather than hiding this and fearing reprisals from those who would accuse you of regressing to a traditional approach, it is better to have the courage to take a pragmatic approach to using agile in your situation.

Effective application of DAD certainly requires discipline and skill, but in our experience the key determinant of success is the ability and willingness of the team to work well together and with stakeholders, both within and external to the team.

We hope this book has shown you how the agile delivery process works from start to finish. Some of the reviewers of our book suggested that we have not been as forceful as we should be in making certain recommendations about what exactly should be done to be agile. However, this was our approach by design. As we have said, it takes discipline to learn and become self-aware about what alternative approaches might be used and which make sense for you. It would be presumptuous for us to assume that we can write a book to tell you exactly how to apply agile most effectively for your unique situation. If this book helps you to adapt and use a goals-driven approach to delivering valuable solutions for your stakeholders, we have done what we set out to do. Good luck with your DAD adoption.

We plan to continue the discussion on DAD on its community Web site www.DisciplinedAgileDelivery.com. There are some topics that we would like to have addressed in this book but ran out of space, such as scaling agile beyond DAD projects, and how to apply lean thinking toward an advanced DAD approach. We will build on the material in this book and continue the discussion there. We encourage you to subscribe to this blog and join the discussion.

Additional Resources

If you have come this far in the book (first of all thank you!), you should have a good understanding of how DAD differs from traditional approaches such as a waterfall methodology. We include some diversions that you may find add some humor should you be in a position of not being able to effect positive change in your organization:

- **Overcoming impediments to agile adoption.** YouTube. Julian Holmes (of UPMentors) and Carson Holmes (of Fourth Medium Consulting) created a hilarious video titled "I Want to Run an Agile Project" describing typical impediments to running agile projects. We link to this video from www.DisciplinedAgileDelivery.com.

- **The Waterfall conference.** Waterfall 2006, www.Waterfall2006.com, was a fictitious conference Web site devoted to making fun of the waterfall methodology. This Web site is very well done and looks legitimate. Mark joked to one of his customers that he would be attending. This senior IT executive said "It looks good. Book a meeting with me when you return to review the key points." That was awkward.

- **Scott's April Fool's escapades.** Finally, if you receive a new article in your inbox from Scott on April 1 it may not be as serious as it appears at first glance. Links to previous articles can be found at www.ambysoft.com/onlineWritings.html.

Index